ATTACHMENT AND THE THERAPEUTIC PROCESS

ATTACHMENT AND THE THERAPEUTIC PROCESS

Essays in Honor of
Otto Allen Will, Jr., M.D.

Editors
James L. Sacksteder, M.D.
Daniel P. Schwartz, M.D.
Yoshiharu Akabane, M.D.

INTERNATIONAL UNIVERSITIES PRESS, INC.

Madison   Connecticut

Library of Congress Cataloging in Publication Data

Attachment and the therapeutic process.

   Includes bibliographies and indexes.
   1. Psychoanalysis. 2. Will, Otto Allen.
I. Will, Otto Allen. II. Schwartz, Daniel P.
III. Sacksteder, James L. IV. Akabane,
Yoshiharu. [DNLM: 1. Psychoanalytic Theory.
2. Psychoanalytic Therapy. WM 460 A883]
RC504.A88 1987   616.89′17   87-3347
ISBN 0-8236-0447-0

Manufactured in the United States of America

To Otto Allen Will, Jr., M.D.
analyst, teacher, investigator, and
colleague who has inspired us through
his life's work

Contents

Contributors   ix
Acknowledgments   xi
Introduction   1

PART I: THEORY

1. The Point of View of Psychoanalysis: Energy Discharge or
   Person—MERTON M. GILL   17
2. The Emotional Basis of Attachment and Separation—J. P.
   SCOTT   43
3. Defensive Processes in the Light of Attachment Theory—JOHN
   BOWLBY   63
4. Mutuality and Pseudomutuality Reconsidered: Implications for
   Therapy and a Theory of Development of Relational
   Systems—LYMAN C. WYNNE   81
5. Language, Psychosis, and Spirit—JOHN P. MULLER   99
6. Intrapsychic Structure and Interaction—DANIEL P. SCHWARTZ   117

PART II: RESEARCH

7. Engagement of Schizophrenic Patients in Psychotherapy—JOHN
   G. GUNDERSON   139
8. To Err Is Human: The Role of Error in Creativity and
   Psychotherapy—ALBERT ROTHENBERG   155

PART III: THERAPY

9. Illuminations of the Human Condition in the Encounter with the
   Psychotic Patient—GAETANO BENEDETTI   185
10. Suicide and the Impact on the Therapist—BEATRIZ FOSTER   197
11. The Changing Picture of an Illness: Anorexia Nervosa—HILDE
    BRUCH   205
12. The Struggle Toward Ambivalence—CLARENCE G. SCHULZ   223

PART IV: OTTO ALLEN WILL, Jr., M.D.

13. Illuminations of the Human Condition—Otto Allen
        Will, JR., M.D.   241
14. Human Relatedness and the Schizophrenic Reaction—Otto Allen
        Will, JR., M.D.   263
15. The Reluctant Patient, the Unwanted Psychotherapist—and
        Coercion—Otto Allen Will, JR., M.D.   299
16. The Schizophrenic Patient, the Psychotherapist, and the
        Consultant—Otto Allen Will, JR., M.D.   333

Chronological Bibliography of Otto Allen Will, Jr., M.D.   361
Author Index   000
Subject Index   000

Contributors

Gaetano Benedetti, M.D.: Professor of Psychiatry, University Psychiatric Institute, Basel, Switzerland

John Bowlby, M.A., M.D. Sc.D.: Honorary Consultant Psychiatrist, The Tavistock Clinic and Tavistock Institute of Human Relations, London, England

Hilde Bruch, M.D.: Professor Emeritus of Psychiatry, Baylor College of Medicine, Houston, Texas

Beatriz Foster, M.D.: Private Practice, Los Angeles, California; Former Staff Member, Chestnut Lodge, Rockville, Maryland, and the Austen Riggs Center, Stockbridge, Massachusetts

Merton M. Gill, M.D., Ph.D.: Professor of Psychiatry, Abraham Lincoln School of Medicine, University of Illinois, Chicago, Illinois; Former Staff Member, Menninger Clinic, Topeka, Kansas, and the Austen Riggs Center, Stockbridge, Massachusetts

John G. Gunderson, M.D.: Associate Professor of Psychiatry, Harvard Medical School; Director of Psychotherapy, McLean Hospital, Belmont, Massachusetts

John P. Muller, Ph.D.: Senior Researcher, Austen Riggs Center, Stockbridge, Massachusetts

Albert Rothenberg, M.D.: Director of Research, Austen Riggs Center, Stockbridge, Massachusetts; Clinical Professor of Psychiatry, Yale University School of Medicine, New Haven, Connecticut

J. P. Scott, Ph.D.: Regents Professor Emeritus of Psychology, Bowling Green State University, Bowling Green, Ohio; Research Professor, Tufts University, Boston, Massachusetts

Clarence G. Schulz, M.D.: Senior Psychiatrist and Director of Residency Training, Sheppard and Enoch Pratt Hospital, Towson, Maryland; Former Staff Psychiatrist, Chestnut Lodge, Rockville, Maryland

Daniel P. Schwartz, M.D.: Medical Director, Austen Riggs Center, Stockbridge, Massachusetts; Former Medical Director, Yale Psychiatric Institute, New Haven, Connecticut

Otto Allen Will, Jr., M.D.: Private Practice, Point Richmond, California; Former Medical Director, Austen Riggs Center, Stockbridge, Massachusetts; Former Staff Psychiatrist and Director of Psychotherapy, Chestnut Lodge, Rockville, Maryland

Lyman C. Wynne, M.D., Ph.D.: Professor of Psychiatry and Director of the Division of Family Programs, University of Rochester School of Medicine and Dentistry, Rochester, New York

Acknowledgments

We wish to thank the editor of *Psychiatry* for permission to reprint ''Human relatedness and the schizophrenic reaction.'' This paper originally appeared in *Psychiatry*, Vol. 22, No. 3, August 1959, pp. 205–223. We would also like to thank the editor of *Contemporary Psychoanalysis* for permission to reprint ''The schizophrenic patient, the psychotherapist and the consultant,'' which originally appeared in *Contemporary Psychoanalysis*, Vol. 1, No. 2, Spring 1965, pp. 110–135; and ''The reluctant patient, the unwanted psychotherapist—and coercion,'' which originally appeared in *Contemporary Psychoanalysis*, Vol. 5, No. 1, Fall 1968, pp. 1–31.

We wish also to thank the Museum of Modern Art for permission to reproduce from color material provided by the Museum the following work of art: Henri Matisse, *Bather* (summer 1909). Oil on canvas, $36\frac{1}{2} \times 29\frac{1}{8}''$ (92.7 × 74 cm.). *Collection, The Museum of Modern Art*, New York. Gift of Abby Aldrich Rockefeller.

Introduction

Psychoanalytic investigators beginning with Freud have been led by the findings of their clinical work to formulate general theories of human growth, development, and experience. Originally, of course, there was only one paradigm for ordering the data of human living psychoanalytically—the one formulated by Freud. Over time, many additional paradigms, each arising from data generated by psychoanalytic therapy and research, have been formulated and have become the focus of scientific attention and development. Multiple psychoanalytic viewpoints have developed and now include ego psychology, Kleinian psychology, self psychology, object relations theory, interpersonal theory, and structuralist theory. Each view offers its own paradigm of what is central and what is peripheral to a psychoanalytic conception of human development. Some of these paradigms complement and augment one another and thus appear mutually assimilable. Others, however, offer fundamentally different and opposing points of view. It is the intent of the editors of this volume to contribute to the current dialogue about different points of view in contemporary psychoanalysis by providing the reader a selected range of original papers written by distinguished theoreticians, clinicians, and researchers that address some of the valuable attempts to impose these paradigms in areas of current interest and controversy.

Each of the authors has a distinct perspective that has evolved naturally out of his or her area of clinical investigation. The phenomena investigated are quite diverse and include animal research, naturalistic observations of mothers with their infants, family research, research into the nature and function of speech and language, research into creativity, and research into the processes operative in psychoanalytic therapy. Given the very different data bases these investigators have relied on, it should come as no surprise that their very different types of investigations have led them to espouse different points of view about the nature of man, human relatedness, and psychoanalytic theory and technique. It is the hope of the editors, though, that the papers collected in this volume will help the reader clarify the origin and nature of the differences between the different paradigms and the boundaries between them, and thus how and why they either complement and enrich or contradict one another.

The first section of this volume gathers together six papers that address the very basic question of how the paradigm of psychoanalysis articulated in terms of drive and defense should be modified. Each of the authors feels a major modification is indicated, but that is where their agreement ends.

Merton Gill opens the volume by asserting that psychoanalysis must choose between a person and an energy discharge point of view, as well as between a hermeneutic and a natural science framework for organizing the data of psychoanalysis. He clarifies some of the differences between the different schools of psychoanalysis by using these contrasting conceptual points of view, emphasizing especially their different understandings of transference and countertransference phenomena and their different recommendations with regard to psychoanalytic technique.

Gill's paradigm derives from his perspective as a teaching, training, and supervising analyst engaged in scientific research into the nature of the analytic process. His recent work has aimed at a clarification of the nature of transference and its analysis through careful scrutiny of actual recorded transactions between analyst and analysand. Data derived from research into his own and others' analytic work have led him to conclude that a body schema with its sexual and aggressive imperatives must certainly be taken into account by psychoanalytic theorists and therapists; nonetheless, he feels that supraordinate to the body schema, which is itself different from the traditional Freudian drive paradigm, is a person paradigm. He explicates here the ways in which this "person point of view" calls for a fundamental reorganization of psychoanalytic theory and technique.

John Scott and John Bowlby agree with Gill that a fundamental reorientation in psychoanalysis is called for, but the paradigm they advocate is conceptualized in terms of attachment and separation. Both Scott and Bowlby, in a series of elegant and comprehensive studies of attachment and its disruptions, have described the biologically based beginnings of relationship processes.

Professor Scott has devoted his life to research into animal development and its implications for human behavior and development. He details the basic animal research evidence for "site" and "social" attachment, the evidence for the importance of "critical periods" for forming social attachments, and the implications of these phenomena for the characteristics and consequences of "separation distress." He then preliminarily explores the implications of this basic animal research on attachment and separation processes for human behavior in general, and psychotherapy in particular, an exploration extended by Bowlby.

Dr. Bowlby's work on attachment, separation, and loss, especially in terms of the origin and evolution of the child's tie to the maternal figure, is well known. In it he brought his scholarly knowledge of animal studies, his training as an analyst, and his concern with such central analytic concepts as the object ties, anxiety, and defensive processes and their implications for growth, development, and structure formation to his naturalistic observations of children with their mother or maternal figure. His lifelong effort has been to clarify the nature of the forces leading to attachment and to study the effects on the developing child of instances of separation and loss once attachment has been effected.

His findings, over time, led him, like Gill, to be critical of psychoanalytic explanations in terms of psychic energy and drive discharge. In contrast to Gill, however, but in agreement with Scott, his findings led him to advocate explanations in terms of attachment and its vicissitudes and in terms of systems theory, information theory, and cognitive psychology. In his chapter he explores in addition the implications of his point of view for conceptualizations of psychopathology, defensive activity, and psychotherapy.

Lyman Wynne's chapter builds explicitly on those of Gill, Scott, and Bowlby. Wynne is an analyst who brought an analytic perspective to his pioneering research into normal and pathological family functioning. His data base thus includes psychoanalytically informed research into the forces operative in both dyadic and family relationships. Noting Gill's advocacy of a person paradigm supraordinate to the traditional body paradigm of psychoanalysis, Wynne for his part outlines a "relatedness paradigm" that he suggests can be viewed from within a systems theory perspective as supraordinate to the person paradigm. Here he elaborates an epigenetic theory of relatedness or, more precisely, of relationship systems that progressively unfold over the life cycle. Wynne feels relatedness has its beginnings in attachment and caregiving, and uses the contributions of Scott, Bowlby, and others to clarify the nature of this early type of relatedness. He then sketches out an epigenetic sequence of types of relatedness leading to mutuality and compares it to Erik Erikson's stages of individual development, postulating an epigenesis of relationship systems that parallels the epigenesis of the individual's intrapsychic and social development throughout the life cycle. He then uses this paradigm to reexamine psychopathology and is able to suggest various therapeutic interventions that such a conceptual scheme indicates would have a useful impact on pathological developments in relatedness.

With John Muller's chapter the focus shifts. Like the others, he feels the basic psychoanalytic paradigm is in need of major revision, but the revision he suggests is quite different. Muller's work has been primarily concerned with explicating the function and field of speech and language in psychoanalysis. He has devoted himself particularly to exploring the contributions and implications of the work of Jacques Lacan to contemporary psychoanalysis. Here Muller calls for a radical reconceptualization, based on the work of Lacan, of what is central to psychosis and its treatment. Using a literary text, an account of a native American healing ceremony, and the account of psychotherapeutic work with a psychotic individual, Muller explicates what Lacan refers to as the three essential dimensions, or registers, of human reality: "the real," "the imaginary," and "the symbolic," and reinterprets the nature of psychosis and its therapy within this theoretical framework.

Daniel Schwartz's chapter completes the theoretical section of this volume. Schwartz's data base consists of analytic work with seriously disturbed patients and psychoanalytically informed observations and work with children. Long concerned with an effort to formulate a psychoanalytic concept of action, he is interested in the relationship between the general conditions of "actions" which are necessary for the development of intrapsychic structure and for their alteration, either in the course of development or in psychotherapy. He believes he has articulated supraordinate conditions applicable to each psychosocial and psychosexual stage but not confined to any one of them. These are the opportunity to represent the psychic structure's evolving nature, the describable range of action for the exercise of the structure, the limits of the range of action, and conditions which facilitate fusion and which are asymmetrical. He then proposes that change in intrapsychic structure during the course of psychoanalysis or psychotherapy requires similar conditions which help arrange the integration of action's possibilities prior to the full organization of symbol formation in words.

The next section of this volume consists of two chapters focusing on areas of ongoing empirical research in psychoanalysis. John Gunderson is a psychoanalyst currently conducting a multihospital psychotherapy outcome study designed to evaluate the mechanisms and context in which schizophrenic patients can benefit from psychotherapy. Here he provides a preliminary report of some of the results of this study. His work represents a critically important research effort to empirically study the characteristics of the schizophrenic patient, the characteristics of the therapist, and of the types of engagement between therapist and patient that lead to favorable change. He also investigates the contextual influences within families and hospitals that promote or interfere with engagement, continuation, and favorable outcome of psychotherapy with schizophrenic patients.

Albert Rothenberg's chapter draws on material from his previous and ongoing research into the domains of aesthetics and creativity, and applies his findings about particular cognitive functions involved in the creative process to psychotherapy. After defining the process of "articulation of error" and demonstrating its importance as a factor operating widely in creativity, he discusses the central importance of "the creative articulation of transference errors" in the psychotherapeutic action of psychotherapy, both in general and as applied to work with schizophrenics.

Four chapters focusing on clinical issues follow. These contributions reflect ongoing efforts to clarify and specify both the difficulties seriously troubled individuals have and the processes of engagement with them that promote favorable change. They thus reflect ongoing psychoanalytic efforts to broaden and deepen understanding of human development and interaction as these features are revealed during the course of intensive work with deeply troubled individuals.

Gaetano Benedetti opens the section with a description of a successful treatment of a psychotic patient. Benedetti, an Italian analyst living and working in Switzerland, is a pioneer in long-term, intensive psychoanalytic work with psychotic individuals. Once an assistant of Professor Manfred Bleuler, his psychoanalytic training and perspective were greatly influenced by his association with the existential analysts Gustav Bally and Medard Boss. This existential background brings to Benedetti's analytic work a special emphasis on the reciprocity and mutuality of the relationship between patient and therapist and on the extent to which the psychotherapeutic encounter is potentially transformative for both. He stresses that what is meaningful and transformative in the psychotherapeutic work with a psychotic individual is both interpretation and the patient's coming to know that he has an impact on the therapist, that he actually changes him. For this to occur, the therapist must be open to being inhabited by various aspects of the patient and his experience, including both dead or deathly aspects and wholly original and vital aspects of the patient. Similarly, the analyst must permit parallel aspects of himself to dwell in the patient for variable periods. Benedetti argues that both patient and therapist must learn to accept this as part of the process of therapeutic change, as it leads to the creation of shared symbols vital to the success of the work.

The next chapter continues the exploration of the ways in which the experiences of the analyst in the psychotherapeutic encounter are crucial data, to be unflinchingly scrutinized, if analysts are to deepen their understanding of disorders of human relatedness and of the factors that either promote or interfere with their amelioration. Beatriz Foster has devoted herself to work with deeply troubled people. She often works with individuals with previously unsuccessful therapy experiences—individuals who are felt by others and by themselves to be hopelessly ill—and brings to this work a capacity to immerse herself in the patient's experience. Like Benedetti, she allows their experience to inhabit her, affect her, disturb her, in order that whatever experience is stirred in her may be used as part of the data of the treatment, to be examined and understood by patient and analyst alike. She thereby conveys a willingness to share in someone's experience, however hazardous, traumatic, failed, disturbed, regressed, or disorganized it may be, in order to help them endure it, and struggle to understand and alter it, if that is their wish. She is deeply respectful of the dignity of the people with whom she works and is determined to respect their autonomy and freedom, mindful and accepting of the anxiety, uncertainty, and pain that this will at times evoke. Dr. Foster demonstrates these qualities by providing a riveting account of the impact on her of the suicides of two of her patients. Her very personal paper describes the steps she took to understand, resolve, and integrate these experiences into her ongoing life and work.

In the following chapter, Hilde Bruch describes the changing picture of anorexia nervosa. A psychoanalyst treating deeply disturbed people with eating disorders, she describes how her work forced her to alter her conception of human development, especially with regard to such basic issues as how one acquires a sense of separateness and effective autonomy, a body image, a sense of thinness or fatness, and a capacity to identify accurately states of hunger and satiety. Prior to her work with individuals with eating disorders, she had assumed, as do analysts generally, that these perceptual and conceptual abilities unfold in some innate, genetically prescribed manner. But, as she discovered, all this must be learned, an insight that helped her begin to explicate the complicated interrelationships between perception, social learning, and the development of intrapsychic structure and functioning. She has been a pioneer explorer of clinical states that reflect developmental arrests, regressions, and distortions secondary to, or contingent upon, social and personal learning within a family context. Her work with individuals with eating disorders led her to reconceptualize the nature of their difficulties in terms of their relationship to schizophrenia, pathological narcissism, and borderline personality organization. She notes that in all of these conditions one sees, in addition to intrapsychic conflicts, defects of intrapsychic structure and functioning, and defects in perception and conception of bodily, emotional, and social realities due, in large part, to faulty learning in social contexts. In a concluding section she outlines some of the modifications of technique required for work with such individuals.

In the last chapter of the clinical section, Clarence Schulz draws on his experience as psychoanalyst, educator, hospital administrator, and therapist of seriously disturbed patients to explicate a carefully individualized, multidisciplinary treatment approach to the difficulties of the seriously troubled. He addresses the current emphasis on symptoms, considered apart from the total person, and the pressures on hospitals and individual therapists to develop symptom-specific treatment approaches to provide rapid symptom relief. The approach he advocates does not ignore these emphases and pressures, but maintains a psychoanalytic developmental perspective with regard to both the nature of the psychopathology and its treatment. He illustrates this orientation and process by discussing a coordinated, individualized treatment approach focusing on the promotion of one developmental advance: the advance from splitting and recourse to other all-or-none phenomena to a higher level of integration that includes, and is marked by, the acquisition of ambivalence.

This volume evolved out of an International Symposium entitled "Illuminations of the Human Condition: Perspectives Arising from Psychoanalytic and Psychological Sciences," convened by the Trustees and Staff of the Austen Riggs Center in Stockbridge, Massachusetts, October 1–3, 1982, to honor Dr. Otto Allen Will, Jr., former medical director of the Center, for his lifetime of effort and achievement, particularly his many contributions to the psychoanalytic understanding and treatment of psychotic individuals. The symposium brought together distinguished clinicians and researchers who have devoted themselves to exploring various aspects of human experience that directly relate to this central concern.

Otto Will is one of a handful of psychoanalysts who has chosen to devote his entire professional life to attempting to understand and help psychotic individuals by entering into long-term, intensive psychotherapeutic relationships with them. In addition to individual psychotherapeutic work, he has spent his life supervising other therapists' work with these individuals. He has also been, and remains, a therapist to therapists engaged in this difficult work. The knowledge gleaned from his work with patients and supervisees constitutes both the data and the method of his ongoing research into the nature of psychotic and nonpsychotic ways of life and into the nature of the conditions and processes necessary for useful, that is, transformative psychotherapeutic work with psychotics.

Dr. Will came to psychiatry, psychoanalysis, and the psychoses somewhat circuitously. After completing medical school, he took postgraduate training first in pediatrics and then in internal medicine. However, World War II and active duty in the Navy interrupted his medical training and, following the war, he again changed specialties. It was at this point that he began his training as a psychiatrist and psychoanalyst. He chose as his training analyst Harry Stack Sullivan. Frieda Fromm-Reichman became a valued colleague when early in his career he joined the staff of Chestnut Lodge, a private psychiatric hospital in Rockville, Maryland, specializing in long-term, intensive, psychoanalytically oriented work with psychotic and other seriously troubled individuals. The relationships with Sullivan and Fromm-Reichman and what he learned from them about the origin and function of psychotic processes and about the nature of psychotherapy have been enduringly important influences on Dr. Will's thought and work.

In addition to the associations with Sullivan, Fromm-Reichman, and other pioneers in the field of intensive psychotherapy with psychotic individuals, his ongoing work at Chestnut Lodge, first as a staff psychiatrist and later as Director of Psychotherapy, provided countless opportunities to learn firsthand about psychotic phenomena and what facilitated or interfered with his own and others' efforts to understand and impact therapeutically on such phenomena. During his years at the Lodge, Dr. Will's reputation as a clinician, supervisor, and teacher steadily grew, and it was during these years that he began to publish papers on his experiences with psychotic individuals. A complete bibliography of Otto Will's published papers is included in this volume and in addition we have elected to reprint three of his papers for the benefit of readers unfamiliar with his writings. These papers highlight his work as clinician, consultant, and supervisor. We have included them in addition to the original paper he presented at the symposium. This later paper is typically wide-ranging, thought-provoking, and very personal, and it fittingly encompasses the complex issues grappled with in the various contributions to this volume.

In 1967 Dr. Will left Chestnut Lodge to become Medical Director of the Austen Riggs Center in Stockbridge, Massachusetts. Like the Lodge, Austen Riggs is a private psychiatric hospital specializing in long-term, intensive, psychoanalytically oriented psychotherapy with psychotic and nonpsychotic but very seriously disturbed individuals. Unique to the Austen Riggs Center, though, is its totally open and totally voluntary character. It has as well an extraordinarily rich psychoanalytic tradition, having had on its staff pioneers in psychoanalytic ego psychology and treatment techniques. Its experimental yet psychoanalytic tradition invited Dr. Will to further explore the possibilities and limitations of long-term psychotherapeutic work with individuals with severe difficulties. For the next eleven years, Dr. Will continued his activities as therapist, supervisor, teacher, researcher, and writer, working to refine, deepen, and expand his ongoing efforts to grasp and report on some of the essential aspects of human experience as these are revealed in the psychotherapeutic encounter. One of Dr. Will's unique capacities has been his ability to look at psychotic experience from a psychoanalytic developmental perspective and to find revealed there something of normal life that has been overlooked. Thus, one source of his originality and creativity has been his capacity to relate reciprocally psychotic and normal experience. He can approach psychosis and freshly illuminate it in terms of normal developmental considerations. He can also derive from psychotic experience insight into what we need to look at as important in normal development that has been overlooked or taken for granted, but that in fact requires a developmental exploration and explanation. Dr. Will retired as Medical Director of the Austen Riggs Center in 1978. He continues as a Trustee of the Center and contributes to its teaching program periodically, as he does at other centers. He is currently in private practice in San Francisco, California, and his work and contributions to the field continue.

Having acquainted the reader with Otto Will, we would like to quote and paraphrase some passages from his papers that might serve to convey enough of how Dr. Will conceptualizes the nature of psychopathology and psychotherapy to make clear the interrelation of his work and that of the contributors to this volume.

On the nature of psychiatric disorder

"Psychiatric disorders themselves may be thought of as destructive, inadequate, inappropriate, unduly complicated, or overly simplified forms of human behavior, exhibited in interpersonal situations, and arising from experiences in a variety of previous interpersonal fields. Although we do not disregard man's genetic-biological foundation, we consider the behavior that we call 'sick' as having been developed largely in response to social, cultural, and existential necessities, as learned, and as having purposes and goals" (Will, 1976, p. 363).

"Man may be seen as a participant in multiple, serial, and concomitant social fields—being molded by these and, in varying degrees, molding them in turn" (Will, 1976, p. 362).

The most serious maladaptive behaviors originate in the first relationship between the infant and his mother, and in the relationship of the infant to his family as a system.

"The human infant depends for a long time on those who care for him; he is exposed to their anxieties, beliefs, values, emotions, ways of living, and personal idiosyncracies. During his early life he is bound to a narrow space, physically and socially, from which he cannot escape" (Will, 1980, p. 1230).

"The beginnings of low self-esteem, insecurity, lack of trust, perceptual defects, disfigurements of body image, may stem from the infant's involvement in a disturbed, anxiety-laden, unclear social system (the family) before the establishment of a reliable concept of self and others and the refinement of speech skills" (Will, 1980, p. 1230).

". . . each of the family groups from which those people came seemed to be normal on the surface but disturbed on closer view. Here 'disturbed' refers to strong ambivalences regarding relationships within the family, odd and private views about the world, interferences with the development of independent and reliable identities in its members: and resistance to the growing up of the children" (Will, 1980, p. 1222).

Thus, the future patient struggles to find security and satisfaction, to establish and maintain required human relationships, to keep anxiety within tolerable limits, to maintain self-esteem, and to discover a way to communicate meaningfully, without destructive self-revelation, but his efforts are hampered from the beginning.

> ". . . the upset condition is derived from an accumulation of failing adjustive efforts beginning in early life . . . failure to acquire the social, interpersonal skills usually formed in one developmental era handicaps the learning of skills in succeeding eras. Thus, the learning defects in childhood contribute to the difficulties of learning in the juvenile era, and deficiencies in the juvenile era contribute to the problems of adolescence" (Will, 1980, p. 1229).

Defensive operations required to maintain self-esteem and freedom from anxiety and other dysphoric affects lead to increasing isolation and/or to increasing dissociation of major aspects of one's personality; i.e., those thought to be incompatible with the need to maintain security and secure satisfaction. Bothersome behaviors, all learned, increasingly reflect this progressive isolation and dissociation, and also, of course, reflect "in miniaturized, distorted, or accurate ways the social system in which the patient grew up and in which he currently exists" (Will, 1980, p. 1226). Breakdown ultimately occurs when the person is confronted by tasks and stresses he simply is not able to cope with.

> At this point the individual's behavior "often becomes so complex and devious—or so stereotyped and simplified—that its primary goal-directedness is lost, communication becomes increasingly defective, relationships are attenuated or give way to fantasy, anxiety increases, and despair and panic supervene." [Will, 1976, p. 363]

Serious adult psychopathology thus is looked upon as the expression of the culmination of interpersonal insults, learning defects, and dissociations of experience, vital to satisfactory adult living, uncorrected from infancy. It is the representation of human-biological-social development and an expression of the individual's effort to establish, maintain, and further evolve a personal identity that will enable him to function satisfactorily in interpersonal and social situations. The different types of serious psychopathology are, in short, "ways of human living, multiply determined, modifiable for better or worse, and in varying degrees, through interpersonal-social experience" (Will, 1976, p. 363).

On the nature of the psychotherapeutic process
> "The psychotherapeutic process is a special instance of an interpersonal relationship and is thus well suited for intervention in disorders that in themselves have their origins to a large extent in such relationships and reflect current difficulties in them. The procedure is one of learning in social situations. It is designed to correct misadventures of earlier years through which important aspects of experience have been shut off from awareness, grave misapprehensions of the self and others have developed, and dangerous oversimplifications or complexities of behavior have been formed." [Will, 1980, p. 1232]

New learning and changes are encouraged and made possible by examining the development and evolution of the relationship between the patient and the therapist. "Psychotherapy is based on the planned use of the human relationship as an agent of change" (Will, 1980, p. 1227).

The theory and practice of psychotherapy is predicated on the biology and psychology of the processes associated with attachment, dependence, growth, change, separation, and loss as they evolve in evolving human relationships.

> "In or out of the hospital, the therapist must attend to the various social fields in which the patient has his existence—the family, the school, the ward, people with whom he or she lives, and the one-to-one relationship with the therapist himself." [Will, 1980, p. 1228]

To be especially noted are distortions in perceptions of the sense of self and of others and adaptive and maladaptive ways of interacting, including the emergence of forms of thinking and behavior that decrease anxiety but interfere with accurate perception of reality and with personality growth. In the course of this work, intense feelings will be stirred up in the patient and in the therapist. They are the invariable accompaniments of the growing relationship and are part of the data to be observed, learned from, and put to use in the service of developing an understanding of the processes that promote and inhibit the growth of the patient. With frequent meetings, attachment increases. Hitherto dissociated aspects of experience are brought into awareness and are integrated into the concept of self and others. When things go well, the patient learns about himself, gains confidence, discovers abilities, and accepts limitations.

> "In general terms the goal [of psychotherapy] is the attainment of a form of personal freedom in which the major aspects of the self are available to awareness and recognized as being a part of one, the ways of relating to others are known, the aloneness of existence is accepted without resort to restrictive mythologies, interpersonal attachment and separation are understood as necessary and inevitable, change and uncertainty are tolerated, and choices can be made from those options for action that may be open." [Will, 1973, p. 153]

Thus, a sickness is not cured, "but a way of life and a manner of looking at the world and the self" (Will, 1980, p. 1219) are altered.

We hope these passages have made clear how the various contributors to this volume reflect, have influenced, and are influenced by the work of Otto Will. This volume is meant to honor Dr. Will and his life's work as well as to reaffirm the enduring value of the continuing unique contributions that psychoanalysis has to make to understanding the full range of human experience, whether it be labeled normal, neurotic, psychotic, or creative.

References

Will, O. A. (1973), Psychotherapy: Changing styles as exemplified in the treatment of schizophrenia. *Amer. J. Psychiat.*, 130(2):152–155.

——— (1976), Psychiatry at the Austen Riggs Center. In: *Long-Term Treatments of Psychotic States*, ed. C. Chiland. New York: Human Sciences Press, pp. 361–374.

——— (1980), Schizophrenia: Psychological treatment. In: *Comprehensive Textbook of Psychiatry III*, Vol. 2, ed. H. Kaplan et al. Baltimore: Williams and Wilkins, pp. 1217–1240.

Part I

Theory

1

The Point of View of Psychoanalysis: Energy Discharge or Person

Merton M. Gill, M.D., Ph.D.

It is common to believe that one's own era is one of particular ferment. We believe that about psychoanalysis today. There do seem to have arisen a number of foci of active challenge to received wisdom. Some of the important issues of debate are these: (1) Is psychoanalysis a hermeneutic discipline, a natural science, or both? Or, alternatively, what is the proper role of psychoanalytic metapsychology? (Ricoeur, 1970; Gill and Holzman, 1976). (2) On the assumption that it must include a natural science metapsychology, should the energy metapsychology be replaced by an information theory metapsychology? (Gill, 1977; Peterfreund, 1971; Rosenblatt and Thickstun, 1978). (3) Is psychoanalysis a linguistic discipline, as Lacan (1977) maintains, and does Schafer's proposal for an ''action language'' (1976) have the same implication? (4) Is an object relations theory subordinate to Freud's paradigm or a replacement for it, and exactly what is that paradigm? (Mujeeb-ur-Rahman, 1977). And how are the recently promulgated theories of self psychology (Kohut, 1977) related to object relations psychologies (Sutherland, 1980) on the one hand and Freud's

I am indebted to my colleague Irwin Z. Hoffman, for specific suggestions as well as for our continuing conversations.

17

paradigm on the other? (5) What is the appropriate balance of transference and extratransference interpretations, of attention to the here-and-now and to the past? (Gill, 1982a). (6) Are psychoanalysis and psychotherapy on a continuum or are they dichotomous techniques? (Gill, 1984; Joseph and Wallerstein, 1983). How important a role may appropriately be played by the relationship between patient and analyst as a mutative factor in the analytic result (Dewald, 1976; Loewald, 1960), and to what extent can one reasonably expect the transference neurosis to be resolved? (Norman, Blacker, Oremland, and Barrett, 1976; Schlessinger and Robbins, 1983). (8) Does the recent emphasis on the analytic process as a construction of a narrative (Schafer, 1980; Sherwood, 1969) imply that we cannot reconstruct the past in any significantly veridical sense? (9) Can the several schools of analysis be differentiated in terms of their position on a single central issue?

These controversies need to be sharply delineated. An important part of that task is to establish the pertinent hierarchical relations. I suggest that the supraordinate question under which this confusing array of controversies can be subsumed is whether the appropriate point of view for psychoanalysis is that of energy discharge or of persons. I will elaborate the implications of this issue for only some of the controversies I have mentioned, though it has implications for all of them. In what follows I opt for the person point of view. My position is that the basic integrating point of view of psychoanalysis should be that of relations between people, not that of energy discharge. I make bold to reaffirm this anticlimactic pronouncement—and it is a commonplace—because I believe I can clarify some of the issues involved.

It is not easy to fix on an appropriate label for this overarching integrative concept. I have just chosen *point of view*. I have considered *paradigm*, with its connotation, established by Kuhn (1963), of a basic and shared integrative concept of a discipline. I have considered *matrix* because of its connotations of ''that within which something is embedded,'' as well as of ''framework,'' and furthermore because it has the same root as ''mother''—my position here will be that the point of view of psychoanalysis should be interpersonal, and the relationship with mother is of course the primary and abiding one for human beings. Frame of reference and point of view are much the same. For the present at least I have settled on the latter in deference to the fact that psychoanalytic metapsychology has long been described in terms of points of view. Though I have argued for the abandonment of psychoanalytic metapsychology (Gill and Holzman, 1976), the cogent objection has been made that any system of thought must have a "meta" organizing principle, whether implicit or explicit. I can only have meant the abandonment of the present metapsychology. Schafer (1976) has been especially clear on this point in his criticisms of the prevailing metapsychology and his advocacy of action language as a differing and consistent point of view. I believe that his concept of a language parallels what I am calling here a point of view, and that his action language implies the person point of view I am espousing (Friedman, 1976a, b). In Schafer's discussions of action he always insists that a person, not a drive, is acting. Freud was saying much the same thing when he wrote, "we become aware that the attitudes of love and hate cannot be made use of for the relations of *instincts* to their objects, but are reserved for the relations of the *total ego* to objects" (1915, p. 137).

It is also not easy to fix upon appropriate terms to designate the opposing points of view I discuss. I have just labeled them the energy discharge and the person points of view. Probably more usual is the characterization of this dichotomy in terms of interpersonal relations and drive. However, I reject drive as a term for one side of the dichotomy. It is taken by many to mean that the distinction is between the bodily and nonbodily, and interpersonal relations, I would argue, may partake of both. The intended contrast is rather between bodily relations meaningful in interpersonal terms and those conceptualized as discharge of energy. If drive is conceived of as an innate biological urge rather than more specifically as an energy-seeking discharge, there is no reason one cannot postulate an innate drive toward interpersonal relations, both bodily and nonbodily. Indeed this is a postulate for which we are indebted to John Bowlby (1960) and, before him, Imre Hermann (1936), as well as to the work of the Harlows (Harlow and Harlow, 1965). This postulate stands in contrast to the Freudian conception of interpersonal attachment as secondary to the gratification of somatic drive—what Bowlby calls the cupboard-love theory.

I have chosen the term *person* rather than "interpersonal" because for so many the latter automatically means Sullivan's theory, to which I will turn later. The less encumbered *person* implies interpersonal relations and is less subject to the implication that interpersonal relations derive solely from experience imprinted on a blank slate, a conception I reject. Person seems to me on the one hand to encompass self, object relationship, and interpersonal theories, and on the other to be relatively free of the connotations these terms have acquired in our battles. I shall later argue, however, that the term interpersonal is more restrictive in its implication for the range of human motivation than is the term person.

An especially confusing and potentially misleading issue in establishing the terms of the dichotomy is that of sexuality. For many analysts sexuality is well-nigh equivalent to what I have spoken of as the bodily. Sexuality can become the focus of serious misunderstandings in efforts to discuss the psychoanalytic point of view because to some it means interpersonal bodily relations while to others it means energy discharge. Indeed it is easy to slip from one meaning to the other. It is for this reason that a rejection of the energy discharge point of view is so often misunderstood to be a rejection of the centrality of sexuality in human psychology.

My course in this essay is as follows: I will first outline the difference between the two points of view. I will then sketch the implications of the acceptance of the person point of view for the following issues: the controversy over whether psychoanalysis should be a hermeneutic or a natural science; the position of several schools of analysis on the point of view; the understanding of transference which follows from the person point of view and some of the implications for technique of this understanding; the controversy over the difference between psychoanalysis and psychotherapy; and, finally, how the acceptance of the person point of view might improve the prospects for systematic research in psychoanalysis. The range of these topics is so broad that I can offer only an outline in the space of this essay.

I shall not attempt a precise definition of the two points of view. I will assume the reader knows essentially what I mean and that my meaning will become clearer as I sketch the implications of the person point of view for the issues mentioned. In broadest terms, the energy discharge point of view sees the person as concerned primarily with the gratification of bodily needs while the other sees the person as concerned primarily with his relations with other people. I deny that psychoanalysis requires both, but I insist that the person point of view subsume the data which might lead to adoption of its rival.

There is a vast body of evidence which points to the enormous importance of the body in human development, to bodily experiences as templates for complex modes of human interaction, and to the clarification of these complex interactions when they are understood as disguised expressions of these bodily templates. When one considers that from the genetic standpoint human interaction *is* bodily interaction, this does not seem so surprising. That man is a biological entity with somatic needs, as well as the subjective sense of urgency and the discharge (both literal and metaphorical) that so often accompany the arousal and gratification of these needs, makes it easy to understand the persuasiveness of the energy discharge point of view. For one who espouses the other point of view, therefore, a major problem is how to give due recognition to the influence and centrality, both in development and throughout life, of these bodily templates and yet to make them subordinate to the psychological, interpersonal meanings that bodily experiences have for the person.

A crucial consideration in the clarification of the hierarchical relationship between energy discharge and person, as well as between bodily and non-bodily interpersonal interaction, is the symbolic representation of bodily considerations. It must be recognized that the body as such does not influence the person but only as that influence is meaningfully represented in the psyche. Freud said as much when he distinguished between the instinctual drive and its psychic representation. But his metapsychology describes the vicissitudes of these representations in the natural science dimensions of force, energy, and locus, while his clinical theory describes them in the hermeneutic dimensions of purpose, intention, and position in a psychical context. A somatic stimulus acquires meaning in an interpersonal context. It cannot be otherwise, because psychological man exists only in an interpersonal context.

An important difficulty preventing consensus on the person point of view is that its rival does not reject the data which in my opinion speak for the person point of view but on the contrary subsumes and thus in a sense coopts them. It is for this reason that an insistence on the person point of view will seem to many like banging on an open door. The very emphasis it currently enjoys in psychoanalysis makes it more difficult to argue for its hierarchical primacy, as it seems already adequately taken into account.

I offer a quotation from Freud to show how close he could come to a statement of the person point of view. In the introduction to "Group Psychology and the Analysis of the Ego" he wrote, "In the individual's mental life someone else is invariably involved, as a model, as an object, as a helper, as an opponent; and so from the very first individual psychology, in this extended but entirely justifiable sense of the words, is at the same time social psychology as well" (1921, p. 69).

But I must quote him again to show how even a passage which comes close to the person point of view, and even more so with regard to sexuality, that shibboleth of those who insist that the supraordinate point of view must be energy discharge, remains ambiguous as to the relation between the points of view. In " 'Wild' Psycho-Analysis" he wrote,

> In psycho-analysis the concept of what is sexual . . . goes lower and also higher than its popular sense. This extension is justified genetically; we reckon as belonging to "sexual life" all the activities of the tender feelings which have primitive sexual impulses as their source even when those impulses have become inhibited in regard to their original sexual aim or have exchanged this aim for another which is no longer sexual. For this reason we prefer to speak of *psychosexuality*, thus laying stress on the point that the mental factor in sexual life should not be overlooked or underestimated. We use the word "sexuality" in the same comprehensive sense as that in which the German language uses the word *lieben* ["to love"]. . . .
>
> Anyone not sharing this view of psychosexuality has no right to adduce psycho-analytic theses dealing with the aetiological importance of sexuality. By emphasizing exclusively the somatic factor in sexuality he undoubtedly simplifies the problem greatly,

but he alone must bear the responsibility for what he does. [1910, pp. 222–223]

I suggest that "goes lower and also higher" bespeaks the ambiguity as to the relationship of the points of view.

Now to show how Freud can be guilty of the very simplification he deplores, I quote a formulation of his which sounds very much as though written from the energy discharge point of view alone. It is from one of his last works, "An Outline of Psycho-Analysis": "Modifications in the proportions of the fusion between the instincts have the most tangible results. A surplus of sexual aggressiveness will turn a lover into a sex-murderer, while a sharp diminution in the aggressive factor will make him bashful or impotent" (1940, p. 149).

It is impossible to say how much of a role the perspective of this last quote plays in ordinary analytic work as compared to that of the first, but it is not hard to believe that the temptation to resort to the energy discharge point of view can become great in times of stress in the transference, about which I will have more to say.

There is frequent reference in the Freudian literature to the genetic fallacy, by which is meant the reductionist equation of a complex, multidetermined phenomenon with a primitive phase of but one of its many aspects. I consider the energy discharge point of view in large measure responsible for the prevalence with which the genetic fallacy goes unrecognized; it reduces a complex human interaction to a sexual formulation.

As one of the bases for my speaking more generally of the body, rather than more specifically of sexuality, as a central consideration in psychoanalysis, as well as for my choice of the person point of view, I refer to Bowlby's criticism of Freud's specification of the primitive somatic basis for later interpersonal interaction. Bowlby finds the basis for such interaction rather in social attachment, in a literal sense, from the beginning of life. He counterposes this position to the Freudian ascription of social attachment as anaclitic to bodily needs and gratifications. Another way of pointing to the priority of personhood is to emphasize that the same bodily (including sexual) apparatus is used, like attachment, to express both love and hate.

I have suggested that Freud's emphasis on the data which for me bespeak a person point of view makes it more difficult to show the primacy of that point of view. I must add that a major difficulty standing in the way of the acceptance of the person point of view is that so often those who espouse it neglect the bodily data emphasized by those who espouse the energy discharge point of view. I will return to this point in my discussion of the schools of psychoanalysis.

Hermeneutics or Natural Science

I turn to the implication of the person point of view for the controversy as to whether psychoanalysis should be a hermeneutic or a natural science. I could logically have chosen this issue as supraordinate to the specific points of view I am counterposing. The hermeneutic position is that psychoanalysis deals with meanings, while the natural science position is that psychoanalysis deals with the neurochemical, physiological, or biological dimensions. If one asks what kinds of meanings psychoanalysis deals with and answers, interpersonal meanings which take account of natural science events in terms of their interpersonal significance, then one is opting for the person point of view; whereas if one answers that psychoanalysis deals with the discharge of drives and takes account of interpersonal meanings in terms of their significance for such discharge, then one has opted for the energy discharge point of view.

Since I consider it possible to refer to Freud without implying that he must of necessity be right, and since I believe that as the founder of psychoanalysis his views merit special attention, I will offer a quotation from Freud which distinguishes between the psychological and the organic and proposes the centrality of meaning as the dimension of psychology:

Anything that is observable in mental life may occasionally be described as a mental phenomenon. The question will then be whether the particular mental phenomenon has arisen immediately from somatic, organic, and material influences—in which case its investigation will not be part of psychology—or whether it is derived in the first instance from other mental processes, somewhere behind which the series of organic influences begins. It is this latter situation that we have in view when we describe a phenomenon as a mental process, and for that reason it is more expedient to clothe our assertion in the form: 'the phenomenon has a sense.' By 'sense' we understand 'meaning,' 'intention,' 'purpose,' and 'position in a continuous psychical context.' [1916–1917, pp. 60–61]

"Position in a continuous psychical context" is a particularly important concept because it provides the basis for inferring unconscious processes. It was the interruptions in a continuous psychical context which Freud considered irrefutable evidence that there must be dynamic unconscious mental processes, to complete the psychical context. He never tired of saying that these unconscious processes are psychological in the same sense in which conscious mental processes are.[1]

While we may agree that intention and purpose give psychoanalysis an unmistakably teleological cast, can we agree on what kinds of intentions and purposes are pursued in this continuous psychical context? I have taken the position that they are interpersonal meanings. I believe that the data of psychoanalysis point unmistakably to this conclusion, but I make no pretense to rigorously demonstrate the claim. Rather, I am discussing some of the consequences of such a conclusion, partly in the hope that the cogency of the consequences will themselves help to establish the validity of the original claim.

Hermeneutics is a term that does not sit well with American psychoanalysts. It conjures up visions of exegetical hairsplitting, of abstruse philosophical jargon unrelated to palpable facts. Together with

---

[1]It is sometimes objected that the failure to emphasize that this is an assumption based on conscious experience may lead to too ready an equation between conscious and unconscious processes. Freud discussed whether the dynamic unconscious is best conceived of as physical or psychical perhaps most clearly in the late work, "An Outline of Psycho-Analysis" (1940, pp. 144–207). Contrary to my thesis in this paper he held the view that the fact "that the unconscious is psychical in itself, enabled psychology to take its place as a natural science like any other" (p. 158). I believe that the error of his conclusion that psychoanalysis is thus a natural science is exposed in his immediately following remark that the processes with which psychology is concerned are just as unknowable as those dealt with by sciences like chemistry and physics. Perhaps not just as unknowable and, in any case, not unknowable in the same sense. Freud may be equating natural science with all science.

such disciplines as phenomenology and existentialism it seems to por-
tend a flight from the body and the familiar oral, anal, and phallic
realities. But hermeneutics is the discipline of interpretation and it is
impossible to deny that interpretation lies at the heart of psychoanalysis.
Interpretation is devoted to discovering hidden meanings. Psychoanalysts surely are occupied with finding such meanings.

I must take a little time for definitions of metapsychology and
hermeneutics. I use metapsychology as synonymous with the natural
science position and with the energy discharge point of view as supraordinate. My license for doing so is that this is by far the most
prevalent sense in which Freud used the term, that it was he who
introduced the term to psychoanalysis, and that it is the most prevalent
meaning of the term in contemporary psychoanalysis. I believe this
to be true even for those who say they use it to mean simply psychoanalytic theory in general (Brenner, 1980) or simply as the highest
order of abstraction from clinical data. Of course I believe that theory
is necessary and that general laws must be sought, but I argue that
metapsychology as presently constituted is in a different universe of
discourse from that of meaning, namely the natural science universe
of force, energy, and space. As such it is incompatible with a hermeneutic science. I reiterate that I believe the energy discharge point
of view is conceptually parallel to the generally accepted psychoanalytic metapsychology and the conception of psychoanalysis as a natural science.

I realize that there are variants of hermeneutics which are anti-
scientific, antirational, antiempirical, and, with specific reference to
psychoanalysis, anti-the unconscious and anti-the body. But I use the
idea of hermeneutics only in its meaning of human psychological
meaning in contrast to natural science, and I hold that psychoanalysis
can and should be a hermeneutic science which obeys all the canons
of science but deals in the dimensions of human meanings, not in those
of natural science.

In this connection I must emphasize that psychoanalysis is a science with limitations and boundaries. It is not a complete science of
man. It is in this vein that I would reply to the general perspectival
objection to my thesis here. That objection holds that while the person
point of view has merit for psychoanalysis as a therapeutic technique

it is a mistake to apply it to psychoanalysis as a whole. Definitions of psychoanalysis can differ of course. I believe it heuristic to define it as a psychology elaborated from the person point of view. The natural science point of view is not specifically psychoanalytic, although psychoanalytic propositions must be consistent with man seen from the natural science point of view. I believe psychoanalysis should not even aspire to be a complete psychology. It has its contribution to make to an understanding of perception, cognition, and the other concerns of general psychology, but it does not constitute a general psychology. Kris (1952, p. 16) is often quoted as having said that psychoanalysis is psychology from the point of view of conflict. I believe that is too restrictive a definition and also fails to specify what I would call the basic unit of psychoanalytic consideration—the person.

One more word regarding hermeneutics. It has become associated with the idea that psychoanalysis is the construction of a narrative and that one narrative is as good as another. That contention is not a necessary concomitant of a hermeneutic science. It confuses the fact that multiple narratives, each with its own truth, are possible with the idea that any narrative is necessarily a truth and is as good as any other.

George Klein stated the hermeneutic versus natural science issue most clearly and simply when he said psychoanalysis has two theories, the metapsychology and the clinical theory (Klein, 1973), or, as Holzman and I preferred to state the dichotomy in the volume we edited in Klein's memory (Gill and Holzman, 1976), the metapsychological and the psychological. The metapsychology purports to explain the psychology. I believe it no more does that than metaphysics explains physics.

Would it suffice then to simply discard the generally accepted psychoanalytic metapsychology? Yes, but metapsychology and psychology have become so intertwined that the person point of view will not be consistently and clearly elaborated until they have been disentangled. As Leo Goldberger and I said in our introduction to George Klein's posthumous book (Klein, 1976), in which he tried to free the psychology from its metapsychological shackles, Klein had the unusual courage to deny that scientific progress is necessarily a synthesis of opposing views; he believed the situation called for a disengagement rather than a synthesis.

The Psychoanalytic Schools

In discussing the position of various psychoanalytic schools in relation to the two points of view I have distinguished, I shall have to restrict myself to considering how the increasing attention directed to object relations is a progressive move toward the person point of view.

The term object relations calls for some unpacking, as the philosophers say, because it is used in various senses (Sutherland, 1980; Mitchell, 1981). It is in fact employed with opposite meanings with regard to the relation between the innate and the acquired (Gedo, 1981).

The several groups of object relations theorists take different positions on the hierarchical relationship between the person point of view and energy discharge, more usually referred to as the relationship between object relations and drive; as I said above, however, the concept of drive is ambiguous as to whether it means bodily behavior that acquires meaning in interpersonal relations or bodily behavior understood as energy discharge. I distinguish four positions.

First is that of the followers of Melanie Klein (Segal, 1979), in which despite the emphasis on object relations it is metapsychology that explains psychology. Though the Kleinian theory postulates innately based object relations fantasies from the beginning, these fantasies are considered to derive primarily from the drives within; energy discharge is supraordinate to object relations. A second principal feature of the Kleinian position is that the object relations with which it deals are to a very large extent only internal object relations. Internal object relations are the intrapsychic representation of object relations in contrast to the here-and-now enactment of object relations. The latter may be called external object relations or, alternatively, interpersonal relations, although the latter term is more ambiguous. It is the failure to give due weight to external relations that is responsible, at least in part, for the fact that Klein's ideas have remained outside the psychoanalytic mainstream. Of course the actual practice of any particular Kleinian pays some degree of attention to external object relations.

In a second position, developed by Fairbairn (1952), object relations become supraordinate to energy discharge. Fairbairn's formula that libido is object-seeking rather than pleasure-seeking might mislead one into thinking that he makes libido a primary and independent force. In fact his theory is explicitly formulated from the person point of view. (For an excellent summary and discussion of Klein and Fairbairn see Mitchell, 1981.) Winnicott (1965) approached a person point of view but did not attempt a systematic and consistent formulation in terms of points of view. Loewald (1978) describes drive as developing in the matrix of object relations rather than as the matrix within which object relations develop, but his concept of drive remains ambiguous between the person and energy discharge points of view and he does not propose the major reorientation his formulation requires.

A third position is Kernberg's. He uses both points of view and says he fails to see any incompatibility between them (1980, p. 81; Mitchell, 1979). The classical Freudians Jacobson and Mahler occupy a fourth position. Jacobson (1964), in her discussion of the self and the object world, and Mahler (Mahler, Pine, and Bergman, 1975), in her studies of separation-individuation as a crucial dimension of development, have laid great stress on object relations but without confronting the question of whether doing so necessitates any rethinking of the role of energy discharge.

An important consequence of the fact that Freudian clinical theory of object relations is the dog wagged by the tail of metapsychology is the repeated ascendance in psychoanalysis of revisionist theories reaffirming the centrality of object relations. Adler insisted that man is a social animal. Perhaps it was this that gave him the heart to see earlier than Freud how hateful man can be. Ferenczi's experiments with supplying the love he believed his patients had been denied may have been ill-advised, but was he not trying to remedy what he found missing in the object relation between patient and analyst? Alexander may well have been too impatient with the pace of classical analysis and may have needed to exploit the force of his personality, but is not his corrective emotional experience also an effort to supply a missing object relationship? What does it mean that the term ''corrective emotional experience'' has acquired such pejorative connotations that it cannot be used even by analysts who argue that insight alone does not adequately characterize what takes place in a successful analysis?

Balint's position in this matter is succinctly captured in the phrase "primary object love." I have already mentioned Fairbairn and Winnicott. Kohut's self psychology lays great stress on object relations and it is clear that one of his primary goals was to make the atmosphere of psychoanalysis more friendly and more freely interactive. He insists that narcissism shapes a particular kind of object relationship that has its normal and necessary place in human existence alongside other forms of object love. I would criticize him as failing to recognize that a form of mutuality in object love is present from the beginning. Kohut explicitly rejects energy discharge metapsychology but blurs this rejection by distinguishing between narrow and broad theories of the self. An important theoretical task yet to be accomplished is the clarification of the relationship between self theories and object relations theories. Gedo makes a stimulating contribution to this task in his two recent monographs (1979, 1981). His concept of self (like person) allows for a broader range of motivations than is implied by the designation interpersonal relations or object relations, but I have expressed objections to what he calls organismic in contrast to subjective aims (Gill, 1981).

Sullivan

I turn next to a theorist who has been a special inspiration and guide to Otto Will, whom we are honoring in this volume. I mean Harry Stack Sullivan (1953), the interpersonalist. Sullivan's theory, formulated from the interpersonal point of view, differs from Freudian object relations theory, and even more so from that of the followers of Melanie Klein, in at least two major respects. It emphasizes external rather than internal object relations, and it rejects the primacy of sexuality as the determinant of object relations. I will discuss these two differences separately.

I believe that Sullivan's failure to give adequate attention to internal object relations is one of the reasons his scheme has failed to make a greater impact on the psychoanalytic mainstream. It is not true that Sullivan failed to recognize intrapsychically represented object relations, but his concern about remaining empirical and dealing with what actually went on between himself and his patient led him to deny the relevance of idiosyncratic individuality to the therapeutic process in his much debated paper on the illusion of individuality (Sullivan, 1950; Bromberg, 1980). He was so intent on describing man as a social animal that he placed great emphasis on defining personality in terms of *ongoing* social relationships. In that sense I would say that Sullivan is the progenitor of the here-and-now as the focus of the therapeutic process. But he did not reach an integration of internal and external object relations in the way a comprehensive psychoanalytic theory must. It is also true that despite his exquisite sensitivity to what was going on interpersonally in the therapeutic process, he did not do much by way of making it explicit. In other words, he did not adequately analyze the transference. It should be pointed out that many present-day Sullivanians do interpret the transference. It is pertinent in this connection to refer to a paper by Will and Cohen (1953) which pioneered in the publication of audio-recorded psychotherapeutic sessions and in which the analysis of the transference in the here-and-now is given primary attention; both of these issues are central preoccupations of my own (Gill, 1982a; Gill and Hoffman, 1982a, b).

A second major divergence of Sullivan from Freudian theory lies in his views on sexuality. He explicitly rejected the conceptual extension of sexuality to prepubertal life. He rejected Freud's enlarged concept of sexuality, which Freud equated with love. But it is a serious injustice to Sullivan to believe, as many people do who have never read him, that he ignored the phenomena that led Freud to expand the concept of sexuality, or that he failed to recognize how important sexuality is to human beings. Sullivan had much to say about infantile bodily phenomena, but he organized his concept of these phenomena in the context of the interaction between mother and infant rather than in the context of the discharge of bodily tension. And he made much of what he called the "lust dynamism" as another major mode of interpersonal integration. He regarded this dynamism as so important that he considered success in achieving a reasonably comfortable heterosexual gratification the central task dividing adolescence from adulthood. Sullivan's position makes possible a much sharper distinction between attachment and lust than does Freud's. At the same time it must be recognized that Freud's complex findings about the role of the body, findings mistakenly elevated to the role of point of view in

Freudian psychoanalysis, are not comprehensively integrated in Sullivan's theory, a statement I realize requires detailed explication and justification.

Kohut

The criticism often voiced, with considerable justice, by Freudian analysts against revisionist schools is that they underplay the role of the body and its manifestations. This is true not only of Sullivan's theory but also of a revisionist movement currently the subject of much attention among psychoanalysts, namely Kohut's self psychology (1977). Kohut explicitly acknowledges the phenomena conceptualized under bodily drive in normal development, but in fact he accords them relatively little attention either in what he calls the narcissistic personality disorders or in the context of understanding psychopathology, unless they rise to prominence, as in perversions for example. He then calls them disintegration phenomena and understands them primarily in terms of their interpersonal significance. Freudian analysts read this as a denial of bodily drive and feel confirmed in this conclusion by Kohut's general emphasis on experience as against innate urges. They feel further justified in their assessment in the light of Kohut's belief that the normal Oedipus complex is a relatively untroubled, even joyful stage of development.

But many Freudians will not concede that a major revision of the Freudian paradigm can still encompass the crucial issues relating to the body and sex. George Klein (1969) has been especially systematic and comprehensive in demonstrating that the phenomena relating to sexuality which Freud discovered can be encompassed by a theory which abandons drive in the metapsychological sense. From a somewhat different point of view Schafer has made the same argument in terms of a ''psychoanalysis without psychodynamics'' (1975). He insists that his action language in no way diminishes the centrality of the Freudian clinical emphases, and his case illustrations bear him out.

Psychoanalysis must not only integrate the intrapsychic with the interpersonal, but it must also reach a synthesis between bodily and interpersonal interaction, recognizing all the time that interpersonal interaction can symbolize bodily interaction, understanding symbol in the wide sense, as denoting any signifier.

Implications for the Blank Screen Model and Transference

Our understanding of transference and its implications as regards psychoanalytic technique is affected by the conclusion that man exists in an interpersonal context, that he is indeed defined in an interpersonal context. It is this interpersonal context to which Sullivan referred in calling the therapist a participant-observer. I consider this insight to be his most important contribution to psychiatry and psychoanalysis. It is a mark of the deterioration of technique after Freud that the analyst can be described as ideally only an observer while insofar as he is a participant he is viewed as beset by unfortunate countertransference.

My colleague Irwin Hoffman (1983) has made an important contribution to the model of the therapist as participant-observer by spelling out with admirable clarity the distinction between conservative and radical critiques of the blank screen model. In its crude form—the analyst as a mirror reflecting only what is shown him—this model is the very antithesis of the participant-observer model. But in this crude form it is a straw man set up by those who would caricature analysis; it is unlikely that it is adhered to by any real analyst. The standard model of the analytic situation in fact holds that a degree of realistic perception of the analyst by the patient is necessary for the analytic process to take place. Even this standard model is often subjected to what Hoffman calls conservative critiques, which take two main forms. One is that the therapist's real, benign interpersonal influence is underemphasized. It is in response to this critique that such concepts as the therapeutic alliance have been proposed. The other conservative critique is that countertransference is far more prevalent than commonly recognized. But the critique in either case remains conservative, because the transference itself, the main focus of exploration in psychoanalysis, is viewed as developing in a social vacuum. The critique is built upon an asocial view of the psychotherapeutic situation, that is, the basic integrating concept for understanding the transference is considered to be intrapsychic bodily drive rather than interpersonal interaction.

The radical critique, on the other hand, is based on a social or person point of view. It is accompanied by a relativistic and perspectival view of interpersonal reality. However much the two participants in the therapeutic situation may differ in their evaluation of their interaction, it can never be that one of them is all right and the other all wrong. Each always has a point, that is, some degree of plausibility in his perspective, including the perspective arising from neurotic transference. In this sense it is misleading ever to regard the patient's perspective as simply a distortion of an interaction correctly perceived by the analyst.

The patient's perspective, even if his neurosis, the therapist's posture, or both succeed in blinding him to it, will be that the therapist is also human. The therapist may deny he is reacting to the patient, but it is impossible for him to entirely avoid such a reaction, although it may be confined to a subjective response with no external cue perceptible by the patient. As Hoffman (1982) points out, the therapist who does not recognize the inevitably social nature of the analytic interaction is in the grip of the companion illusion to the illusion of himself as blank screen, even as corrected by a conservative critique. It is the illusion that the patient is naive. Not only is the average expectable patient not naive, his sophistication is such that he has enough sense to deny, or to pretend to deny, what he can plausibly believe the therapist would want him to be oblivious to, whether or not the therapist provides overt cues (of which the therapist himself may be unaware) to what he wants the patient to ignore.

It is important to be clear that the conclusion that the therapeutic situation is an interpersonal one does not imply that the therapist is necessarily affectively involved in a sense similar to that in which the patient is, whether this be shown in the therapist's overt behavior or in his subjective state (Gill, 1983). He may be much or little involved. He may be pathologically or nonpathologically involved, but he is always involved in some kind of personal response and the patient is on solid ground in assuming so. It is true that if one accepts this view of the therapeutic situation as anxiomatically interpersonal, one will probably see the appropriate and ordinary involvement of the therapist as greater and more subject to what could be described as countertransference than one would otherwise. An important reason for this lies in the nature of interpersonal interaction. Each participant behaves in ways designed to elicit from the other confirmation of the patterns of interpersonal interaction he has come to expect. And each participant inevitably responds in a way which to a greater or lesser degree confirms the expectation of the other. The more crucial the issue the more each participant is disposed to influence the other and the more is each likely to be influenced by the other. The therapist who accepts an expectable participation will search the patient's associations for disguised expressions of how the patient is experiencing him and thus come to a better understanding of what is usually discussed as his countertransference. He will be less disturbed by becoming aware of it and by that very fact will be less likely to remain unaware of it.

If one accepts the social, interpersonal, or person point of view, one is inevitably forced to reach a conception of transference and countertransference different from the prevailing one. In the prevailing, asocial point of view transference and countertransference on the one hand and reality on the other are dichotomized. Transference and countertransference are described as distortions of reality. The social paradigm, as Hoffman (1982) suggests, leads to a rejection of the differentiation of transference and nontransference on the grounds that the former distorts reality whereas the latter does not. Transference is distinguished from nontransference not by being a distortion of reality but by the rigidity with which the person maintains his views of reality as shown in his relative obliviousness to external circumstances and changes and to alternative modes of relating to others which in turn have the potential of evoking different kinds of responses and new forms of interpersonal experience. The person in the grip of a transference is blind to such potential.

Implications for Technique

The implications of the person point of view for the technique of psychoanalysis and psychotherapy depend on whether the therapy aims to make patterns of interpersonal interaction as explicit as possible. For me the acceptance of that aim defines psychoanalysis. There are of course other therapies, with their own usefulness, which deal with patterns of interaction by other techniques. They include the suppression of undesirable behavior by various countermeasures, both friendly and unfriendly, both witting and unwitting. It should also be pointed out that the more comprehensively one seeks to make patterns of

interpersonal interaction explicit, the greater the likelihood that errors
in perceiving what they are can be corrected. A therapist can not be
sure he is correctly understanding a patient unless he submits his
understanding to the challenge of the patient's response to his interpretations.

If the therapist operates on the assumption that psychologically
determined psychopathology is a matter of interpersonal relations, if
he further believes that for purposes of the psychotherapy the most
accurately demonstrable pattern of interpersonal interaction is that
being enacted between the patient and himself, and if he further believes that the explication of this pattern of interaction will result in
the most far-reaching and stable beneficial influence on the patient's
patterns of interaction, he will conclude that the elucidation of the
transference or, to use an expression less encumbered by the prevailing
connotations I am criticizing, the patient's experience of the relationship should be his primary goal. In pursuit of this goal he will be alert
to disguised references by the patient to his experience of the relationship with the therapist in the here-and-now; he will make such
references explicit, ever mindful that he may be mistaken; he will look
first for the role the patient is attributing to him in this experience; and
he will attempt to make that role explicit in a spirit of seeing the
plausibility of the patient's experience even if that experience and the
role attributed to him do not agree with what he subjectively considers
his role to be. Only after the patient's experience has been explored
from this point of view will he raise questions about possible alternative
interpretations of the ongoing interaction, with the goal of elucidating
the patient's transference contribution to his experience. The therapist
will recognize that the patient's contribution is significantly related to
his past and that this past needs to be explored from the same perspective the therapist employs in his examination of the here-and-now
interaction of the therapy; that is, he must view these past experiences
as having taken place in a similarly interpersonal context. But he will
be ever mindful of a temptation, on both his part and the patient's, to
flee to an exploration of the past from the probably more stressful
examination of the present; he will therefore be biased toward attention
to the present rather than the past. In the most general terms, a therapist
who accepts the perspective I have described will conduct therapy in

a manner very different from that prevailing today. Its emphasis will shift toward the relationship in contrast to the patient as an intrapsychically organized entity, toward the therapist as a participant rather than simply an observer, toward the present rather than the past; it will view the patient's experience of the relationship as plausible before seeing it as a distortion of correctly ascertainable reality. Therapy conducted within this perspective will also reject the prevalent conception that free association and regression will in time lead to the relatively direct expression of bodily urges little related to interpersonal interaction, whether with others in the past or with the therapist in the present.

Range of Applicability of Analytic Technique

Two further issues for which the person point of view has important implications may be briefly noted. One is the controversy over the range of applicability of psychoanalytic technique viewed in terms of frequency of sessions, chair or couch, type of patient, and experience of therapist. I believe it can be demonstrated that with the revised view of transference consequent on the person point of view and the concomitant recognition of the centrality of the analysis of the transference as the decisively defining feature of psychoanalysis, the range of applicability of psychoanalytic technique can be much extended (Gill, 1982b).

Implications for Research

The second issue is that of systematic research in psychoanalysis. Although there are many reasons for the paucity of such research in the psychoanalytic situation I believe an important one is that the inapplicability of natural science dimensions has acted as a deterrent. I believe also that with acceptance of the social model and the accompanying recognition of their inevitable involvement in the analytic situation, analysts will be less fearful of exposing themselves and will permit their work to be audio-recorded in order to provide the necessary raw data for systematic research in the psychoanalytic situation.

Otto Will

A last word directed to the work of Otto Will (1979). He has devoted himself to the intensive psychotherapeutic investigation of very sick people. Work with such people can have either inhibiting or facilitating effects on recognizing and employing the perspective I have outlined. The facilitating effects come from the fact that very sick people force the centrality of the relationship and the contribution of the therapist into the open. The inhibiting effects arise from the fact that the very intensification and clarity of the centrality of the relationship and the involvement of the therapist tempt the therapist to flee to the safety of the patient's past, if not even farther—to organic explanation and psychopharmacological interventions. I am not denying the value of the latter in its proper place but I believe it is especially important to keep alive in our day the kind of perspective I have sketched when it threatens to be overwhelmed by the progress being made in the neurosciences. I believe that Otto Will's work has in fact conformed in significant measure both to the person point of view and to the implications of that point of view for technique. He has done so in what is one of the most difficult arenas for its employment, the attempt to help psychologically very disturbed human beings. That was possible not least as a natural outgrowth of his own character as a human being.

References

Bowlby, J. (1960), Grief and mourning in early infancy and childhood. *The Psychoanalytic Study of the Child*, 15:9–52. New York: International Universities Press.

Brenner, C. (1980), Metapsychology and psychoanalytic theory. *Psychoanal. Quart.*, 49:189-214.

Bromberg, P. (1980), Empathy, anxiety, and reality. *Contemp. Psychoanal.*, 16:223–236.

Dewald, P. (1976), Transference regression and real experience in the psychoanalytic process. *Psychoanal. Quart.*, 43:213–230.

Fairbairn, W. R. D. (1952), *An Object-Relations Theory of the Personality*. New York: Basic Books, 1954.

Freud, S. (1910), "Wild" psychoanalysis. *Standard Edition*, 11:221–227. London: Hogarth Press, 1957.

———— (1915), Instincts and their vicissitudes. *Standard Edition*, 14:111–140. London: Hogarth Press, 1957.

———— (1916–1917), Introductory lectures on psychoanalysis. *Standard Edition*, 15:9–239. London: Hogarth Press, 1963.

———— (1921), Group psychology and the analysis of the ego. *Standard Edition*, 18:67–143. London: Hogarth Press, 1955.

———— (1940), An outline of psychoanalysis. *Standard Edition*, 23:144–207. London: Hogarth Press, 1964.

Friedman, L. (1976a), Problems of an action theory of the mind. *Internat. Rev. Psycho-Anal.*, 3:129–138.

———— (1976b), Cognitive and therapeutic tasks of a theory of the mind. *Internat. Rev. Psycho-Anal.*, 3:259–275.

Gedo, J. (1979), *Beyond Interpretation*. New York: International Universities Press.

———— (1981), *Advances in Clinical Psychoanalysis*. New York: International Universities Press.

Gill, M. M. (1977), Psychic energy reconsidered: Discussion. *J. Amer. Psychoanal. Assn.*, 25:581–598.

———— (1981), The boundaries of psychoanalytic data and technique: A critique of Gedo's *Beyond Interpretation*. *Psychoanal. Inquiry*, 1:205–232.

———— (1982a), Analysis of Transference, Vol. I: Theory and Technique. *Psychol. Issues*, Monogr. 53. New York: International Universities Press.

———— (1982b), Merton Gill: An interview. *Psychoanal. Rev.*, 69:167–190.

———— (1983), The distinction between the interpersonal paradigm and the degree of the therapist's involvement. *Contemp. Psychoanal.*, 19:200–237.

———— (1984), Psychoanalysis and psychotherapy: A revision. *Internat. Rev. Psycho-Anal.*, 11:161–179.

———— Hoffman, I. Z. (1982a), Analysis of Transference, Vol. II: Studies of Nine Audio-Recorded Psychoanalytic Sessions. *Psychological Issues*, Monogr. 54. New York: International Universities Press.

———————— (1982b), A method for studying the analysis of aspects of the patient's experience of the relationship in psychoanalysis and psychotherapy. *J. Amer. Psychoanal. Assn.*, 30:137–168.

———— Holzman, P., Eds. (1976), Psychology vs. Metapsychology. *Psychological Issues*, Monogr. 36. New York: International Universities Press.

Harlow, H., & Harlow, M. (1965), The affectional systems. In: *Behavior of Non-Human Primates*, Vol. 2, ed. A. Schrier, H. Harlow, & F. Stollinitz. New York: Academic Press.

Hermann, I. (1936), Sich Anklammern—auf Suche gehen. *Internationale Zeitschrift für Psychoanalyse*, 22.

Hoffman, I. (1983), The patient as interpreter of the analyst's experience. Unpublished.

Jacobson, E. (1964), *The Self and the Object World*. New York: International Universities Press.

Joseph, E., & Wallerstein, R. (1983), *Psychotherapy: Impact on Psychoanalytic Training*. New York: International Universities Press.

Kernberg, O. (1980), *Internal World and External Reality*. New York: Aronson.

Klein, G. (1969), Freud's two theories of sexuality. In: *Psychoanalytic Theory*. New York: International Universities Press, 1976, pp. 72–120.

———— (1973), Two theories or one? *Bull. Menn. Clin.*, 37:102–132.

———— (1976), *Psychoanalytic Theory*. New York: International Universities Press.

Kohut, H. (1977), *The Restoration of the Self*. New York: International Universities Press.

Kris, E. (1952), *Psychoanalytic Explorations in Art*. New York: International Universities Press.

Kuhn, T. (1963), *The Structure of Scientific Revolutions*. Chicago: University of Chicago Press.

Lacan, J. (1977), *Ecrits: A Selection*, trans. A. Sheridan. New York: Norton.

Loewald, H. (1960), On the therapeutic action of psychoanalysis. *Internat. J. Psycho-Anal.*, 41:16–33.

———— (1978), Instinct theory, object relations, and psychic structure formation. *J. Amer. Psychoanal. Assn.*, 26:493–506.

Mahler, M., Pine, F., & Bergman, A. (1975), *The Psychological Birth of the Human Infant*. New York: Basic Books.

Mitchell, S. (1979), Twilight of the idols. *Contemp. Psychoanal.*, 15:170–178.

———— (1981), The origin and nature of the "object" in the theories of Klein and Fairbairn. *Contemp. Psychoanal.*, 17:374–398.

Mujeeb-ur-Rahman, M., ed. (1977), *The Freudian Paradigm*. Chicago: Nelson-Hall.

Norman, H., Blacker, K., Oremland, J., & Barrett, W. (1976), The fate of the transference neurosis after termination of a satisfactory analysis. *J. Amer. Psychoanal. Assn.*, 24:471–498.

Peterfreund, E. (1971), Information, Systems, and Psychoanalysis. *Psychological Issues*, Monogr. 25/26. New York: International Universities Press.

Ricoeur, P. (1970), *Freud and Philosophy*. New Haven: Yale University Press.

Rosenblatt, A., & Thickstun, J. (1978), Modern Psychoanalytic Concepts in a General Psychology. *Psychological Issues*, Monogr. 42/43. New York: International Universities Press.

Schafer, R. (1975), Psychoanalysis without psychodynamics. *Internat. J. Psycho-Anal.*, 56:41–55.

———— (1976), *A New Language for Psychoanalysis*. New Haven: Yale University Press.

———— (1980), *Narrative Actions in Psychoanalysis*. Worcester, MA: Clark University Press, 1981.

Schlessinger, N., & Robbins, F. (1983), *A Developmental View of the Psychoanalytic Process*. New York: International Universities Press.

Segal, H. (1979), *Melanie Klein*. New York: The Viking Press.

Sherwood, M. (1969), *The Logic of Explanation in Psychoanalysis*. New York: Academic Press.

Stone, L. (1981), Some thoughts on the "here and now" in psychoanalytic technique and process. *Psychoanal. Quart.*, 50:709–733.

Sullivan, H. (1950), The illusion of personal individuality. *Psychiatry*, 13:317–332. Reprinted in H. Sullivan, *The Fusion of Psychiatry and Social Science*. New York: Norton, 1964, pp. 198–226.

———— (1953), *The Interpersonal Theory of Psychiatry*. New York: Norton.

Sutherland, J. (1980), The British object relations theorists: Balint, Winnicott, Fairbairn, Guntrip. *J. Amer. Psychoanal. Assn.*, 28:829–860.

Will, O. A. (1979), Comments on the professional life of the psychotherapist. *Contemp. Psychoanal.*, 15:560–576.

————— Cohen, R. (1953), A report of a recorded interview in the course of psychotherapy. *Psychiatry*, 16:263–282.

Winnicott, D. W. (1965), *The Maturational Processes and the Facilitating Environment*. London: Hogarth Press.

2

The Emotional Basis of Attachment and Separation

J. P. Scott, Ph.D.

Attachment

Evolution

Site attachment, or attachment to physical objects and geographical localities, is widespread in the animal kingdom and occurs almost universally among vertebrates. It is an important and fundamental adaptive capacity and seems to have undergone relatively little change in the course of evolution of various species.

Social attachment, defined as attachment to species mates, is on the other hand a phenomenon that appears only in animals that maintain continued contact with each other. A simple and plausible theory of the origin of social attachment is that it was evolved from the older and more basic capacity of site attachment. This is supported by the fact that in such animals as dogs the behavior and emotional expression associated with site attachment and social attachment appear to be virtually indistinguishable. This theory would also explain the observation that attachment in birds and mammals is strikingly similar. This could be a case of convergent evolution, but it could also be explained on the basis of a common origin from the general vertebrate capacity for site attachment.

The Development of Social Attachment in Mammals

A critical period for social attachment occurs early in life in all species that have been adequately studied. The period may occur almost immediately after birth, as in some precocial animals such as sheep and cattle, or it may occur somewhat later in life, as in dogs and humans. The period is of relatively brief duration, lasting for a few days in the case of sheep, a few weeks in dogs, and a few months in humans. During this critical period, the young animal has the capacity to form an attachment to any social object with which it has more than momentary contact. In the case of dogs, changes in behavior can be observed within as little as two hours after initial contact (Cairns and Werboff, 1967). Fleener and Cairns (1970) demonstrated similar capacities for making rapid attachments in human infants during the critical period, the babies reacting differentially after seven and a half hours of contact.

In terms of theory, a critical period (called by some authors a *sensitive period*) is one in which a rapid organizing process is going on (Scott, 1979). Such a process is vulnerable to change and modification. The critical period begins when the organizing process either begins or becomes rapid, and ends when the process either ceases or is markedly slowed down. In the case of attachment, the evidence shows that infant animals beyond the critical period can still form attachments but at a much slower rate, indicating that the process is markedly slowed but still existent. The result of such a critical period is that the young animal rapidly becomes attached to members of its own species, usually to the parents but also to any other individuals with whom it may be in prolonged contact.

Corresponding to the critical period for infantile attachment, there may be a similar period for parental attachment. This is particularly marked in such species as sheep or goats, where the mother becomes attached to her offspring within an hour or two after birth and thereafter rejects any other infant animals with which she comes into contact. A similar period for parental attachment has been demonstrated by Klaus and Kennell (1976) in human mothers. These results have been confirmed by de Chateau (1980). Both the intensity and the quality of attachment is different in human mothers who have contact with their infants immediately after birth as opposed to those for whom contact is delayed for several hours by hospital procedures. It is obvious, however, that attachment can still develop, although at a slower rate, at later times.

At times other than the critical period, attachment takes place quite slowly, or if contact time is short, not at all. In one of our experiments with dogs, we allowed puppies to maintain contacts with their mother and litter mates throughout the critical period but prohibited contact with humans until afterward. Such puppies react toward humans like little wild animals (Freedman, King, and Elliot, 1961). While they can be tamed with patience and the use of techniques such as enforced contact and hand feeding, they never develop the type of intense attachment that readily develops with human beings in a few hours during the critical period. To summarize the behavior of such a dog: if he is standing on the street midway between another dog and his human master when the latter calls, the dog is more likely to go to the other dog than to the human. Attachments developed at later ages are always less strong than those produced during the critical period.

One of the phenomena that can be observed in mothers, ovine or human, is that of intense emotional excitement during the birth of an infant. While there has been no physiological analysis of the process of attachment in mothers, one obvious possibility is that the intense emotion experienced by them may facilitate attachment at a time other than in the infantile critical period. The occurrence of rapid attachment associated with mating behavior and intense sexual emotion also suggests this hypothesis.

The Physiological and Emotional Basis of Attachment

An earlier theory regarding the process of infantile attachment was that it was produced by food rewards offered by the mother. However, it has been repeatedly shown in both dogs (Brodbeck, 1954; Stanley, 1963) and monkeys (Harlow, 1958) that attachment is entirely independent of food rewards; for example, a puppy that has never been fed by hand will become firmly attached to humans with no more than continued contact and social interaction. Motherless monkeys given a choice between an inanimate model that provided comfortable contact but no food, and an uncomfortable wire model that provided food, became attached to the comfortable model. Therefore, attachment is an internal process that depends externally only on the perception of objects or individuals. Of course, behavior involved in attachment can be altered by reward and punishment. For example, feeding an animal may cause it to remain in contact long enough so that the attachment process can go on. Once attached, the behavior of the attached animal can be modified by food rewards in other ways.

Furthermore, attachment is not inhibited by external punishment. This was first shown by Fisher (1955), who reared puppies in isolation except for regulated hours of contact with the experimenter. In one group of puppies he punished all behavior that involved social contact, and these puppies indeed maintained their distance from him. However, when the punishment was discontinued, the puppies maintained closer contact than those that had previously experienced either indifferent or positive treatment. Later Harlow and Harlow (1965) and their associates demonstrated in the case of motherless monkeys that actually abused and mistreated their offspring, that the infants nevertheless made every effort to maintain contact with the mother. The point is that maintaining social contact and forming attachments is so necessary for life in a social mammal that nothing will interfere with it.

Although attachment is an almost totally internal process, we know very little about the underlying physiological changes that must accompany it. Likewise, we know little about the physiology of the accompanying emotional responses. Subjectively, humans report that attachment is accompanied by a mild and pleasurable form of affect that they call love. They also report that "falling in love" (sometimes objectively labeled "sexual bonding") may be accompanied by pleasurable emotion so intense as to be almost unbearable. At the present time, love appears to be better understood by poets than by physiologists.

Theoretical Conclusions and Implications

If two or more individuals either maintain contact or are forced into close contact for long periods, they will inevitably become attached to each other. This conclusion, borne out by observation, has widespread implications. Such long-continued contacts are common in any social species, including man.

To begin with the primary interests of psychoanalysts, the quality and duration of the contacts between patients and therapists may vary considerably. On the one hand the average physician attempts to have about fifteen minutes of contact with a patient during an office visit and to send him or her away cured. Obviously, such brief contact will lead to little or no attachment. On the other hand, most psychotherapeutic relationships, no matter what the nature of the therapy, usually involve long continued and repeated contacts. Mutual attachment under such conditions should be almost inevitable, and if it does not occur this in itself is an indication of pathology (Will, 1959).

Attachment should occur in any working situation, including both site attachment and social attachment. Such attachments occur between pupils at any level of education, and likewise between teachers and students, depending on the degree of contact that is permitted. A professor who lectures to a group of several hundred students once or twice a week is not going to develop any degree of attachment toward them, but a teacher who conscientiously works with individual students, as is almost universal with graduate students, will develop strong ties with them and they with him. Similar attachments are bound to develop in any work situation in which there is not a continual turnover of personnel.

Among the situations of direct interest to therapists, there is the obvious one of long-term care of patients such as may occur in nursing homes and to some extent in any sort of nursing care. Attachments will develop under these circumstances and should be recognized and respected.

In addition to voluntary associations, many human institutions involve enforced contact. Among them are military service, prisons, the institution of slavery (now nearly defunct), and religious institutions such as convents and monasteries. Whatever the quality of the relationship, one would expect that attachment would nevertheless occur, and this would explain the paradoxical attachments that have been reported between prisoners and jailers, masters and slaves. The internal and largely uncontrollable nature of the attachment process will thus explain the curious relationships that have been described as involving both love and hate.

Marriage is of course another institution that involves prolonged contact and inevitably some degree of attachment. This would explain the occurrence of relationships in which people cannot get along with each other but still do not wish to separate.

Finally, the observation that attachment in later life is facilitated by intense emotions suggests the general hypothesis that the process of attachment may be facilitated by *any* kind of strong emotion, including anger, pain, and fear as well as sexual emotions. While this hypothesis is as yet largely untested experimentally, it raises many interesting questions and problems.

The most important of these is, Do intensely unpleasant or painful emotions facilitate attachments? If so, danger, fear, anger, and pain might have such an effect, with obvious implications for the development of maladaptive as well as useful relationships. This is an area of intense theoretical and practical importance, and it deserves experimental exploration.

A second question is, Does the phenomenon of facilitation of attachment by intense emotion occur early in life as well as in adulthood? Elliot and King (1960) found that underfeeding, and hence hunger, caused puppies fed by hand to become more rapidly attached to them than puppies that were overfed. If other intense emotions cause similar effects, infants subjected to them during the normal critical period might become overly attached in such a way as to produce pathological behavior. The same considerations would apply to individuals beyond the critical period, as in the case of abused children. If such experiences do indeed produce pathological attachment, we need to develop methods of dealing with this phenomenon.

Separation

Evolution

In any highly social species, survival of infants and also to some extent of adults is dependent on maintaining contact with species mates. Correlatively, separation in social species produces an almost immediate, intense, and unpleasant emotion, often expressed as distress vocalization. Such vocalization has the obvious functions of attracting the attention of parents or species mates and giving a cue as to the location of the vocalizing animal. This behavior has such an important function that it permits very little variation, even in a domestic species like the dog. In the course of testing hundreds of puppies, I have never found one that would not give this reaction, although the actual rates of vocalization may differ from individual to individual. Also, the quality of the vocalization has certain unique properties. It is not uniform in either loudness or tone and consists of a variety of noises: barks, whines, yelps, and even howls. The result is that it is practically impossible to accommodate to this noise and disregard it. We can conclude that the quality of vocalization has a strong functional basis, and that the emotion has strong effects upon the animal that experiences it, as well as upon those who hear it expressed.

Development

Separation distress in infant animals occurs only after attachment has taken place. Therefore it is a direct and reliable measure of attachment. The only confusion that can arise is that distress vocalization may also occur for other reasons, such as pain or hunger, but these kinds of vocalization are, at least in dogs, readily distinguishable. As the infant animal grows older, there is a tendency for the rate of distress vocalization in response to separation to decrease, although it may never go down to zero. In adult animals of some species, distress arising from separation is usually expressed in forms other than vocalization, although in herd animals like sheep a separated adult individual will still call to the others.

Does separation distress increase or decrease with development? In species that are semisolitary as adults, as are raccoons, it is probable that distress from separation decreases markedly in adults. Among species that are social throughout their lives, as are humans and canines, separation distress can be observed at all ages.

From the general principles of reinforcement, we might conclude that repeated experience of separation distress should result in intensification of the emotion. If this were true, adults should feel more intense distress after separation than do infants. On the other hand, we have experimental evidence that repeated experience of separation of a mild and temporary nature will result in a lessening of observed emotional responses, presumably because of the phenomenon of desensitization (Scott, Stewart, and DeGhett, 1973). Also, infants and adults may develop coping responses to separation distress. An obvious coping response noted by Bowlby (1973) in his work with separated infants was the conscious realization that the separated individuals would return after a few hours. That is, it is easier to bear the pain of separation if one knows that it will have a definite endpoint.

Physiological and Emotional Bases of Separation Distress

Beginning with observational evidence, the emotion of separation distress does not readily die out as do some other emotions. In the case of fighting mice, physiological reactions to a fighting experience die out in a few hours, or at the most twenty-four hours (Eleftheriou and Scott, 1971). But when we isolate a young puppy, vocalization begins within a few seconds after separation and continues unabated for at least twenty-four hours. We have not tried to continue separation for longer periods because of the obviously severe physiological effects on the separated animal.

In adult animals that have been separated from a familiar environment and familiar individuals, the emotional effects have been observed to continue for months or years. In one Shetland sheep dog adopted by a family at the age of six months, the owners never saw this animal wag its tail as long as they owned it, over a period of many months. In the case of certain beagles that were transferred as adults from another laboratory to ours, these animals showed indications of separation distress for as long as three years thereafter. If left in a familiar pen with familiar animals, they behaved reasonably normally, but if they were removed from this area, or if strange humans approached, the dogs showed signs of intense fear.

Thus, separation distress appears to be an emotion that persists as long as the separation lasts, never fading out entirely. It is particularly evident whenever situations occur that remind the separated individual of the original circumstances of separation. This has several consequences for a human sufferer from separation. One of these is that because the emotion is so persistent it may be difficult to trace it to its source. The individual simply knows that he or she feels bad, and may not realize why.

For several years my colleagues and I have pursued a program of pharmacological research on the nature of separation distress (Scott, 1974). Our first thought was to investigate the tranquilizers, both major and minor. The results were negative. Excessive doses might render the animal unconscious, but there was no evidence that lower doses would lessen the emotion. For example, a puppy given chlorpromazine might be sedated and fall fast asleep if left with its litter mates, but if separated would immediately arouse itself and begin to vocalize. With one of the minor tranquilizers, meprobamate, we gave doses at various levels and saw no effect until we got into the toxic level and one of the puppies became unconscious. Similar results were achieved with other sorts of major and minor tranquilizers. Since the clinical use of tranquilizers is chiefly to reduce anxiety, defined as the fear of some anticipated event, I conclude that separation distress is not equivalent to anxiety, although some authors have referred loosely to this phenomenon as separation anxiety. The point is that separation distress is not a response to an anticipated future event but to an ongoing immediate event.

As Bowlby (1973) has pointed out, the term "separation anxiety" appears frequently in the human literature, often without a clear definition. He himself observed that anxiety was an *outcome* of separation distress, i.e., a child would come to fear separation after having experienced the distress associated with it.

In a second line of research, which was never carried out in depth, we investigated the effects of an antidepressant drug, imipramine. We reasoned that this substance might be effective because separation is known to produce depression in human subjects. In beagle puppies, but not in breeds such as the Telomians and Shetland sheep dogs, imipramine given at relatively moderate doses was 100 percent effective in reducing distress vocalization. These animals were not only quiet but appeared to be normal, happy puppies. The results suggest strong genetic effects on the response to this drug. An obvious line of research would have been to try out other antidepressant drugs (in humans it is frequently found that some individuals are more responsive to certain drugs than others), but for various reasons we were unable to continue this research.

We were also interested in the effects of the stimulant drug amphetamine sulfate. When we gave this drug to puppies that were vocalizing at a maximum rate (about one hundred per minute or higher) there was no effect until toxic levels were reached, when some reduction of the vocalization rate occurred. When we gave the drug to puppies that had been isolated in their home pens and hence were vocalizing at moderate rates of thirty per minute or so, we found that amphetamine would increase the rate of vocalization. Amphetamine does not appear to be a specific for reducing separation distress.

On the other hand, amphetamine sulfate can reduce certain behavioral effects of separation in adult dogs. In a series of experiments concerned with hyperactivity in dogs, we found that F_1 hybrids between beagles and the Telomian breed, were normally quite active animals and that under certain circumstances they were almost untrainable with respect to any activity involving motor inhibition. Amphetamine had a beneficial effect, but only under certain special circumstances, namely after the hybrids had as adults been separated from their home environment and developed the separation or kennel dog syndrome. One of the characteristics of this syndrome is intense activity. Given amphetamine sulfate, such dogs showed dramatic improvement in their capacity to sit quietly. Thus amphetamine seems to have the property of modifying the results of separation distress in some interactive fashion as yet not understood (Corson et al., 1980).

Finally, Panksepp and his colleagues (Panksepp, 1981; Herman and Panksepp, 1978; Panksepp, Meeker, and Bean, 1980) have investigated the effects of morphine and naloxone in a variety of animal species, including dogs. In both chicks and guinea pigs, low doses of morphine will inhibit distress vocalization resulting from separation, and naloxone will increase the rate of such vocalizations.

In the dog, low doses of morphine will moderately decrease the rate of distress vocalizations in puppies, but not to zero. However, tail wagging in response to a human caretaker is reduced by morphine and dramatically increased by naloxone (Davis, 1980).

These experiments imply that brain opioids are concerned with the emotion of distress induced by separation. From an evolutionary viewpoint, the brain opioids are primarily concerned with pain, and it is reasonable to suppose that when an emotional response to separation was first evolved, the organisms concerned made use of the already present emotional response to physical injury and elaborated a different set of controls to elicit essentially the same affective response. Certainly, the emotion of separation distress in humans is subjectively a painful one, although distinguishable from pain in that sensations associated with the emotion of pain are usually localized in particular parts of the body, while separation distress is not.

The next problem is to discover the biochemical and physiological basis of separation distress. Does it activate the same set of brain opioids as pain, or is there a special opioid related to it? Also, what are the nerve connections within the brain that activate the opioid response? With respect to the latter problem, Herman (1979) found that electrical stimulation of the ventral septum preoptic area and dorsomedial thalamus would reliably elicit distress vocalization in guinea pigs. Herman and Panksepp (1981) found that simultaneous stimulation of analgesic sites in the periventricular gray area inhibits vocalization. But stimulation of nearby areas elicited the kind of screams associated with pain.

These results demonstrate that there are special circuits in the brain that activate distress vocalization in response to separation, but there is no evidence as yet as to the circuits that lead into these from outside stimulation. At any rate, this is the best evidence we have concerning the physiological bases of separation distress, and it adds another mammal (the dog being the other) that can serve as an experimental model of such distress.

In another line of research, we investigated the nature of separation distress in the dog by combining it with other kinds of affect. Emotions occurring at the same time might interact antagonistically, independently, additively, or might show facilitation or interaction in a multiplicative fashion.

One of the easiest emotions to induce is that of hunger. When hungry puppies are separated they vocalize at a rate which is similar to that which they show if separated but not hungry; the two emotions do not produce additive effects. Also, such puppies can rarely be induced to eat, from which we conclude that separation distress is incompatible with hunger.

On the other hand, separation distress arising from different sources (e.g., social separation and separation from physical surroundings) reacts in an additive fashion, the highest rates being obtained by a combination of the two.

We were unable to devise an experiment in which anger and separation distress were combined, for soon as the puppy sees another puppy that arouses anger, it is no longer separated. Bowlby (1973) suggests that the anger in human infants that develops following separation arises from frustration. An alternative explanation (not necessarily excluding Bowlby's) is that the separated individual attempts to punish the apparent cause of its distress. At any rate, one of the manifestations of the separation syndrome in adult dogs is attacks on human caretakers or bystanders. From these lines of indirect evidence I tentatively conclude that separation distress and anger are compatible.

The problem of studying the interaction between separation distress and fear is technically easier because fear can be aroused in an isolated animal. Our studies with fear in dogs, however, indicate that there is no such thing as general fearfulness, but rather that fears are specific to certain objects or situations (Scott and Fuller, 1965). Working with the fear of loud noises, we found that the two emotional reactions appeared to be independent (Davis, Gurski, and Scott, 1977). Fears of strange places or strange individuals, on the other hand, appear to be facilitated by separation distress, as observed in the separation syndrome.

My general conclusion from these three lines of research is that separation distress is a unique kind of emotional state and therefore has a different physiological basis from that of every other sort of emotion. As opioid research indicates, its basis may be related to that of pain.

A fourth line of evidence is that derived from experiments with the alleviation of separation distress. As a base line, reunion with the individuals or return to the places from which separation has taken place is 100 percent effective in reducing distress. A puppy that has been vocalizing at a rate of one hundred times or more per minute will quiet down almost immediately when restored to its home pen and litter mates, and exhibit a zero rate. We then tested the effectiveness of various calming or partially alleviating factors upon the expression of distress vocalization in puppies (Pettijohn, Wong, Ebert, and Scott, 1977). Food had little or no effect. If the animals ate at all they stopped vocalizing only while eating. Hard toys had no effect, these being the sorts of toy bones and other objects with which puppies are supposed to amuse themselves. Soft toys had some effect, especially a toy woolly lamb that in some respects resembled a puppy. Also, a towel produced some reduction in rate; the puppies dragged it around and one animal actually went to sleep on it.

Interaction with live individuals, either species mates or humans, was much more effective. Some puppies responded to their own mirror images and became considerably quieter. Interaction with other dogs was effective, depending on the degree to which the other animal permitted such interaction. In an experiment designed to test the effectiveness of human contact, the experimenter was at first surrounded by a fence that prohibited contact, and sat quietly within it. The puppies approached and were moderately quiet. Removing the fence and allowing the puppies to make direct contact was more effective, and active playing with the puppy was the most effective treatment of all.

Fuller (1967) had found with his experiments on puppies reared in isolation that active interaction with a playful puppy was the most effective alleviating agent for separation distress. Therefore, active social interaction is the most effective alleviating agent, presumably because it sets up some sort of counteracting emotional response. It is effective in proportion to the degree of familiarity, the degree of contact (visual or tactile), and the intensity of social interaction.

In general, these experiments lead to the conclusion that separation distress is an emotion that is highly dependent upon external circumstances, not arising internally from spontaneous metabolic reactions, as does hunger. It is nevertheless an intense and painful emotion that is unique in its degree of persistence. It is therefore an emotion that should be of significance in problems of mental health. This is borne out by Bowlby's review of the clinical literature (1973). He notes that ''the experiences of separation and loss, occurring recently or years before, play a weighty role in many clinical conditions'' (p. 30).

Separation Distress and Maladaptive Behavior

As with any other strong emotion, a situation in which this emotion becomes chronic may lead to maladaptive behavior. In dogs, the major form of maladaptive behavior in response to separation is the separation or kennel dog syndrome (Scott, 1970). If a puppy is reared in a restricted environment such as a kennel until the age of six months or older and is then separated to go to a new home as a pet, it will develop certain symptoms. These take two general forms, depending on whether the animal belongs to a nonaggressive breed or to a more aggressive one. Two case histories will illustrate this point. In the first case a male Shetland sheep dog puppy was reared in our laboratory until the age of six months. It was observed to be somewhat fearful but otherwise showed no unusual behavior. The puppy was sold to a family but the owners returned it after five days. They were afraid it was going to die, as it had not eaten, slept, drunk, or moved during the entire time. This behavior is strikingly reminiscent of the hospitalized human infants described by Bowlby (1973), except that this older puppy did not vocalize.

On its return to the laboratory, it recovered and began acting normally within a few hours. I then took this puppy to my own home and observed that it indeed behaved as reported, taking a position underneath a sofa and remaining alert but refusing to move or respond in any way. I therefore undertook therapy by taking the animal back to the laboratory each day and bringing it home in the evening. After approximately two weeks it began to show the first signs of response in this strange situation, and shortly afterward I transferred it permanently. By way of additional therapy I also introduced a young and playful puppy of the Telomian breed, which I brought out of the laboratory at the optimum age of eight weeks. The Shetland sheep dog gradually became more normal in behavior, but I never saw it act like a "happy" dog except on one occasion when I showed it a mirror. It responded as if to a familiar animal, leaping and wagging its tail, and stopped only when it went behind the mirror and discovered that no other dog was there. The sequel to this therapeutic endeavor was not a happy one. This dog ran away from its adoptive home several months later and was never found. Presumably it was trying to find its way back to its old home but never made it.

A second case history was that of a Telomian with a similar early experience. Telomians are like terriers in that they readily attack strange animals. This one was adopted by a family that had owned many dogs, but they reported after several months that it was unsatisfactory, having bitten three members of the family seriously enough to break the skin. I took my assistant out to test this dog in the home site and, sure enough, when he suddenly approached the dog it attempted to bite him. While this dog showed relatively little sign of fearfulness, it did not appear ''happy.'' It was not strongly afraid of people but would react aggressively if suddenly approached, especially by a stranger, but also in response to individuals that lived in the home and should have been familiar.

Such behavior in human individuals would be described as paranoid. In the dog, the behavior is maladaptive if one assumes that the adopted animal has to remain separated from its familiar environment. From the dog's point of view, either mode of behavior described above would, in noncaptive animals, lead to the avoidance of new attachments and to searching for ways back to the old familiar environment. Fearful reactions would keep an animal constantly active, and one would predict that if such an animal were turned loose it would eventually find its way back home if it were not too far away and no difficulties were encountered. One can also postulate another adaptive function for aggressive behavior: the dog reacts as if the humans present were responsible for its continuing emotional distress, as of course they were.

Therapy, in the sense of reducing the symptoms, can be very easily achieved by simply restoring the dog to its home and familiar others, and is 100 percent effective. When the aggressive Telomian was brought back to the laboratory it began behaving normally in a few hours and never bit anyone again.

Most human owners, however, attempt to modify the dog's behavior in the new environment by reducing its fearful or aggressive reactions by what are essentially desensitization techniques. As a result, the dog will lessen its fearful responses under most circumstances. But if a stranger enters the door, the dog is likely to run upstairs, hide under the bed, and urinate on the floor. In short, such techniques are only partially effective. The best therapy, of course, is preventive. The

  J. P. SCOTT

separation syndrome never occurs if the puppy is separated from its home environment for adoption at the optimum time during the critical period for primary socialization, namely at approximately eight weeks of age (Scott, Stewart, and DeGhett, 1974).

I have never attempted to experimentally induce depression in puppies because of the severity of the symptoms that a separation of even a few hours will produce. However, I have repeatedly observed depression in older dogs whose owners have left them in a boarding kennel. In fact, if one wishes to observe the effects of separation, such a facility provides plentiful material.

In humans there are many situations that can lead to chronic separation distress. The most serious and irreversible of these is the death of a person to whom a deep attachment has been made. Every human culture that has been studied has ceremonial ways of attempting to lessen the impact of such separations. Other common situations that lead to separation distress are permanently moving to another locality, as in emigration to a new country, to cite the most drastic form, or moving to a different locality within the same society, to cite a milder form. Then there is the total destruction of a home that may occur as the result of warfare, fire, flood, or earthquake, and, in modern history, the resettlement of city dwellers whose homes have been destroyed in order to bring about some form of city improvement.

Finally, there is retirement from active work. The circumstances vary from one occupation to another, but the retiree will usually be suddenly separated from a familiar work area and daily contacts with work associates. If the person is not prepared for this, the consequent emotional reaction may be a serious problem. A psychiatrist of my acquaintance remarked that about six months after the retirement party, the retiree shows up in his office.

With respect to the symptoms arising from chronic separation distress, the most commonly reported is that of depression. About 25 percent of clinical cases of depression are reported to be associated with separation caused by either death of a family member or by physical removal to a different locality (Klerman, 1979).

This brings us to the problem of therapy. The basic clinical problem associated with separation distress is how to reduce an attachment that is no longer functional and useful. This is a problem about which we have little or no experimental information. The most that we can say, on the basis of what we know from animal experiments, is that active social interaction should eventually lessen the impact of permanent and chronic separation.

Attachment and Separation in Psychotherapy

The process of therapy itself may now be considered from the viewpoint of what we know about attachment and separation. From what has been said above, any long-continued patient-therapist relationship should result in mutual attachment. This would in part depend upon the amount of time spent together. A few short sessions might result in only a weak attachment, but if we are talking about the usual weekly or monthly sessions for an hour or so, it is obvious that a relatively strong degree of mutual attachment will eventually result. Will (1959) has described the relationship that develops under these circumstances.

A complicating factor in the development of the therapeutic relationship may arise from the nature of the difficulties that the patient is experiencing. These may or may not involve separation distress, but if they do, interaction with the therapist will itself constitute the active social interaction that appears beneficial in treating such conditions.

A special problem involving separation arises in connection with hospitalization. The new patient is separated from familiar physical surroundings and frequently from family and friends as well. One would expect separation distress to follow, and unless some steps are taken to alleviate it, this strong emotion will automatically complicate the problems of therapy.

Incidentally, the physical surroundings and management system at Austen Riggs should be favorable in that many of the patients are of college age, and the Institute resembles the college setting with which many patients are already familiar, thus lessening some of the impact of separation.

Inevitably, a long stay in a hospital will bring about new attachments, so that a departing patient should again experience separation distress. The impact can be lessened in various ways. The patient can be told what to expect and can also be encouraged to leave for short periods prior to final departure.

I have no suggestions to make concerning the effects of the mutual attachment processes during the treatment of conditions other than those involving separation. They might facilitate treatment or they might hinder it. In any case, attachments appear to be inevitable, but on the conclusion of successful therapy mutual attachment may no longer be functional. Should an attempt be made to reduce attachment—a process about which we know little—or should both parties recognize a continuing relationship that can be broken off at will by either patient or therapist? It is the nature of people to become permanently attached to each other, a fact that must be recognized by all of us, and especially by those who have a scientific bent and would like to look at human relationships in a purely impersonal fashion.

From a different point of view, it is obvious that if patient and therapist do not become attached to each other, therapy will be difficult or impossible. What are the factors that facilitate attachment? This is a question that calls for research, but one hypothesis is that attachment will be easier with individuals who are nonthreatening and who resemble other individuals to whom attachments have been made in the past.

Another hypothesis is provided by our finding that the best way to alleviate separation distress is active social interaction. For a puppy this may mean playing with a rag dangled by an owner or an experimenter. Translated into human terms, active interaction becomes "making friends," and is not dissimilar to "making love," which makes still another problem for the therapist.

If I were a therapist, I would review all the situations involved in therapy from the viewpoint of attachment and separation, and act accordingly. Furthermore, I would routinely discover what a patient's experience has been with respect to attachment and separation, both currently and in the more distant past. Separation distress is a powerful emotion that may produce maladaptive behavior, and it may be so persistent and omnipresent as to escape notice.

In summary, attachment is a normal and fundamental process in social animals, including humans. Separation distress is likewise a normal and functional response to situations which threaten the loss of contact with objects or individuals with whom a person may be attached. As with other emotional processes, attachment and separation can give rise to dysfunction. There are many conditions which might usefully be analyzed as disorders of either the attachment process or the response to separation. Among these are autism, various love-hate relationships, overdependence, and maladaptive responses to permanent and unavoidable separation such as is produced by death or major disasters.

References

Brodbeck, A. J. (1954), An exploratory study of the acquisition of dependency behavior in puppies. *Bull. Ecol. Soc. Am.*, 35:73.

Bowlby, J. (1973), *Attachment and Loss, Vol. II: Separation, Anxiety, and Anger.* New York: Basic Books.

Cairns, R. B., & Werboff, J. A. (1967), Behavior development in the dog: An interspecific analysis. *Science*, 158:1070–1072.

Corson, S. A., Corson, E. O'L., Becker, R. E., Ginsburg, B. E., Trattner, A., Conner, R. L., Lucas, L. A., Panksepp, J., & Scott, J. P. (1980), Interaction of genetics and separation in canine hyperkinesis and in differential responses to amphetamine. *Pavlovian J. Biol. Sci.*, 15:5–11.

Davis, K. L. (1980), Opioid control of canine social behavior. Ph.D. dissertation, Bowling Green State University.

———— Gurski, J. G., & Scott, J. P. (1977), Interaction of separation distress with fears in infant dogs. *Devel. Psychobiol.*, 10:203–212.

de Chateau, P. (1980), Parent-neonate interaction and its long-term effects. In: *Early Experiences and Early Behavior: Implications for Social Development*, ed. E. C. Simmel. New York: Academic Press.

Eleftheriou, B. E., & Scott, J. P., Eds. (1971), *The Physiology of Aggression and Defeat*. New York: Plenum.

Elliot, O., & King, J. A. (1960), Effect of early food deprivation on later consummatory behavior in puppies. *Psychological Reports*, 6:391–400.

Fisher, A. E. (1955), The effects of differential early treatment on the social and exploratory behavior of puppies. Ph.D. dissertation, Pennsylvania State University.

Fleener, D. E., & Cairns, R. B. (1970), Attachment behavior in human infants: Discriminative vocalization on maternal separation. *Develop. Psychol.*, 2:215–223.

Freedman, D. G., King, J. A., & Elliot, O. (1961), Critical period in the social development of dogs. *Science*, 133:1016–1017.

Fuller, J. L. (1967), Experiential deprivation and later behavior. *Science*, 158:1645–1652.

Harlow, H. F. (1958), The nature of love. *American Psychologist*, 13:673–685.

———— Harlow, M. K. (1965), The affectional systems. In: *Behavior of Nonhuman Primates*, ed. A. M. Schrier, H. F. Harlow, & S. F. Stollnitz. New York: Academic Press.

Herman, B. H. (1979), An exploration of brain social attachment substrates in guinea pigs. Ph.D. dissertation, Bowling Green State University.

———— Panksepp, J. (1978), Effects of morphine and naloxone on separation distress and approach attachment: Evidence for opiate mediation of social affect. *Pharmacology, Biochemistry, & Behavior*, 9:213–220.

—————— ————— (1981), Ascending endorphin inhibition of distress vocalization. *Science*, 211:1060–1062.

Klaus, M. H., & Kennell, J.H. (1976), *Maternal-Infant Bonding*. St. Louis: Mosby.

Klerman, G. L. (1979), Stress adaptation and affective disorders. In: *Stress and Mental Disorders*, ed. J. E. Barrett, R. M. Rose, & G. L. Klerman. New York: Raven Press, pp. 151–160.

Panksepp, J. (1981), Brain opioids: A neurochemical substrate for narcotic and social dependence. In: *Theory in Psychopharmacology*, Vol. 1, ed. S. J. Cooper. London: Academic Press, pp. 149–175.

————— Meeker, R., & Bean, J. (1980), The neurochemical control of crying. *Pharmacology, Biochemistry, & Behavior*, 12:437–443.

Pettijohn, T. F., Wong, T. W., Ebert, P. D., & Scott, J. P. (1977), Alleviation of separation distress in three breeds of young dogs. *Devel. Psychobiol.*, 10:373–381.

Scott, J. P. (1970), Critical periods for the development of social behavior in dogs. In: *The Post-Natal Development of Phenotype*, ed. S. Kazda & V. G. Denenberg. Prague: Academia, pp. 21–32.

————— (1974), Effects of psychotropic drugs on separation distress in dogs. *Proc. 19th Int. Congress CINP*, Paris. Excerpta Medica International Congress Series No. 359, pp. 735–745.

————— (1979), Critical periods in organizational process. In: *Human Growth, Vol. 3*, ed. F. Falkner & J. M. Tanner. New York: Plenum, pp. 223–241.

————— Fuller, J. L. (1965), *Genetics and the Social Behavior of the Dog*. Chicago: University of Chicago Press.

————— Stewart, J. M., & DeGhett, V. J. (1973), Separation in infant dogs: Emotional response and motivational consequences. In: *Separation and Depression: Clinical and Research Aspects*, ed. J. P. Scott & E. C. Senay. Washington, D.C.: American Association for the Advancement of Science, pp. 3–32.

————— ————— ————— (1974), Critical periods in the organization of systems. *Developmental Psychobiol.*, 7:489–513.

Will, O. A. (1959), Relatedness and the schizophrenic reaction. *Psychiatry*, 22:205–223.

3

Defensive Processes in the Light of Attachment Theory

John Bowlby, M.A., M.D., Sc.D.

Every analyst in his day-to-day work finds himself confronted by his patient's defenses. One patient has no memories of what happened before he was six. Another avoids thinking about human relationships and experiencing human feeling by throwing himself frantically into his work or into some social or political cause. A third abuses and alienates anyone who attempts to be kind to him. A fourth is given to idealizing one person and scapegoating another. Examples are legion. While as a clinician I have been concerned with the whole range of defenses, as a research worker I have directed my attention especially to the way a young child behaves toward his mother upon returning home after a spell in a hospital or residential nursery without having been visited. In such circumstances it is common for a child to begin by treating his mother almost as though she were a stranger but then, after an interval, usually of hours or days, to become intensely clinging, anxious lest he lose her again, and angry with her should he think he may. In some way all his feeling for his mother and all the behavior toward her that we take for granted, keeping within range of her and most notably turning to her when frightened or hurt, have suddenly vanished—only to reappear again after an interval. This was the condition that James Robertson and I termed detachment (Bowlby, 1960),

63

and that we believed was a result of some defensive process operating within the child. How best to conceptualize that process is a problem I have been wrestling with ever since.

When Freud first tackled problems of defense during the 1890s (e.g., Freud, 1894), the conceptual model he brought with him from the natural sciences of the day required that all phenomena, physical or biological, be explained in terms of the disposition of energy. As a result Freud, eager from first to last to formulate psychoanalysis along scientific lines, advanced his theory of defense to conform with those requirements. Two quanta of energy were postulated, one invested in the repressed impulse that strives for release, the other invested in the repressing agency (the countercathexis) that strives to maintain the repression. A dam holding back the flow of a river is his familiar metaphor.

Over the years dissatisfaction with this type of theorizing has increased among analysts, not least because it has proved impossible to specify the properties of, and therefore to measure, the special form of energy that Freud postulated. As a concept, moreover, the construct of psychic energy has not led to productive research. But it is one thing to be dissatisfied with an existing theory and quite another to replace it with something better. Yet, if we are ever to see psychoanalysis take its place as a major component within a comprehensive psychology that Freud clearly hoped it would become, I believe it essential we try to do so. My aim in this contribution is to give a sketch of one approach that chimes closely with a great deal of Freud's clinical theorizing (in contrast to his metapsychology) and that I believe to be promising.

The first thing to note is that natural science no longer expects all explanations to be couched in terms of energy and its disposition. Nowadays explanations draw on such interrelated concepts as organization, pattern, and information, while the purposeful activities of biological organisms are conceived in terms of control systems structured in certain ways. With supplies of physical energy available to them, these systems become active on receipt of certain sorts of signal and become inactive on receipt of signals of other sorts. Thus, the world of science in which we live is radically different from the world Freud lived in at the turn of the century, and the concepts available to us immeasurably better suited to our problems than were the very restricted concepts available to Freud. It is hardly arrogant therefore to suppose that we may be able to improve on some of the traditional theorizing. Indeed, it would be rather pitiful were we not.

Let me return now to the empirical problem I set out to solve: how to understand and explain the dramatically changed behavior observed when a young child returns home after a spell in a strange place with strange people. As I remarked earlier, in these circumstances all the behavior toward his mother that we take for granted, keeping within range of her and turning to her when frightened or hurt, are suddenly missing. Before trying to explain its absence, however, we have to be able to explain its presence. Why should a young child behave so as to remain within range of his mother or some familiar mother substitute? How do we explain the contented play in which he engages, even in a slightly strange place, when his mother is present and the sharp change that ensues when she leaves him? And how do we explain the readiness with which he resumes his play on her return—provided her absence has not been long?

Now it is evident that there is no way of explaining these rapid changes of behavior in terms of a buildup of psychic energy which is then discharged. On the other hand, the postulate of a control system set to maintain him within range of his mother-figure, to reduce distance when he's frightened or distressed, and to ease up once he's comforted and reassured, is an obvious possibility. This, of course, is how I explain a child's tie to his mother (Bowlby, 1969). Further central features of this type of theory are the notions that keeping proximity to a familiar caregiver reduces the risk of the child's coming to harm, and that the presence in human beings of a system, or set of systems, producing attachment behavior is due to the operation of Darwinian evolution. Many other patterns of behavior that have traditionally been regarded as instinctive—for example, eating, sexual behavior, and parental behavior—can be understood in analogous ways.

Yet another distinctive feature of the theory derives from the observation that attachment behavior soon becomes focused on one person, or a small hierarchy of familiar people. Whereas the different patterns of behavior are constantly being activated or inactivated according to whatever is happening in the child's world, his overall relationship to his mother clearly persists. Very evidently he builds up in his mind a representational model of his mother, of her likely whereabouts and movements and, in particular, of the ways in which she is likely to respond to him when he seeks her care. This representational model of his mother, which he builds up on the basis of his experience, is another way of describing what is traditionally referred to as an internal object. This is a term I much dislike not only because it is so impersonal but because it fails to link the internal representation to the living reality of another person who thinks, feels, and acts in highly significant ways.

That completes a very rough sketch of how it is possible to account for a child's libidinal tie to his mother—and with some modifications for libidinal ties of later life (Weiss, 1982)—in terms of concepts nowadays widely used throughout biology and cognitive psychology. And it is with these and related concepts in mind that we can take a fresh look at problems of defense.

Let us start with the strange detached behavior a young child shows after being away for a time with strange people in a strange place. What is so peculiar about it is of course the absence of attachment behavior in circumstances in which we would confidently expect to see it: even when he has hurt himself severely such a child shows no sign of seeking comfort. Thus, signals that would ordinarily activate attachment behavior are failing to do so. This suggests that in some way and for some reason the signals are failing to reach the systems responsible for attachment behavior, that they are being blocked off. Furthermore, the way a detached child behaves toward his mother often suggests that he only half recognizes her. This suggests that the sensory inflow his eyes are transmitting fails to be matched to the internal representation he has of his mother, as would normally occur. Here again there is a blockage.

Before going further with this line of thinking let me give another example, this time from the treatment of an adult patient whose clinical condition was also one of emotional detachment. For this material I am indebted to the contribution made by Thomas Mintz (1976) to a symposium, organized by the American Psychoanalytic Association, on the effects on adults of object loss during the first five years.

The problems for which Mrs. G. came for analysis were that she felt irritable, depressed, and filled, as she put it, with hate and evil. In addition she found herself frigid with her husband, emotionally detached, and wondering whether she was capable of loving anyone.

Mrs. G was three years old when her parents divorced. Her father left home and her mother, who began working long hours, had little time for her daughter. A year later, when Mrs. G. was four, her mother placed her in an orphanage where she remained for eighteen long months. Thereafter, although she was back with her mother, family relationships continued to be disturbed and unhappy. As a result Mrs. G. left home during her teens and, before she was twenty-one, had already been married and divorced twice. Her present husband was her third.

In the early phases of the analysis Mrs. G. was extremely reluctant to recall the painful events of her childhood; and when she did so she broke down into tears and sobbing. Nevertheless, her analyst encouraged her to reflect on them further and to do so in minute detail since he believed this would help her. At the same time he paid at least equal attention to her relationship with himself, in which, as would be expected, all the interpersonal difficulties she had had in other close relationships recurred.

Among much else in her childhood that was painful, Mrs. G. recalled how sad she had felt on being parted from her pets when she was sent away. Sometimes she dreamed about her time in the orphanage and her feelings of being overwhelmed. She recalled feeling very small among the many children, how there were no toys, the harsh treatment meted out, and how she had sometimes misbehaved deliberately in order to get smacked, which at least meant that she was given some attention.

After four years of analysis Mrs. G.'s financial difficulties led to the decision to end treatment in six months' time. Inevitably, the emotional conflicts she had in her relationship with her analyst became more acute. She now dreamed and day-dreamed more openly of him. From the first she had realized that parting would be painful. Separations had always made her angry and, as she put it now, "anger makes me sad because it means the end . . . I'm afraid you'll leave me or kick me out or put me away." The analyst reminded her of how she had felt when sent to the orphanage. Struggling to think of herself as self-sufficient, she exclaimed: "I'm clinging on to me . . . I'm taking care of me all by myself."

A few months later, as termination approached, she linked how she felt about her analyst with how she had felt earlier about her mother: "I don't want to release my mother—I don't want to let her go—she's not going to get rid of me." By this stage of her analysis her active yearning for love and care had returned together with her anger at those who had denied it her.

The radical change that had occurred in this woman was confirmed in other episodes. For example, during the early days of the analysis her cat had died but she had felt indifferent about it. As she had then explained: "If I let it hurt me, I'd be saddened by everything. One will trigger off the rest." But now, toward the end of the analysis, when another cat died she wept.

Although therapy had restored this patient's feeling life and had resulted in her becoming able to make improved relationships, including that with her mother, a follow-up five years later showed, as would be expected, that she remained vulnerable to situations that arouse anxiety and sadness, such as separation and loss.

Let us examine the change that had occurred in this woman, whose condition might be described clinically as schizoid (Fairbairn, 1940), or as false self (Winnicott, 1965, 1974), or as narcissistic (Kohut, 1971). Before the analysis she had felt emotionally detached and had wondered whether she was capable of loving anyone; a loss left her feeling indifferent. Now she had become aware how deeply she longed for love and care, and how angry she felt at not being given it; and a loss led to tears. Thus, in situations where they were missing before, responses laden with deep affect now appeared.

To account for such a change, one of the traditional explanations has used the hydraulic metaphor. Affect has been dammed up and has now been discharged, the dam being regarded as a defense against an excessive quantity of excitation that is in danger of overwhelming the ego. Other explanations invoke processes postulated to occur in earliest infancy, for example fixation in a phase of narcissism or a split in the ego resulting from the projection of a death instinct.

An alternative explanation follows the approach I have already outlined. First, it sees Mrs. G.'s initial psychological state as being an example of the emotional detachment already described in young children following certain sorts of separation, and, secondly, it attributes this detachment, whether in child or adult, to the systems responsible for attachment behavior having been immobilized as a result of the separation experiences. In the case of Mrs. G., I see the immobilization and consequent emotional freezing as being a response to the intense pain caused during her early years by the prolonged and probably oft-repeated frustration of her attachment behavior, experienced by her as rejection of her urgent desire for love and care.

A key concept in this explanation is the notion that a behavioral system in certain circumstances can be partially or even wholly immobilized, that is, rendered either temporarily or permanently incapable of being activated, and with it the whole range of feeling and desire that normally accompanies it rendered incapable of being aroused. By what means, we may then ask, is it proposed that this deactivation, as I term it (Bowlby, 1980), is produced?

In answering this question I turn to the work of the cognitive psychologists (Erdelyi, 1974; Norman, 1976; Dixon, 1981), who during the past twenty years have revolutionized our knowledge of how we perceive the world and how we construe the situations we are in—a revolution that, among much else that is clinically congenial, accords unconscious mental processes the central place in mental life that analysts have always claimed for them.

Now the simplest way in which to deactivate any control system dependent on signals for its activation is to block off the signals before they reach their destination. Thus, we can imagine an animal being rendered incapable of feeling hungry, and so never being motivated to eat, by an experimenter severing all the neural and other pathways that conduct hunger signals to the higher centers. But it is clear that there are also means other than surgery for achieving the same end. This is where I turn to the cognitive psychologists. Their work has shown unmistakably that the mental apparatus is quite capable of blocking off sensory inflow of specific sorts—indeed that in the course of daily life it is doing so every minute of the day.

Studies of human perception have shown that before a person is aware of seeing or hearing something the sensory inflow coming through his eyes or ears has already passed through many stages of selection, interpretation, and appraisal, during the course of which a large proportion of the original inflow has been excluded. The reason for this extensive exclusion is that the channels responsible for the most advanced processing, being of limited capacity, must be protected from overload. To ensure that what is most relevant gets through and that only the less relevant is excluded, selection of inflow is under central, or we might say ego, control. Although this processing is done at extraordinary speeds and almost all of it outside awareness, much of the inflow has nonetheless been carried to a very advanced stage of processing before being excluded. The results of experiments on dichotic listening provide striking examples.

In this type of experiment two different messages are transmitted simultaneously to the person, one message being transmitted to one ear and the other to the other ear. The person is then told to attend to one of these messages only, say the one being received by the right ear. To ensure he gives it continuous attention, he is required to "shadow" that message by repeating it word for word as he is hearing it. Keeping the two messages distinct is found to be fairly easy, and at the end of the session the subject is usually totally unaware of the content of the unattended message. Yet there are significant exceptions. For example, should his own name or some other personally significant word occur in the unattended message he may well notice and remember it. This shows that the unattended message is being subjected to continuous and fairly advanced processing during which its meaning is being monitored and its content being appraised as more or less relevant; and all this without the person being in any way aware of what is going on.

In the ordinary course of a person's life the criteria applied to sensory inflow that determine what information is to be accepted and what is to be excluded are readily intelligible as reflecting what is at any one time in the person's best interests. Thus, when he is hungry, sensory inflow concerned with food is given priority, while much else that might at other times be of interest to him is excluded. Yet, should danger threaten, priorities would quickly change so that inflow concerned with issues of danger and safety would take precedence and inflow concerned with food be temporarily excluded. This change in the criteria governing what inflow is to be accepted and what excluded is effected by evaluating systems central to the personality.

In thus summarizing the findings from a neighboring discipline, the main points I wish to emphasize are, first, that throughout a person's life he is engaged in excluding, or shutting out, a large proportion of all the information that is reaching him; second, that he does so only after its relevance to himself has been assessed; and, third, that this process of selective exclusion is usually carried out without his being in any way aware of its happening. Thus, there is no longer any difficulty in imagining, and describing in operational terms, a mental apparatus capable of shutting off information of certain specified types and of doing so without the person being aware of what is happening.

In the emotionally detached individuals we have been discussing, children and adults, the information being excluded is of a very special type. So far from its being the routine exclusion of irrelevant and potentially distracting information that we engage in all the time and that is readily reversible, what is being excluded in these pathological conditions are the signals, arising from both inside and outside the person, that would activate their attachment behavior with its related thoughts, feelings, and desires and that would enable them both to love and to experience being loved. In other words, the mental structures responsible for routine selective exclusion are being employed—one might say exploited—for a special and potentially pathological purpose. This form of exclusion I refer to, for obvious reasons, as defensive exclusion, which is of course only another way of describing repression. And, just as Freud regarded repression as the key process in every form of defense, so I see the role of defensive exclusion. Furthermore, just as Freud insisted that what is repressed is constantly ready to return, so I emphasize that any system which has been deactivated in this way is constantly ready for reactivation. Thus, whenever the cognitive system responsible for defensive exclusion of relevant information operates with less than complete efficiency, the behavioral system in question together with its related thoughts, feelings, and desires, will become active, if only incompletely and for a limited spell. It is along these lines that the theory proposed is able to account for all those phenomena that led Freud to advance his theory of a dynamic unconscious.[1]

---

[1] The role in this conceptual framework of feeling and emotion, and their relation to cognition and behavior, are outlined in Attachment (1969), Chapter 7.

Let us turn now to consider the process of therapeutic change as it occurred in Mrs. G. As I see it, thanks to the relatively secure base provided by the analyst, this patient managed to develop sufficient courage to permit some of the information she had hitherto excluded to go forward for processing. This included both information stemming from the present situation, for example evidence of her analyst's genuine concern to help her and the conflicting thoughts, feelings, and behavior that that aroused, and also information stored in her memory, for example, memories of the very painful events of her childhood and the thoughts, feelings, and behavior aroused by them. As so often happens, with this patient information from the two sources was recovered as a chain in which information from the present, especially the transference, alternated with information from the past, with each link leading on to the next. Once the relevant information had become accepted, Mrs. G.'s attachment behavior was reactivated, together with the urges and desires, thoughts, and feelings that went with it. In traditional terms, the unconscious had been made conscious and the repressed urges and affects had been released.

I remarked that it was only with the analyst's support that Mrs. G. managed to muster sufficient courage to look afresh at events and experiences that had caused her so much suffering in the past and also to permit herself to become attached to her analyst in the present. What a person in this frame of mind dreads most is permitting themselves to become attached to someone only to be rejected yet again. Because of this these people have no sooner begun to relax their guard and to allow themselves some feeling than they shy away. For some years I treated an extremely disturbed and hostile woman who had presented suffering from severe agoraphobia and depression. At one phase in her analysis she was apt to needle me unceasingly about my shortcomings in ways that ultimately led me to be fairly irritable in return. This seemed to satisfy her. After we had recognized the sequence, known as ''getting under my skin,'' I asked her why she had to do it. To this she replied with a phrase I have never forgotten. ''I can't take kindness,'' she explained; and she went on to describe how it was after I had done something that she had felt was kind that she became possessed of this urge to needle me unmercifully. What she was afraid of, it seemed clear, was becoming attached to me; in her experience, to become attached to someone could lead only to rejection and further suffering. Once I had become irritable any warm feelings she might have felt in response to my kindness were snuffed out. Then she felt safe again, though of course terribly isolated.

It is to this tragic condition of emotional isolation that Otto Will has so insistently called attention. As it happens, he and I in our professional work have chosen very different routes. The source of his ideas has been the psychotherapy of adolescents and young adults who are suffering from very serious disorders, whereas I have focused on the diverse pathways along which personality can develop and on the real-life experiences responsible for which path it follows. Yet our tracks have converged in a most striking way. As a result of his experiences, Otto Will emphasizes the abyss of loneliness in which so many of his patients are living, how during therapy they show "both a great need for, and a fear of, intimacy," and how he regards therapy as being designed to expose their need for friendship and love, and "to encourage the formation of trust in another person" (Will, 1980). Need I say how heart-warming I find it that, having started along such different-seeming routes, we should now find ourselves at precisely the same destination? When we are not blinded by misleading theory the facts of experience can indeed be compelling.

There are, I know, many analysts who regard the ideas I have outlined with the greatest reserve, but there are others who see them as presenting essentially the same traditional drama, only in an unfamiliar, modern dress. I myself believe the case for seeing them in that light to be very strong.

First, it is important to recognize that, although Freud adopted a model of the mental apparatus in which psychic energy plays a central part, a great deal of his theorizing is couched in terms hardly different from those of present-day cognitive psychology. Thus, in the opening sentence of his paper "The Unconscious" Freud writes, "the essence of the process of repression lies, not in putting an end to, in annihilating, the idea which represents an instinct, but in preventing it becoming conscious" (1915, p. 166), and that the reason or purpose for doing so is to prevent the person from experiencing some form of psychological pain. Later in the same paper he points out that "repression results not only in withholding things from consciousness, but also in preventing the development of affect and the setting-off of muscular activity'' (p. 179). In support of the theory I am advancing, it can be said that the defensive exclusion of anything capable of activating the control systems that mediate attachment behavior and the thoughts and feelings that go with them achieves just that.

Moreover, not only are Freud's central ideas on theory catered for by the conceptual scheme I am proposing but also his ideas on treatment. For example, in his 1913 paper ''On Beginning the Treatment,'' he advises that ''the first aim of the treatment [of a patient] is to attach him to it and to the person of the doctor,'' and that, given time and the absence of mistakes, ''he will of himself form such an attachment and link the doctor up with one of the images of the people by whom he was accustomed to be treated with affection'' (pp. 139–140).

I have dealt at some length with the defensive organization that I believe can account for emotional detachment because that was the problem I set out to solve many years ago. But there are several other situations that can give rise to information of great significance to a person being excluded from consciousness.

Elsewhere (Bowlby, 1979) I discuss two such situations, to both of which I should like to refer briefly again. On that occasion I took as my starting point a generalization made by Freud (1914) in one of his early papers on technique: ''Forgetting impressions, scenes or experiences nearly always reduces itself to shutting them off. When the patient talks about these 'forgotten' things he seldom fails to add: 'As a matter of fact I've always known it; only I've never thought of it' '' (p. 148).

Since we have already discussed the means whereby memories can become shut off and apparently forgotten, let us consider what special features characterize the ''impressions, scenes and experiences'' that tend to become shut off in people suffering from neurosis, and the causal conditions, internal and external to the personality, that activate the shutting off processes.

Children not infrequently observe scenes that parents would prefer they did not observe; they form impressions that parents would prefer they did not form; and they have experiences that parents would like to believe they have not had. Evidence shows that many of these children, aware of how their parents feel, proceed then to conform to their parents' wishes by excluding from further processing such information as they already have; and that, having done so, they cease consciously to be aware that they have ever observed such scenes, formed such impressions, or had such experiences. My reasons for calling attention to this cause of information being shut away and apparently forgotten is that until recently little attention seems to have been given to it by leading thinkers of any of the major psychoanalytic groups, in either their theorizing or their practice.

Evidence that parents sometimes press their children to shut off from further, conscious processing information the children already have about events the parents wish they had never observed comes from several sources. Perhaps the most vivid concerns the efforts made by a surviving parent to obliterate his or her child's knowledge of the other parent's suicide.

Cain and Fast (1972) report findings from their study of a series of forty-five children, aged between four and fourteen, all of whom had lost a parent by suicide and all of whom had become psychiatrically disturbed, many of them severely so. In reviewing their data the authors were struck by the very large roles played in the children's symptomatology by their having been exposed to pathogenic situations of two types, namely situations in which intense guilt is likely to be engendered (not discussed here) and situations in which communications between parent and child are gravely distorted.

About one quarter of the children studied had personally witnessed some aspect of the parent's death and had subsequently been subjected to pressure from the surviving parent to believe that they were mistaken in what they had seen or heard, and that the death had not been due to suicide but to some illness or accident. "A boy who watched his father kill himself with a shotgun . . . was told later that night by his mother that his father had died of a heart attack; a girl who discovered her father's body hanging in a closet was told he had died in a car accident; and two brothers who had found their mother with her wrists slit were told she had drowned while swimming" (Cain and Fast, 1972, p. 102). When a child described what he had seen, the surviving parent had sought to discredit it either by ridicule or by insisting that he was confused by what he had seen on TV or by some bad dream he had had. Such confusion was sometimes compounded, moreover, by the child hearing several different stories about the death from different people or even from his surviving parent.

Many of the children's psychological problems seemed directly traceable to their having been exposed to situations of this kind. Their problems included chronic distrust of other people, inhibition of their curiosity, distrust of their own senses, and a tendency to find everything unreal.

In the situations so far described the information a parent is pressing a child to shut away is information relating to events in the outside world. In other situations the information to be shut away relates to events in the child's private world of feeling. Nowhere does this occur more commonly than in situations of separation and loss.

When a parent dies the surviving parent or other relative may not only provide the children with inadequate or misleading information but may also indicate that it would not be appropriate for the child to be distressed. This may be explicit: Miller (1979) describes how, when a six-year-old's mother died, his aunt told him: ''You must be brave: don't cry; now go to your room and play nicely.'' At other times the indication is only implicit.

There are in fact many situations in which a child is expressly told not to cry. For example, a child of five whose nanny is leaving is told not to cry because that would make it more difficult for nanny. A child whose parents leave him in the hospital or residential nursery insist he not cry, otherwise they will not visit him. A child whose parents are frequently away and who leave him with one of a succession of *au pair* girls is not encouraged to recognize how lonely, and perhaps angry, he feels at their constant absence. When parents separate it is often made plain to a child that he is not expected to miss the departing parent or to pine for his or her return. Not only are sorrow and crying condemned as inappropriate in such situations but older children and adults may jeer at a distressed child for being a crybaby. Is there any wonder that in such circumstances feeling should become shut away?

All these situations are plain enough but have, I believe, been seriously neglected as causes of information and feeling becoming excluded from consciousness. There are, however, other situations also, more subtle and hidden but no less common, that have the same effect. One such is when a mother, who herself had a childhood deprived of love, seeks from her own child the love she has hitherto lacked. In doing so she is inverting the normal parent-child relationship—requiring the child to act as parent while she becomes the child. To someone unaware of what is going on it may appear that the child is being "over-indulged," but a closer look shows that the mother is placing a heavy burden on him. What is of special relevance here is that more often than not the child is expected to be grateful for whatever care he receives and not to notice the demands being made on him. One result of this is that, in conformity with his mother's wishes, he builds up a one-sided picture of her as wholly loving and generous, thereby shutting away from conscious processing much information also reaching him that she is often selfish, demanding, and ungrateful. Another result is that, also in conformity with his mother's wishes, he admits to consciousness only feelings of love and gratitude toward her and shuts away every feeling of anger he may have toward her for expecting him to care for her and for preventing him from making his own friends and living his own life.

A related situation is one in which a parent, having had a traumatic childhood, is apprehensive of being reminded of past miseries and thus becoming depressed. As a result her children are required always to appear happy and to avoid any expression of sorrow, loneliness, or anger. As one patient put it to me after a good deal of therapy: "I see now that I was terribly lonely as a child but I was never allowed to know it."

Most children are indulgent toward their parents, preferring to see them in a favorable light and eager to overlook many deficiencies. Yet they do not willingly conform to seeing a parent only in the light the parent requires or to feeling toward him or her only in the way demanded. To ensure that, pressure must be exerted. Pressure can take different forms but all forms depend for their effectiveness on the child's insistent desire to be loved and protected. In some families the message remains unspoken, but implicitly it runs: "Either you think about me as I wish or else expect nothing further from me." In others pressures are less subtle. One form, threatening to abandon the child as a means of disciplining him, is an extremely powerful weapon, especially with a young child. Faced with such threats, how could a child do other than conform to his parents' wishes by excluding from further processing all that he knows they wish him to forget? Elsewhere I have given reasons for believing that threats of this sort are responsible for much acute and chronic anxiety (Bowlby, 1973) and also for a person responding to bereavement in later life with chronic depression in which the dominant feeling is one of having been deliberately abandoned, as a punishment, by the dead person (Bowlby, 1980).

In all such cases, of course, an early task for the analyst is to first recognize that his patient still feels under duress not to think anything his parents expect him not to think nor to feel anything his parents expect him not to feel and then to raise with him the possibility of thinking and feeling about those very things—a large issue that merits a full discussion.

In recent years the cognitive components of analytic theory and analytic therapy have been given much more attention than formerly. I have found myself in close agreement with the views on the therapeutic process expressed by Gedo (1979) and Peterfreund (1982), and also with views expressed in recent times by a number of child analysts, for example Rees (1978) and Koch (1980). It is reassuring to find so many beginning to think along these same lines.

References

Bowlby, J. (1960), Separation/Anxiety. *Internat. J. Psycho-Anal.*, 41:89–113.
———— (1969), *Attachment and Loss, Volume I: Attachment.* 2nd ed., 1982. London: Hogarth Press; New York: Basic Books.
———— (1973), *Attachment and Loss, Volume II: Separation: Anxiety and Anger.* London: Hogarth Press; New York: Basic Books.
———— (1979), On knowing what you are not supposed to know and feeling what you are not supposed to feel. *Can. J. Psychiat.*, 24:403–408.
———— (1980), *Attachment and Loss, Volume III: Loss: Sadness and Depression.* London: Hogarth Press; New York: Basic Books.
Cain, A. C., & Fast, I. (1972), Children's disturbed reactions to parent suicide. In: *Survivors of Suicide*, ed. A. C. Cain. Springfield, IL.: Charles C Thomas.
Dixon, N.F. (1981), *Preconscious Processing.* New York: Wiley.
Erdelyi, M. H. (1974), A new look at the New Look: Perceptual defense and vigilance. *Psychol. Rev.*, 81:1–25.
Fairbairn, W. R. D. (1940), Schizoid factors in the personality. In: *Psychoanalytic Studies of the Personality.* London: Tavistock; New York: Basic Books, 1952.
Freud, S. (1894), The neuro-psychoses of defence. *Standard Edition*, 3:45–61. London: Hogarth Press, 1962.

———— (1913), On beginning the treatment. *Standard Edition*, 12:123–144. London: Hogarth Press, 1958.

———— (1914), Remembering, repeating and working through. *Standard Edition*, 12:147–156. London: Hogarth Press, 1958.

———— (1915), The unconscious. *Standard Edition*, 14:166–215. London: Hogarth Press, 1957.

Gedo, J. E. (1979), *Beyond Interpretation: Toward a Revised Theory for Psychoanalysis*. New York: International Universities Press.

Koch, E. (1980), Self-observation, insight and the development of "knowing" in a child analysis. *J. Child Psychother.*, 6:5–22.

Kohut, H. (1971), *The Analysis of the Self*. New York: International Universities Press.

Miller, A. (1979), *Prisoners of Childhood*. New York: Basic Books (English translation, 1981).

Mintz, T. (1976), Contribution to panel report on effects on adults of object loss in the first five years. Reported by M. Wolfenstein. *J. Amer. Psychoanal. Assn.*, 24:662–665.

Norman, D. A. (1976), *Memory and Attention: Introduction to Human Information Processing*. 2nd ed. New York: Wiley.

Peterfreund, E. (1982), *The Process of Psychoanalytic Therapy: Models and Strategies*. Hillsdale, NJ: Lawrence Erlbaum.

Rees, K. (1978), The child's understanding of his past: Cognitive factors in reconstruction with children. *Psychoanalytic Study of the Child*, 33:237–259. New Haven, CT: Yale University Press.

———— (1974), Fear of breakdown. *Internat. Rev. Psycho-Anal.*, 1:103–107.

Weiss, R. S. (1982), Attachment in adult life. In: *The Place of Attachment in Human Behavior*, ed. C. M. Parkes & J. Stevenson-Hinde. London: Tavistock; New York: Basic Books.

Will, O. A. (1980), Comments on the "elements" of schizophrenia, psychotherapy and the schizophrenic person. In: *Psychotherapy of Schizophrenia*, ed. J. S. Strauss et al. New York: Plenum.

Winnicott, D. (1965), Ego distortion in terms of true and false self. In: *The Maturational Processes and the Facilitating Environment*. London: Hogarth Press.

4

Mutuality and Pseudomutuality Reconsidered: Implications for Therapy and a Theory of Development of Relational Systems

Lyman C. Wynne, M.D., Ph.D.

> Alice stood without speaking, looking out in all directions over the country—and a most curious country it was. . . . "I declare it's marked out just like a large chess-board!" Alice said at last. "There ought to be some men moving about somewhere—and so there are! . . . It's a great huge game of chess that's being played—all over the world—if this *is* the world." . . .
>
> —Lewis Carroll, *Through the Looking Glass*

During the past twenty-five years, two worlds of therapy for disorders of the human condition have grown almost in parallel. Individual psychotherapy, rooted in psychoanalysis, and family therapy, taking off from systems theory, have for the most part gone their separate ways, sometimes with frankly deprecatory attacks and counterattacks, and sometimes with recognition of the other's existence in a manner that is polite and, as I would call it, pseudomutual. Pseudomutual recognition, that is, engagement limited to the level of appearances, negates recognition of more fundamental qualities of the other.

Despite infrequent acknowledgment in the literature, it is my observation that a great many respected practitioners of individual

81

psychotherapy and family therapy now commonly use techniques from both fields, but do so in haphazard or abortive ways. For some years I have been troubled that this admixture of individual and family therapy approaches that clinicians actually use in the privacy of their offices and clinics is only vaguely linked to any coherent theory, certainly not to theories that are taught in our residencies, institutes, and other so-called educational programs. Although it is often exciting to proceed with therapy unguided by theory, or to join a therapeutic chess game in an exotic setting, perhaps it would be interesting and even reassuring to some therapists to know what game they are playing and what the rules may be. In a tentative effort to contribute to the clarification of this problem, though surely not its resolution, I have turned to what I call a theory or paradigm of relatedness, or more accurately, of relational systems, especially of family systems.

In Chapter 1 of this volume, Merton Gill describes brilliantly and lucidly a *person* paradigm. He proposes that this paradigm can best be regarded as supraordinate to the traditional *body* paradigm of psychoanalysis. Tentatively, the relatedness paradigm I shall outline here can be viewed as supraordinate to the person paradigm in terms of the hierarchy of systems. In general systems theory (Bertalanffy, 1968; Weiss, 1969) and in the biopsychosocial model of Engel (1977, 1980), the person is unquestionably the system level of focal interest. I believe that this emphasis on individuation reflects the rather special orientation of America and other Western cultures. Oriental cultures, exemplified in the Japanese concept of *amae* (Doi, 1973), an untranslatable experience of reciprocal attachments, tend to give greater attention to relatedness in its own right. America has nurtured, in contrast, the rugged individualism of the pioneers and, in more recent years, what Christopher Lasch has called the culture of narcissism (1979). Psychoanalysis and individual psychotherapies found an exceptionally hospitable reception in America, culminating in recent years in the credo made explicit in Fritz Perls' ''Gestalt Prayer'' (1969):

> I do my thing and you do your thing. . . .
> And if by chance we find each other, it's beautiful.
> If not, it can't be helped.

Such views undoubtedly have a widespread romantic appeal when individuation is uncertain. On the other hand, a thoughtful consideration of the qualities and varieties of relatedness surely has been neglected not only by our culture as a whole but also by psychologic and psychoanalytic theoreticians and therapists. Otto Will and the contributors to this volume, with their explicit attention to human relationships, are among the most noteworthy exceptions to this bias.

Earlier Formulations

The place where I wish to begin my own comments is remote in time, back to a broad formulation my colleagues and I first presented in 1956, in a paper entitled "Pseudo-Mutuality in the Family Relations of Schizophrenics" (Wynne, Ryckoff, Day, and Hirsch, 1958). In that paper we began with a key postulate that mankind faces a "universal necessity for dealing with *both* the problems of relation and identity." We assumed, first, that "movement into relation with other human beings is a fundamental principle or 'need' of human existence." Restating this in psychoanalytic terminology, we noted that "man is inherently object related," in a sense similar to that proposed by Fairbairn (1952) and Balint (1952). The other key postulate for this formulation was that "every human being strives consciously and unconsciously, in a lifelong process, to develop a sense of personal identity" (Erikson, 1956).

Combining these premises, we conceptualized a subjective dilemma and a behavioral dialectic, ranging on a continuum from a relatedness pole to an identity or individuation pole. This hypothetical continuum has been used in my subsequent studies and, independently, as the starting place for several family therapy approaches, for example, that of Bowen (1971), and for formal family system research, most notably in the work of Olson, Sprenkle, and Russell (1979).[1] Interesting as these various ideas have been, I believe that their meaningfulness and usefulness can be considerably enhanced by a reassessment of the

[1]Cf. the formulation of the philosopher Martin Buber, who conceptualized a twofold principle of human life consisting of two basic movements: "the primal setting at a distance" and "entering into relation." The first presupposes the second, for we can only enter into relation with a being that is set at a distance and thereby has become an independent opposite (Friedman, 1955).

basic concepts. Here I shall take a more detailed look at the concept of relationship or relatedness.

First, as a preliminary step toward a generalized theory, in our 1958 paper we identified three forms of relatedness that could result from efforts to solve this dilemma: *mutuality*, in which the identity of each participant is recognized and positively valued; *pseudomutuality*, ''a predominant absorption in fitting together, at the expense of the differentiation of the identities of the persons in the relation''; and *nonmutuality*, role-limited complementarity without a strong investment ''in exploring what the relation has to offer either person'' (Wynne et al., 1958).

In 1959 we described how rigid structuring of family roles in myths and behavior can impede the changes needed for growth, in the quality of family relationships, and in identity development (Ryckoff, Day, and Wynne, 1959). In 1961 I introduced the concept of pseudohostility, proposed as a term to describe intense relating, mostly with negative affect, in families in which turmoil and crisis become a way of life (Wynne, 1961). As with pseudomutuality, the shared, collusive participation in pseudohostile relatedness maintains an enduring level of connectedness, protecting against both dissolution of the relationship and the hazards of intimacy.

In 1958 Singer and I began more systematic and detailed research on these hypotheses, starting with Rorschachs and TAT's of family members (Singer and Wynne, 1963; Wynne and Singer, 1963), as well as with transcribed family therapy interviews (Morris and Wynne, 1965). Experimenting with the applicability of an exploratory psychoanalytic treatment model in order to understand family relationships in greater depth, we met with families three or four times a week for several years, without the addition of either medication or individual psychotherapy for the identified schizophrenic patient (Schaffer, Wynne, Day, Ryckoff, and Halperin, 1962; Wynne, 1965). (This approach to therapy was permanently abandoned in about 1963.) These detailed observations in both research and family therapy impressed us with the fragmentation of the communication in these families, expressed in therapy by a profound uncertainty about the meaning and connectedness of specific events and messages in family life. The problems of relatedness, we observed, were found in the most dysfunctional of these families at many levels: in difficulties in maintaining ''proper distance'' in dyadic emotional ties (Singer and Wynne, 1965a), in fluid triangular and multiperson alignments and splits within the family (Wynne, 1961), in a limited ability to engage in therapeutic and research tasks (Wynne, 1965; Schaffer et al., 1962; Loveland, Wynne, and Singer, 1963), and in the inability to focus attention on the content and meaning of specific messages and actions (Singer and Wynne, 1963, 1965a & b).

In an effort to link these diverse varieties and levels of functioning, Margaret Singer and I adopted a special way of thinking about communication:

> Communication can be conceived as beginning with the efforts of two or more persons to focus their attention selectively on shared percepts, ideas, or feelings. If this attentional phase is aborted or confused, the consequences for the rest of the communicative process will be profound. We believe that communication in the families of schizophrenics is especially disturbed at the attentional level, whereas in the families of borderline, neurotic, and normal individuals, communication disorders are more prominent later on after an attentional focus has been shared. [Singer and Wynne, 1965a, p. 191]

This formulation led in turn to specifying that *sharing* foci of attention is a crucial ingredient in communication, leading, most immediately, to the sharing of meaning. Operationally, what Singer and I called communication deviances were features of ''naming and explaining'' by a subject that distract the attention and befuddle a listener who is attempting to share the meanings conveyed by the speaker. We identified communication deviances, for example, when a statement is both made and denied or partially disqualified, when a referent is ambiguous or inconsistent, and when ordinary words or phrases are used oddly out of context (Singer and Wynne, 1966).

The study of communication deviances in families has proved to be a highly productive research strategy (see Wynne, Singer, Bartko, and Toohey, 1977; Singer, Wynne, and Toohey, 1978; Wynne, Singer, and Toohey, 1976). On the other hand, other aspects of relatedness

were quietly relegated to the background. To be sure, I have made a
number of forays back into my earlier, broader interests (Wynne, 1970,
1972, 1976, 1980). Most comprehensive was a 1970 paper (Wynne,
1970) defining more explicitly three levels of "communication": relationship, task, and focal content or message. I also provided explicit
examples to show how difficulties could start (or first come to notice)
at *any* of these three levels and then permeate the whole of family
transactions; the message and communication deviance level is con-
venient to identify for research purposes but cannot be regarded as
primary.

The Epigenesis of Relatedness

This volume honoring Otto Will, who has influenced me and so
many others in understanding "the planned use of the human relationship" (Will, 1978), has stimulated me to exhume my dormant
theory of relatedness. In so doing, I have been delighted to discover
useful linkages to both my recent research and my current approaches
to treatment.

What I shall describe here are certain major components of relatedness, to be followed by a few brief remarks on disturbances in,
and treatment of, these components. After struggling with various ways
of organizing these components in an integral form, I realized that I
am dealing with developmental processes in relational systems. Although there is a great deal of temporal overlap as these features
develop, there is a certain sequential logic that deserves to be called
epigenetic. Here I discovered an interesting parallel to the epigenesis
of identity described by Erikson. The epigenetic principle, as formulated by Erikson (1968), "states that anything that grows has a ground
plan, and that out of this ground plan the parts arise, each part having
its time of special ascendancy, until all parts have arisen to form a
functioning whole" (p. 92).

Table 1 presents a preliminary scheme for a possible epigenesis
of relatedness. The stages I have identified as prerequisites leading to
mutuality in relatedness are (1) attachment/caregiving, (2) communication (sharing attention and meanings), (3) sharing tasks and role-
structuring, (4) intimacy, (5) establishing and allowing divergence,
and (6) mutuality.

TABLE 1
Epigenesis of Relatedness

Relational Process	Mode of study	Disturbance and pathology
1. Attachment/caregiving (Emotional bonding)	Ethology Mother-child observations	Autism Abandonment
2. Communication (Sharing attention and meanings)	Communication studies	Transactional thought disorder Communication deviances
3. Sharing tasks (I-It) (Role structuring)	Problem-solving studies	Conflictual living
4. Intimacy (I-Thou)	Experiential reports	Pseudomutuality and its transformations
5. Divergence	Behavioral observations	Alienation and violence
6. Mutuality	Family life cycle observations	

Attachment/caregiving (emotional bonding).   In the elegant and comprehensive studies by John Bowlby (1969) and John Scott (Scott and Fuller, 1965) of attachment and its disruptions, they have described the necessary, biologically based beginnings of relationship processes. The term "emotional bonding" can be used to include both the attachment behavior and the complementary behavior of caregiving, as well as all their derivatives in adolescence and adulthood, to which Bowlby rightfully has drawn attention. The emotional bonding, however crucial, is so elaborated in complex cognitive processes, contextual and other events, that it becomes quite reductionistic to view the whole of adult relatedness (including mutuality) of adults as merely an extension of attachment and caregiving.

Attachment and caregiving are periodically reactivated in something like their early form in later life, at times of illness and aging. For many of our most severely disturbed patients, months and years of therapy oriented to the developmental issues of this stage are, in effect, efforts to compensate for the early impairments of attachment. Although human beings are capable of accomplishments that are compensatory for loss, for example, of limbs or vision in early life, therapy of early and profound attachment disorders results in outcomes that are necessarily different from development that has unfolded in an expectable epigenetic sequence. I might add that while the participation of the family in understanding, assessing, and planning therapeutic work on profound disorders arising from attachment difficulties is often very helpful, sustained therapy with an individual therapist in a supportive milieu is usually indicated.

Communication (sharing attention and meanings). The second component in relatedness is communication. Earlier, I, like some others, inflated the concept of communication so that it could be understood as including everything that goes on between people. This was confusing to many people who prefer to define communication as primarily the exchange of signals and messages, largely an attentional and cognitive process. For the sake of improved communication, I am now restricting my use of the term to the sharing of focal attention and content that becomes manifest in the reciprocal transmission of messages and meanings. An emotional bond, enduring beyond the biological givens of early attachment, requires increasingly complex communication to be predictably renewed. Such communication becomes elaborated most rapidly between ages two and four, or can, at that time, become noticeably blocked, or private and unshared.

Sharing tasks (I–It/role structuring). The third component is the sharing and structuring of tasks and goals in joint problem-solving. With any shared meaning there is at least a moment of relatedness, but such moments would be concretistic fragments unless unified around sustained purposes and tasks. Such shared tasks, when repeated, become patterned into role relationships. Reciprocal role behavior alone does *not* constitute a complete relationship of mutuality, but does incorporate and stabilize in a crucial manner the bonding and communication processes that have begun before. In Erikson's schema, industry is postulated as the task of individual development that precedes the consolidation of identity in adolescence (1968).

Martin Buber (1937, 1947), whom I regard as one of the seminal thinkers of this century, has in his poetic manner described the process and the experience of turning to external tasks as the world of I–It. Here objects, events, and ideas external to each person are viewed and considered by each. Relationally, the persons join in a common purpose, but not addressing one another *directly* as in affectional bonding or attachment/caregiving.

From day to day, in our ordinary activities, we live in the world of I–It. We use messages and meanings as tools, usually without focusing attention on specific messages when the supraordinate task is proceeding smoothly. The communicational level is not experienced as such, as a "world," except when we are stuck in controversies and in concrete literalness.

Intimacy (I-Thou).   As affection and meanings and purpose converge, we may then make a transition to another stage of relatedness, the emotional engagement and involvement of adults, to reciprocal empathy and intimacy. Intimacy is properly a term of dyadic relatedness, of a relationship *system*, not of a *person*. Yet intimate relationships, as I understand them, can arise only when a core of personal identity has first been achieved. Thus, Erikson describes intimacy as a developmental stage *after* identity, and it is here that the relational and the individual epigenetic life cycles converge.

The term intimacy is sometimes used to refer to the relatedness of attachment/caregiving. More restrictively, I believe that the term is best reserved for the relatedness of those who have grown beyond the requirements of basic attachment and caregiving, however important this ground plan surely is. Erotic elements, joint inspiration, and the sharing of interests on a reciprocally enduring level surely all can contribute to intimacy beyond the biological starting points of attachment/caregiving.

The quintessential form of intimacy is found in Buber's "life of dialogue" and the world of I-Thou relatedness, that is, "with the whole being," focusing not upon individual objects and their causal connections but upon the "sphere of the between" in which each experiences the other side. (Although Buber speaks of three forms of relation—with nature, man, and God—the relation between man and man is most clearly reciprocal and most pivotal for the I-Thou concept.) Even so, the experience of I-Thou relatedness and intimacy cannot last uninterruptedly.

Divergence.   With contextual and physiological changes, with growth and aging, divergence is inevitable in any relational system.

Such divergence is most commonly accepted as normal in adolescent-parent relationships, but the normality of divergence is not limited to this developmental phase and is just as inevitable in marriage and other adult-to-adult relationships. Mutuality, which becomes possible after divergence is recognized and confronted, encompasses moments, and longer, of the recognition and tolerance of failures, errors, and limitations, both at the level of the sharing of tasks and interests, and at the level of the communication of meaning. I have insisted that there *must* be divergence and noncomplementarity in order to have genuine mutuality. "Genuine mutuality, unlike pseudomutuality, not only tolerates divergence of self interests, but thrives upon the recognition of such natural and inevitable divergences" (Wynne et al., 1958).

Mutuality.   Built out of and enriched by the experiences together of people who each have an established, intact, necessarily divergent personal identity, genuine mutuality involves mutual recognition of one another's identity, including a recognition of one another's goals, abilities, and potentialities and, with growth and situational changes, recognition of areas of noncomplementarity of interests. With divergence, intimacy subsides and the relationship may work back through the world of I-It, through the world of shared tasks and roles, to return again, with good fortune, to the holistic experiences of intimacy. As these relational changes recur and establish a recognizable but evolving pattern, then and only then does the concept of mutuality become applicable. Far from being a precious and delicate, momentary experience, mutuality includes, indeed requires, room for considerable error. As Buber (1947) emphasized, "The life of dialogue . . . does not begin in the upper story of humanity. It begins no higher than where humanity begins. There are no gifted and ungifted here, only those who give themselves and those who withhold themselves" (p. 35). Implicit in the concept of an epigenesis of relatedness is the formulation that *mutuality encompasses over time all of the components previously described.*

Adaptability, flexibility to change, is crucial in mutuality. Separation and divergence actually are important at each developmental level, though not in such full-blown forms as in the achievement of full mutuality. Experiences of at least brief separations strengthen attachment; failures to share attention, if not massive, sharpen the attentional process.

Central in this theory of relatedness is the necessary movement between role-structured tasks and intimacy, between the worlds of I-It and I-Thou. In describing the distinction and the linkages between these two spheres, I must return to a memorable passage from Martin Buber:

> The world of *It* is set in the context of space and time.
>
> The world of *Thou* is not set in the context of either of these.
>
> The particular *Thou*, after the relational event has run its course, is *bound* to become an *It*.
>
> The particular *It*, by entering the relational event, *may* become a *Thou*.
>
> These are the two basic privileges of the world of *It*. They move man to look on the world of *It* as the world in which he has to live, and in which it is comfortable to live, as the world, indeed, which offers him all manner of incitements and excitements, activity and knowledge. In this chronicle of solid benefits the moments of *Thou* appear as strange lyric and dramatic episodes, seductive and magical, but tearing us away to dangerous extremes, loosening the well-tried context, leaving more questions than satisfaction behind them, shattering security—in short, uncanny moments we can well dispense with. For since we are bound to leave them and go back into the "world," why not remain in it? . . . .
>
> And in all the seriousness of truth, hear this: without *It* man cannot live. But he who lives with *It* alone is not a man. [1937, pp. 33–34]

Perturbation of Relatedness

A full-scale discussion of the deviations, both pathological and creative, arising at each stage in the development of relatedness is obviously beyond the scope of this contribution. Some, especially the disturbances of attachment and communication, are too familiar to deserve comment. I shall focus here primarily on distortions of intimacy and on suggestions for their treatment.

The first of these distortions I have previously labeled pseudomutuality. In pseudomutual relationships there is a striving, often willful or forced, to create or to sustain intimacy artificially. The illusion of a close emotional tie will result—illusory in the sense that it does not have a substructure of shared tasks in a role relationship, and perhaps not in an emotional bond, that can carry the relationship forward when divergence comes along.

> In pseudomutuality, the subjective tension aroused by divergence or independence of expectations . . . is experienced as not merely disrupting that particular transaction but as possibly demolishing the entire relation. The alternative outcome is overlooked or cannot be awaited: that the recognition and exploration of difference may lead to an expanded or deepened, although altered, basis for the relation. [Wynne et al., 1958, p. 207]

The result is that the appearance of relationship, the *sense* of relatedness does not have a firm bed to rest upon. This results in overlooking what the other person is really like, what is really going on with the other. This may end up in difficulties of perception in a severe form, even at a schizophrenic level, but much more commonly far short of that.

Thus, a pseudomutual impasse occurs when people get stuck believing that they have a relationship but are unable to deal with the differences. This is true in many marriages as well as in separation problems between adolescents and their parents. With the growth of the adolescent, there is obvious change and divergence. In the case of marriage, there also are life changes; people get older and what was there before is no longer part of the current reality. If people need a relationship very strongly but cannot let it unfold, the relational system will combine with individual inhibitions to constrict growth, including new experiences. Subjectively, there then will be a lack of freshness, a lack of zest. The relationship will be experienced as empty, boring, or barren, bereft of fun, humor, and creativity.

Pseudomutual manifestations take place in many small ways in all, or most all, of our lives, so that we usually overlook them. In fact, if they never occurred, there probably would be an overabundance of assertiveness and contentiousness. But there are families in which pseudomutuality becomes the overarching pattern of relating. This pattern is usually preserved by the "creation of a pervasive familial subculture of myths, legends, and ideology that stress the catastrophic consequences of openly recognized divergence from the fixed family role structure" or may involve a desperate preoccupation with harmony in all family relationships (Wynne et al., 1958). Such pseudomutuality impressed us when we were beginning, in the years 1953–1957, our long-term intensive studies of the families of acute schizophrenics. The families that were willing to stay around for prolonged meetings with us were probably those who also were unusually stuck in their relationships within the family. Our willingness to be patiently reflective, hour after endless hour, in our efforts to grasp and share the "meanings" of the family enabled us to empathize with their despair and anguish (Schaffer et al., 1962). We became emotionally engaged on an intimate, experiential level, but—as I now see it—these "therapeutic" relationships were, for the most part, a shared pseudomutual illusion. Little or no problem-solving, no updating and restructuring of their roles and relationships, and little change in manifest behavioral patterns took place with that approach to treatment. These particular families had evolved a prolonged pseudomutual solution to the difficulties of achieving individuation within relationships. The interpretive treatment model offered to them attempted to move directly from the level of meaning to the level of empathy and intimacy; but by neglecting the world of the I-It we regrettably perpetuated, I now believe, the pseudomutuality of these families.

Fortunately, the lifelong striving for relatedness does not ordinarily lead to fixed pseudomutuality. More commonly, one of these other outcomes emerges, the latter two being less "healthy": (1) the "healthy" recognition of genuine divergence and the redefinition of roles and expectations within the relationship, paving the way for developmentally appropriate new relationships (for example, when adolescents and their parents successfully separate); (2) mutual withdrawal but continuation of the relationship on an increasingly barren and empty basis, often with frustration and despair recognized by one or both, but with an inability to change; (3) an unrelenting, open, coercive, reciprocal demand that the relationship return to a romanticized intimacy and sharing of interests. With this last outcome, the result is perpetually angry, nagging, irritable bickering, or worse, that may go on for the duration of the persons' lives. This type of outcome warrants the term pseudohostility (Wynne, 1961): a shared, collusive defense against the anxiety of enhanced personal identity and divergence, as well as an agreement, usually covert, that neither of them will risk the hazards of genuine intimacy. Pseudohostile relationships are common in marital conflicts that never end. On a continuum, the pseudohostile transformation may take place at a more adaptive level, as good-humored bantering and sparring.

Another important variant in this kind of relationship occurs when one person in a couple or in a family gives up the striving for relatedness and tunes out unresponsively. The other often becomes bitter and strident. The relational pathology is then of a polarized form; only rarely do the persons successfully achieve a new basis for this relationship. More often, the tuned-out partner finds a substitute involvement or interest outside the family, usually in an occupational or amorous affair. The partner who is still fighting for the relationship will most often, in my observation, intensify an intrafamilial tie with someone else, such as an offspring, or establish a quasi-familial relationship with a therapist.

In summary, the paradigm for relatedness sketched out in this paper incorporates, in a hierarchy of systems, the paradigm for persons and for their bodily functions. One cannot properly conceptualize the *reciprocity* of relatedness that most vividly characterizes full mutuality by using only the perspective of individual persons, even when one recognizes, as do Gill, Fairbairn, and others, that persons are social beings. The starting point of psychoanalytic object relations theory and similar efforts is that of subject relating to object rather than that of reciprocal contributors to the relational system from the outset, to be accorded attention as equally balanced as possible.

Therapeutically, in work with individual patients in psychotherapy or psychoanalysis, the experience of the patient is extracted from the enduring social context in which he or she lives. Although the emphasis upon both transference and countertransference in the psychoanalytic relationship creates a relational system very close to what I have described here, it still is not, of course, a "natural" system such as the family. Many additional therapeutic implications of this formulation will need to be discussed elsewhere, but I hope that some of them are self-evident. For example, the epigenetic formulation suggests that development of problem-solving skills and sharing of interests in marital or family therapy must surely be established and given emphasis before intimacy and mutuality can be expected to emerge. Many couples and families seek therapy, or encounters that serve as substitutes for therapy, in the belief that they can create intimacy and mutuality by a direct, willful effort, rather than through the growth of relatedness.

The strategies and rules of relationship therapy are different from those of individual therapy. I strongly believe that we should be quite clear at all times whether we are functioning in the world of individual therapy or that of therapy with relational systems. The patterns of change in these realms are quite different.

I shall conclude by returning to Alice who has just stopped running with the Red Queen behind the looking glass:

> The Queen propped her up against a tree, and said kindly, "You may rest a little, now."
>
> Alice looked around her in great surprise. "Why, I do believe we've been under this tree the whole time! Everything's just as it was!"
>
> "Of course it is," said the Queen. "What would you have it?"
>
> "Well, in *our* country," said Alice, still panting a little, "you'd generally get to somewhere else—if you ran very fast for a long time as we've been doing."
>
> "A slow sort of country!" said the Queen. "Now, *here,* you see, it takes all the running *you* can do, to keep in the same place. If you want to get somewhere else, you must run at least twice as fast!"

So, like Alice, until I can run twice as fast, I must content myself with sharing with you these preliminary views of where I now find myself in the perplexing world of relational systems.

References

Balint, M. (1952), *Primary Love and Psychoanalytic Technique*. London: Hogarth Press.

Bertalanffy, L. von (1968), *General System Theory*. New York: Braziller.

Bowen, M. (1971), Family therapy and family group therapy. In: *Comprehensive Group Psychotherapy*, ed. H. Kaplan & B. Sadock. Baltimore: Williams & Wilkins, pp. 384–421.

Bowlby, J. (1969), *Attachment and Loss, Vol. I: Attachment*. New York: Basic Books.

Buber, M. (1937), *I and Thou* (trans. R.G. Smith). Edinburgh: T. and T. Clark.

——— (1947), *Between Man and Man*. London: Kegan Paul.

Doi, T. (1973), *The Anatomy of Dependence: The Structure of Amae*. Tokyo: Kodansha International.

Engel, G. (1977), The need for a new medical model: A challenge for biomedicine. *Science*, 196:129–136.

——— (1980), The clinical application of the biopsychosocial model. *Amer. J. Psychiat.*, 137:535–544.

Erikson, E. (1956), The problem of ego identity. *J. Amer. Psychoanal. Assn.*, 4:56–121.

——— (1968), *Identity: Youth and Crisis*. New York: Norton.

Fairbairn, W. (1952), *Psychoanalytic Studies of the Personality*. London: Tavistock.

Friedman, M. (1955), *Martin Buber: The Life of Dialogue*. Chicago: University of Chicago Press.

Lasch, C. (1979), *The Culture of Narcissism*. New York: Norton.

Loveland, N., Wynne, L., & Singer, M. (1963), The family Rorschach: A method for studying family interaction. *Fam. Proc.*, 2:187–215.

Morris, G., & Wynne, L. (1965), Schizophrenic offspring and styles of parental communication: A predictive study using family therapy excerpts. *Psychiat.*, 28:19–44.

Olson, D., Sprenkle, D., & Russell, C. (1979), Circumplex model of marital and family systems: I. Cohesion and adaptability dimensions, family types, and clinical applications. *Fam. Proc.*, 18:3–28.

Perls, F.S. (1969), *Gestalt Therapy Verbatim*. Lafayette, CA: Real People Press, p. 4.

Ryckoff, I., Day, J., & Wynne, L. (1959), Maintenance of stereotyped roles in the families of schizophrenics. *Amer. Med. Assn. Arch. Psychiat.*, 1:93–98.

Schaffer, L., Wynne, L., Day, J., Ryckoff, I., & Halperin, A. (1962), On the nature and sources of the psychiatrist's experience with the family of the schizophrenic. *Psychiat.*, 25:32–45.

Scott, J., & Fuller, J. (1965), *Genetics and the Social Behavior of the Dog*. Chicago: University of Chicago Press.

Singer, M., & Wynne, L. (1963), The differentiating characteristics of the parents of childhood schizophrenics, childhood neurotics, and young adult schizophrenics. *Amer. J. Psychiat.*, 120:234–243.

——— ——— (1965a), Thought disorder and family relations of schizophrenics: III. Methodology using projective techniques. *Arch. Gen. Psychiat.*, 12:187-200.

——— ——— (1965b), Thought disorder and family relations of schizophrenics: IV. Results and implications. *Arch. Gen. Psychiat.*, 12:201–212.

——— ——— (1966), Principles for scoring communication defects and deviances in parents of schizophrenics: Rorschach and TAT scoring manuals. *Psychiat.*, 29:260–288.

——— ——— Toohey, M. (1978), Communication disorders and the families of schizophrenics. In: *The Nature of Schizophrenia: New Approaches to Research and Treatment*, ed. L. Wynne, R. Cromwell, & S. Matthysse. New York: Wiley, pp. 499–511.

Weiss, P. (1969), The living system: Determinism stratified. In: *Beyond Reductionism*, ed. A. Koestler & J. Smythies. New York: Macmillan.

Will, O. A. (1978), Responsiveness of the schizophrenic to the planned use of the human relationship. In: *Controversy in Psychiatry*, ed. J. Brady & H. Brodie. Philadelphia: Saunders, pp. 621–639.

Wynne, L. (1961), The study of intrafamilial alignments and splits in exploratory family therapy. In: *Exploring the Base for Family Therapy*, ed. N. Ackerman, F. Beatman, & S. Sherman. New York: Family Service Assn. of America, pp. 95–115.

———— (1965), Some indications and contra-indications for exploratory family therapy. In: *Intensive Family Therapy: Theoretical and Practical Aspects, with Special Reference to Schizophrenia*, ed. I. Boszormenyi-Nagy & J. Framo. New York: Harper & Row, pp. 289–322.

———— (1970), Communication disorders and the quest for relatedness in families of schizophrenics. *Amer. J. Psychoanal.*, 30:100–114.

———— (1972), The injection and the concealment of meaning in the family relationships and psychotherapy of schizophrenia. In: *Psychotherapy of Schizophrenia*, ed. D. Rubinstein & Y. Alanen. Amsterdam: Excerpta Medica, pp. 180–193.

———— (1976), On the anguish and creative passions of not escaping double binds: A reformulation. In: *Double Bind: The Foundation of the Communicational Approach to the Family*, ed. C. Sluzki & D. Ransom. New York: Grune & Stratton, pp. 243–250.

———— (1980), Paradoxical interventions: Leverage for therapeutic change in individual and family systems. In: *Psychotherapy of Schizophrenia*, ed. J. Strauss, M. Bowers, T. Downey, S. Fleck, S. Jackson, & I. Levine. New York: Plenum, pp. 191–202.

———— Ryckoff, I., Day, J., & Hirsch, S. (1958), Pseudo-mutuality in the family relations of schizophrenics. *Psychiat.*, 21:205–220.

———— Singer, M. (1963), Thought disorder and family relations of schizophrenics: I. A research strategy. *Arch. Gen. Psychiat.*, 9:191–198.

———— ———— Bartko, J., & Toohey, M. (1977), Schizophrenics and their families: Recent research on parental communication. In: *Developments in Psychiatric Research*, ed. J. Tanner. London: Hodden & Stoughton, pp. 254–286.

———— ———— Toohey, M. (1976), Communication of the adoptive parents of schizophrenics. In: *Schizophrenia 75: Psychotherapy, Family Studies, Research*, ed. J. Jørstad & E. Ugelstad. Oslo, Norway: Universitetsforlaget, pp. 413–452.

5

Language, Psychosis, and Spirit

John P. Muller, Ph.D.

During a flagrant psychotic episode, a patient described his auditory, verbal hallucinations as "an internal tape recorder that goes on and off," frightening, and not in his control. I want to compare this example to statements made by a French Canadian with whom I shared an afternoon fishing in Northern Lake Huron this past summer. Ray is in his forties, married, with two grown children, and runs a small restaurant in Ontario. He spoke of how he and his wife take part in a weekly, church-sponsored Bible reading group and of how much the charismatic movement has changed their lives, in quite concrete ways. For example, when he was considering going into the restaurant business, after selling a small lumber mill, he debated whether he should buy a downtown restaurant and take on a large debt, or whether he should purchase a small diner in a suburban mall. One day while he was stopped for a red light, the Spirit told him: "Don't go into debt!" He promptly bought the small diner. He gave additional examples of how the Spirit, he said, communicates with him. This man did not seem to be psychotic and, based on the evidence of one fine breakfast at least, he seems to know his work.

Is there a difference between these two linguistic moments? I would like to suggest that they are very different, that the words uttered by the "internal tape recorder" exemplify the status of words that have passed into what Lacan calls "the Real," while the words uttered to

99

Ray by "the Spirit" may represent the process whereby what is just at the border of "the Real" passes into words. But to go further we must step back and try to find some way of talking about "the Real" and what Lacan seems to mean by it, as well as what he means by "the imaginary" and "the symbolic." I'd like to begin by sharing some texts from a marvelous book called *China Men* by Maxine Hong Kingston.

The *New York Times* book reviewer, John Leonard, wrote in 1980: "Fiction, memoir, dream, epic, or elegy—whatever Maxine Hong Kingston is writing, it is certainly art. Four years ago in this space I said: *'The Woman Warrior'* [her first book] was the best book I've read in years. *'China Men'* is, at the least, the best book I've read in the four years since." High praise from a tough critic. *China Men* (a Chinese-American's account of the migration of her ancestors to the U.S., where they helped build the railroads, among other things) is for me the best concrete introduction to Lacan in English, precisely because of the author's ability to move smoothly among the three dimensions or registers of the imaginary, the Real, and the symbolic—"these three registers which," Lacan tells us, "are indeed the essential registers of human reality" (1953a, p. 2).

The imaginary, for Lacan, is defined by the image, where the image is taken to function in a structure governed by point-to-point correspondences, as when an object is placed before a mirror or when an image is projected on a screen (1964, p. 86). When Kingston exposes the imaginary, she makes note of mirrors, movies, reflections, racial stereotypes, and narcissistic preening, this last highlighted in images of flying. These cues denote the arena of visual captivation by a lure that is often erotic. Fantastic scope is given to desire, ferocious images of bodily fragmentation shape hatred. The alluring power of the image has its origin, for Lacan, in the mirror stage of child development. Sometime during the period from eight to eighteen months, the human infant, still neurologically incomplete, becomes capable of recognizing its reflection in a mirror, identifies itself with the exterior, erect, whole form of the human body, becomes narcissistically invested in this visible, external form and thereby alienated from itself, and this identification with its reflected image constitutes the ego. Henceforth the ego will be concerned not with objectivity and adaptation to "reality,'' as the American ego psychologists have proposed, but rather with demands for recognition and with defensive maneuvers to protect self-esteem. Images of oneself and of others dominate this register, images that distort, that promise an illusory happiness, that camouflage basic human longing. An example in *China Men*: With some earned money, the father buys an expensive suit: ''In the three-way mirror, he looked like Fred Astaire. He wore the suit out of the store'' (p. 61). He and his friend ''strolled down Fifth Avenue and caught sight of themselves in windows and hubcaps'' (p. 61). There follow, in the subsequent four pages, references to posing, to photographs (nine times), two more references to movies, another reference to mirrors, and a reference to flying (pp. 61–64). At the end of this episode, the three other partners cheat the father out of his share in the laundry business and the ''perfectly legal'' theft sends the author's disillusioned parents to search for a new life in California.

Kingston also structures the imaginary register by using symmetries that undercut racial stereotypes. For example, the father's difficulties in China in teaching Chinese children ''who were more bestial than animals'' (p. 35) is mirrored later in the book by the teacher brother's ''surprise at how dumb the students were'' in his class in America (p. 277). There are at least eight such symmetrical, corresponding episodes involving birth, death, migration, and longing, and Kingston seems to be telling us that stereotypes on both sides are in a mirror-relationship, that they stem as reflections from the same source; this source, in a Lacanian framework, is the imaginary order, the register of images that lure and captivate and shape what we call reality.

In distinction from ''reality,'' the register of ''the Real'' has not been easy to comprehend in the work of the Lacanians, who variously refer to it as ''always in the same place'' and ''already there'' (Faladé, 1974, p. 33), as that ''which lacks nothing'' (p. 30), the undifferentiated, unspoken, brute facticity that invades us from time to time but to which we usually have a relationship mediated by language. Such mediation transforms our contact with the Real into ''reality,'' something very different from the Real, for reality is ''a montage of the symbolic and the imaginary'' (p. 36). When there is ''loss of reality,'' as in psychosis, then contact with the Real can be horrifying and maddening. The Real, then, must somehow be filtered or shielded from experience. There is a kind of "struggle against the Real" (M.-L. Lauth, 1982, p. 62). There is a tearing-out or "uprooting from the Real by the symbolic" (p. 61), the Real must be "made to draw back" (p. 63). This "struggle against the Real" is precisely what Kingston provides a metaphor of in the labor of the China men cutting away jungle to establish sugar cane on Hawaii. And the Real is even more forbidding as the China men cut through mountains building a railroad:

> Beneath the soil, they hit granite. Ah Goong struck it with his pickax, and it jarred his bones, chattered his teeth. He swung his sledgehammer against it, and the impact rang in the dome of his skull. The mountain that was millions of years old was locked against them and was not to be broken into. . . . He hit at the same spot over and over again, the same rock. Some chips and flakes broke off. The granite looked everywhere the same. It had no softer or weaker spots anywhere, the same hard gray. . . . This rock is what is real, he thought. This rock is what real is, not clouds or mist, which make mysterious promises, and when you go through them are nothing. When the foreman measured at the end of twenty-four hours of pounding, the rock had given a foot. [p. 132]

We touch the Real in the violent deaths of the men blown up by explosives, men falling thousands of feet. The unburied corpse was an unbearable intrusion of the Real: "After a fall, the buzzards circled the spot and reminded the workers for days that a man was dead down there. The men threw piles of rocks and branches to cover bodies from sight" (p. 130). The horror of unburied corpses—corpses denied a place in the symbolic order—haunted the living as they began to learn to use dynamite:

> The men who died slowly enough to say last words said, "Don't leave me frozen under the snow. Send my body home. Burn it and put the ashes in a tin can. . . ." "Shut up," scolded the hearty men. "We don't want to hear about bone jars and dying." "You're lucky to have a body to bury, not blown to

smithereens. . . .'' ''Aiya. To be buried here, nowhere.'' ''But this is somewhere,'' Ah Goong promised. ''This is the Gold Mountain. We're marking the land now. The track sections are numbered, and your family will know where we leave you.'' But he was a crazy man, and they didn't listen to him. [p. 136]

But this ''crazy man'' clearly realized that the only way to overcome the Real is by marking it, cutting into its mass with signifier, transforming its undifferentiated fullness through a kind of negation so that divisions appear and mediated relationships become possible. Frontiers can then be established making repression possible, graves can and must have markers so that the dead can be forgotten and not haunt the living. And the railroad was a budding symbolic network making such markings possible. Again, when the Kingston storybook character Lo Bun Sun shipwrecks against an unknown shore, he manages to retrieve many useful items over several days, but: ''One morning, he awoke and the ship was gone. No man-made hulk served as a marker against all that sea'' (p. 226). Totally alone, he immediately orders his life by putting marks on the Real: he marks the days with notches on a board, he writes in his diary, he fires clay pots and decorates them, he teaches a parrot to say his name, ''so that he would hear a voice other than his own, a voice calling him by name'' (p. 229). This socialization of the Real so that it becomes reality is, Lacan tells us, the effect of the signifier, marking the Real, the effect of the symbolic order.

The symbolic register is the network of language and ritual. The decisive feature of this register, or order of symbols, is that it consists of a relatively closed system of reciprocally differentiated units, each of which has no meaning in itself but is differentiable solely with reference to all the other units in the system. This system is language, structurally understood as a system of phonemes or signifiers related by convention to what they signify but only in the context of the ensemble. Unlike the imaginary register, there are no one-to-one correspondences in the symbolic order. The symbolic order with its polyphonic and polysemic structure is the source of meaning; it roots, it sustains subjects, it even contains ghosts. Kingston introduces the register of the symbolic by calling attention to words, syllables, phonemes, names, and a variety of speech acts such as cursing, blessing, chanting, singing, screaming, as well as speaking, writing, and the force of silence. In Kingston's text more than one out of two pages deals explicitly with these signifying elements, and they occur in clusters, more frequent serially when the register of the symbolic is in play, absent when the imaginary is given its day. Even the book's title—*China Men*—is used in the text to emphasize the symbolic network, as distinct from what Kingston calls "the slurred-together word" chinamen, reflecting the stereotypic image the whites have for the Chinese.

It is the act of speech that overcomes the Real and sustains us, and Kingston provides numerous examples of this. While crossing the ocean with a stowaway in a crate, the smuggler periodically comes and knocks "a code on the wood, and the stowaway father signalled back. This exchange of greetings kept him from falling into the trance that overtakes animals about to die" (p. 49). Forbidden to speak while clearing Hawaii for sugar cane, the great-grandfather coughed out his cursing syllables in the dust: "He felt better after having his say. He did not even mind the despair which dispelled upon his speaking it. The suicides who walked into the ocean or jumped off the mountains were not his kindred" (p. 102). Later, another grandfather enables the author to name an aspect of the Real in an example that shows how the three registers articulate:

> Say Goong took my hand and led me to a cavernous shed black from the sun in my eyes. He pointed into the dark, which dark seemed solid and alive, heavy, moving, breathing. There were waves of dark skin over a hot and massive something that was snorting and stomping—the living night. In the day, here was where the night lived. Say Goong pointed up at a wide brown eye as high as the roof. I was ready to be terrified but for his delight. "Horse," he said. "Horse." He contained the thing in a word—*horse*, magical and earthly sound. A horse was a black creature so immense I could not see the outlines. [p. 165]

This is a good example of how the Real, initially undifferentiated as the living night, opens up in a look, a seeing and being seen that is compelling and frightening when the child's eye meets the horse's look, unleashing the captivating power of the image, and then the experience is given a boundary, a frontier, once it is contained in the word *horse*, so that a mediated relation is now established.

The author does not hide her admiration for the China men, but the true hero of the book is language, for language alone sustains these men and women (as well as writer and reader). As she narrates the psychotic episodes of six of her relatives, she shows us that what is central to psychosis has to do with slippage in the symbolic order, failures in ritual, social upheavals, and cultural outplacements, and how ritual itself is restorative.

In her first example, a grandfather goes in and out of madness while blasting the American railroad out of rock, far away from home: "When he stumbled out" of the tunnel, writes Kingston, "he tried to talk about time. 'I felt time,' he said. 'I saw time. I saw world' " (p. 132). The second, a great-grandfather, begins to see visions and hear ghosts on Hawaii and wonders: "Now that he was in a new land, who could tell what normal was?" (pp. 107–109). The third, a cousin with a home and family in California, receives letters of horror from his starving mother in China, imploring him to sell his daughters and return to China. When she dies, she haunts him day and night, accusing him of letting her starve to death. Finally, he buys a boat ticket and returns, talking with her all the while, to her grave:

"Here you are mother," he said, and the villagers heard him say it. "You're home now. I've brought you home. I spent passage fare on you. It equals more than the food money I might have sent. . . . Rest, Mother. Eat." He heaped food on her grave. . . . He poured wine into the thirsty earth. He planted the blue shrub of longevity, where white carrier pigeons would rest. He bowed his forehead to the ground, knocking it hard in repentance. "You're home, Mother. I'm home, too. I brought you home." He set off firecrackers near her grave, not neglecting *one* Chinese thing. "Rest now, heh, Mother. Be happy now." He sat by the grave and drank and ate for the first time since she had made her appearance. . . . He boarded the very same ship sailing back. . . . to America, where he acted normal again, continuing his American life, and nothing like that ever happened to him again. [pp. 178–179]

A fourth relative, an older cousin in America, gets caught up in the great postwar upheavals in China and becomes delusional about wheat germ and communism: "When he connected his two big ideas [wheat germ and Communism], he touched wrong wires to each other, shot off sparks, and shorted out. He had become a paranoiac. 'They are trying to poison me,' he said, running into the laundry . . ." (p. 195). He calms down when he decides to return to Communist China. The fifth, an uncle by marriage, was torn between remaining in Hong Kong with his shoe factory, or coming to the U.S., where his wife was living. After a brief visit to the U.S., he persuaded his wife to return with him, despite fears of a Communist takeover. One day he became sensitive to light and sounds: "He explained later how he understood the stopping quality of red light and the go of green. . . . He passed a book store. Jets of colored lights jumped along the books' spines; he wanted to stop and see whether *Red Chamber Dream* and Communist books were red . . ." (p. 213). He went to a bank, withdrew all his money and left it with strangers. Twice he did this, recovered, and then returned once again with his wife to the U.S., having "said goodbye properly, goodbye forever" (p. 216). The sixth, the author's father, became severely depressed after the police closed down the Chinese gambling house and social hall he had managed in Stockton. He stopped shaving, sat and stared, drank whisky, no longer went out, and screamed in his sleep (p. 246 ff.). In her seventh example, a "wild man" is found living alone in a Florida swamp. When the police have him speak with a Chinese interpreter, he tells how he left Taiwan and his seven children to sail on a Liberian freighter to earn money; how, becoming homesick and screaming and weeping as they tried to return him on a plane, he was hospitalized and then later escaped into the swamp. After being recaptured, he hangs himself in jail (pp. 222–224).

All of Kingston's examples of psychotic states involve the link between madness and some catastrophe in the social order, and we shall return to this. To recapitulate: what we do as humans is structured by reflected images that lure our desire and soothe our egos, but we remain grounded in a symbolic network that pervasively supports our speech, ritual, and even our perception of the world, and we from time to time come to the edge and touch upon the nameless, the Real that is always there but usually mediated by language. Now what if language does not function as such a recourse against the Real? What if the Real is experienced without the mediation of language? What if words themselves lose their referential context and are experienced as *in* the Real? To say that words are in the Real is to say that words have become like things: whether they come from the therapist or the titles of books or the "internal tape recorder," they can strike the patient's ears, eyes, forehead, chest, like objects. They do not mediate and refer to objects. Mediation involves a distancing whereby the person has a status as distinct from surroundings, precisely through having a relationship to words, which themselves comport relationships with other words. The word, the name, is taken as a substitute for the object, not identified with it, and correlatively oneself is taken as distinct from the word and the name. But in psychotic states the mediation language gives us is problematic, and I would like to approach a discussion of psychosis by moving from Kingston to Canada and drawing upon a meeting held in August 1982 on an island in Georgian Bay.

This five-day meeting was sponsored by the Niobrara Institute in order to bring together American therapists, Lacanian analysts, and native people, including medicine men, all of whom have an interest in the nonpharmaceutical treatment of psychosis—that is, whose practice relies essentially on the use of words. We met in a native setting (the Whitefish River Ojibwa Reserve) in order to question our accustomed modes of thinking, and we all shared the experience that working with psychotic patients challenges notions about reality. Unfortunately, Otto Will (who has a long-standing interest in Plains and Southwest Indians) could not be there this time—maybe next time, we hope, as much of his work exemplifies our concerns. We read, for example, in one of his papers that "the psychotic process, bizarre as it may be, reflects conflict, is problem-solving, and is goal-directed" (1972, p. 35). He writes of "dissociated representations of experience" as "processes that lack the refinement (in terms of time, logical sequences, cause and effect, space, and identity of self and object) of the ordinary day-by-day forms of thought," and "are not to be approximated in language" (pp. 37–38). From this point of view, "schizophrenia is not looked upon as a disease, but as a reaction to, and an expression of, the social scenes in which an organism"—with adequate biological endowments—"has its being" (Will, 1958, p. 218). This view was supported by what emerged as we discussed the nature of psychotic experience, and the remarks made at that meeting may clarify our two examples of the tape recorder speaking and the Spirit speaking.

The French Lacanian analysts Françoise Davoine and Jean-Max Gaudillière stressed through case presentations that psychosis is not a function of the individual personality but rather always involves a relationship, of a special kind. The patient in psychosis relates by putting death between himself or herself and the other. If this other is the analyst, the patient will attempt to force the analyst to that special place in the transference where the death can be interposed. What death is this? It has to do with a catastrophe, personal as well as social. This catastrophe occurred originally in the presence of an other who simply registered it without responding, without naming it. The patient in turn registered it, as on a photographic plate or tape recorder, on his or her own body—that is to say, in the Real. Unable to name it, the patient attempts to interpose it so that it can be named in the analysis. Often the catastrophe is of gigantic social proportions: the horrors of war, massacres, the holocaust, genocide of native peoples, the radical changing of national boundaries, the disappearance of entire nations. Of personal proportions is the disappearance, death, suicide, mutilation, or prolonged depression of a parent or other close relative. For the psychotic the experience has no name and no image. The experience remains foreclosed from the imaginary and symbolic registers. It is in the Real, and it is to this place the patient leads the analyst, who tries to resist by a variety of secondary process activities—theory-building, fine interpretations, encouragement to get on with life—failing to see that the psychotic is embarked on a way of knowing, on a path where the terrain does not become intelligible through ordinary concepts of time, space, identity, and causality. The exploration of this field exists in a different time, a sort of timelessness, and in a space without usual boundaries.

Madness is the only reasonable way to respond to the unnamed catastrophe, and, once in treatment, the psychotic is insistent on exploring it with the analyst, thus interposing some kind of death as the central field of the work. But all too often the patient explores this field on his or her own body, since there is no alternative cultural form for doing it. And, as we read in Kingston, madness always says something about the disharmony in one's relationship to the social fabric, which itself may be torn by large-scale deceit and failures in social ritual. There are ghosts of unburied ancestors that haunt the living, and they play havoc until they can be put to rest by being named.

Lacan (1953b, p. 104), following Hegel, insists that there is an intimate link between death and naming, for the act of naming a thing amounts to a kind of ''murder of the thing.'' How is this so? Because in the name, or the concept of the thing, the object is contained independent of its immediacy and its physicality. The philosopher Sokolowski, in a book titled *Presence and Absence*, writes:

A vocal response can become a name when I not only have the object before me, but appreciate it as present. I recognize that the object here does not have to be here; it could have been absent instead. I appreciate its presence as contrasted to its absence. I not only enjoy the object, I enjoy the object as present. Then I can name it; I am no longer limited to making a voiced response to it. I am said to have acquired some distance towards the object. But the distance in question is not spatial, it involves only the intrusion of the ''as present'' between the object and me. This is what makes the object nameable.

I now can ''have'' the object in mind as something to be spoken about; I no longer merely have it to be consumed, fondled, or provoked. Things can be said about an object only when it is so held by a name. [1978, p. 4]

To so hold or contain something or someone by a name destroys its immediacy; that is, the name gives us a mediated relation to the thing. Recall Kingston's example of the horse whose fearsome image becomes instantly transformed into a part of her world: ''He contained the thing in a word—*horse*, magical and earthly sound. A horse was a black creature so immense I could not see the outlines'' (p. 165). Even though the child could not see the outlines, she now, given the name, knew they existed, and she could, furthermore, name the horse in its absence (p. 167). Sokolowski stresses that such naming is not simply a matter of images or representations:

> When we name something absent, we do name what is absent. We do not name a copy, an image, a fantasm, or some other present representative of it. Names stretch into what is not here. They can do so because they are constituted precisely as the masters of both the presence and the absence of what they name. Even when they name what is present, they do so with a sense of its capacity to be not present. [1978, pp. 28–29]

Such naming, furthermore, is not solipsistic. Lacan writes: "Naming constitutes a pact whereby two subjects in the same moment agree to recognize the same object" (1954–1955, p. 202).

Now in the treatment of psychosis the heart of the problem is the struggle to kill, to destroy the catastrophe as imprinted on the body by naming it, by the creation of a signifier for what has remained unnameable because it remains embedded in the Real. What is in the Real is neither present nor absent: it is immediate, that is, unmediated. "There is no absence in the Real," Lacan tells us (1954–1955, p. 359). To render a thing present or absent requires negating it through naming it: presence and absence are a function of the symbolic register. This is not a matter of lifting a repression, as with an experience that is forgotten because it has been inscribed in memory. On the contrary, the task is to create boundaries that make it possible to have repression. Psychotics, the French stress, are conscious of the catastrophe; they are, in fact, haunted by the thing. What must be done in naming is to make an inscription of it so that it *can* be forgotten. "Otherwise," Françoise Davoine (1981) writes,

> this thing without a name will return through hallucination to persecute the living by asking for rest and oblivion. So that when, for any reason, it has been impossible to accomplish this naming of the thing, to accomplish the inscription of its disappearance in order to change it into a signifier, one will necessarily have to make it disappear a second time in order to stop the return of its ghost, which Lacan calls the return of the Real. Well, the only way to make it disappear is to kill it, to destroy it. . . . The exploration of the psychotic search consists in the creation and destruction of limits in this space of the Real, even if these limits

> should be those of the body itself. . . . This lasts until something
> is definitely destroyed and gives place to a new signifier.

The therapeutic frame must hold on long enough so that the patient's body survives and the catastrophe can be truly forgotten, that is, inscribed in the unconscious. Davoine continues: "Freud defines the unconscious as a compromise between oblivion and memory. It is the only place where the paradox of memory comes to a resolution, the paradox being that nothing is more present than an unspeakable disappearance. On the other hand, the only way to let it go is to have it written somewhere in order to forget it through memory." She gives the name on a tombstone as an example of the function of such inscription: "Not so much that one will forever remind somebody because it is written, but rather that we will forget thanks to this inscription." (For a resumé of the many texts in Freud dealing with inscription, see Derrida, 1966.)

In summary, the psychotic patient's report of being dead, decayed, or empty, the negativism, thought disorder, and disturbed family communication patterns that are well identified have as their context a specific field in a relationship where the representation of an unnamed catastrophe has to be killed: better for this killing to be symbolic rather than real, and the symbolic killing occurs through naming. Such naming can be done in words or ritual, even by gesture or by the use of transitional objects. When we met in Canada we all witnessed another kind of naming, as enacted by a practicing medicine man. Joe Eagle Elk, a Lakota Sioux in his fifties, from Rosebud, South Dakota, described how he had become a medicine man, how he experiences his relationship to what are called "spirits," and how he practices.

Joe described how the same dream recurred to him four times, beginning when he was twelve years old, when his father scolded him for having such dangerous dreams, until his thirties, when he finally brought it to a medicine man for interpretation. The medicine man prepared Joe to make a vision quest, whose outcome made clear that Joe had to become a medicine man, and he began his rigorous training. He is currently very respected and very busy. In describing his work with patients, he says, quite simply, that he has no power of his own. The spirits tell him what is the nature of the problem and what has to be done about it. Often they do not tell him the cause. When he conducts a ceremony, he calls the spirits into the room, by name, for they are his friends. That is the general name for them: friends. Each spirit is called by its own individual name, and when they enter the room they speak to him. He in turn articulates what they have to say about the patient and what the patient has to do. We witnessed his healing ceremony for an allegedly hexed Ojibwa woman who, by her own report, had suffered from multiple somatic symptoms, including diabetes, liver dysfunction, vision problems, and severe headaches that had been ascribed by physicians to cerebral tumors. At one point in the ceremony Joe put on the light and asked the woman to stand in a special place while holding the ceremonial pipe. He asked her to tell the thirty-five or so of us what her problem was. Then, in total darkness, we each voiced our concerns for this woman, ourselves, and others. Then there was further chanting while the spirits spoke to Joe. (The manifestation of the spirits' presence in the darkness consists of small movements of phosphorescent-like light.) Then he again turned on a light and asked the woman to stand as before and told her, through a translator, that the spirits said: ''There is nothing wrong with you. You have just been confused by what others have told you.'' In subsequent discussion with Joe about the actual Lakota words spoken, he said the spirits told him her problem lies in her *wowacin*: the Lakota word means a combination of thought and desire. It is the word used in the phrase, ''to lose one's mind,'' but this was not her condition. The spirits said, through Joe, that her problem is what she allowed herself to assume from others, namely the thoughts and desires of others about her; she accepted their labels into her *wowacin*, and she took these labels and exaggerated them into her symptoms. She was to leave her fears and worries in the spot where she was standing, and the spirits instructed Joe to prepare an herbal medicine, for which she was to return the next day. She did, and at last report, one year later, she was said to be fine.

Numerous psychoanalytic authors have described such an event in terms of projection and introjection, or even paranoia (Ducey, 1976); others have invoked notions of group dynamics, suggestion, and non-verbal communication (Erikson, 1950, pp. 174–175); some call it outright trickery or magic, where the medicine man is no more than a master illusionist or conjuror who takes advantage of the so-called "primitive" beliefs of the people (Boyer, 1964, pp. 403–404). Such approaches fundamentally assume "reality" as given and do not adequately take into account what Lacan draws our attention to as "the Real," and how language shapes "reality." Even the cognitive psychologist Jerome Bruner and his associate write that speakers "come into a world already constituted by language" and that the child cannot learn to speak "until the child is inducted into a social world where language has already made a deep impression in shaping and even in constituting the reality to which speech will refer" (Bruner and Feldman, 1982, p. 36).

We can attempt to conceptualize the medicine man's practice in another way. The medicine man, after rigorous discipline, is enabled to stand at the edge of the Real in highly specific, community-based rituals. Standing at the edge without being terrified, he is at the point where, through him and the ritualized space, the Real passes into language. In his culture and in those carefully defined moments, this passage of the Real into language takes the form of named spirits who become articulated through his voice. In this way the patient, who addresses her demands to the Real, the Real of part of her body, the Real of death, destruction, and cultural catastrophe, receives a response, through the medicine man, from this Real. The response is framed by the entire symbolic structure that includes, in this place and time, what are called spirits. They are part of the group's reality once their presence is named. Standing at the edge of the Real, the medicine man *names*: he exercises what Sokolowski calls the mastery of presence and absence; his articulation establishes for himself, the patient, and the community a mediated relation with the Real.

In this context what we do in the analytic moment of the psychotic transference is similar: with whatever disciplined ways we possess, we stand at the edge of the Real to which our patients have led us. This may well be experienced as the patient's attempt to drive us crazy, and our discipline will often fail us as we resist. But eventually we do stand at the edge, and now and then we name: we name the death the patient brings between us, we find, usually without forethought, some signifier, gesture, or object that overcomes the immediacy of the Real, that frees the patient from a fusion with us and the surroundings, that renews perspective on his or her body, that eventually leads to an unconscious inscription that allows the catastrophe to begin to be repressed, that puts a stop to "the internal tape recorder."

What now can be said of the two examples with which we began? For the patient in the psychotic state, words no longer function in the symbolic order: they have passed into the Real, and the patient is left with only the fantastic quality of images to try to grab hold of their import. These images alternately terrify or seduce, promising destruction or paradise. The community no longer has a mediating role; the sense of isolation is extreme. For Ray, in his community of charismatics, it appears quite different. He remains firmly embedded in a structure of ritual in which standing at the edge of the Real has its own discipline and safeguards. Native religion itself can be viewed as the universal human effort to find ways to stand at this edge so that the Real can pass into language, can receive an articulation that is fresh and that challenges the complacent notions of reality to which we all too readily become adapted. The voice of the Spirit, then, may be the particular manifestation of this languaging process, particular to Ray's community (a rather large and growing one) with its specific rituals.

To speak in this way may remind some of us of Carlos Casteneda and Don Juan's exploits of seeing and flying: but it has nothing to do with Casteneda, for the pervasive absence in his work of community ritual undercuts his whole fictional enterprise. As Gerry Mohatt (1982), a psychologist who has spent fifteen years working on the Rosebud Sioux Reservation, writes:

> The medicine man does not expect that we common people are confronted with spirits only for idiosyncratic reasons. This experience says something about us in relationship to our community. Was a ritual of grieving not accomplished? Was the group in jeopardy because of disharmony and unrepaired rips in family relationships? In addition, common people aren't expected to interpret and meet spirit phenomena in everyday life. Ritual is the proper place, the medicine man the proper person. Too often current literature has encouraged a romantic idea that spirit experience can free a person or is the stuff of mystical experience.

To the medicine man, the solitary spirit experience for the common man is dangerous. [p. 14]

Spirits, then, may perhaps be conceptualized as the mode of passage of the Real into language in a specific context of culture and ritual. To name them is to engage them as present, in the way names allow things to be present, in the way they are presented to us by Ray, Maxine Hong Kingston, and Joe Eagle Elk. Spirits need not be thought of as substances but rather as processes, perhaps an aspect of the incomplete process of the Real as Being coming into presence through language in a particular way, particular to a cultural setting of place and ritual moment of time. Such coming into language recalls the Heideggerean notion of Being as "perpetually under way to language" (Heidegger, 1947, p. 239). But such coming into language, as Heidegger shows, is problematic, for he writes: "But if man is to find his way once again into the nearness of Being he must first learn to exist in the nameless" (p. 199). Few of us can do that: perhaps the most we can do is to acknowledge with our patients that there *is* a nameless and from time to time stand at its edge.

In any case, to pronounce that spirits are impossible within our narrow day-to-day conceptual framework or to reduce them to projections is to pretend to know the Real. We do not and cannot know the Real. In our usual frames of reference we know about reality, this necessary construction that allows us to maintain what we call sanity, on this side of the Real, and it is language that makes this possible. The Mexican poet Octavio Paz (1974) writes:

The reality that poetry reveals and that appears behind language—is literally intolerable and maddening. At the same time, without the vision of this reality, man is not man, and language is not language. Poetry is the necessarily momentary perception (which is all that we can bear) of the incommensurable world which we one day abandon and to which we return when we die. Language sinks its roots into this world but transforms its juices and reactions into signs and symbols. Language is the consequence (or the cause) of our exile from the universe, signifying the distance between things and ourselves. At the same time it is our recourse against this distance. [p. 132]

References

Boyer, L. B. (1964), Folk psychiatry of the Apaches of the Mescalero Indian Reservation. In: *Magic, Faith, and Healing: Studies in Primitive Psychology Today*, ed. A. Kiev. New York: The Free Press, pp. 384–419.

Bruner, J., & Feldman, C. F. (1982), Where does language come from? *New York Review of Books*, June 24, pp. 34–36.

Davoine, F. (1981), Freud's death-drive reconsidered. Paper presented at the symposium Adaptation as Negation, Annual Convention of the American Psychological Association, Los Angeles.

Derrida, J. (1966), Freud and the scene of writing. In: *Writing and Difference* (trans. A. Bass). Chicago: University of Chicago Press, 1978, pp. 196–231.

Ducey, C. (1976), The life history and creative psychopathology of the shaman: Ethnopsychoanalytic perspectives. In: *The Psychoanalytic Study of Society*, vol. 7, ed. W. Muensterberger. New Haven, CT: Yale University Press, pp. 173–230.

Erikson, E. H. (1950), *Childhood and Society*. 2nd ed. New York: Norton, 1963.

Faladé, S. (1974), Sur le Réel. In: *Lettres de L'École Freudienne, 16*. Bulletin intérieur de L'Ecole Freudienne de Paris. Proceedings of the 7th Congress of the Ecole Freudienne of Paris, Rome, October 31–November 3, 1974. Paris, 1975, pp. 30–36.

Heidegger, M. (1947), Letter on humanism. In: *Martin Heidegger: Basic Writings*, ed. D.F. Krell (trans. F. Capuzzi and J. Glenn Gray). New York: Harper and Row, 1977, pp. 193–242.

Kingston, M. H. (1980), *China Men*. New York: Ballantine.

Lacan, J. (1953a), Le Symbolique, l'Imaginaire, et le Réel. Unpublished manuscript.

——— (1953b), The function and field of speech and language in psychoanalysis. In: *Ecrits: A Selection* (trans. A. Sheridan). New York: Norton, 1977, pp. 30–113.

——— (1954–1955), *Le Séminaire—Livre II. Le moi dans la théorie de Freud et dans la technique de la psychanalyse, 1954–1955*, ed. J.-A. Miller. Paris: Editions du Seuil, 1978.

——— (1964), *The Four Fundamental Concepts of Psycho-Analysis*, ed. J.-A. Miller (trans. A. Sheridan). New York: Norton, 1978.

Lauth, M.-L. (1982), Et si le Réel insiste. . . . In: *Resumé des Scéances de Travail Pour Les Journées d'Avril, 1982*, ed. S. Faladé. Groupe d'Étude sur l'Enseignement. Unpublished manuscript. Paris, pp. 61–65.

Leonard, J. (1980), Review of *China Men* by Maxine Hong Kingston. *New York Times*, June 3.

Mohatt, G.V. (1982), Psychic power or spiritual power: False dichotomies and spirit phenomena in psychotherapy with native people. Unpublished manuscript. Crookston, NB: Niobrara Institute.

Paz, O. (1974), *The Monkey Grammarian* (trans. H.R. Lane). New York: Seaver Books, 1981.

Sokolowski, R. (1978), *Presence and Absence: A Philosophical Investigation of Language and Being*. Bloomington: Indiana University Press.

Will, O. A. (1958), Human relatedness and the schizophrenic reaction. *Psychiatry*, 22 (1959):205–223.

——— (1972), Catatonic behavior in schizophrenia. *Contemporary Psychoanalysis*, 9:29–58.

6

Intrapsychic Structure and Interaction

Daniel P. Schwartz, M.D.

The context for this paper is the general attempt to develop a concept of action congruent with psychoanalytic knowledge.[1] This involves, I will contend, action's dimensions as they reciprocally evolve and are governed by intrapsychic structure, the necessities for exercise of such intrapsychic structure, its imposition of those actions upon behavioral space, and its tendency toward fixity (F. Schwartz, 1981). The conditions of action's range, limit, asymmetry, place in representation, and opportunity for fusion are examined in relation to intrapsychic structures evolution and change (D. Schwartz, 1983).

We say of our patients that they teach us, and we mean much more. We mean that each patient in our presence relentlessly imposes upon our thoughts and behaviors, for whatever time, the stamp of his or her inner complex organization (Schafer, 1959; Greenson, 1960). Here's an example. An analytic patient who was making considerable

---

[1]This necessary and incomplete development in psychoanalytic thinking has been noted by Rapaport (1960)—''we must establish how processes turn into structures, how a structure once formed, changes, and how it gives rise to and influences processes'' (pp. 98–99)—as well as by Hartmann (1947), D. Schwartz (1959), Loewald (1970), and Schafer (1976). Schafer would, I imagine, regard my treatment of action-structure relationships as too mechanistic, biological, and anthropomorphic. I believe Schafer's conception of action does not give sufficient weight to structural considerations, delay phenomena, and developmental processes.

117

progress nonetheless disagreed, overtly for a number of years, with every single interpretation her analyst presented. Finally, one day she left the hour after the analyst had noted this relentlessly dismissive phenomena in her again. As she got to the door she said, "Doctor, I think you have truly known what it means to meet my mother." This regular imposition in its various forms determines the possibilities of our knowledge, invites and indeed largely limits the character of our interpretive analytic response.

This imposed organization we understand as the result of the patient's intrapsychic structure even as it delays, modulates, and shapes the drives, thoughts, and affects of a particular patient, as it arranges in uniquely individualized form stereotypes in the nature of their action and narrows the range of possibilities of actions of a particular therapist (Rapaport, 1958). Indeed, as teachers of psychotherapy we rely on this governing relation. We are not surprised when novices in our field, though rather unknowledgeable about the complexities of the unconscious, ignorant about much of human developmental processes, bumbling in their therapeutic techniques, still "say the right thing," "interpret" correctly to the patient. The patient's material, not requiring our teacherly knowledge or permission, without the guidance of analytic wisdom, unfolds as it were of its own accord in the beginner's therapy. In other contexts we note the imposition of this structure when we discuss such analytic issues as the "nature of the resistance," "the repetition compulsion," the evolution of transference arising in the therapy, the form in which the patient determines the countertransference in the analyst, and the character of therapeutic impasses. Indeed we complain privately to each other how day after day we have been regularly immobilized, constricted, and persecuted from the couch.

Examining that imposed structure and its attributes, one notices the relentlessness of its exercise by the person and the rigidity of its form (Freud, 1914). Each hour begins characteristically; each transference's style of relationship evolves in an orderly pattern. One notices this of course not only within the analytic hour; these central organizations are exercised in relationships with one's spouse, employer, children, and occupational activities as well.

We observe that a fellow we know treats his wife and his automobile and his analysis in like fashion, and that in the absence of any of them what he misses seems not simply the person or object involved but the opportunity to exercise his structure. We say he misses not so much the person of the analyst as his experience in the analysis. We read in Dear Abby a letter from a woman—"It isn't my husband particularly I miss, it is really that I wish to take care of someone"—and we are not surprised. We joke about such extremes of this inner exercise of structure and its necessities. There is the "workaholic" executive or the "crazy clean" obsessive housewife down the street. The exercise of aspects of their inner structure become the most prominent feature in such persons' lives. At the other extreme we notice that where such exercise is interfered with, as in some retirees, there are those who suddenly die. There was that woman at the church who gave up playing the organ and had a stroke the next week. There was that foreman who died shortly after he received his gold retirement watch. And, by contrast, where the exercise of structure is permitted and supported we note those wonderful musicians who conduct their orchestra into very advanced years though the orchestra can apparently conduct itself without them, even in the person's presence. It appears it is not simply loss of the object but loss of the opportunity to exercise the intrapsychic function that is crucial to such vitality (Lynch, 1977).

It is clear that the requirement for exercise applies to such a person's invested central structures. Other organizations of memory, old skills, can of course lie dormant for years and return unimpeded with little evidence of disuse atrophy or loss of vitality. And most retirees do not die; indeed many of them bloom. It is, however, not infrequently observed that when vital exercise of inner function is interfered with, particularly abruptly, for instance through unemployment, divorce, or removal from executive function, a withering action related to intrapsychic structure sets in and a decrease in vitality in that person is a common accompaniment (Freud, 1923).

If an intrapsychic structure once established does require exercise, if it imposes itself upon the behavioral space, if it tends to evolve in rigid forms, what does this mean for human relationships? What consequences are there for marriages, mothers and children, for group structure formation, and for those kinds of psychotherapy that are interested in personal change? Is there a relationship between the general conditions of development of such intrapsychic structure and the necessities of the conditions under which change can occur?

It is my contention that the conditions of development of intrapsychic structure, well described in the analytic literature, require for their *full* description certain specifiable conditions. These are the opportunity to represent the structure's evolving character, a describable range of action, and limits to that action, conditions that facilitate fusion and are asymmetrical. Change too, I believe, requires similar conditions as well as the added condition of a limit that interferes with existing psychic structures and their usual function.

Let me illustrate a patient's complexly leveled intrapsychic structure as it is exercised and determines an interaction in therapy. It involves her organizations of memory, defense, object relationship, transference, regressive pulls upon the ego, superego constraints, varieties of drive controls, and possibilities of identity formation. They all run me, as the therapist. These structures exercise themselves, they represent themselves, and rigidly order our therapeutic interaction.

As a therapist I meet five times a week with an intelligent, at times charming young white woman from the South. An artist, she is recovering from schizophrenia and is a patient at the Austen Riggs Center. She comes to her appointments in my office from her private room at the Inn wearing, under her coat, the first crumpled thing she can grab to put on. She does not wash her face or comb her hair prior to her arrival in my office. This costume is not alluring. She says she hates coming to my office, the hours bore her. Sitting on my couch makes her sleepy, she says. She gets up and walks around the room, tries another chair, finds it too far away, and says she has nothing to talk to me about. Occasionally she says she notices she has an impulse to torture me, to taunt me in some way, though she can't put that more clearly into words. She is not happy much of the time, nor is she sleeping well. Last night, she said, she had a "stupid" dream. In it she saw herself as a child drawing a picture with crayons. She was in a class with a teacher. She tried to draw a house and was surprised as she realized it was the sort of house one might find in a ghetto. At that moment she became aware that she was or was becoming a black child. The dream ends. My attempts to encourage her to explore more fully her thoughts and feelings in regard to the dream and its "stupidity,'' her Southern childhood, its surrounding black people, her art work, her home, her developing ambivalent and regressive attachment to her therapist, the fact that his surname is the German word for black do not engage her. They are treated by the patient with all the powerfully dismissive contempt of a bored, spoiled, and stubborn child, perhaps with all the sullen dissembling ''ignorance'' of a young black and its white master (Erikson, 1946).

Other meetings intervene across the days. In them she conveys what she as a person might wish to be and fears she might become. She notes that she hates the way another patient in the hospital eats, in a ravenously hungry, childlike fashion. He is, she says, like a baby shoveling food into its mouth and letting it spill down its sides for its mother to clean up. She is disgusted by his dependent and infantile slovenliness. She does not want to be a child, she says, and yet she does not want to grow up either. She does not want to become a woman like her mother. She might, she thinks, become a fierce Israeli sabra.

She oversleeps an hour, phones in her apology, and then appears—face washed, neatly dressed—for her next appointment. She is occupied with thoughts and questions as to whether another therapist at the Austen Riggs Center might have left his job at the hospital because he found the patients spoiled, indulged, and therefore not worth working with. At times, she says, she feels that I am indulging her in some way. She doesn't wash up or dress for our appointments; she comes to me as if I were her employee. She thinks it is her couch, her hour, she says, and she can bore me with it. She can fall asleep on my couch, she can do whatever she likes, she can walk around the room, and I have to sit there and take it. I am, in a certain sense, a servant of hers. Like a maid to her, she says. In fact, I am like that black maid, Marie, of her childhood. Marie took care of her throughout her childhood years. She can torment me, truly, and I have to do everything for her. She can, in practice, hardly sew on a button, she says, with some pleasure, and she hates, in fact, to do it. Her delight in my submissive, attendant posture—a partially accurate characterization—make us both laugh, a joke suddenly revealed. Here I am, a presumably successful doctor and psychoanalyst, supposed to be doing something important for her, and I am revealed as a black woman servant, submissive and attendant to her various wishes. There she is, reduced by her view of herself as a dependent mental patient, subject to analytic actions of various sorts, scheduled and attendant upon my office, revealed in fact as a powerful Southern lady, enjoying and tormenting, and in charge of this demeaned woman servant. I tease her somewhat about the high cost of having me as an employee at the Austen Riggs Center, and she reminds me that the meals she receives are included in what she pays and are pretty good as well. Then we proceed. Her wish and fear of becoming my "black" child, her constraints on her therapist, her artistic talent, her crayons' symbolic portents, and much more are left to be slowly evolved.

This sequence of events occurs with such regularity in any moving psychoanalytic treatment that we call it "the work."[2] All of us educated by Freud's extraordinary discoveries of the nature of the mind and its restraints and forces finds such examples familiar. We note a regressively avoided sexuality represented in the controlling, castrating Southern belle and her eunuch slave. The infantile forms are represented in the dependent and warded-off disgusting orality and the sexuality viewed in the analyst as woman and servant and caretaker. The conscience's critical view of permission and indulgence is there, as well as the ego's regressive and controlling defensive postures, its identificatory particulars, and aggression's regular search for the choice of either torture or heroic display (the fierce Israeli sabra). One notes repression's collaboration with the unwashed face, the avoided associative pathways of the dream, and more. I mention these portents and conceptions not to put them aside but to remind you of the complexity of the inner structure and the context of its currents and imposition (Rapaport and Gill, 1959; Schafer, 1967).

I would like to call your attention to the fact that the patient is involved in living out this complex intrapsychic structure. This structure, as it exists, is also an organization of the patient's actions and capacities for action in therapy. It determines the nature, the shape of the interaction with the outside world. And it tends to represent itself

---

[2]The *differences* between classical psychoanalytic treatment and psychoanalytic psychotherapy as a treatment are from many points of view crucial and significantly different. Here, however, in terms of structure-action relationships, their imposition in action, and their representational necessities, I am regarding psychoanalysis and psychoanalytic psychotherapy as they exhibit a continuum involving lawful relatedness (Wallerstein, 1979).

(Pious, 1961). It has a stability to its organization and appears to extend and exercise its actions.

For myself as a therapist, there is no way to escape the imposed stereotype, the rigid forms of her interaction. I am treated to repetitive boredom and thereby tortured. I cannot escape participating in forms of indulgence if I am to sit quietly and listen. I am caring of this part child within the patient's processes of its becoming mine. I am treated to disgust in action—the mess of body and dress and face and knowledge—even as I help her examine her fear of these pregenital and dependent conditions of early object relation, their constraints and longings. I am effectively castrated in part by her fright of her own and my body, and on and on. Most important, she ensures by this imposition of structure—its relentless exercise, its rigidity of form, its necessities of representation in dream and action, in thought and word, in art and resistance—that if I am to comment relevantly on my experience and these actions within the hour, I must comment on the structure she imposes. I must put into words her fear of being my child, her enslavement, indulgence, and torture, her regressive and repressive defenses, her identification, her identity fragments. She compels and she invites my response by the very nature of her imposition of this intrapsychic structure organizing the stereotype of her action and the manner in which it imposes upon and limits mine within our common space.

Such intrapsychic structure exists, of course, not only in patients or in therapies. The stereotypes of their action forms are exercised relentlessly and impose themselves with rigidity upon the behavioral space in all intimate and invested relationships. These processes are the central forces of our understanding of the determinants of child development, and in their disordered consequences occupy our detailed exploration in psychotherapy.

Adopted babies followed by Dr. Sally Provence rapidly begin to look and act uniquely like their mothers.[3] Engel's esophageal atresia baby "Monica" (1978), fed through a gastric fistula as an infant, upon

---

[3]This was a common observation among those privileged to observe Dr. Sally Provence at work in the Yale Child Study Center. There she did serial neuropsychological testing of adopted children and their mothers, observable through a one-way mirror, as one part of her creative longitudinal research activities.

herself becoming a mother feeds her own baby flat across her lap unhandled, in a manner identical to the way she was fed as a child, though that she cannot remember.

In adults, of course, we notice the exercise of this structure most often in marriage. Our observations range from the felicitous outcome of Jack Sprat and his wife, who together licked the platter clean, to such disordered couples as the following. A man would regularly mow the lawn twice, the second time at right angles to the first mowing, and would pick up the cut grass as he went so as to leave the path unblemished; his wife, meanwhile, would vigorously follow him, weeding her garden and tossing the weeds haphazardly upon each finished area. Some couples fuse, look alike and think alike, while others oppose each other relentlessly and with vitality. We notice this structural exercise and its modulating adjustments similarly in bosses and their good secretaries, who think for them as if a part of them, as well as in teachers and their students, leaders and disciples. This is the stuff of novels, and we enjoy it, watching TV shows such as *The Odd Couple*. Much of it is an everyday occurrence.

A fifteen-year-old boy feels uprooted from his town, the home of his childhood, as he moves with his parents to a different section of the state. He feels and is foreign to the new school system, the social group, to the ground he walks on. In this new town, with all the bravado and rebelliousness of a developing youth, he makes friends with two older, French-speaking immigrant boys, newer than he, working nearby him at his summer job. He invites them to his home for dinner and visits them, indeed, at their temporary residence with their aunt. One night he sings to them in English the anthem "My Country 'Tis of Thee" and describes his experience in school for their education and amusement. He had, he says, to recite the Pledge of Allegiance every morning in grade school, and as he instructs these "foreigners" in the rooted ways of his land, he obviously repairs his own uprootedness. He describes this to his father, with whom he is largely and currently in rebellious relation. He says these French boys asked whether he personally had to say this patriotic pledge, whether he had a choice. He says he now realized that at that time in grade school he had had to say the pledge. There was no other option available to him within his thoughts. "Now," he says to his father, "I could say no.

I could even feel like a Communist.'' ''I guess,'' he says, ''you have to be rebellious in your teens, so that when you mellow out later on you have an independent mind.'' His teacherly father listens, educated by this young fellow. I suggest to you the obvious, that this living out, this exercise of these inner developing structural forms which these serious behaviors contain are essential in their exercises, and crucially evolved in the process of representation, to himself, to this boy, most of all, in all aspects of his evolving intrapsychic structure.[4]

Representation is important in relation to man's intrapsychic structure and its state. We have no well-established developmental series of observations on introspection and how one knows oneself, of what Freud (1911) called ''endopsychic perception.'' We're not even sure how important this is. What role does it normally play in integration? We don't know its relation to language; we don't treat it as learned, but more as a given in human development. There is the illusion but for the barriers of defense, of repression, that we would be ''conscious'' of all our inner life. Yet this is clearly and functionally an oversimplified assumption.

We treat our data often more in relation to what is excluded, defended against from our awareness, rather than inquiring how we come to know ourselves at all. Still, in dream and symptom, in forms of behavior, in talking to oneself or a friend, and in creative activity, we at times come to find ourselves representing and thereby coming to know an aspect of ourselves in a fashion that is in all probability essential to our full function.

A young man dreams that he unwittingly pulls his analyst's arm off that analyst's body, and comes to know his own ''disarming,'' castrating, touching exercise of intrapsychic structure and outer organization. He learns of his defensive and aggressive charm. A young woman develops an inexplicable burning sensation in the sole of her foot which then leads her to seek analytic consultation. There she puts into previously unavailable words the certainty that it had been time (for her soul's sake?) for her to ''hot foot'' it down to her analyst for

---

[4]Representation is a complex process. See Gill (1967) and Holt (1967). I am dealing here with what I believe to be the role of representations in the organization of an intrapsychic structure. ''The considerations of representability'' (Freud, 1900) in this regard appear to me to be a portion of the necessary processes of structure formation.

help. Slogans on T-shirts and ritualized clothing for work, signs indicating an organization which supports such inner changes as "black is beautiful," and sharpened pencils on the writer's desk appear necessary as signs to represent the states or organization of inner life and its exercise in particular action. Such representations seem necessary to the experience, the vital pursuit of that activity.

Rigidity, indeed fixity, is another important and wide-ranging character of much of human intrapsychic structure, though we regard ourselves personally as extremely flexible. There is much about organizations of the intrapsychic structure in a person, and in the ego, in the conscience, and in memories, that is very like those eggs one cannot unboil. This relative fixity is not confined to the delusion, to the "idée fixe," but exists throughout the range of intrapsychic structure from memory onward (Frosch, 1967; D. Schwartz, 1978). Shakespeare (1623) reminds us of this fixity when Macbeth says, "Canst thou not minister to a mind diseased, / Pluck from the memory a rooted sorrow, / Raze out the written troubles of the brain?" (Act V, Scene II). Neurotic symptoms from globus hystericus, the obsessive ritual, and modes of work for men and women have in many aspects these evolved and fixed inner organizations. Acute and chronic trauma of sufficient severity similarly tends to form fixed inner organizations (Berman, 1979). Combat soldiers with traumatic neuroses were among the first groups in which this was noted, though of course developing children who suffer severe trauma are affected most (Freud, 1920). A young girl in a German concentration camp asks where her mother is and the guard points to a wisp of smoke rising from the nearby gas chamber. He says to her that this is where her mother is—in that smoke. The girl loses her voice, and this event alters the nature of her inner organization and vocal expression to some degree forever, though she later becomes a wonderful and gifted professional person. Repetitive traumatic persecution, poverty, and abandonment, particularly but not only at a young age, organize the mind around the consequences of that trauma embedded in an inner organization and an outer stereotype of behavior.

Given such a view of structure, and of its exercise, rigidities, and impositions upon the nature of human beings, the consequences for social processes and their rigidities seem obvious and difficult. It is no surprise that total removal from many social processes are necessary before change can occur in some individuals. Thus, leaving home and school are almost always necessary, and for some the liberating effect of the death of a parent or of divorce from a spouse is well known. The organizational problem of progressive rigidities in groups, of the formation of bureaucratic structures, rigid ideologies, and dictatorships among leaders in any social organization, to the detriment of its vitality, may indeed relate to such forces as well (Kohut, 1976).

But as there are processes which form structure for an individual, there are also processes (other than total removal) which facilitate change in those structures. We are most familiar with the process called psychotherapy, of which analysis is the clearest model (educational and conversion techniques are among the others). Let us examine, in terms of action, the similarities between the conditions of development of intrapsychic structure and the processes which facilitate change in those structures during a therapy. The complex conditions of intrapsychic development in terms of psychosocial and psychosexual stages detailed by psychoanalytic research are well known (Fenichel, 1945; Adatto, 1980; Erikson, 1980; A. Freud, 1980). The overriding conditions of action-structure relation include five in my view: asymmetry, facilitation of fusion, assurance of range of action, the organization of limits, and the conditions for representation. These conditions appear to exist apart from psychosexual and psychosocial developmental stages (Pine, 1976).

Asymmetries are of course obvious (Post, 1980). There is asymmetry between the baby searching for the mother's face and the mother's responsive glance; between the eighteen-month-old little girl's exciting muscular exercise of her ability to say no and the distraught mother's gathering her up in her arms; between the five-year-old boy and his parents having after-dinner coffee when the boy says, "Guess who I love most," and quickly points his adoring finger at his mother while running over to sit on his father's lap; between the sullen teenager who has not cleaned his room, wants to use the car that night, and tries to engage his father in an argument about his own belief in the existence of UFOs, and the father's inevitable impotent rage. These are the regular and expected asymmetries of invested action.

And, of course, in therapy and analysis when one examines the realities of action in the analyst's schedule, the fixities of time, fee, and use of the couch, the attempted free association of the patient, and the restriction of information and action and response from the analyst, the asymmetry is crucially arranged (Macalpine, 1950; Eissler, 1953). Who has not heard such things as issued from the mouth of a young psychotic woman once she became less frightened of her therapist? "I am bored here and in therapy." "I don't like this office. It looks like a doctor's office. The office of my other doctor was wonderful. It was like a pad, it had beautiful things all over the walls and much more modern furniture. I called him by his first name and I loved him; it was fun to go to therapy. I used to show him all my journals and write poetry for him. You're no fun at all. You look like a minister. I hate your bow ties; they're old-fashioned. I get sleepy just coming over here; just thinking about our appointments. Every day it's like you defeat me in mental health. You're the healthy doctor; I'm the sick patient . . ."—and so on and on and on.

We are, I believe, so accustomed to the asymmetrical conditions of development that we are not surprised by the fact that the absence in childhood of this asymmetry of structure leads to big trouble. "My father wanted to be a pal to me rather than a father." "My mother told me all her troubles." "I could hardly have any troubles within my own self." These are but a few everyday expressions of such absence (Lidz, Fleck, and Cornelison, 1965).

A second condition are responses that facilitate union or fusion between the participants. In development we know this is both very simple and very complex in its forms. That is, we have every reason to believe this union or fusion in the developing child's mind exists from the very beginning and that his objects—his self and mother as objects, his body as object—develop in fact out of a unity, an undifferentiated state. In that sense it is deceptively simple. But of course the work of analysts studying the organization of a self out of the mother's smiling responsiveness—the child defines her as separate out of her playful organization of the world as part of *his* "good self," and out of *her* "good self" an object is evolved—documents and clarifies the complexities (see Freud, 1920; Winnicott, 1951; Loewald, 1976; and Klein and Riviere, 1937). These complexities include the necessities of the variously located aggression of the child in part objects of the mother, in aspects of her which are frustrating, in the projective fusion required in order for that aggression to be modified and later reintrojected in a more usable fashion for the organization of a self and other. Fusion, too, is inherent in the truths involved in Erikson's notion of mutuality (1950), in the organization of an identity, in Kohut's variously described mirroring stages (1977), and in the necessity of the mother's responsiveness to the child. These all suggest and demand acknowledgment that fusion in action, play, thought, and image is no simple phenomenon. Still in various forms, from the baby's delight at playing peekaboo, through the fourteen-month-old child's walking on the couch and continuing to walk right off the edge until caught by an alert parent (as if he could walk on air), through the three-year-old who tells his mother she is the bad one, not he, as he spills his cereal, through the seven-year-old who thinks her mother is a sex maniac who sleeps with her father at least once a year in order to try and make babies, to the adolescent's morose condemnation of the materialistic self-centeredness of his parents, there is a fusion of various complex forms arranged and experienced. And in analysis the silence, the visual absence, the recumbent position, the anonymity of the person of the analyst, the limitlessness of time, the centered attention upon the feelings and thoughts of the patient himself, the lack of conventional responsiveness in the analyst—all simply facilitate a fusion with the image of the analyst as determined by the capacity of the patient to organize and imagine that.

A third condition in normal development is a fairly wide range of permissible action and behavior toward the person of the mother or the father by the developing child. These are crucial for the development of normal intrapsychic structure. Evidence of death rates in babies and failure-to-thrive syndromes in foundling homes run scientifically but ascetically, gathered by Spitz (1946), Provence and Lipton (1962), where babies are fed but cannot actively "love" the mother's person, is overwhelming. There is abundant analytic evidence showing that a child's appreciated love affair in action, managed aggressive and sexual actual behaviors—not simply mental events occurring within a home—are necessary for that child to develop manageable internal organizations of defense, affect expression, and integrated internal organizations regarding sexual or aggressive aspects of an object relationship (Searles, 1959). You really do have to be able to exercise some range of aggressive action at home toward the important family member for one to develop an internalized conscience which modulates and permits such usable control structures in fully developed adults. And who in a psychotherapy or analysis has altered, or even become acquainted with, their intrapsychic structure without actions of a truly aggressive, however modulated kind toward the analytic situation, the analyst, and his endeavors? What successful patient has come out of a therapy without having behaved, in some crucial and repetitive way, in an adoring, cherishing, loving fashion toward the analyst? It is not that the analyst arranges this. It is that when he says, "I gather you are very embarrassed to tell me you are feeling loving toward this aspect of me," he notices the range of behavior such an organization imposes and allows it to be deployed specially within its own structure, in an organizing context.

The fourth condition of action-structure relation is that of limits. Limits are most crucial in all of this; they have a similar signal importance in both human development and therapeutic change. They are a chapter all to themselves, wondered about throughout Freud's writing and described in normal development variously and invariably, at least if such data are examined closely. The limiting actions of child and mother and father are involved in defining memory, separation-individuation, and object loss and object constancy; in weaning and the modulation of the drives of both aggression and sexuality; in defining the Oedipus complex and its passing; in dealing with the delineation of the body and its gender; in internalization; and in the adolescent's reworking of separation, reality testing, his organization of identity, and more. There is no structure formation that can occur without involving a limiting action of one's own or another's part. And where these limits are fudged by families, by the father who cannot say no to the child, by the parent who cannot be absent, formidable pathology appears in the developing person.

In therapy, limits are of course central. The formal structure of the hours, as defined by regular time to begin and to stop, the limit on information available about the analyst, the limit on analyst responsiveness, the basic rule—all are limits related to the common task.

They also, by their rigidity and invariance as limits, do three things crucial to therapy and different from development. Limits permit, by virtue of the stereotypy of the behaviors, the invariance of the therapist's behavior. They permit a variance in the behavior of the patient and allow it to be noticed. "You were late today and I wonder if that had a relation to what you were talking about differently at the end of the last hour," says the analyst. This could not be said by the analyst, or noted by the patient, without the hour's invariant beginning, and often without the analyst's silence; this limit on his previous hour's behavior allows the patient's variable behavior at the end of that hour to be noted. Limits in analysis are involved also in changing the nature of consequence for patient and analyst. The patient's feeling, thinking, and acting rebelliously and forcefully largely occurs as a consequence *within* the analytic hour; he does not, as the analyst's child might do, crack up the analyst's car and the analyst can "listen" by virtue of that limit. And finally, the limits upon the analyst include the proviso that he not act; he is silent. He may only inquire and communicate responsively. These allow analyst and patient a flexibility of response enormously wider than conventional behavior allows.

For example, early in an hour, a patient is very angry with the therapist. He is ideologically rigid, she says. He doesn't know anything about dance therapy, which she is involved with, and which she says can help patients. He, she says, wants all the therapeutic help to be located in his office. He thinks he is so important. She hates him. Then slowly she shows him a gift she has bought for a girl friend; it is a pretty little box containing a number of tiny men and women dolls. "I feel like smoking here," she says. She likes men who smoke cigars. Her grandfather smoked cigars. He would give her the boxes. They smelled wonderful. She had seen her therapist on some occasion with a cigar. She says she wishes she could bring a small ceramic pipe to her hour to smoke. "I gather," her analyst says, "that would make you feel good." "Yes," she says, pleased; "we could smoke together." He says, "A part of that pleasure would be as if you and I were enjoying sort of being men together." "That's right," she says. As the hour ends she mistakenly leaves one tiny man doll from her gift behind her in the office.

Without analytic limits the possibility of arranging and *attending to* anything like this easy flexibility, to such flow of hourly context, is difficult indeed. This young woman is criticizing her therapist angrily for what she considers the rigidity of his authoritarian male position and ideology. This young woman shares with him a complex and symbolic gift. She allows behaviors which acknowledge pleasures in their being united in a similar act and an imagined shared gender. Such flexibility of response, safe and examined, is difficult to arrange in the normal conditions of human relatedness. It is notable that the very flexibility of the patient's behavior and analytic response are in fact guaranteed by the rigidities of the action's limit, the inflexibility of the analytic situation and its permissible behaviors.

Finally, childhood developmental play is much concerned with representation. It is so much concerned with such representation that we tend to neglect it as an early form of thinking (Greenspan, 1981). But when words are not available (and not only to children), then gesture and play, experimental action and charade with things, people, bodies, and particularly loved objects, including self and other, are central to representation and integration in one's life. From a child's presenting the gift of her feces to her mother as she evolves an internal view of herself, her mother, her capacity to defecate, and her body's capacity to give, to the little boy spanking his toy animal for being bad, to the little girl dressing up in her mother's clothes, and the little boy zooming around shooting things on his bike, the development of inner structures is accompanied by and requires representation. Most often it occurs in action first and language only much later. In analysis and psychotherapy, in dreams, and in "acting out," it is the case that much of patients' behavior is an *appropriate* attempt to represent, to give some form to aspects of their inner life and outer situation which they are in the process of attempting to know and integrate. Often the words come later. It is often only after the patient finds you, the therapist, to be indestructible within the therapeutic framework (you won't change the hour, alter your furniture, take back your irritating interpretive remark; you won't back off from what seems true) or he finds you to be lovable within the limitations of the hours (you are not embarrassed that he told his wife that he loved you) that he then can say, "I just had this crazy idea that I would destroy you somehow if I really care."

One notices here that the integration involved action and preceded consciousness, that the organization *evolved* into language, as it *represented* itself in more final form. But first it required action to represent and negotiate the provisional integration. In that sense it may be that consciousness and language are among the highest levels of organization available to integration, and that defensive operations, only at their most mature level, are involved with repression and consciousness. If, then, integration is what is truly crucial, language is an exquisite tool in its service, and consciousness represented in words is fully possible only where integration is far advanced. In that sense the unconscious may indeed be structured like a language, but only to the degree that it approaches those higher levels of organization and representation at which some degree of integration is not beyond action's negotiated possibilities.

Summary

We have reminded you that *intrapsychic structures exist*. That they *organize in a stereotyped way* the nature of thought and interaction with the world around them. That they *represent themselves*, and are *resistant to change*. That they *tend toward rigidity* and expand to *fill the behavioral space*. That they *must be exercised* or the person and their vitality may wither. That understanding their *conditions of development* requires acknowledging the *necessities for representation*, the *range of action*, the conditions which facilitate *fusion*, the *limits* of action out of which structures evolve, and the *asymmetry* in invested action between the people involved in their development. The conditions of change involve an appreciation of these factors as well as the necessities of limits required to notice and *interfere* with existing structure. The nature of therapy, the conditions of human development, the relationships between marital parties and the problems of groups involve consideration of these forces and their impact. Degrees of integration of actions' organizations may precede consciousness and their representation in language forms. States of fixity and flexibility in action and intrapsychic structure need to be more thoroughly explored by psychoanalytic observers.

References

Adatto, C. P. (1980), Late adolescence to early childhood. In: *The Course of Life*, vol. 2, ed. S. I. Greenspan & G. H. Pollock. Adelphi, MD: Mental Health Study Center, U.S. Dept. of Health & Human Services, pp. 463–476.

Berman, S. (1979), The psychodynamic aspects of behavior. In: *Basic Handbook of Child Psychiatry*, vol. 2, ed. J. D. Noshpitz. New York: Basic Books, pp. 3–28.

Eissler, K. R. (1953), The effect of the structure of the ego on psychoanalytic technique. *J. Amer. Psychoanal. Assn.*, 1:104–143.

Engel, G. L. (1978), Monica: A 25-year longitudinal study of the consequences of trauma in infancy. Panel report to the American Psychoanalytic Assn. *J. Amer. Psychoanal. Assn.*, 27 (1979):107–126.

Erikson, E. (1946), The ego development and historical change. *The Psychoanalytic Study of the Child*, 2:359–396. New York: International Universities Press.

———— (1950), *Childhood and Society*. New York: Norton.

———— (1980), Elements of a psychoanalytic theory of psychosocial development. In: *The Course of Life*, vol. 2, ed. S. I. Greenspan & G. H. Pollock. Adelphi, MD: Mental Health Study Center, U.S. Dept. of Health & Human Services, pp. 11–61.

Fenichel, O. (1945), *Psychoanalytic Theory of Neurosis*. New York: Norton.

Freud, A. (1980), Child analysis as the study of mental growth (normal and abnormal). In: *The Course of Life*, vol. 1, ed. S. I. Greenspan & G. H. Pollock. Adelphi, MD: Mental Health Study Center, U.S. Dept. of Health & Human Services, pp. 1–10.

Freud, S. (1900), The Interpretation of Dreams. *Standard Edition*, 4 & 5. London: Hogarth Press, 1953, pp. 339–349.

———— (1911), Psychoanalytic notes on an autobiographical account of a case of paranoia. *Standard Edition*, 12:9–82. London: Hogarth Press, 1958.

———— (1914), Remembering, repeating, and working through. *Standard Edition*, 12:145–156. London: Hogarth Press, 1958.

———— (1920), Beyond the pleasure principle. *Standard Edition*, 18:7–64. London: Hogarth Press, 1955.

———— (1923), The ego and the id. *Standard Edition*, 19:12–66. London: Hogarth Press, 1961.

Frosch, J. (1967), Delusional fixity, sense of conviction, and the psychotic conflict. *Internat. J. Psycho-Anal.*, 48:475–495.

Gill, M. M. (1967), The primary process. In: Motives and Thought, ed. R. R. Holt. *Psychological Issues*, Monogr. 18/19. New York: International Universities Press, pp. 259–298.

Greenson, R. (1960), Empathy and its vicissitudes. *Internat. J. Psycho-Anal.*, 41:418–424.

Greenspan, S. I. (1981), *Psychopathology and Adaptation in Infancy and Early Childhood*. New York: International Universities Press.

Hartmann, H. (1947), On rational and irrational action. In: *Essays on Ego Psychology*. New York: International Universities Press, 1964, pp. 37–68.

Holt, R. R. (1967), The development of the primary process: A structural view. In: Motives and Thought, ed. R. R. Holt. *Psychological Issues*, Monogr. 18/19. New York: International Universities Press, pp. 344–383.

Klein, M., & Riviere, J. (1937), *Love, Guilt, and Reparation.* New York: Norton, 1964.

Kohut, H. (1976), Creativeness, Charisma, Group Psychology: Reflections on the Self-analysis of Freud. *Psychological Issues,* Monogr. 34/35. New York: International Universities Press.

——— (1977), *The Restoration of the Self.* New York: International Universities Press.

Lidz, T., Fleck, S., & Cornelison, A. (1965), *Schizophrenia and the Family.* New York: International Universities Press.

Loewald, H. (1970), Psychoanalytic theory and the psychoanalytic process. *The Psychoanalytic Study of the Child,* 25:45–68. New York: International Universities Press.

——— (1976), Primary process, secondary process, and language. In: *Papers on Psychoanalysis.* New Haven, CT: Yale University Press, 1980, pp. 178–206.

Lynch, J. J. (1977), *The Broken Heart.* New York: Basic Books.

Macalpine, I. (1950), The development of the transference. *Psychoanal. Quart.,* 19:501–539.

Pine, F. (1976), On therapeutic change. In: *Psychoanalysis and Contemporary Science,* 5:537–569.

Pious, W. (1961), A hypothesis about the nature of schizophrenic behavior. In: *Psychotherapy of the Psychoses,* ed. A. Burton. New York: Basic Books, pp. 43–68.

Post, S. (1980), Origins, elements and functions of therapeutic empathy. *Internat. J. Psycho-Anal.,* 61:275–293.

Provence, S., & Lipton, R. (1962), *Infants in Institutions.* New York: International Universities Press.

Rapaport, D. (1958), A historical survey of psychoanalytic ego psychology. In: *Collected Papers of David Rapaport,* ed. M. M. Gill. New York: Basic Books, pp. 745–757.

——— (1960), *The Structure of Psychoanalytic Theory. Psychological Issues,* Monogr. 6. New York: International Universities Press.

——— Gill, M. (1959), The points of view and assumptions of metapsychology. In: *Collected Papers of David Rapaport,* ed. M. M. Gill. New York: Basic Books, 1967, pp. 795–811.

Schafer, R. (1959), Generative empathy in the treatment situation. *Psychoanal. Quart.,* 28:342–373.

——— (1967), Ideals, the ego ideal, and the ideal self. In: *Motives and Thought,* ed. R. R. Holt. *Psychological Issues,* Monogr. 18/19. New York: International Universities Press, pp. 129–174.

——— (1976), *A New Language for Psychoanalysis.* New Haven, CT: Yale University Press.

Schwartz, D. P. (1959), The integrative affect of participation. *Psychiat.,* 22:81–86.

——— (1978), Aspects of schizophrenic regression: Defects, defense, and disorganization. In: *Psychotherapy of Schizophrenia,* ed. C. Muller. Amsterdam & Oxford: Excerpta Medica, 1979, pp. 79–87.

——— (1983), The open hospital and the concept of limits. In: *Psychosocial Intervention in Schizophrenia,* ed. H. Stierlin, L. C. Wynne, & M. Wirsching. Berlin & New York: Springer-Verlag, pp. 83–92.

Schwartz, F. (1981), Psychic structure. *Internat. J. Psycho-Anal.,* 62:61–72.

Searles, H. F. (1959), Oedipal love in the countertransference. In: *Collected Papers*. New York: International Universities Press, 1965, pp. 284–303.
Shakespeare, W. (1623), *Macbeth. The Complete Works of Shakespeare*, ed. I. Ribner & G. L. Kittredge. New York: Wiley, 1971, pp. 1292–1323.
Spitz, R. (1946), Hospitalization. *The Psychoanalytic Study of the Child*, 2:113–117.
Wallerstein, R. S. (1979), Conceptualizing the nature of the therapeutic action of psychoanalytic psychotherapy: Panel report. *J. Amer. Psychoanal. Assn.*, 27:127–144.
Winnicott, D. (1951), Transitional objects and transitional phenomena. In: *Collected Papers: Through Paediatrics to Psycho-Analysis*. New York: Basic Books, 1958, pp. 229–242.

Part II

Research

7

Engagement of Schizophrenic Patients in Psychotherapy

John G. Gunderson, M.D.

In 1960, when the first empirical studies on the effects of psychotherapy with schizophrenics were initiated, it was considered unethical to withhold psychotherapy from patients under circumstances where it would potentially be available to them. By 1970, at the conclusion of these empirical studies, the ethical issue became whether—considering the expense involved—psychotherapy should be provided to schizophrenic patients in the absence of any evidence to support its effectiveness (Feinsilver and Gunderson, 1972). This indictment of the value of psychotherapy for schizophrenic patients was sufficiently contrary to what I had learned from such honored teachers as Elvin Semrad and Otto Will that it provided the impetus for my having spent most of the past decade engaged in empirical studies on this issue. Viewed more dispassionately now, a decade later, I believe that the results of the earlier empirical studies were correct insofar as they raised questions about the widespread application of various forms of individual psychotherapy to schizophrenic persons and made clear the need for further examination of the indications for such treatment.

The present chapter is the first in a series of reports on the Psychotherapy Outcome Study collaboratively conducted at Boston University, the Bedford, Massachusetts, Veterans Administration Hospital, and McLean Hospital since 1974 under the joint direction of Dr. Alfred Stanton, Dr. Peter Knapp, and myself (Stanton, Gunderson, Knapp, Frank, Schnitzer, Vannicelli, Rosenthal, 1984). In this study non-chronic, carefully diagnosed schizophrenic patients were randomly assigned to one of two psychotherapeutic modalities. The first was exploratory insight-oriented therapy (EIO) conducted by experienced, analytically trained or oriented therapists with a past record of success and a commitment to this treatment. The second was a reality-oriented, adaptive/supportive therapy (RAS). This was also provided by experienced therapists committed to the approach. Patients receiving EIO therapy were seen three or more times a week, while those given RAS therapy were seen once a week at most. All patients received drug therapy, monitored and continued on an individualized clinical basis. Patients were followed at six-month intervals, at which times they received extensive assessments lasting six hours or longer. These included such traditional areas as signs and symptoms, role functioning, and social interactions, but in addition special indepth attention was given to psychological changes that might more specifically reflect the impact of insight-oriented psychotherapy.

In what follows I will examine our data with an eye to identifying what characterizes patients who become engaged and continue in their assigned therapy; what factors in the therapist and in the nature of the therapy itself relate to continuance and engagement; and, finally, what contextual factors within family and hospital influence continuance and engagement. To this end, a series of correlational analyses are made and then supplemented by more specific, hypothesis-testing studies. Some analyses are similar to those reported earlier by Stanton, Boutelle, Gomes-Schwartz, Gunderson, Katz, Knapp, Mintz, Schnitzer, and Vannicelli (1979), before completion of our sample collection.

Magnitude of the Problem

In the course of our study we selected and followed 164 patients. Of these, 64 dropped out within six months; the remaining 100 comprise our study sample proper insofar as we expected that less than six months' treatment was an inappropriate test of the effectiveness of an individual psychotherapy. Of the 100 patients who remained in their assigned treatment for more than six months, about 50 continued for two or more years. These figures document that under circumstances where assignment to individual psychotherapy is not based on a specific clinical indication, only about a third of the patients can be expected to continue into the period at which the effects of that psychotherapy might be expected to occur. This finding is consistent with the findings of Rogers, Gendlin, Kiesler, and Truax (1967), who concluded that less than half of a continuously hospitalized group of schizophrenic patients actually became engaged with their assigned therapist—despite the contextual support provided by the hospital. Similarly, O'Brien, Hamm, Ray, Pierce, Luborsky, and Mintz (1972) found that only 40 percent of outpatients assigned to individual therapy at the time of discharge continued over the next two years. In a study where schizophrenic patients were first clinically evaluated for suitability for individual therapy, Alanen, Rakkolainen, Rasimus, Laakso, and Jarvi (1981) found that over half of their sample were assigned individual therapists and that approximately 80 percent of these continued in treatment over the next couple of years. This indicates that indiscriminate assignment of psychotherapy to schizophrenic patients—even under optimal conditions, where it is socially and financially supported—is not a wise deployment of professional resources and that thoughtful evaluation can enhance the likelihood that assignment of individual psychotherapy will result in meaningful engagement.

Characteristics of Patients Who Become Engaged and/or Remain in Individual Therapy

In these analyses we looked for baseline characteristics that differentiate dropouts from those who remained in therapy beyond six months, and also for baseline characteristics that correlated with therapist ratings on engagement in the first six months. Our own clinical experience and a review of the available literature suggested a number of hypotheses with regard to selection criteria for schizophrenic patients to be assigned individual therapy. We hypothesized that the following characteristics would predict subsequent engagement and continuance in individual therapy: more education, better work achievement, higher sociability, greater insight, capacities deemed useful in EIO therapy, and the presence of subjective distress and dissatisfaction (see Table 1). Of these, only a past history of more education and a capacity for adaptive regression as measured by the Rorschach were significantly correlated with continuation in therapy beyond six months. More remarkably, many of these characteristics actually appeared to have a negative relationship with therapists' subsequent judgments of their patients' engagement. For example, all of the indices of subjective distress and the assessment of sociability from the Phillips were negatively correlated with engagement.

In our subsequent summary of baseline correlates of continuance and engagement, these negative results to our predicted relationships found added confirmation. Moreover, we found that our broad viewpoint that healthier patients were better candidates for psychotherapy was also disconfirmed. By many measures (Menninger, Camarillo, IMPS morbidity 2 and 3, PSS macro 1 and 4, Phillips and Vaillant total scores, WAIS vocabulary scatter, Rorschach percent primary process), patients who dropped out or were rated as less engaged in their psychotherapy emerged as healthier! Another finding of particular interest was that therapists rated those patients higher on engagement who had lower baseline IQ performance (WAIS verbal, performance, and full scale).

Another unexpected relationship was that the amount of previous psychotherapy for patients who remained in therapy (3.1 months) was significantly greater than for those who dropped out (1.3 months). It is my impression that many schizophrenic patients need to have repeated exposures to psychotherapy before they remain in it. This may not simply be due to a lessening of denial or an increase in motivation, but also to the process of becoming more comfortable within the psychotherapy situation.

A more detailed examination of two hypotheses has been completed by Ann Rosoff (1982). She tested the hypotheses that TAT measures of high emotional distancing and low level of interpersonal relatedness would correlate with dropping out of therapy. To highlight any differences, she used as a dropout sample (n = 19) patients who left therapy within three months of their own choice and a sample of remainers (n = 19) who stayed in therapy for over a year—also by choice (i.e., without external coercion or support for continuation).

TABLE 1

Predicted Characteristics of Patients Who Will Remain and/or Become Engaged in Therapy

Characteristic	Measure & scale which tests	Continuance	Engagement		
			Alliance	Productivity	Values Rx
More education	Years completed	.05	.01(−)[a]	NS	.005(−)
Better work achievement	PSS—good wage earner	NS	—	—	—
More sociable	Phillips—more involvement	NS	NS	.05(−)	.05(−)
	PSS—low social isolation	NS	NS	NS	NS[b]
Insight	Soskis—integrates illness	NS	NS[c]	NS[c]	NS
	Camarillo—high insight	NS	NS[c]	NS	NS
	PSS—low denial	NS	NS	NS	NS
Capacity for therapy	Rorschach—adaptive regression	.05	NS	NS	NS
	Camarillo—high motivation	.10	.05(−)	NS	NS
Subjective distress	PSS—high subjective distress	NS	NS	.05(−)	NS
	PSS—high depression/anxiety	NS	NS	.05(−)	NS
	KASS—high symptom discomfort	NS	.05(−)	.05(−)	NS
Emotional availability	TAT—low emotional distance	.0002[d]	NS	.05	NS
Interpersonally oriented	TAT—high level of interpersonal relatedness	.09(−)[d]	NS	NS	.05(−)

[a] (−) indicates correlation was in opposite direction to prediction.
[b] Indicates it was positively correlated (p = .05) at 1–3 months but not subsequently.
[c] Indicates it was negatively correlated (p = .05) at 4–6 months but not for months 1–3 or overall for first 6 months.
[d] These analyses were done on restricted matched samples (see text).

The samples were matched by hospital treatment modality and length of hospitalization. Rosoff's hypotheses were confirmed. Emotional distancing in particular was very significantly greater among dropouts than remainers. The issue of the number of interpersonal relationships was nearly significant, but in a direction opposite from that predicted; i.e., dropouts appeared to have more interpersonal relations as evidenced on the TAT than did the remainers. These results were consistently supported in analyses using our full sample.

In sum, then, our results indicated that the baseline characteristics of patients who are more likely to continue in individual therapy and to be considered more engaged in it by their therapist are a somewhat surprising group. They are a socially isolated, emotionally flat group with considerable internal disorganization (PSS disorientation, Rorschach primary process), but perhaps are more consistent role performers (PSS roles, KASS expected performance, number of years of prior education) than those who drop out. All in all, those who are more likely to engage and remain in individual psychotherapy are duller, quieter, and more stable than the dropouts. These results find some support in a report by Beck, Golden, and Arnold (1981), who also found that schizophrenic patients who remained in long-term psychotherapy were less functional and had received more previous treatment than those who dropped out.

Characteristics of Therapists Whose Patients Remain in Treatment

Both the opinions of clinicians experienced with schizophrenic patients and prior research in this area (Gunderson, Schulz, and Feinsilver, 1975) suggest that personal and professional characteristics of therapists may have powerful effects on the ability to engage patients in the initial phase of treatment.

To study this, we have correlated ten personality dimensions in our therapists (initially developed into reliable scales by Feinsilver and myself) with indices of continuance in therapy (see Table 2). We found that therapists judged to be more gentle, grandfatherly, and comfortable with depression were more apt to have patients who dropped out. Therapists whose patients remained in therapy were less apt to externalize and were somewhat more active. These findings combine to

TABLE 2
Comparison of Dropouts, Terminators, and Study Patients in Terms of Their Therapist's Personality Characteristics[a]

	Dropouts $\bar{x}$	Terminators $\bar{x}$	Remainers $\bar{x}$	F
Activity	3.36	3.77	3.58	2.21[b]
Comfort w/aggression	3.30	3.22	3.42	0.55
Externalizing	3.14	3.47	2.97	5.23[c]
Sociopathy	2.89	2.91	2.68	0.99
Gentleness	3.40	2.71	3.16	4.49[c]
Grandfatherliness	3.04	2.50	2.92	3.78[d]
Comfort w/depression	3.75	3.35	3.57	2.31[b]
Optimism	3.17	2.84	3.16	2.04
Composure	3.73	3.47	3.81	1.63
Comfort w/dependency	3.57	3.63	3.72	0.43

[a]Dropouts = less than 6 months Rx, n = 55;
terminators = 6–18 months Rx, n = 39;
remainers = more than 18 months Rx, n = 52.
[b]p .10
[c]p .01
[d]p .05

suggest that continuance in psychotherapy is more likely with active therapists who are relatively intolerant of their patients' symptoms.

How Type of Therapy (RAS or EIO) Effects Engagement and Continuance

To study this, we compared the intensive, insight-oriented treatment to the supportive therapy to see whether there were differences in how receptive patients were to them. We found some systematic differences in the nature of the patients who were likely to remain and become engaged in each type of therapy. Patients who dropped out of the insight-oriented treatment tended to be sicker than those who stayed (as measured by Vaillant, IMPS, PSS). The suggested that the intellectual and interpersonal demands made by the insight-oriented therapy were not well tolerated by sicker patients. Also, the patients who remained in the EIO treatment had a less optimistic or "Pollyanna-ish" view of their psychosis at the time of admission than did those who dropped out.

These characteristics of patients who remained in or dropped the EIO therapy contrast with what was found when we looked at the supportive therapy group. Patients who remained in RAS treatment were somewhat sicker than those who dropped out (as measured by baseline indices of thought disorder on the IMPS and Rorschach and emotional distance on the TAT). Moreover, patients who remained in the supportive treatment were likely to have an optimistic view of their illness as a positive event and were judged more motivated (as measured by the Soskis and the Camarillo, respectively) than patients who dropped out. These results seem to concur with the clinical impression that RAS therapists tend to offer patients a well-specified and clearly positive expectation about their treatment which seems particularly well suited for patients who have thought disorder and emotional distancing. The treatment itself places relatively less interpersonal and emotional demands on patients than insight-oriented therapy. We had the impression that patients who dropped out of the RAS treatment showed more interest and involvement in relationships than those who remained.

Similar impressions prevailed in looking at the correlations between dropouts and remainers for each of the two types of therapy and the therapists' ratings on their engagement. Many scales of the Camarillo (insight, motivation, object relations, identity, affective contact, and ego strength) showed that the degree of sickness correlated positively with engagement in therapy as noted by RAS therapists, i.e., the sicker patients were considered more engaged in treatment by their supportive therapists. This contrasted with the less dramatic but nonetheless conspicuous trend whereby EIO therapists scored patients who were healthier on these scales as more engaged in therapy. This again suggests that supportive therapists felt more positively about the progress of the treatment when patients fit into a traditional medical symptom-oriented treatment model.

When looked at from the point of view of their behavioral/symptom pictures, once again RAS therapists scored patients higher on engagement who were more disturbed. In contrast, EIO therapists rated healthier patients as more engaged—patients who had the best reality testing and role performance regardless of their level of behavioral disturbance. Allowing for the fact that insight-oriented and supportive therapists may have rated similar phenomena differently, the issue of fit comes clearly to the fore in these results. It is quite clear that patients whom supportive therapists are more likely to rate as positively engaged, and whom they are more likely to maintain in treatment, are a sicker group of patients than those who drop out. By contrast, insight-oriented therapists are more likely to keep in treatment patients who have better ego strengths and ego functioning, and to score their behavior within the treatment positively.

Contextual Influences on Engagement/Continuation

Our appreciation of the powerful factors in the social context in which the psychotherapy was carried out grew during the course of this study. Now it would seem to us misleading to suggest that factors in either the patient's psychopathology or the therapist's orientation and skill accounted for more variance in the subsequent engagement and continuation than do some contextual factors. Regression analysis indicated that four such contextual factors (families, life events, the milieu program, and milieu-therapist interactions) account for 20 to

25 percent of the variability in the subsequent length of stay in psychotherapy. More specific impressions about the impact of such factors on the course of therapy are based on three data sources: (1) records of the incidence of dropping out in various hospital settings; (2) in-depth case reviews by expert clinicians, and (3) an empirical examination of therapist-milieu interactions (within McLean).

Effects of hospital setting. Patients were seen in three quite different types of hospital: a large, private hospital, McLean; a short-term university hospital unit, Boston University Medical Center; and the Veterans Administration Hospital in Bedford. The VA hospital had the highest frequency of dropouts (53 percent) and McLean the lowest (30 percent). This parallels the relative level of interest and customary practice of psychotherapy for schizophrenic patients at the three institutions. Even with administrative support, financial remuneration, and high-status therapists, it was not easy to introduce changes into usual clinical practices. In milieu programs where psychotherapy is uniformly either given or not given and all patients are on the same research protocol, dropouts will be few within a hospital. May (1968) reported that only 4 percent of his sample dropped out within such milieu programs during the first six months of continuous hospitalization. Where the options of other treatments are openly available or even suggested, dropouts become frequent. Within our project, approximately fourteen patients were lost at McLean either because of rivalries with other professionals for such patients or because of administrators who had righteous opinions regarding the superiority of one treatment over the other. By contrast, no patients were lost for these reasons at the other two hospitals. There patients more frequently took the initiative in discontinuing the treatment than was the case at McLean.

We also found significant relationships between dropping out and the length of hospitalization. Not surprisingly, dropouts had considerably shorter hospitalizations. It is unclear at this point whether this is because people who dropped out of therapy also dropped out of the hospital or because longer-term hospitalization is necessary to engage schizophrenic patients.

Interactions between therapies. Two experienced hospital psychiatrists (Drs. Eldred and Teschke) made extensive retrospective reviews of each case at McLean Hospital. These reviews included interviews with families and treatment personnel, as well as reviews of the chart. From this systematic examination, ratings were made of the positive or negative effects of seven factors in the treatment (see Table 3). Of these seven factors, the most powerful impact was from the family and milieu treatments. Both—but especially the family—often exerted powerful negative effects as well as beneficial ones. Analysis of the first thirty cases showed that patients who remained in therapy for more than eighteen months had more family support for treatment and fewer harmful life events than either terminators or dropouts. Moreover, they were perceived as deriving the most benefit from medications. Finally, a situation emerged whereby patients who remained in their assigned therapy more frequently had therapists who were in conflict with either the patient's family or the patient's milieu. From this and other analyses it tentatively appeared as if there were a competitive relationship between therapy and milieu programs whereby therapy is more likely to be terminated if the milieu is exerting powerful positive effects. Conversely, when the milieu is judged harmful, therapy is more likely to continue. More definitive conclusions will be drawn when the whole sample is available for these analyses (Teschke, Eldred, Gunderson, and Frank, 1983).

A study of psychotherapy-milieu interaction. Independent of the above study, we have completed an evaluation of hypotheses related to interactions between the type of therapy (insight-oriented versus supportive) and the type of milieu program (control-oriented versus insight-oriented) (Frank and Gunderson, 1984). This study tested and confirmed our hypotheses that when supportive therapists were on insight-oriented halls and insight-oriented therapists on control-oriented halls, there would be a significant negative effect manifest in more dropouts and lower engagement in therapy. We found, in fact, that such mismatches significantly decreased the length of time patients continued in therapy and increased the number of dropouts, but that this relationship existed only insofar as the therapists were overt and explicit in their disagreement with the milieu program. Mismatches failed to have negative impact when therapists were administratively uninvolved and quiet about their differences. This study gives empirical documentation for a type of Stanton-Schwartz phenomena that results in dropouts and early discontinuance of psychotherapy.

TABLE 3

Mean (Total)[a] Influence on Treatment of 7 Contextual Factors for Therapy Dropouts, Terminators, and Remainers

	Dropouts 6 months Rx n = 6	Terminators 6–18 months Rx n = 11	Remainers 18 months Rx n = 12	F
Family	3.00	3.30	4.42	0.77
Milieu	3.67	5.18	3.33	2.25
Family × therapist	3.83	4.00	3.08	0.93
Milieu × therapist	3.50	3.82	2.67	1.86
Life events	3.17	2.09	3.67	5.50[b]
Medications	5.00	5.09	5.42	0.17
Psychotherapy	4.50	4.91	3.75	0.93

[a]Scores reflect amount and type of influence combined and range from (1) strong harmful to (7) strong beneficial influence.
[b]$p < .01$.

Discussion

Our research group takes pride in being composed of clinically experienced and analytically trained people who can appreciate the complexities of the clinical situation. Had our results merely confirmed our best clinical judgments about psychotherapy with schizophrenics, it might have been satisfying, but we would have learned little. If we measure the present research by whether it brings to light unexpected relationships which can inform clinical judgment, I believe we have succeeded.

To my mind, the most striking results from this study concern (a) the high frequency with which schizophrenic patients discontinued psychotherapy even under conditions of institutional and financial support; (b) the striking differences between patients who seem well suited for supportive therapy and continue in it and those who seem well suited for and continue in insight-oriented therapy; and (c) the clearly demonstrable effects that contextual factors in the family and milieu have upon continuation of psychotherapy. Each of these observations carries the implication that no simple answer to the question of whether psychotherapy with schizophrenic patients is effective can ever be possible. This conclusion seems unassailable if one accepts the idea that only long-term individual psychotherapy can be expected to have either measurable or specific effects for schizophrenic patients.

One clinical implication of the present study is that institutions or individuals who practice psychotherapy with schizophrenic patients should select patients only after a careful clinical judgment regarding their suitability has been made—perhaps aided by the report from this study. A second is that selection of the patient should be based in part on the nature of the therapy being offered. Therapists providing supportive treatment would do better to select patients who are emotionally distant and thought-disordered but who have an optimistic view of their illness. In contrast, therapists providing insight-oriented therapy would do better to select more interpersonally and affectively related patients who have better reality testing and who see their psychosis as an unfortunate event. This does not mean that patients will necessarily profit who are selected in this way, but only that they are more likely to remain in therapy sufficiently long for it to be effective.

Finally, the messages to therapists with respect to contextual factors are themselves quite complex. While support for psychotherapy by a patient's family is a strongly positive factor in continuance, there appear to be occasions when the therapist's alignment with the patient, against either the milieu or the family, can also sustain and consolidate the therapy. Finally, it is useful for therapists to know that when they disagree with the milieu orientation it is better to keep silent than to become involved and attempt to change the hall—at least from the point of view of continuing as the patient's therapist.

References

Alanen, Y. O., Rakkolainen, V., Rasimus, R., Laakso, J., & Jarvi, R. (1981), Developing the treatment of schizophrenia in a community-psychiatric setting: A psychotherapeutic and family-centered approach. Unpublished manuscript.

Beck, J. D., Golden, S., & Arnold, F. (1981), An empirical investigation of psychotherapy with schizophrenic patients. *Schiz. Bull.*, 7:241–247.

Feinsilver, D. B., & Gunderson, J. G. (1972), Psychotherapy of schizophrenia: Is it indicated? A review of the literature. *Schiz. Bull.*, 6:11–23.

Frank, A., & Gunderson, J. G. (1984), Matching therapists and milieus: Effects on engagement and continuance in psychotherapy. *Psychiatry*, 47:201–210, 1984.

Gunderson, J. G., Schulz, C., & Feinsilver, D. (1975), Matching therapists with schizophrenic patients. In: *Psychotherapy of Schizophrenia: Current Theory, Research and Practice*, ed. J. Gunderson & L. Mosher. New York: Aronson, pp. 343–360.

Karon, B. P., & Vandenbos, G. F. (1972), The consequences of psychotherapy for schizophrenic patients. *Psychotherapy: Theory, Research and Practice*, 9:111–119.

May, P. R. A. (1968), *Treatment of Schizophrenia: A Comparative Study of Five Treatment Methods*. New York: Science House.

North, C., & Cadoret, R. (1981), Diagnostic discrepancy in personal accounts of patients with schizophrenia. *Arch. Gen. Psychiat.*, 38:133–137.

O'Brien, C. P., Hamm, K. B., Ray, B. A., Pierce, J. F., Luborsky, L., & Mintz, J. (1972), Group vs. individual psychotherapy with schizophrenics: A controlled outcome study. *Arch. Gen. Psychiat.*, 27:474–478.

Rogers, C. R., Gendlin, E. G., Kiesler, D. J., & Truax, C. B. (1967), *The Therapeutic Relationship and Its Impact: A Study of Psychotherapy with Schizophrenics*. Madison: University of Wisconsin Press.

Rosoff, A. (1982), Unpublished thesis, University of North Carolina.

Stanton, A. H., Boutelle, W., Gomes-Schwartz, B., Gunderson, J. G., Katz, H., Knapp, P., Mintz, M., Schnitzer, R., & Vannicelli, M. (1979), An evaluation of individual psychotherapy with schizophrenic patients: Determinants of engagement in therapy. Paper presented at the 123rd Annual Meeting of the American Psychiatric Association.

——— Gunderson, J. G., Knapp, P., Frank, A., Schnitzer, R., Vannicelli, M., &

Rosenthal, R. (1984), Effects of psychotherapy on schizophrenic patients. I. The design and implementation of a controlled study. *Schiz. Bull.*, 10:520–564.
Teschke, G., Eldred, S., Gunderson, J. G., & Frank, A. (1983), Contextual influences on treatment course. Paper presented at Annual Meeting of American Psychiatric Association, New York, May 6, 1983.

8

To Err Is Human: The Role of Error in Creativity and Psychotherapy

Albert Rothenberg, M.D.

I am, both in substance and in form, involved in risk. The topic I have chosen is value-laden and complex, and it requires me to draw on material from the rich, risky, and dazzling domain of aesthetics and creativity on the one hand, and, on the other, from the equally rich, risky, and—in its way—dazzling work of psychoanalytic psycho-therapy. Not that this is the first attempt to relate creativity to the practice of psychotherapy—this difficult theoretical leap has been pre-viously attempted in various ways. These have ranged from general formulations such as Edith Weigert's notion (1970) of therapist and patient as reconstructive artists, to more specific formulations such as David Beres's analogue (1957) between communication in the creative process and communication in psychotherapy, to my own quite specific application to psychotherapy of my research findings about particular cognitive functions in the creative process (Rothenberg, 1972, 1983a). Before the full measure of success with the theoretical leap has been taken, however, I am risking the inclusion of yet another domain and a third area of conceptual complexity. I am adding the domain of the psychology of errors, and attempting to relate error to the practice and theory of psychotherapy as a creative process.

What does error have to do with creativity, or, more complicated than that, with the creative practice of psychotherapy? Some years ago, in one of my research explorations of the creative process in visual art, I met with a woman sculptor who did large-scale abstract work in perfectly smooth white plastic material. These sculptures had perfectly clean lines and perfectly even coloration and were obviously proportioned according to exact specifications. I marveled at their seeming perfection, and she described to me the detailed engineering process involved in creating such elaborate and elegant works. Then she took me over to look at one of the large surfaces more closely. Pointing to a gnarled and slightly raised blemish on the surface on one of her works, she said, "Do you see that blip on the surface there? Well, that's me." This sculptor's dramatic and metaphoric reference to the single error on an otherwise absolutely perfect constructed sculpture may readily be related to poetic and philosophical conceptions of the human condition. To err is indeed to be human, and the sculptor's equating of her self and of her own individuality with the error on her creation is consistent with aesthetic and philosophical emphases on celebration of humanness, and of individual style and performance. There are surely other meanings, too, both aesthetic and psychodynamic, but we can surmise that she may also have felt uncomfortable and disavowing about the mechanistic and technological perfection of her creations. The unbroken sleek lines and machine-produced smooth surface in those works of art certainly produced some discomfort in me.

There is, I believe, more than personal psychological issues to be taken from this sculptor's remark, however. It is not only that erring is human and that artists assert their humanness or individuality in the errors they make, but, as I shall presently clarify, error itself, and a special orientation to error, is intrinsic to the creative process. Both commission of errors and the handling of errors are important and special matters in creative processes. First, errors are not merely allowed but, given a requisite very high level of technical skill, they are actually courted to some extent in the process of creating products in art, and in other fields as well. Second, in a significant way errors are linked and integrated into such created products. The sculptor was not merely acknowledging an error in her creation, she was embracing that error and including it as a significant part of the product itself. Indeed, she considered it to be the sign of her handiwork and her style, and she thereby indicated what is referred to as the artist's "signature." Broader in meaning than the literal name written on a canvas or a sculpture pedestal, her signature was the error that figuratively represented herself in her creation. This way of handling, thinking about, and using error in the creative process involves a factor I have called *articulation*. Articulation is a major factor in creative processes, and the process of articulation of error is a particular manifestation of this factor.

Articulation of Error

I am using the term "articulation of error" in a specific way. Literally, the word articulation means a joint, but it is a word with a double sense. The articulation or joining of one element with another produces at the same time both a connection or coming together and a separation. When we call someone an articulate speaker, we mean that that person speaks clearly and distinctly, and also that his words and thoughts flow in a smooth, connected stream. Thus, the articulate person separates the words and thoughts from each other, but he also connects them, both in sense and in syntax. Such articulation, with its connecting and separating, is a cardinal feature of creative processes in art, science, and many other fields. There is constant bringing together and separating in many different dimensions—conceptual, perceptual, volitional, affectual, and physical. Articulation is an ego function involving specific creative cognitive operations. As I have discussed elsewhere, in relation to empirical data derived from research interviews, experiments, and manuscript studies of the creative process, the creation of poetic metaphors, or completed novels, poems, and plays, and of paintings and sculpture, as well as of scientific theories—in this regard, I have presented specific data about Einstein's general theory of relativity (Rothenberg, 1979a) and Bohr's principle of complementarity (Rothenberg, 1983b)—have all involved a constant separating and bringing together by specific creative cognitive operations. These operations function in an overall process of articulation.[1]

---

[1]Although the term articulation does not appear in those earlier cited works, the creative cognitive operations described (janusian and homospatial process) are factors in the articulation process. The term articulation, as used here, has appeared in Rothenberg (1979b, 1983a).

The creative person—artist, scientist, or other—separates out critical aspects of the abstract or tangible material he works with and concomitantly fuses or brings these elements together in producing a creation. In the course of a creative process, errors that appear are also articulated; the articulation of error involves both separation and connection of various aspects of abstract and tangible material.

Before saying any more about the way in which articulation of error operates in creative processes, I will turn to a brief consideration of error as a topic in itself. To do so, I come straight away to the creative achievement of Sigmund Freud.

Freud on Error

Although there had been some scholarly work on speech and hearing errors prior to the work on Freud, most notably that of such linguists and philologists as Paul (1880), Delbrück (1887), von der Gabelentz (1891), Jespersen (1894), and, especially, Meringer (1908; Meringer and Mayer, 1895). Freud's analysis of the psychological meaning of such errors was ground-breaking. Moreover, his work on the psychopathology of everyday life (Freud, 1901), though an early exploration, was systematic and well documented, and in the years to follow it has been repeatedly confirmed. It stands today as a well-established scientific discovery, even among persons who otherwise are severe critics of psychoanalysis. Although there are modern linguists who challenge the idea that every speech error must necessarily be the product of the unconscious, of repression, and of the primary process, these factors are accepted as operative and important in many errors and are included in theoretical and empirical linguistic analyses (Ellis, 1980; Motley, 1980).

Freud's interest in error, of course, went beyond the slips of tongue and pen with which his name has come to be associated in everyday parlance, and in the corpus of his work he showed the operation of unconscious factors in forgetting, bungled actions, chance actions, and errors of memory. A general principle implicit in his work, therefore, is that any erroneous effect consisting of a discrepancy between intent and execution results from the operation of unconscious factors (Rothenberg, 1969).

Freud's search in the realm of error in hope of discovering general psychological laws was a type of action characteristic of his genius, a persistent feature of his scientific creativity. In the lowly regarded and disrespected areas of human experience, he often looked to discover meaningful truths. Dreams were for him a major focus of interest at a time when, as he himself noted (Freud, 1900), the prevailing professional attitude was "Traume sind Schaume" (dreams are froth), and sexuality had quite surely been considered an area unworthy of professional concern. His quotation from Virgil, which he cited in a letter to Fliess and which he used as an epigraph for the entire study on dreams, is important and revealing: "Flectere si nequeo superos, acheronta movebo" (If I cannot bend the Higher Powers, I will move the infernal regions). Although Freud used the quotation initially to refer to symptom formation (Freud, 1896, p. 132), I believe he was really citing a broader principle characteristic of his creative thinking. Typically, he turned from the unbendable higher levels of psychic functioning toward the lowest (the "infernal") levels in order to understand both simultaneously. With error, he had combed the wastebaskets of human action in order to understand critical aspects of both pathological and nonpathological cognitive functioning.[2]

Freud focused a good deal on the role of primary process mechanisms in parapraxes and other types of error, but I am concerned here with his broader finding that erroneous actions are produced by unconscious factors, and that the substance of a particular erroneous action derives from, and to some extent represents, the unconscious factor itself. This finding points the way to a clarification of one of the routes by which unconscious representations appear in creative works. For, while many theorists have rushed forward with a dogged insistence that unconscious representations appear regularly in creative works, few have provided more than teleological or *post hoc ergo propter hoc* explanations of the psychodynamic mechanism for the phenomenon. Errors provide a route for unconscious material to appear in creative works because of the special management of errors in the creative process. This applies to creative work in art and in other

[2]Freud characteristically used the janusian process, actively conceiving multiple opposites or antitheses simultaneously, in his creative thinking (Rothenberg, A., and Sledge, W., "The Creative Thinking of Sigmund Freud," in preparation).

intellectual fields and, as I shall show later, it applies in some measure to creative work in therapy as well.

Although Freud could not possibly follow up on all the ramifications of his brilliant early work on error, he added to his specific examples over the next twenty years. Only toward the end of his life did he return to error as a specific topic, in a short and seldom noticed note entitled, "The Subtleties of a Faulty Action" (Freud, 1935). In this piece he discussed his own mistaken insertion of a word with a double meaning in a salutation accompanying a birthday present. In addition to a rich and interesting analysis of the particular error, which I will not repeat, Freud introduced a new conception and pushed the general understanding of error further. In this case, he said, "a mistake gained its purpose not by being *made*, but only after it had been *corrected*. . . . A variant, not without interest, of the mechanism of a parapraxis" (p. 234, Freud's italics). Thus, the purpose of an error may be realized *after* the error has been made, specifically in the act of correcting it. With regard to articulation of error, I too am referring to a process in which realization or representation of unconscious meaning and other material occurs after the error is made. Although articulation of error and correction of error are not the same process, there is a psychodynamic relation between them. I stand, and hopefully walk ahead therefore, on solid Freudian ground. Moreover, in a broad sense, Freud's scientific creative processes in his early and later work on error are themselves instances of the creative articulation of error. In the earlier work he articulated the entire topic of error within a body of psychological knowledge, and in the later he focused on a specific error and subsequently developed and clarified its psychological meaning and overall psychodynamic structure.

The Process of Articulation of Error in the Creative Process

Creative people have an orientation to error that is out of the ordinary. Most people when engaged in highly skilled difficult work tend to be quite careful or controlled, and they are wary of making errors. Mistakes are irritating and bothersome, and sometimes are of a type and magnitude to provoke discouragement and cessation of the task. Although creative work itself is almost always quite difficult, and is very highly fraught with error, creative people characteristically deal with errors and mistakes in a different way. While engaged in the creative process they think in a highly free and wide-ranging fashion, and they take risks and chances that invariably lead to error. When errors occur, they may or may not be subjectively felt as bothersome, but characteristically they are directly noticed, assessed, and, if possible, articulated with the creative work in progress. Valuable or interesting elements within the error are clarified and elaborated, and they are joined with the developing product as a whole. The error elements may be connected and incorporated within the product, or they may lead the development of the product into new directions. Articulation of error is not a matter of rejecting material because it is wrong, or a matter of turning away from an incorrect approach. Unlike what is generally called trial-and-error thinking, in which errors are removed or corrected, articulation of error involves preservation in the whole work of new, interesting, or valuable elements within a miss or a mistake. In the creative process, the articulation of error involves both separation and connection simultaneously.

To illustrate how the process operates in artistic creative work, I shall present an example from a painting by the modern artist Henri Matisse. This is the painting entitled "The Bather" (Figure 1, following p. 181). In the major portion of his works, Matisse was interested in organizing color and pattern on a two-dimensional surface. He was a master of constructing patterns, and one of his achievements was the invention of the collage style of painting. In this oil on canvas painting done in 1909, it is rather easy to see the use of a bright, strong color design, and the emphasis on the nude body of the male bather as a pattern of lines on an essentially two-dimensional surface. While the body is presented with some traditional line perspective, and there is some degree of depth and solidity, this effect is somewhat secondary to the effect of strong lines, contours, and especially a sense of movement on the flat surface. How is this latter aesthetic effect achieved? First, of course, the lines outlining the body contour are thick and black: they stand out. But did Matisse draw out these lines all at once with a perfect unbroken motion, much as we have seen Picasso do in his filmed demonstrations of spontaneous drawing using penlights in the empty air? Not at all. Close inspection of the painting shows numerous repetitious and erroneously placed lines: in the hand region, behind the back, and on the legs. And now, it is important to note, that when I say erroneously placed, I am not describing the aesthetic effect of this painting, because these lines do not appear to be unnecessary or wrong in the total context of this work. Indeed, these seemingly stray lines emphasize and enhance the rounded contour of the body, and they impart dynamism and a feeling of movement to the whole. That is precisely the point of such articulation of error. While a careful examination of the painting indicates that Matisse's hand strayed several times while drawing the nude figure, he was able to articulate these strayings with the overall final pattern he produced. Not only are the strayed lines part of the aesthetic form of the painting, but one could also infer philosophical and psychological content from the crude and erroneous lines, notions such as those involved in the sculptor's remarks I quoted earlier.

Other illustrations of the principle of articulation of error in visual art come from artists of different styles, times, and schools. In the school of abstract expressionism, the working approach of Jackson Pollack, the founder, exemplifies the use of this principle. Although we know that Pollack planned his patterned canvases carefully, and that he dripped buckets of paint on them with a highly skilled and practiced hand, much occurred that was not intended. These so-called "chance" or erroneous developments of lines, textures, and color effects were immediately articulated by him into the overall design. With brilliant proficiency, Pollack and other abstract expressionists who have come after him introduce lines and colors which connect their errors to other aspects of the design. These errors become articulations within the whole design because they appear as separations which are, at the same time, connected.

It is difficult to distinguish between error and either chance or randomness in such events because, as I shall make clearer later, these factors are interrelated. For the moment, however, I shall refer only to error because of the clear-cut deviation of intent, or at least of expectations, in the straying of the artist's skilled and expert hand. Etymologically considered, the word "error" derives from the Latin word for "a wandering" and it is the wandering from a particular contour, line, or texture that introduces an initial separation. This separation is connected with the whole in an articulation contributing to overall integration, and to a final product or creation.

Moving away from modern art to a time-honored instance of articulation of error in visual art, there is the process of creative water coloring. With the water coloring technique, as even a beginning water colorist knows, the trick is to be able to work with thin liquid paint that runs down the surface of the paper as it is applied. Increasing skill with this medium allows the water colorist to anticipate the direction and extent of the run, and also to have an idea of the effects of running paint merging with surrounding lines and colors. However, there is no way to be sure of these effects beforehand—and this is where articulation of error comes in. The creative water colorist learns especially to capitalize on the dripping, runny effect, and to use it as a means of producing an overall aesthetic result. In the course of producing this result, merged and connected lines and colors may, for instance, be separated out and emphasized by repeating them in an approximate way on other parts of the paper. Separated and dripping lines and colors may be immediately brushed into, and connected with, other lines and colors. The process is one of continual recognition and assessment of error and wandering, with both separation and connection into an integrated whole.

In literature, a telling and immortal example of articulation of error appears in a passage from Shakespeare's *The Merchant of Venice*, which Freud (1916–1917) cited as an example of creative writers' understanding of parapraxes. Portia says to Antonio: "One half of me is yours, the other half yours— / Mine own, I would say; *but if mine, then yours*, / And so all yours" (Act III, Scene ii, author's italics). In her elaboration of the error, Portia clarified the separation of the first person and second person pronoun referents and she connected herself together with Antonio at the same time.

With respect to the process of creation in literature, writer research subjects I have worked with directly in regular, structured, and intensive interviews—focused on the creative process—over periods of months and years (Rothenberg, 1972, 1979b) have consistently indicated, or shown me, the process of articulation of error during the writing of poems, novels, and plays. The playwright Arthur Miller, for example, talked once of freeing himself up and making mistakes in order to use those mistakes to develop his ideas and his writing. Sometimes he felt he needed to try to write like a novice in order to generate emotion and error. The novelist John Hersey told me at one point of the importance of ''blurts'' and ''inner mistakes'' as the essence of what a writer did that made himself unique and idiosyncratic. He believed that mistakes allowed a writer to bring emotion into his work and, like Miller, he thought that novice writers sometimes brought more emotion than experienced writers into their work as a direct result of aesthetic mistakes.

A detailed illustration of the articulation of error during the literary creative process comes from the work of Hersey on a novel about an alienated college student of the 1960s entitled *Too Far to Walk* (1966). In a passage describing the hero's interaction with a sophisticated young college-town whore he had ironically and rebelliously brought home to meet his parents, the author first wrote the somewhat discordant following description:

She was a sharp girl, one who, it could surely be said, lived by her wits, and her conversation was far more intelligent than (at random) Wagner's or Gibbon's [friends of John, the hero]. She was college material—a dropout in the sense that it would never have occurred to her to try to get in. She began talking about Dahomey: something she had picked up from some pipe smoker [faculty member]. As she was talking of this, John suddenly thought of having sat in the Freshman Dean's office, one day the year before, and having caught a glimpse of a number beside his name on his record card on the Dean's desk: 3M242526. He had seen the number only a few moments, but it was seared on his brain. What was it? Was it a code for all his abilities and accomplishments? Or did it stand for *him*—his machine card self? He was at home; his excited mother was trembling upstairs for her cub—yet as Mona [the whore] spoke of the African ritualist bending over the girl with his special knives, John was overcome with a horror of the impersonality, the inhumanity of the big machine of life for which he was being educated. At any moment buttons might be pressed in that machine that would make of his number something for a GI dog tag. . . . [cf. Hersey, 1966, pp. 107–108]

In discussing this passage with me, the author at one point commented on something that would have struck a listener of this very first manuscript draft as discrepant and out of place. Why the reference to the country Dahomey and Africa in the mouth of the young whore? It seems a definite mistake in the passage and the author himself wondered why he put it in. Instead, however, of deciding to delete it, he proceeded to articulate this error by making some changes. He clarified and separated out an issue in the Africa reference, and connected it to the rest of the material in the passage. He changed, ''She began talking about Dahomey,'' to the more detailed and clear, ''She began talking about, of all things, the cicatrization of the faces, arms and thighs of young girls in puberty rites in Dahomey.'' And he also changed the sentence about the number on his record card from, ''He had seen the number only a few moments, but it was seared on his brain,'' to the connected phrasing of the following: ''He had seen the number only a few moments, but it was as if cicatrized across his forehead.''

With these changes he gave the passage a unified and telling metaphorical impact relating the young man's college experience to a violent African puberty rite. Also, of course, the psychoanalyst reader will see the introduction of material referring to cicatrization as suggesting and emphasizing unconscious castration fears which relate meaningfully to a rebellious young man's experience and concerns with a whore. Interestingly, after making these changes—and here we have a dynamic similar to Freud's correction of a faulty action—the author himself became aware of a specific unconscious connection to an event in his life the previous day. He and his wife had been at a meeting of the Institute of Arts and Letters at which awards were bestowed to several outstanding American writers. Because of the large number of people at the affair, some persons got confused about some of the attendees' names, and the author's wife commented that she thought everyone should have his name printed on his forehead. Thus, the textual change to refer to a cicatrix or scar on the hero's forehead brought out, and incorporated, an unconscious issue in the passage. This unconscious issue—pertaining to the author's feelings about the Institute of Arts and Letters award ritual—came to the fore as a result of an articulation of the awkward and initially erroneous use of the idea of Africa. To clarify the psychodynamic structure of this event, it is important to note that it was not a matter of the upsurge of unconscious material which was subsequently subjected to ego modification and control. It was not, therefore, a manifestation of what would be expected according to the traditional "regression in the service of the ego" theory of creativity (Kris, 1952). Instead the unconscious material was gradually brought closer to consciousness; it was rendered into consciousness and represented by means of an ego process of articulation of error. While errors are generally produced by unconscious wishes—and the Africa error was surely no exception—the active representation of unconscious content in the work of art, and in the author's consciousness, is due in large measure to the process of articulation.

Another illustration of the articulation of error in the literary creative process comes from my study (Rothenberg, 1969) of Eugene O'Neill's revisions in manuscript drafts of his 1940 play, *The Iceman Cometh*. As the articulation of error process was not made explicit in my original report (the concept had not yet been formulated), I shall recapitulate that material briefly now. The iceman of O'Neill's title is not a character in the play, or an actual person, but rather the subject of a joke about adultery told by the leading character, a salesman and evangelistic former alcoholic named Hickey. In addition to the joking reference, the nonexistent iceman has other symbolic meanings, both tacit and explicit—he is the iceman of death, and he is Christ the bridegroom, who cometh to the virgins (Matt. 25:5–6). On the basis of O'Neill's explicit comments in his notes for the play, and his specific use of the biblical "bridegroom cometh" phraseology in a play written earlier (*More Stately Mansions*, 1938), there is no doubt that from the first he had in mind a symbolic iceman rather than a real one.

However, in O'Neill's very first reference to an iceman during the writing of the play, he constructed the following: A character, Harry, who is waiting for Hickey to appear, says, "Remember the way he always lies about his wife and the Iceman?" Another character replies: "Maybe that's what's keeping him, Harry. There's an old belief among savages that it's bad luck to call something too much, unless you're sure you want it because, if you keep calling it, it'll come to you. Hickey's done enough calling the Iceman and Fate has a bum sense of humor. Maybe it wouldn't know he was joking.'' Harry then becomes angry and says, ''There was nothing to Hickey's bull about the Iceman. Only a joke, and he wouldn't give a damn if it was true, anyway.'' Without going further into the many references to the iceman of this type throughout the first manuscript draft, I want to point out that O'Neill introduced the idea of a real, corporeal iceman—an actual adulterer—right away in these first references in his first draft. That this suggestion of a real corporeal iceman was an error on O'Neill's part is clearly indicated by his own revisions on the manuscript. O'Neill extensively deleted the dialogue I just quoted except for the very first line, which he changed to: ''Remember that gag he always pulls about his wife and the Iceman?'' More than that, he systematically altered phraseology indicating a real iceman in every single one of the sixteen written contexts in which reference is made to an iceman in the first or later drafts. This systematic alteration of every single context demonstrates the error, and to an investigator of the manuscript material it is a remarkable event. One perceives a virtually uncanny sensitivity in O'Neill, a sensitivity that removed all denotations of a real flesh-and-blood iceman and thereby delineated and established the symbolic feature, but managed at the same time to preserve a certain ambiguity about real and symbolic aspects. In this way, the erroneous initial references to a real iceman adulterer became both separate and connected within the overall context of the play. Particular instances of this articulation process are also seen in the following small, but very specific, alterations. There is a subtle dialect change from the expression ''Cheatin' wit de Iceman or somebody?'' to ''Cheatin' wid de Iceman or nobody?'' In the latter, the erroneous denotation of a somebody, i.e., a real person, as an equivalent alternative to the iceman is removed, but an ambiguity remains. Second, the reply to the question ''How's de Iceman, Hickey? How's he doing at your house?'' is changed from the elaborated and denotative ''Fine! He's moved in for keeps'' to the slightly ambiguous but simple ''Fine.'' Lastly, there is the addition of a protesting emphasis that the whole iceman issue was really all a gag.

A more extensive example of this process is as follows: at the end of the first act, a character says to Hickey in the first draft version, ''I notice you didn't answer me about the Iceman or deny it. Did this

great revelation come to you when you found him in her bed. . . .
Was it you caught the Iceman in the arms of your dear Evelyn at last,
and had to make the best of it and shake hands with him?'' In the first
step of the process of articulation of this passage, O'Neill on the second
draft completely deleted the very vivid reality reference beginning with
the words, ''Was it you caught the Iceman . . .'' and ending with
''shake hands with him.'' In the next version he continued the articulation of his error by deleting the phrase ''found him in her bed'' and
produced the construction used in the play: ''I notice you didn't deny
it when I asked you about the Iceman. Did this great revelation of the
evil habit of dreaming about tomorrow come to you after you found
your wife was sick of you?''

Articulation of error is a creative factor outside of literature and
the visual arts, and it operates widely in creativity. Rather than spell
out further examples in detail, however, I shall merely cite some other
instances to sharpen the point. In music, an empirical exploration by
the psychologist Bahle (reported by Jacobs, 1960) of the compositional
methods of thirty-two European composers, including Schönberg,
Honnegger, Malipiero, Orff, and Richard Strauss, reportedly demonstrated, as an intrinsic part of the musical creative process, ''the
discovery of musical values which at first he [the composer] has not
intended or sought intentionally'' (p. 278). Also, in a unique study by
Reitman (1966) involving the detailed recording of an American composer's vocal description of everything he was thinking and doing
while he worked, the composer was found to engage frequently in
''modifying a plan after the fact, as it were, so as to make it conform
to something the problem solver has discovered or created by accident
and now wishes to preserve'' (p. 177). Shifting to scientific creativity,
the remarkable cases of Sir Arthur Fleming's discovery of penicillin,
Roentgen's discovery of the x-ray effect, and Pasteur's development
of the concept of immunology were particular instances of the articulation of error. All have been at some time cited as instances of
serendipity, a wonderful but mysterious term meaning the productive
use of phenomena appearing by chance. In all of these cases, however,
an error occurred which the scientist was able to use or else to understand in the sense that he connected the substance of the error with
the accumulated corpus of knowledge of his field. Instead of merely

correcting the error or turning away from it toward some other correct direction, these scientists preserved the fact of nature that had been clarified and separated off by the error, and they connected this fact to other facts or data. Thus, Fleming saw that a mold that was erroneously allowed to contaminate a petri dish destroyed the bacteria in its immediate vicinity; he connected this observation with the idea of disease or illness and, reasoning that the contaminating mold would have a beneficial effect in the treatment of illness, he conceived the idea of the penicillin drug. Such an event, involving conversion of error, must be distinguished from the broad range of purely accidental discoveries.

Pasteur suggested the point I am making here in his famous aphorism, "chance favors the prepared mind." I have generally avoided use of the word "chance" in my discussion so far, because I believe "error" more adequately represents the discrepancy between intent and execution in the foregoing events. Also, the term error points to a wandering from a course, and because of the unconscious roots it emphasizes a factor of psychic determinism. That there is a distinct phenomenal relationship between error and chance is indisputable, and it is because of the essential phenomenal similarity that errors can lead to truly new creative events. Chance is critically related to creativity and the appearance of new entities. Mutations are chance events in the biological realm that introduce new qualities that are selected out and subsequently preserved. These are creative events in nature. So, too, chance in the realm of mental operations introduces new material that is selected out, preserved, and articulated into creations.

The Process of Articulation of Error in Psychotherapy

Moving from the realm of science and art to the practice of psychoanalytic psychotherapy requires a shift from tangible productions such as theories, discoveries, and works of art to the realm of intrapsychic and interpersonal interaction. Although somewhat less tangible, a creative process in therapy does occur. As I have discussed previously (Rothenberg, 1983a), a psychoanalytic therapy involves the making of new structures that require the collaboration of therapist and patient in a mutual creative process. Together, patient and therapist engage in creating aspects of the patient's personality. Together they create attributes and structure. Collaborative articulation involving both separating and connecting by patient and therapist plays a major role. The reasons for this creative articulation are complex, having to do with the difference between creative making and pure systematic analysis, and with the difference between the related factors of what may be called "presentational" truth or validity, and propositional or "explicated" truth or validity.[3] Complex also are the psychodynamics of the articulation of error, specifically as this process is applied in psychotherapy. I must therefore be satisfied in this relatively short exposition with trying to sketch some broad, general outlines. I shall suggest the role of articulation of error with regard to transference and countertransference and, with respect to the latter issue particularly, shall describe some applications to the psychotherapy of schizophrenia.

Freud's discovery of the phenomenon of transference, like his discovery of the psychological roots of errors and parapraxes, resulted from a bending of the "higher powers" by approaching the "infernal regions." Bird (1972) describes it as a creative leap and calls it an "unbelievable discovery" (p. 269). As we know, the phenomenon of transference became apparent to Freud during the same period that his colleague Breuer fled in "distaste and repudiation" (Freud, 1914a, p. 12) from his patient, Anna O., and when Freud himself was experiencing his own two patients' excessive feelings of love for him to be quite bothersome. In his first use of the term "transference" he defined it as a "false connection" (Freud, 1893–1895, p. 302) and at that point described it as a resistance. Not long after, in his discussion of the case of Dora, he described transference as the cornerstone of psychoanalytic treatment and called it the treatment's "most powerful ally" (Freud, 1905, p. 117); somewhat later, in the *New Introductory Lectures*, he called it treatment's "best tool" (Freud, 1917, p. 444). In these initial formulations Freud was once again able to see special meaning in apparently senseless and unacceptable behavior. In studying and explicating this phenomenon, he had again connected the

---

[3]Presentational truth is exemplified in artistic works, in which the presentation of metaphors and images instills and reveals truths about the world, whereas explicated truth is exemplified in scientific and philosophical explanation. Further clarification of these concepts is in progress.

"infernal" with a higher function and, in a manner similar to the creative work of Fleming, Pasteur, and others, articulated a false and erroneous matter into a scientific discovery.

As Freud (1917) stated, and Hoffer (1956), Bird (1972), Loewald (1980a), and others (see Weinshel, 1971) have emphasized, transference appears to be the basis for the development of human relationships throughout life, whereas the transference neurosis is a new illness developed within the treatment. In my discussion here, I shall address only the aspect of distortion and error in transference, but what I shall say does not deny the complexities and rich unfoldings involved in the development and resolution of transference in the course of treatment. The discussion shall therefore have bearing on the therapeutic action of psychoanalytic psychotherapy.

That transference involves error and distortion is an intrinsically important aspect of the phenomenon.[4] Because feelings are transferred from earlier persons and earlier experiences onto the person of the therapist, they are essentially erroneous; they are truly "wanderings." It is because these errors appear in the therapy that the therapist knows that transference exists. And for the patient, one of the aspects of the working through and resolution of the transference is a recognition of errors and distortions regarding the therapeutic situation and the therapist. With regard to the concept of an active creative process of therapeutic action, it is important to note that transference, and therefore transference error, is especially induced within the therapeutic situation. Several authors have affirmed that therapy affords, as Freud (1914b, p. 154) said, "especially favorable conditions" for the development of transference because of the formal aspects of the therapeutic situation, the therapist's empathic and interpretive interventions, as well as other factors (see Weinshel, 1971). Transference error is facilitated by the therapy and the therapist, not because of an interest in deceiving or confusing the patient, but because of the functional importance of error in therapeutic action. This action involves a creative articulation of transference errors and distortions.

Recognition of error by the patient is an early aspect of the working through and resolution of transference. This recognition may be clear

---

[4]See Gill (1982), and in this volume, for a somewhat different viewpoint.

and explicit, or only diffusely sensed or felt. Most salient is the recognition of "wandering" involving deviations of feelings and beliefs from the current reality. Once such deviations are recognized they are not merely corrected, but they are then subjected to a creative process of articulation. I say "not merely corrected" in order to emphasize the distinction from trial-and-error thinking and scientific induction. Patient and therapist do not engage in a predominantly intellectual discourse where errors about the therapist are discovered and are then systematically corrected or renounced. Some correction does occur, but other important steps are also undertaken, such as the tracing of the background of the error and its vicissitudes and permutations.

Regardless of the specific sequence and types of steps, and despite the direction of the process—I state this to avoid becoming too doctrinaire or prescriptive regarding technique—articulation of the transference error in which both separation and connection occur is an end therapeutic result. The patient is able to experience the therapist as separate from parental objects and other earlier persons but at the same time is able to connect and recathect real attributes from past and present object relationships. Also, the patient is able to separate and connect internal and external reality, as well as conscious, preconscious, and unconscious ideas and experiences. To do this, he or she has had to separate and identify psychic structures that have been renounced, projected, or disowned, and intrinsically incorporated into pathological thinking and behavior—and to connect these structures with a coherent sense of self, i.e., the sense of being an integrated volitional being responsible for all aspects of one's thought and action. Overall, in articulating transference error the patient achieves a separation between his or her past and present motives and experiences, and at the same time accepts a connection and a continuity between the present and the past. The separation of past and present defeats the repetition compulsion while the connection allows for remembering, as well as volitional, or what Loewald calls, "re-creative" repeating (1980b).

A major point is that transference error is connected and incorporated rather than obliterated in the articulation process. To follow Loewald (1980a) again: "Without such transference—of the intensity of the unconscious, of the infantile ways of experiencing life that have no language and little organization, but the indestructibility and power of the origins of life—to the preconscious and to present day life and contemporary objects—without such transference, or to the extent to which such transference miscarries, human life becomes sterile and an empty shell'' (p. 250). Interestingly, Loewald elsewhere (1980c) describes transference neurosis as a creative repetition of disease, but he is there using ''creative'' in the limited sense of ''newly produced.'' In the more extended sense of the word that I am using—newly produced and highly valued products such as works of art and scientific discoveries—the creative process consists of the working through of transference error.

The creative articulation of error process plays an important role in therapeutic action. Both therapists and patients can, however, limit the therapeutic effectiveness of this creative process because of an unwillingness to hazard error as well as an intolerance of error when it appears. Patients are characteristically unwilling to experience transference error. From the first they usually avoid, deny, and fight off involvements with the therapist that might lead to full-blown development and recognition of transference feelings. Early transference errors and distortions are clung to as especially rigid resistances in order to avoid more extensive development of transference and error. Partly this is because of fear of the impulses, structures, and affects involved in the transference illness itself, but partly—for patients of all types—there is a fear of risk, error, and new experience. On the therapist's side, there may be a fear of facilitating transference errors and a tendency to correct them as soon as they appear. Specific examples of this tendency are denying or arguing with a patient's accusations about the therapist and, a more subtle manifestation, prematurely asking for, or making, connections between a patient's current feeling about the therapist and feelings about persons in the patient's past. Another manifestation of intolerance of error is a protracted and overexhaustive error-eradicating search for each and every root of particular transference feelings.

Creative articulation of error in the therapeutic process involves the same approach to error as in the other creative processes I have described. Like the creative writer or artist, both therapist and patient need to be willing to take chances and to commit errors in both the form and the substance of their relationship. When errors occur, they need to recognize them and then to clarify them as much as possible. As a "wandering," an error provides the beginning of a separation which, through constant clarification, yields up some of its unconscious content and intent. Rather than exhaustive breakdown and analysis—using the latter word in its precise meaning of systematic dissection—the error is connected, usually through interpretive interventions, to issues in the patient's current and past life. When the connections suggested are appropriate or correct, further separations occur in the form of introduction of new material by the patient, and these separations can be further connected into articulated structures. When the connections suggested are inappropriate or wrong, therapist and patient need to clarify these and to examine them as new errors; these too may yield meaningful new separations. An overall result of this continuing process of separating and connecting is the creative integration of the patient's personality.

With regard to countertransference, the process of articulation of error operates in a somewhat different but related way. While countertransference surely involves error and distortion in a manner similar to transference, the therapist by and large articulates countertransference error privately, without the patient's direct collaboration. There are significant exceptions to this which deserve attention in their own right, but first I would like to emphasize that the therapist's continual attention to countertransference—another cornerstone of psychoanalytic therapy—appropriately involves both an inductive process involving recognition with change and correction of error, and a creative articulation process in which countertransference errors are separated and connected directly in the therapeutic work. For example, a therapist may be troubled by growing aggressive feelings toward a patient and he recognizes that they are a response in part to the patient's masochistic stance. While he privately analyzes the roots of his own discomfort, he may also share his recognition explicitly with the patient in order to help loosen masochistic defenses and reduce the patient's resistant stance. Here the articulation process involves the simultaneous separating and connecting of the elements in both the therapist's and the patient's aggressive impulses.

Countertransference error cannot generally be managed privately when the therapist makes an overt mistake, either in the form of forgetting, distortion, or parapraxis, or else in the form of a technical therapeutic error. Such therapist mistakes almost inevitably do become a manifest issue in the therapy. Indeed, a technical point bearing emphasis is that overt therapist mistakes should properly become a manifest issue in the therapy. To some degree, this point follows the well-established therapeutic maxim of making all issues with an emotional charge—which therapist errors inevitably possess—"grist for the mill" in therapy. To go beyond mere acknowledgment of a therapist error, however—or, to take the gristmill metaphor literally, to go beyond a systematic and sometimes sterile grinding down—and attempt a creative articulation of the error is a therapeutic challenge.

When the therapist makes an overt mistake or error, he is vividly provided a clue to his own unconscious concerns and therefore to countertransference matters to be articulated in the therapy. This is so whether or not the patient openly notes the mistake, because almost invariably it is registered, consciously or unconsciously. Overt disregard on the patient's part probably requires attention in its own right as a first step. When the patient does point out or otherwise openly responds to the therapist error, the articulation process can develop actively. For example, a patient became interested in a psychiatry text on her therapist's bookshelf and asked if she could borrow it. The therapist, for various conscious reasons, decided to deviate from routine practice with this quite difficult patient, and he lent it to her. While he had considered this at the time to be possibly a minor technical error, several sessions later he learned of a rather extensive mistake. His patient told him that she had found a passage in the book underlined, with her own name penciled by him in the margin. It was a passage about the dynamics of acting out. Remembering that he had underlined that passage because he thought it applied particularly to that patient, he felt embarrassed and disturbed. Immediately he apologized to the patient and told her he had made a mistake, but she became hostile and derisive toward him for some time afterward.

Later, when he gave some extended consideration to the reason he had made this particular error, his associations led him to the realization that he had recently thought of giving this patient a manual of sexual information because, though she was an adult, she seemed to have very little valid knowledge about sex. This realization led him to recognize distinct feelings of sexual attraction to the patient. The patient seemed also to be struggling with sexual feelings toward him. Now, if this understanding of his feelings had been available to him at the time the patient challenged him with his mistake, could he have articulated the error? Could he indeed have articulated the error even later? Merely acknowledging the error and apologizing served very little therapeutic purpose in this case; it was an instance of pure correcting rather than articulation. Silence, or focusing on the patient's hostile affect, would probably have escalated the patient's hostility and alienation. Under certain circumstances—depending on the level and current state of treatment—the therapist could have acknowledged his error and, touching on his realization of his sexual attraction to the patient, he could have indicated that he was probably responding to sexual feelings in her. This is in part an articulating type of response because it separates a salient factor in the error and connects it to the therapeutic interaction. In most cases, however, such specificity is threatening and counterproductive and the most appropriate articulating response would be the following: ''I think the reason I may have given you that book when you asked for it was that I somehow wanted to convey to you that you have been acting out some feelings that are bothersome to you.'' In response to this, the patient would presumably ask for, and would also provide, further clarification that would eventually articulate the sexual factors in the interaction.

In another instance, a hospitalized patient was erroneously informed by her therapist that Good Friday was a hospital holiday, and that their therapy session that day would be canceled. As it turned out, the hospital had never provided a Good Friday holiday, and in the next therapy session, two days later, the patient angrily confronted the therapist with his mistake. She insisted that the mistake inconvenienced her terribly because she had decided to go home for a visit on the Good Friday weekend, and she was now forced to change all her plans in order not to miss the reinstated therapy session. When the therapist hesitated before responding to her onslaught, she walked out of the therapy session in fury. Thinking about his mistake later, this therapist became aware that he had in fact wished to avoid seeing the patient because of material in her therapy sessions of the previous days. She had been talking about her father's successful suicide, and this had touched on the therapist's feelings about his own mother's suicide attempt many years before.

When the patient returned the next day for her regularly scheduled session, the therapist focused on his mistake and on the patient's response to it. He attempted to get her to clarify why his making a mistake was such an issue for her, and whether she felt that he must never err at all and therefore not be human. He also asked what it was that had made her walk furiously out of the previous session. She responded that she had left the session because the therapist "just sat there and didn't do anything." Realizing that she was referring to his lack of action about her plans for a weekend trip, the therapist said that he thought she had the topic of leaving on her mind and connected that idea with her leaving the session. The patient then indicated that leaving the hospital for the weekend trip to her mother's house was a problem for her, and she revealed her deep ambivalence about going. Talking of feelings of hatred for her mother, she described current suicidal preoccupations of her own.

While there are numerous psychodynamic factors operating in this sequence of events, I want only to point out the matter of articulation. The therapist's rather simple and unelaborate response was a creative, articulating one because it separated and connected salient issues in the error. Connecting the patient's leaving the office to the topic of leaving itself served to separate out the issue of her leaving the hospital to go home. This in turn served to separate out the issue of death, a salient matter involved both in his mistake and in the patient's furious response, and surely also in the symbolic meaning of Good Friday itself. For the patient, death and suicidal feelings were connected with feelings of hatred toward her mother. By recognizing his own countertransference concerns, the therapist was able to focus on his error without guilt and to see its connection to her feelings about leaving on a trip. As with the artistic examples discussed earlier, such articulation does not involve the obliteration or covering up of error, but instead lets it stand and uses it in the overall effect.

Articulation of error may have its greatest therapeutic pertinence in the treatment of schizophrenia. Although the patient I just described was borderline rather than schizophrenic, a particular feature of the therapist's response with that patient has general application and importance in the psychotherapy of schizophrenia. This is the feature of connecting error with humanness and being human. In schizophrenia, as in all narcissistic disorders, there invariably is a preoccupation with perfection (Rothstein, 1980) and, because of primitive fusions and projective identifications, there is an inability to accept any lack of perfection in the therapist. Moreover, disavowal of therapist error together with disavowal of errors by, or in, the patient's self, serves to deny that both therapist and patient are human beings. It is a vicious circle involving omnipotent perfectionism along with the patient's feelings of being a nonhuman entity in the first place. And it is a circle that is in part broken by the therapist's active use of error.

The use of error in the therapy of schizophrenic patients seldom can consist merely of the acknowledgment of error because such patients can neither forgive, nor forget, nor learn from what is not accepted. So important is this matter that there is a sense in which the psychotherapy of schizophrenia seems to move along, and to progress, by means of a coping with, and a handling, of error. To the therapist actively engaged in such treatment it often appears as though the course of therapy consists of a series of encounters that sometimes go smoothly, but which are invariably disrupted or interrupted in some way by a therapist error. Such an error is almost always a very minuscule and hidden one—seldom of the proportions of an overt mistake about canceling a session—but it is experienced as devastating by the patient and leads to major disruption in the therapy. Weeks or months may go by while the disruption continues in the form of patient withdrawal, or regression and flagrant psychotic production, and the patient covertly indicates the nature of the therapist's mistake in seemingly chance or indirect comments or behavior. When the patient is at a relatively high level of integration, or when there is some degree of engagement and understanding in the therapy, the disruptive response may be more gradual and progressive. At first there may only be lateness for appointments, silence, or the actual missing of sessions. If such reactions are not clarified, and the therapist's error is not somehow incorporated into the therapy, more disruption usually ensues.

Lest I be misunderstood on this matter, I do not mean to say that therapist and patient always discuss each error explicitly after a disruption occurs, nor do I mean that the therapist learns the precise nature of each error he has committed. Sometimes a schizophrenic patient may reveal the nature of these errors weeks or months after a disruption has ceased, or sometimes not until the termination phase of the therapy. What I mean is that the therapist recognizes that the patient's disruption is related to something done or not done in the therapy and, when recognizing an error, the therapist does not pull back, either by simple apology or by rapid correction, but attempts both to separate and connect the error in an articulation process.

Errors in the psychotherapy of schizophrenia are by no means errors in ordinary interaction. Such patients are so exquisitely tuned to rejection and so constantly suspicious of others' reactions that they ferret out and attack the slightest whisper of countertransference and, along with that, the slightest suggestion of the therapist's need. They cannot tolerate any lack of omniscience and consequent imperfection and humanity. For instance, take approval by the therapist in a therapy hour. Patients with very low self-esteem sometimes are ambivalent and uncomfortable about a therapist's tacit or explicit approval of something they have done. With the schizophrenic patient, however, there may be regression or actual disruption of treatment following a compliment—on work in an hour, on general progress, on a generous action—or even when the therapist simply appears gratified by the patient's words or actions. Because we cannot always anticipate this in advance, and because we cannot, and should not, monitor all our positive reactions, we must—strange to say—commit errors of approval. In treating schizophrenia, by and large, we are destined to err to such a degree that error itself becomes a major focus. For the therapist, examination of what appears as error allows for the close monitoring and use of countertransference issues and, on a reciprocal basis, insight into the nature of the patient's transference. For the patient, articulation of errors, instead of simple correction, teaches acknowledgment and acceptance of human imperfection. Also, articulation is a key factor in the overall creation of personality structure and integration by therapist and patient working together.

This is not to say that we do not learn from our errors, nor that we do not in some sense actively correct them in the course of therapy.

In recognizing and focusing on our errors, both learning and correcting inevitably occur. But, using the work of creative thinkers as our guide, we should, if we possess the requisite therapeutic skill, be not at all afraid of making errors; we should in fact—especially in the treatment of schizophrenics—allow ourselves a freedom that incurs, even courts, errors and mistakes. We court errors in order to articulate them and so incorporate into the therapy our own and our patient's individuality, and the humanity of both.

References

Beres, D. (1957), Communication in psychoanalysis and in the creative process: A parallel. *J. Amer. Psychoanal. Assn.*, 5:408–423.

Bird, B. (1972), Notes on transference: Universal phenomenon and hardest part of analysis. *J. Amer. Psychoanal. Assn.*, 20:267–301.

Delbrück, B. (1887), Amnestische aphasie. *Sitzungsberichte der Jenaischen Gesellschaft fur Medizin und Naturcerssenschaft*, 10:91.

Ellis, A.W. (1980), On the Freudian theory of speech errors. In: *Errors in Linguistic Performance*, ed. V.A. Fromkin. New York: Academic Press, pp. 123–132.

Freud, S. (1893–1895), The psychotherapy of hysteria. *Standard Edition*, 2:255–305. London: Hogarth Press, 1955.

—————— (1896), Letter to Fliess, April 12, 1896. In: *The Origins of Psychoanalysis*, ed. M. Bonaparte, A. Freud, & E. Kris. New York: Basic Books, 1954.

—————— (1900), The Interpretation of Dreams. *Standard Edition*, 4/5. London: Hogarth Press, 1953.

—————— (1901), The psychopathology of everyday life. *Standard Edition*, 6:1–279. London: Hogarth Press, 1960.

—————— (1905), Fragment of an analysis of a case of hysteria. *Standard Edition*, 7:7–122. London: Hogarth Press, 1953.

—————— (1914a), On the history of the psycho-analytic movement. *Standard Edition*, 14:7–71. London: Hogarth Press, 1957.

—————— (1914b), Remembering, repeating, and working through. *Standard Edition*, 12:146–156. London: Hogarth Press, 1958.

—————— (1916–1917), Introductory lectures on psychoanalysis (Parts I and II). *Standard Edition*, 15:15–239. London: Hogarth Press, 1963.

—————— (1917), Introductory lectures on psychoanalysis (Part III). *Standard Edition*, 16:243–463. London: Hogarth Press, 1963.

—————— (1935), The subtleties of a faulty action. *Standard Edition*, 22:233–235. London: Hogarth Press, 1964.

Gabelentz, G., von der (1891), *Die Sprachwissenschaft: Ihre dufgaben Methoden, und Bisherigen Ergebnisse*. Leipzig: T.O. Weigel.

Gill, M. M. (1982), Analysis of Transference. *Psychological Issues*, Monogr. 53. New York: International Universities Press.

Hersey, J. (1966), *Too Far to Walk*. New York: Knopf.

Hoffer, W. (1956), Transference and transference neurosis. *Internat. J. Psycho-Anal.*, 37:377–379.

Jacobs, C. (1960), Psychology of music: Some European studies. *Acta Psychologia*, 17:273–297.

Jespersen, O. (1894), *Progress in Language with Special References to English.* London: Sonnenchein.

Kris, E. (1952), *Psychoanalytic Explorations in Art.* New York: International Universities Press.

Loewald, H. W. (1980a), On the therapeutic action of psychoanalysis. In: *Papers on Psychoanalysis.* New Haven, CT: Yale University Press, pp. 221–256.

——— (1980b), Some considerations on repetition and the repetition compulsion. In: *Papers on Psychoanalysis.* New Haven, CT: Yale University Press, pp. 87–101.

——— (1980c), The transference neurosis: Comments on the concept and the phenomenon. In: *Papers on Psychoanalysis.* New Haven, CT: Yale University Press, pp. 302–314.

Meringer, R. (1908), *Aus dem leben der sprache.* Berlin: Behr.

——— Mayer, C. (1895), *Versprechen und verlesen, eine psychologisch-linguerstische studie.* Stuttgart: Göschense Verlagsbuchhandlung.

Motley, M.T. (1980), Verification of 'Freudian Slips' and semantic prearticulatory editing via laboratory-induced spoonerisms. In: *Errors in Linguistic Performance*, ed. V.A. Fromkin. New York: Academic Press, pp. 133–148.

——— (1938), *More Stately Mansions.* New Haven, CT: Yale University Press, 1964.

O'Neill, E. G. (1940), *The Iceman Cometh.* In: *The Plays of Eugene O'Neill.* New York: Random House, 1954.

Paul, H. (1880), *Prinzipien der Sprachgeschichte.* Halle a.d.s.: Niemeyer.

Reitman, W. R. (1966), *Cognition and Thought.* New York: Wiley.

Rothenberg, A. (1969), The iceman changeth: Toward an empirical approach to creativity. *J. Amer. Psychoanal. Assn.*, 17:549–607.

——— (1972), Poetic process and psychotherapy. *Psychiat.*, 35:238–254.

——— (1979a), Einstein's creative thinking and the general theory of relativity: A documented report. *Amer. J. Psychiat.*, 136:38–43.

——— (1979b), *The Emerging Goddess: The Creative Process in Art, Science, and Other Fields.* Chicago: University of Chicago Press.

——— (1983a), Creativity, articulation, and psychotherapy. *J. Acad. Psychoanal.*, 11:55–85.

——— (1983b), Janusian process and scientific creativity: The case of Niels Bohr. *Contemp. Psychoanal.*, 19:100–119.

Rothstein, A. (1980), *The Narcissistic Pursuit of Perfection.* New York: International Universities Press.

Weigert, E. (1970), The goal of creativity in psychotherapy. In: *The Courage to Love.* New Haven, CT: Yale University Press, pp. 73–107.

Weinshel, E. M. (1971), The transference neurosis: A survey of the literature. *J. Amer. Psychoanal. Assn.*, 19:67–88.

FIGURE 1: Henri Matisse: *Bather* (summer 1909). Oil on canvas, 36½ × 29⅛″ (92.7 × 74 cm.). *Collection, The Museum of Modern Art, New York.* Gift of Abby Aldrich Rockefeller.

Part III

Therapy

FIGURE 2: The Christ symbol.

FIGURE 3: The Christopher symbol. The patient can add to her negative self-identity, represented by the devils' horns, the therapeutic aura, since the therapist introjects the aggressivity of the patient and ''adds'' her devils' horns to his aura.

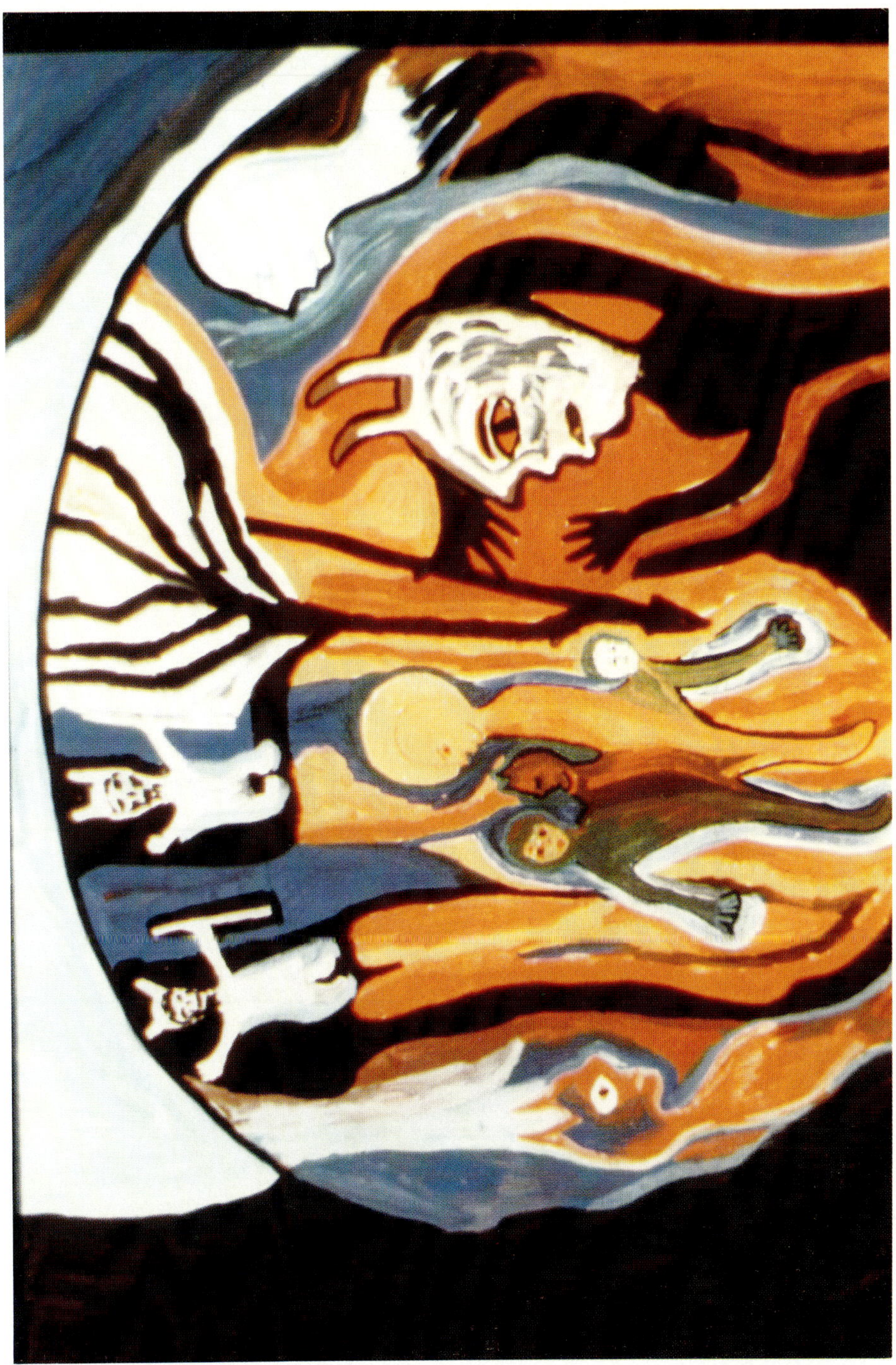

FIGURE 4: The symbiosis symbol. The therapist is in the patient's hell, fused with her. He is, however, taller than the split parts of the patient and so can organize them in a unity.

FIGURE 5: The symbiosis symbol. The therapist is able to differentiate himself from the patient, who appears therefore less frightened. The therapist is still in the patient's hell: ''descensus ad inferno.''

FIGURE 6: The resistance symbol. Between the therapist—who appears like a mother—and the fragmented dark parts of the patient is still an iron wire. But a part of the patient has already gone through the wire and has become a unified bright identity.

FIGURE 7: The destructiveness symbol. Self-perpetuation through birth is interrupted by the eye of insight.

9

Illuminations of the Human Condition in the Encounter with the Psychotic Patient

Gaetano Benedetti, M.D.

In his presentation at the Fourth International Symposium on Psychotherapy of Schizophrenia in Turku, August 1971, entitled "Psychotherapy and Schizophrenia: Implications for Human Living," Otto Allen Will (1972) said in conclusion: "What we call psychotherapy is an aspect of interpersonal events and has a greater significance than the term 'therapeutic procedure' might imply." Also: "I find myself once again suggesting that the study of schizophrenic phenomena from an interpersonal-social point of view offers further promise of increasing our knowledge of human living."

I hope the following eight points will show how this promise has been fulfilled in my own work during the past ten years.

I. Psychotherapy in general, and that of the psychotic patient in particular, with which this paper is concerned, is, on the one hand, a "technical" approach to a psychopathological subject. It is also, however, for *us*, an experience which mirrors our ways of relating with our patient, and for this reason a new discovery of ourselves, and of the world in the mirror of our contact with him.

This kind of *reciprocity* is fundamental to the success of a psychotherapist. It would not be possible to work on a patient through

185

our own self if this—our self—did not discover in the contact with the patient the possibility of a dual meaning, which then becomes our message to the patient. We communicate to him not only what he, "objectively" speaking, appears to us to be, that is to say, the object of psychodynamic mechanisms; we also communicate to him *the meaning his existence holds for our own*: enrichment, surprise, reflection. It is only in this way that we can communicate to him an image which is not only reductive of himself, but prospective, and we communicate to him also an image of ourselves which may enrich and transform his image of himself. In this act of communication, which is reflected by him to us, we too are changed, and it is this, our very ability to let ourselves be transformed, deepened, and enriched, which has an effect upon him.

If, therefore, this type of therapy is for the patient a modification of his existence which allows him to gain greater fulfillment from his life, it is for us an illumination of our common human existence. Perhaps it is really our very "gain" from the "contact" with the patient that constitutes a mainspring of his improvement, insofar as he thus undergoes the fundamental experience of giving as well as receiving.

This reciprocity constitutes one of the very essentials of the treatment, for no one is as disillusioned as the psychotic patient is with the whole range of social formulas that have been offered him over the course of time. What is really meaningful for him is not only interpretation, but also the experience of it that he, a being who is otherwise lacking in impact, can still instigate in others; in us, his therapists and his partners.

II. This first illumination opens our eyes to a second "interpersonal field." We help the patient not only by showing him the psychodynamic linings of the clothes of his illness, and not only by the reciprocity of the relationship, but also *by confronting him with his potential image in ourselves*: an image which is almost beautiful, an image of wholeness in fragmentation, of transparency in autism, of soundness in delusion. It is, however, an image that he must find in us in order to break through the confines of the splitting, the autism, the delusion. It is as if there were, at the base of the psychotherapy, the capacity for seeing the defects, the shortcomings, the wretchedness, and ugliness of a patient who is always mirrored by a spiritual transcendence that is like the reflection of the suffering of Christ (Figure 2, preceding p. 185). The patient bears his own cross, he helps us to bear the weight of the suffering of the world.

But such a reflected image does not exist in the ego of the patient; it does not exist even in his unconscious, where, as Freud stated, the object representations are dissolved; it is first formed in ourselves, and then in him only to the extent that we can become close to him. Through the psychotherapy is built up the potential image that transcends the mental misery. At this point comes the second human illumination in the encounter.

A patient relates his dream of finding himself in a void, of sitting on a coffin, the contents of which are unknown to him. In the patient's image there is the terrible ''real-life'' experience of nonexistence. Why are the contents of the coffin unknown? Because they consist of nothing, or at most a skeleton, in other words, a definite message of death which the patient desperately represses.

The interpretation of repression in psychoanalysis is significant, because in the content of the repression, however fearful it is, there is always life, and this must be recovered in order to be assimilated.

In such a case, however, the interpretation meets a nothingness into whose vacuum the therapist may feel himself being dragged; from this springs up fear of, and social aggression toward, psychotics.

The therapist offered here to the patient not an interpretation, but a symbol of transformation. She suggested to him that in the coffin might be hidden an ancient family manuscript, a lost document on which his life depended. From this image ensued a dialogue in which the patient eventually expressed his wish to undertake a long journey in the desert, together with the therapist, to search for the manuscript.

The desert was the transformation of the symbol of autistic death into a symbol which, while connoting emptiness and barrenness, was open to dual experience—to travel, to movement, to the accompanying presence of the therapist.

The creation of symbols, one may object, is not objective, not scientific enough; it is the work of a fertile imagination. But, basically, is this not also true of their interpretation? The discovery of explicatory models is a creative act based on certain factual observations. The factual observation present here is not simply the result of objective examination; it is also the potential image of the patient formed in the therapeutic mirror.

III. If the potential image of the patient is first developed in the psychotherapist, then the patient's turning into this image, the discovery that he makes himself into this, first rejecting it, then listening to it, trying it out, feeling it, little by little making it his own through the "appersonating" emotions of the partner, is the out-and-out creation of a new self. This *work of "self-creation" by the affixing of parts of the therapist* can be seen in the image of Christopher (Figure 3, preceding p. 185), visualized by one of my female patients, in which she "added" to her negative self-identity, represented by devils' horns, my own psychotherapeutic aura. This became a part of her, a part of what otherwise belonged to a world disassociated from the patient, and which then returned into her by way of a "therapeutic symbiosis" (Figures 4 and 5, preceding p. 185).

In the delusion of a paranoid patient the universe was a malign ramification of tubes that sucked his blood and were connected to the other pole, the persecutor, the "deus ex machina" of the destructive labyrinth. When, during the course of the psychotherapy, this demon gradually took on the features of the therapist, the patient at first had iron defenses against it; but then, to the extent that some messages of love succeeded in getting through this defense and reaching the patient, a gradual transformation of the persecutor took place: he no longer "robbed" the patient of his blood, but now, as the patient stated, "introduced" drops of his own into the common metabolism. The blood of the therapist now created a new self-image in the patient, and it was able to do this because it was, metaphorically speaking, the introjection by the therapist of the potential positive image of the patient.

The new self is thus created from "transitional objects," which arise in the space between the patient and the partner. The former, out of touch with the real world, which influences him and persecutes him with images that are alienating for him, is now nourished by this process, with positive images arising in the mind of the therapist, but originating, in the first place, from the patient himself, from his impact upon his partner. He receives from the therapist a self-image that has been positivised during its transplantation onto the partner, and which is reintrojected after having passed through his own psychic metabolism.

A patient feared the eyes of his therapist. He felt he was being hypnotized and killed by them. The following night the therapist dreamed that he saw the eyes of his patient, which were staring at him. They were enormous and terrible, as the therapist's eyes had been in the patient's experience. The therapist trembled with anxiety, but could withstand the look because it seemed to him, in his dream, to be that of eternity itself. We see here a reversal of the death experience of the patient into a fearful but grandiose life experience of the therapist.

IV. This creation of the new self is the fruit of the processes of the patient's identification with the therapist. These processes have become possible due to the analyst's ability to find himself within the delusion of the patient, to the peregrinations in his own dreams through the backstreets of madness, or to his dressing himself in the patient's clothes, hearing himself called in his sleep by the patient's own name. The partial reciprocal identification results, because of the fermentative process of duality, in an increase in value, a "positivisation" of the two partners. Thus, one of my patients, Hans Peter, dreamed that he was visited at the hour of his death by two people, one of whom was called Hans and the other Peter; both—said the patient, looking at me—were blind in one eye, "just as you, yourself, are!"; and I was of help to them.

The development of the identification process is based upon the therapeutic experience of putting oneself in the patient's own shoes as he is in his delusion, while respecting this delusion, his resistance and autistic withdrawal.

I have discussed my experiences of sharing the psychotic delusion with a few therapist colleagues who firmly reject any type of identification with the psychotic experience. These colleagues stick doggedly to the scanty areas of awareness and retention of ego that are never totally lacking in the schizophrenic, even if only traces of them are present. By identifying with these fragments of the functioning ego, they strengthen them, they broaden them, and thus they make possible a slow and progressive weakening of the delusion. Reflecting on the positive therapeutic results of these two different approaches, we have realized that the "therapeutic constant" present in both is the ability to share aspects of the psychotic personality that society is not capable of sharing.

The discovery by the patient of his own potential positive image, within the persona of the therapist, leads to an act of partial identification of the patient with the therapist, a move I call *counteridentification*. Whereas in the psychoanalysis of neurosis the countertransference is a reaction to the patient, in the psychotherapy of psychoses the first constructive step is taken by the therapist. The counteridentification of the patient signals his approach toward coherence and soundness, as represented in the therapist, which then serves as a matrix for the new structuring of the patient's self. Instead of wanting to adapt the patient to society or to the norm of reason, we, by sharing his symbols, adapt ourselves to him, so that the patient approaches the model of an other who does not alarm him with his reason and coherence, for the very reason that he has intentionally made himself like the patient.

V. I remember a schizophrenic patient whose fundamental psychotic experience was that of being enclosed in an autistic shell that prevented her from knowing that other people existed inwardly, transforming them into so many lifeless "clay models." Naturally, the process of "reification" involved the patient's ego no less than it did the world; just as she saw everywhere, in her daily life, a lifeless pseudonormality, so had she, lacking life in her duality experience, become a clay figure, without a spirit, without even a living body.

During the course of therapy the patient discovered that her experience was partly the consequence of early experience with a destructive mother. Afterward "something inside her" had continued to deny the reality of any human message. When, during a psychotherapeutic sitting composed of bursts of aggression and destructive negation, the patient at last developed a positive transference, her greatest suffering consisted of the perception of an internal "voice" that repeated the denial, including in its field of application even myself. A good part of the psychotherapy, and of the experience of the patient, now assumed the form of a continuous protest against the "false wall" that separated her from me as the result of her negativism. In spite of this, the patient developed a transference that was not just a transfer of past behavioral patterns onto a new partner, but rather something totally new in the patient's history. This patient "lived" waiting for just a few minutes of conversation with me. Without my physical presence she remained dead, clay; in my presence there was a drop of life in her; the fragmented parts of her ego recomposed themselves. I do not believe that in any truthful, friendly relationship such total dedication to the other as was shown by this patient is possible. It was the extreme intensity of this experience that made her "die" now, to the same extent as she had "lived" the clay death. It was a death by unsatisfiable longing for communication, inasmuch as the internal denial of the psychotic voice continued to separate her from me (Figure 6, preceding p. 185). It was her desire to communicate, the like of which I have never otherwise felt in a human being, that could finally erode, break down the density of the autistic wall that had held her prisoner for so many years.

It was as if the psychopathological phenomenon—in this case, autism—had evoked in the patient, who was capable of contending with it, the realization of a different and opposing existential plane, just as intense as the psychopathological one. Psychopathology inverted itself. This change in direction, in its departure from the norm, showed psychopathological features, but it contained an opposing trend as well, one headed toward duality, and thus transcended psychopathology itself. Our contact with the psychotic sets us squarely before positive phenomena found at the edges of existence; and in this fact lies another illumination born of this type of psychotherapy.

VI. It is here that the concept of *progressive psychopathology* enters. By this I mean a type of psychopathology that is not marked by a return to infantile forms of experience as is the purely regressive type, or rather, as psychiatry understands it, by disintegration of the higher levels of cognitive and behavioral organization into lower levels. Progressive psychopathology is marked, rather, by the fact that, in the persistence of behavioral patterns still definable as psychopathological, new intentionalities grow forth that go beyond psychopathology. Let us describe these intentionalities as psychosynthetic, restorative, communicative—in a word, as antipsychopathological. However, these cannot be brought out other than by respecting the psychotic design within which they arise.

Splitting becomes progressive, for example, wherever the patient is separated into a psychopathological half, his old self, and a new half that bears the characteristics of the therapist but is already part of the patient.

Appersonation is progressive when the patient takes on features of the outside world, of the therapist, but these no longer as alienating forces which estrange him from himself, but rather as features which permit him to arrive at a state of greater self-integration.

Hallucination is progressive when the patient listens from afar to the voice (which is therefore internal) of the therapist which communicates to him interpretations which in reality are never spoken, but which, within the reality of the therapy, could not be better than the ones he hallucinated.

Transitivism is progressive when the patient notices some internal self-searching motions as if these were movements of the therapist looking for him.

Hallucinatory memory is progressive when the patient, suffering from derealization, experiences for the first time the richness of reality by hallucinating the memory of a past conflict.

Delusion is progressive when within it occurs an act of synthesis between the good and bad parts of himself.

At this point I cite the case of a patient who, after having at the start of his psychosis hallucinated a fantastic spaceship that was to have taken him back to his ''true homeland''—a planet of violence and terror—at least accepted the therapeutic validity of standing back from these terrifying specters, of which he was both the master and the persecuted; the following delusion then ensued: The aforementioned planet was, in the new delusion, the earth of forty years before, when he had imagined himself to have been a Nazi officer who had sown terror around him. Now the patient no longer wanted to regress to that earlier way of life, but to pay for the suffering he had then caused others. The patient thus became depressed. In the new delusion, which was in fact ''progressive,'' was to be seen Melanie Klein's depressive position, or rather the *synthesis* of the patient's bad parts with the good ones which had been reintegrated by means of the therapeutic experience.

Thus, the discovery of a progressive psychopathology is an illumination of the human condition.

VII. In almost every point of view considered until now, the underlying principle is therapeutic love. This feeling, otherwise well hidden in the folds of the psychoanalysis, must, in the experience with the psychotic patient, courageously bare itself in order to become, in the dialectic of its motivations and limits, an illumination of the human condition.

However, since Freud has opposed hate to love in the polarity of existence, I would like to reflect upon the problem of countertransferential *aggression*. What do we learn here about man, in the extreme situation represented by contact with the psychotic patient?

The origins of countertransferential aggression are almost impossible to "individuate" here. We know that a patient unconsciously *causes* our countertransference; that our perception of aggressive psychic tendencies, which are evoked in ourselves by the patient's behavior, may constitute a piece of useful information concerning the state of the patient's unconscious. This is perceived by us even before it is within our capabilities to examine it cognitively. However, the introjection is reciprocal, interpersonal. Aggressions of the patient can be due to an unconscious aggressivity in the therapist. This double introjection seems to be an example of how self-awareness is fundamentally structured in duality. Furthermore, cases do exist in which we gain information about the unconscious state of the patient not only by sensing an "irrational" feeling of aggression toward him, but also by becoming aware of an "unusual" aggression (which may be rational or irrational, but different from our characteristic reaction patterns) toward certain aspects of the world. The following example will illustrate this.

A psychotherapist observes an aggressivity in his daily life, toward objects other than his patient, which is foreign to his character and his usual reactions. He is surprised at himself; he is not able to understand this phenomenon, which he has not yet connected with his patient or his countertransference. Later it becomes clear that the patient is coming into a new phase of his development, one characterized by a release of an emotion—in this case, aggression—which had disturbed the therapist. The patient becomes more aggressive; he is less afraid to express his aggressivity and to integrate it after the therapist has partially taken this emotion into his own daily life.

Examination of these cases has shown us that our own counter-transferential aggressivity is not only an "unconscious appersonation" of that of the patient, but that it is also a "substituting" phenomenon that demonstrates, so to speak, the amenability of our unconscious to occupy a place in an existence that is important for the future of the patient. Indeed, the latter progresses, developing soon after we do a psychic role consisting of constructive aggressivity, which was until that moment impossible for him, taking shape around his empathetic perception of our unconscious.

The study of these phenomena is significant in that it makes us aware of the structure of empathy. This structure shows us how the birth of the self is composed of a mixture of interchangeable parts of oneself and others. As this interchange, which we shall liken to a physiological birth, repeats and magnifies itself in the psychotherapy of psychosis, it is, as is no other type of psychoanalysis, an illumination of the human condition.

I see a triple function of countertransferential aggressivity as long as it is well moderated. To start with, it is restricted by the love for the patient and so it is always, implicitly, a proposal of human aggressivity to the patient. The omnipotence of the persecutor is the tragic omnipotence of the patient, and so it is, at the same time, the tragic powerlessness of the victim. Therapeutic aggressivity is, on the contrary, a bearer of the suffering caused by having to be like this, by the tragic sense of life.

Second, therapeutic aggressivity is not only restricted by love, but is also compatible with it; in other words, it is always subject to a psychosynthesis between "good self" and "bad self," "good object" and "bad object." This psychosynthetic pattern urges the patient to overcome his desolating split state wherever the continued offer of the good therapeutic self *alone* makes the psychotic feel the full weight of the difference and inevitability of his bad self.

Third, there is not only the possibility of psychosynthesis in the presence of splitting in others, but also the opposite. Countertransferential aggressivity may indeed split the therapist between that part of him which identifies with the patient and that which rejects him; between that part which understands the patient before words are spoken and the other which remains confused about him, which cannot find any sense in what he says; between that part which experiences the patient's sitting as a waste of time, and the opposite which feels his suffering as if it were the pivot of all worldly suffering. The therapist is therefore "split." He has taken upon himself the patient's splitting in order to relive it within a coherent model, his own self; to reproduce it within a framework that will not break; to transform it from inside and give it back, new, to the patient.

VIII. We do not know how destructiveness originates, neither psychotic destructiveness (which is said to be due to the family, to society, to physical constitution, or even to a prenatal phase of being in the patient), nor human destructiveness generally. At the edges of theoretical reason it is brought up against, to paraphrase Kant, the power of practical reason; the power of "knowing" destructiveness by being involved in the clash with it, which is a much deeper knowledge than that which makes it a topic of natural science.

During the contact with the psychotic patient, his destructiveness is experienced in all its manifestations—raving, hallucination, splitting. These are always the perpetuation of an original destructiveness, the roots of which, for me, are at the base of the very psychosis, whether schizophrenic or depressive.

Now, in the psychotherapy, we interpret this destructiveness in all the details of its tragic interactions. We urge the patient to see his destructive impulses and to set himself at a distance from them. But no interpretation, however careful and intelligent, would ever have the power to induce the patient to dislodge himself once and for all from that destructive iceberg, to disidentify himself from his impulses, if there were not something fundamental which permitted a new knowledge of it. *We expose ourselves to this, we undergo the impact, we share it.* We accept feeling the impossibility of the accusations, the autistic wall, the coldness of the psychosis, the horror of the delusion, the boredom and the terror of the void, the barrenness and inanity of so many sittings with the patient; we even run the risk of his being physically violent. And what is more, by exposing ourselves to his direct assaults, fortunately mostly verbal, *we tragically introject his aggressivity*, developing counteraggressive impulses which are still useful, very, from a therapeutic viewpoint, because they are bearers of a form of contact, because they are messengers of a dual reality.

However, they still threaten to damage the patient, while we, on the other hand, see him in all his fragility. We are somehow ''contaminated'' by the patient's aggressivity.

Well, in all this, we have shared the seeds from which psychosis springs; and by not ceasing, in this state, to love our patient, we have proved to him the possibility of uniting and integrating good and bad objects, so that he may do this with us. That is to say, we have in a sense eliminated that frenzied terror of destructiveness that belongs to the realms of psychopathology and is a fount of its perpetuation (Figure 7, preceding p. 185).

Of course, all this is not specific to the psychotherapy of psychosis. Psychoanalysis is also concerned with these problems. But no type of treatment exposes us to such horizons as does the treatment of the psychotic patient. Aggressivity is transferred, above all, by our own internal transformation of it, not without a battle, and with the longing to be different. And the psychotic patient, in this light, becomes our teacher.

Reference

Will, O. A. (1972), Psychotherapy and schizophrenia: Implications for human living. In: *Psychotherapy of Schizophrenia: Proceedings of the Fourth International Symposium on Psychotherapy of Schizophrenia, Turku, Finland, 1971*, ed. D. Rubinstein & Y.O. Alanen. Amsterdam: Excerpta Medica, pp. 130–155.

10

Suicide and the Impact on the Therapist

Beatriz Foster, M.D.

Four years ago a patient of mine died. She was the second patient of mine in a period of two-and-a-half years to commit suicide. Since that second suicide, of which I was informed in Europe, where I had arrived the previous night to give seminars, I have not given a paper, participated in meetings, or been part of any professional group. Whenever I was invited to participate, I declined on the grounds that I had nothing to say.

When I was asked to share in honoring my friend Otto Will, I accepted without hesitation. The yes was to the honoring of my friend. I still felt I had nothing to say.

One night, a few weeks after accepting the invitation, I awakened from a dream. I don't recall the dream. I was sitting up, and saying out loud, ''The void awaits all those who weave the wind,'' and my first thought was about the suicides. I realized then that the impact they had had on me was, perhaps, what I had to offer at this time. This is a very short presentation and it is presented to you as a question or a number of questions for which I am still seeking answers. The questions are, How does suicide affect and transform the life of therapists, nurses, and others who have experienced it, and what steps have they taken to understand, resolve, and integrate the experience as they continue to work?

I shall divide this presentation into three parts: (1) a brief de-

197

scription of the patients and my relationship to them; (2) what I experienced just prior to their deaths; and (3) what followed.

Both patients were female, one twenty-one years old, the other twenty-seven. Both were very bright and beautiful. They came from outstandingly successful families. One was the child of famous parents, the other the child of a well-known professional. Both fathers were dead. Both had close previous contact with suicide: in one case, one parent and one sibling had made unsuccessful suicide attempts; in the other, the father and a brother had killed themselves two years apart, and the mother was alcoholic. Both came to me for treatment because they had heard about me from other patients. They came into treatment with idealized views of what I might be like and what I could do for them. They were bound to be disappointed.

Both were hospitalized: one during treatment with me for uncontrollable anxiety before I left on a trip; the other previous to my knowing her, after her brother's suicide, became overtly psychotic. She was delusional and hallucinating, had been picked up by the police, taken to a psychiatric hospital, and given electroshock with parental consent. She was discharged without further therapy.

Both, in the conventional sense and in the eyes of others, did well in therapy. Their lives became organized. The child of the famous parents lived with a family and went to college; the other had her own apartment and returned to law school. But neither one felt she could follow in her parents' footsteps, nor could either meet the ideals that had been set up for her, or that she had set up for herself. Both developed an intense attachment to me; it seemed they wouldn't make a move without first consulting and discussing it with me.

Mary, the twenty-one-year-old, became more competent, both academically and otherwise, and was accepted by her peer group in her own right and not on account of her famous parents. At the same time she became depressed and overweight. She also resumed an old hobby she had had since she was twelve, which was to walk on the ledges of high-rise buildings. She had done this off and on for years, and now it became a compulsive need for her to do so before coming to her appointments with me. She chose the highest building in West Los Angeles, from which she could see my office, and would balance herself before coming to her appointment. A few days before dying, she mentioned that she was going to give this up because if she didn't she was going to end up dead. And in her diary (which she kept for me and which was found in her car), her last entry read: "Should I have fallen, I can't help but think how much I would have hurt you, Mother" (and she mentioned a few others). She died the day after what would have been her father's birthday and the day before mine. She had repeatedly said: "I will find a way to stay with you and you will never forget me." And so she did. When I went to pick up her personal effects at the coroner's office, I noticed that her glasses were broken. She had fallen with them. Even now, years later, there are times when I really believe she accidentally fell and didn't intentionally kill herself. When I talk about this patient, even to you, I feel I must give her the benefit of the doubt. Yet in the last two sessions with her I experienced some incongruous feelings that seemed odd at the time, and that I will mention later, but that I recognized vividly in the second case.

Lily, the second patient, went to law school in what seemed an attempt to become her father's favorite son, but I think of it more as an effort to right the wrongs in the family, legal and otherwise. It was the week after she started law school that her father killed himself, but she still managed to finish her first year. When she started therapy with me, she took off a year from school. When she returned, she did well, developed some superficial friendships, and lived alone in an apartment. But when the time came for her to take the bar examination, she regressed and, without warning me, moved to her mother's home, though she had had little contact with her of late. Notwithstanding her high level of anxiety, she took the examination.

After the examination, she rented an apartment that she disliked but that was close to my home, took a job as a filing clerk, and became inaccessible. In her hours with me, she said little and was constantly angry. I think that with her graduation from law school she had expected the magic return of her father and brother, the family reunited, the wrongs righted, and it had *all* failed. She became increasingly paranoid, and I increasingly concerned.

It was then that I experienced with her the odd feelings I had had with Mary, except that with Mary they were less clear or maybe just unfamiliar. But with Lily they were very vivid and extremely unpleasant. They were uncanny feelings, and I look upon them now as sub-liminal communications. I experienced physical coldness, although it was summer. I found myself looking intently at the patient because otherwise I felt I was alone in the room. I felt, physically, at a great distance. The room was like an echo chamber and the light seemed very dim. I realized I was talking quite loudly, as if I were not heard, and no matter what I said I could not reach her, and I knew it. A glass wall had come up, through which I could see her but could not get close. The feelings were so marked that I had to fight fatigue and force myself not to withdraw. It had the quality of sensory deprivation. I suspect this was something akin to what the patient felt.

I had had these feelings once before, and now I recognized them. I called the therapist Lily saw during my absences and told him how serious I felt the situation was, and that he might have to hospitalize her. I called him so many times he said he felt I was unduly anxious about leaving her, and that I had done such a wonderful job that I shouldn't worry. That just didn't sound right. There were many pre-vious times when I was going on a trip that Lily got frightened and upset. But this didn't feel at all like the other times. She appeared removed, aloof, and I felt I had become one more of the people she mistrusted and hated. Never before or after have I seen a patient transform in that way with me, in my very presence, and I was unable to do anything to reach her. Finally the interim therapist suggested I take my plane and go, which I did, and immediately after takeoff I fell asleep for a few minutes and dreamt that Lily broke into my home, ransacked it, and that I returned to its ruins. I woke up from the dream, and the rest of the trip was sleepless and restless.

While I was leaving, Lily's mother called the other doctor, who saw Lily immediately (it was a Sunday). After seeing the therapist, her mother dropped Lily at the supermarket, where she purchased some food. The next morning, when her mother was unable to reach her by phone, she went to Lily's apartment. It would seem that Lily had returned home, put some fruit to rinse under running water (where the mother found it), and smoked one cigarette; her handbag, with wallet and identification, were by the ashtray. It would seem that she then walked away, leaving the door of the apartment open, went to the top floor of a high-rise building being constructed a few doors away, took off her glasses, folded them, and jumped.

When I arrived in Stockholm, I got a telephone call and was informed of her death.

I had set aside four days before the seminars, intended for rest. Instead I walked around the countryside with a friend, trying to understand. I had to give some papers and seminars, but Lily's death was constantly with me, and it stayed with me until things began to fall into place.

When Mary died, I felt deep sorrow: I had deeply cared for that girl and, since for some time I had denied her suicide, I grieved for all that was lost. Eventually I asked myself the unavoidable questions. Where did I go wrong? What could I have done differently? Should I have hospitalized her? How could I have prevented it? I suppose I could have done many things differently, and I could have hospitalized her, but I don't think I could have prevented it. I read and reread her diary looking for clues, but got no answers.

In the meantime I continued to work. When eventually the news hit the press, and since it was well known that I was this girl's therapist, my other patients brought it up and asked questions in a variety of ways. But this time, with Lily, I felt quite numb, and it seemed the questions didn't affect me.

When Lily committed suicide there was no denying it, and all that I had not allowed myself to feel previously was compounded. I felt for a long time worthless and incompetent as a therapist. I don't usually talk much during the hours, but I was unusually silent now, as if afraid of saying the wrong thing, or making a wrong move. My patients complained that I was becoming "like an analyst." I also became quite detached; I wasn't particularly interested in what my patients were doing, nor did I want to get involved.

In short, I removed myself as much as possible from the dyad. I was like an onlooker who walks by and sees things through a window.

I did, though, find myself tempted to be seductive, to get patients to do what I wanted. Since it was clear enough to me, I resisted it. But there was a temptation to test and abuse my power.

Finally, the fear surfaced: fear that another patient might commit suicide. I had several (about five) seriously suicidal patients, and sometimes after they left my office the phone would ring, and I would feel cold fear that once again it was the coroner's office. The police called many times on matters regarding patients, and it took time for me to get accustomed to receiving their calls again.

In my personal life I became socially unavailable. I had a good excuse. I worked about fifteen hours a day. I took on more cases, especially high-risk ones. I know now that I had to prove to myself that I was strong and capable and needed by others.

I went through a period of hating both Mary and Lily. At first I hated them for what they had done to themselves, but in time for what they had done to me. I ceased to want to understand. I just wanted to release the whole experience, which had brought with it an overdue loss of innocence—to which, frankly, I wasn't entitled at this stage of my life. I wanted back the hope for each of my patients and myself, and to relinquish my rather prevalent view at that time, of the darkness of the heart of man.

I had lost interest in the things I enjoyed most. Instead I watched TV, where terrible problems start on the hour, and are resolved flawlessly one hour later. In an odd way, I went to sleep, a sleep that lasted several months. I didn't feel it connected to the suicides. It just seemed I was fatigued, and understandably so because I was overworked. I didn't feel like entertaining or being entertained. It was as if I was sleepwalking and, in that state, I made it possible for myself to heal.

And heal I did, though things are never quite the same. Psychiatry deals mainly with life, and rarely with death and dying. When patients used to ask me, what will you do if I kill myself, I used to reply something to the effect that they would not be around to see it, but that after their burial things would go on more or less as they had been, though they wouldn't be the same. Now I keep silent. I dislike platitudes, especially my own.

When I stopped sleepwalking and things became clearer again, and a longed-for familiarity took over, I was able to try to make some sense of what had happened and, more important, what might happen in the future.

I have since had to deal with several suicide attempts, which have confronted me once again with the eternal problem of the patient's freedom and the therapist's power.

As a therapist I have the possibility of being seductive with a patient, overlooking the task at hand, meeting their wants and not their needs, to avoid a suicide. That seems to me disrespectful and unethical. It is hanging on to the patient's life for my own peace of mind.

It is the patient's prerogative to kill himself, suicide being a human (and only human, as far as I know) option, that nobody has the right to take away—particularly in some devious, self-serving manner. I realize that those of us who have dealt with suicide directly learn to bargain for life. One must become acutely aware not to collude with the patient in order to keep him alive, for a while at least, so he won't do it to us, though maybe later to some other therapist. The collusion would be to help cover up and help repress whatever pain or desperation might move him to want to take his life. We're like gamblers, where the highest stake is human life, and where if we don't win, at least we might not lose, by luring the patient away from dealing with the pain that might otherwise become so intolerable he might want to die.

Hospitalization is, many times, a solution for the immediate problem. The presence of others, and the possibility of sharing with hospital staff, can help both patient and therapist. But we must keep clear as to why we hospitalize. The hospital can be used to allay the therapist's anxiety, not to meet the patient's needs. When hospitals are used for this purpose, they become jails for the soul. And the therapist's soul is incarcerated too, for we pay a high price for tampering with another's freedom. But the temptation to hospitalize can be great, particularly in private practice, where there is no support system and where, at times, the burden and the solitude seem intolerable.

I am not advocating or promoting suicide, mind you; all I am saying is that for me there is a great difference between walking a tightrope helping someone desperate find a good reason to live, and interfering with their right to die.

It has been said that suicide is prepared within the silence of the heart, as is a great work of art, and that the person might himself be ignorant of it. I don't personally think of it like this. I think of it as a great act of violence, sometimes insured not to fail, as was the case with these two young women, who chose a foolproof method, who didn't leave notes that might explain why, who risked killing someone in their fall, and who made their silence haunting.

It demands much more of me, now that I know how it feels, to sit and witness the struggle between the choice of life and death. But

I know of no greater triumph than the choice for life made with just a glimmer of hope, apparently little to look forward to, when the choice to live is strictly a choice of risk and pain.

Not long ago I was talking with a friend about these suicides, and I told him about the first time I went snorkeling. After looking for a few seconds underwater, I looked up because I felt acutely anxious with no apparent reason. Then I realized that as I snorkeled I was on the boundary of two worlds, and that once I really looked down nothing would ever be quite the same again. I had seen something I hadn't known through personal experience before. It is similar when you mountain-climb. You also look up and look down. You are like a chess piece and, without limits, can decide your moves. One of the moves can help you get off the mountain. The other, no matter what the fatigue, the fear, and the pain, will want to make you keep going up.

I think that with certain human experiences, suicide being one of them, we are "dealt a severe mercy," as C. S. Lewis called it. We see and we feel things we were not aware of before. We will ask questions that shall remain forever unanswered. Our omnipotence is diminished and our insecurity increased. And so we enter another phase of growth. And we either grow or pay a higher price to stay the same.

So with these suicides—I have looked into darkness. Through it, I have grown to respect my patients' freedom differently and to be keenly aware of my limitations. I still feel discomfort when I talk about them, though less than before, but I have chosen to continue the struggle, come what may. Maybe what enables me to continue is related to something Camus said (and I am paraphrasing): that to a man devoid of blinders, there is no finer sight than that of the intelligence at grips with a reality that transcends it. That discipline that the mind imposes on itself, that will conjured up out of nothing, that face-to-face struggle, have something exceptional about them. To impoverish that struggle is tantamount to impoverishing man himself, to relieve him of the weight of his own life, which, after all is said and done, he must carry alone.

11

The Changing Picture of an Illness:
Anorexia Nervosa

Hilde Bruch, M.D.

In 1958 Otto Will presented a paper, "Human relatedness and the schizophrenic reaction" at the Second Annual Frieda Fromm-Reichmann Memorial Lecture (Will, 1959). There he described in moving terms the misery of a young woman, Catherine, who had been a psychiatric patient for many years and had received the currently popular treatment with insulin and electricity, not only without benefit but with considerable worsening. She was said to have been an amiable, good, and intelligent child, more than adequate as an athlete, and an excellent student and participant in social affairs.

In her late teens she became markedly preoccupied and depressed, showed a dislike for the company of others, and attempted to kill herself. Her apparent depression was then obscured by symptoms suggestive of a physical illness; she suffered from constipation, loss of appetite, and persistent weight loss. The diagnosis of a pituitary disorder—Simmonds disease—was made, but endocrine medication effected no cure. She was finally hospitalized as a "mental" patient, was moved from one institution to the other, and became increasingly withdrawn, hostile, and emaciated. In various reports she was described as "empty," "hollow," "unable to love," and "hopeless."

When she became Will's patient she spent a good part of her time in a closed room, barricaded against intruders, and would run from visitors; her behavior reflected severe anxiety, fear, and loneliness. She was of slight build, having not eaten freely for many years, and regurgitating whatever food was given her. In therapy he found her exceedingly aloof toward his efforts to establish therapeutic rapport, until, as he described it, "one day as I sat in silence Catherine suddenly turned and struck me. I held her arms and she wept, saying: 'I haven't been able to hear you. You've been staying behind that wall of glass. It had to get broken somehow' " (p. 207).

This image is used not infrequently by patients suffering from anorexia nervosa. Will did not use the term "anorexia nervosa" in his lecture, but the description of this emaciated woman's symptoms are in accord with those of anorexia nervosa—the perfect childhood, the adolescent depression, constipation, loss of appetite, decline in weight, increasing withdrawal, and hostility.

Will's report on his contact with Catherine's parents resembles that observed in anorexic families. He found them evasive, uneasy, and seemingly under some unclear but powerful pressure to "change things." The mother expressed it as, "I want it to be like it used to be when we all seemed all right together. She's getting different now—she doesn't seem to be a part of us any more" (p. 208). The wish that an anorexic daughter should be the way she used to be is common in these families. Various family members make attempts to terminate treatment when improvement does not come fast enough or is not what they wish it to be, namely going back to the former stance of compliance. Will's patient was in treatment for several years and responded well to his approach, with its emphasis on human related-ness. In 1971 I inquired about her long-range development and Otto replied: "We stopped work about seventeen years ago, after which she finished college, worked, and at present has a busy and as far as I know satisfying life, both personally and professionally." This suggests that treatment had been terminated in 1954. No definite figure is given for the pretherapy period, but it seems fair to assume that the onset of her illness occurred somewhere around 1944. This figure is important for the point I wish to make.

During the 1940s, and even the 1950s, anorexia nervosa was so rare that it was practically an unknown illness; patients with what we now consider characteristic anorexic symptomatology were apt to be diagnosed as suffering from an endocrine, specifically a pituitary, disease. This leads to misdirected treatment efforts, and many anorexics whose underlying essential problems have been severely neglected show in the long run marked autistic withdrawal, reflecting the corroding effects of social isolation. In Will's patient the psychosocial symptomatology, which added up to a schizophrenia-like picture, developed following the anorexic phase; this was not a schizophrenic patient who lost weight because she refused to eat.

I emphasize the significance of the time of the patient's illness to illustrate that medical interest in anorexia was at a low ebb at the time she became sick. Things changed rapidly afterward. During Will's directorship of the Austen Riggs Center he and his staff accepted referrals and undertook the treatment of the most seriously disturbed anorexics, and I have been impressed by the success they achieved with some of these hopeless-sounding patients (Story, 1982). I have been particularly appreciative of Dr. Will's having himself undertaken the treatment of some of the most discouraging patients I had occasion to refer to Austen Riggs.

I should like to give a brief sketch of the history of anorexia nervosa and various efforts to understand it. It is a complex and still enigmatic condition that was first described as a clinical entity somewhat more than a hundred years ago (Gull, 1874). Opinions about the relative importance of various factors have fluctuated. Early opinion emphasized ''nervous'' causes, referring to some rather unspecific psychological factors, and in 1914 was superseded by the assumption that it was of pituitary origin. This was based on the autopsy findings on certain cases of cachexia, and this opinion dominated the field for the next three or four decades (Simmonds, 1914). During the 1930s a psychogenic form of anorexia nervosa was rediscovered, and the diagnostic criteria were recognized as distinctly different from those of cachexia of pituitary origin.

Psychoanalysis played an important role in bringing about this new understanding. Investigative focus was on the disturbed eating function, the ''oral'' component. Anorexia nervosa was conceived of as a form of conversion hysteria and as symbolically expressing repudiation of sexuality, specifically or ''oral impregnation'' fantasies

(Waller, Kaufman, and Deutsch, 1940). This view dominated the field during the 1940s and 1950s, and has not yet completely disappeared. Classical psychoanalysis was considered the treatment of choice, though some analysts expressed doubts about "insight" producing favorable changes in these patients; they stressed that the mental disturbance in anorexia nervosa was more severe than that observed in neurosis (Eissler, 1943; Meyer and Weinroth, 1957).

I wish to quote from a discussion only recently published, in which Helene Deutsch in the 1940s called her approach "so-called" analysis, implying the need for considerable modification of the classical procedure (Deutsch, 1981). She speaks of certain features of the clinical picture as delusional or psychotic and mentions the overcompliance of her patient, how she would accept all her interpretations as true but without any change in her thinking or behavior.

Though the condition was exceedingly rare, most physicians had heard about anorexia nervosa in medical school; few, however, even those with a special interest, saw more than an occasional patient. This has changed during the last two or three decades. Today the increased frequency of anorexia nervosa is reflected in greater medical interest and is expressed in an endless stream of publications. It has also aroused great popular curiosity. Even more attention is given to bulimia, which has practically been invented by the media.

As to my own experience, I actually saw as an intern a case of anorexia nervosa, for whom the professor claimed a pituitary origin recognizable by the O-shape of the space between the thighs. This may serve to illustrate the ease with which at that time an endocrine label was attached to a puzzling condition. I became therapist to an anorexic girl when I was a psychiatric resident during the 1940s. Studying the rather scanty literature on anorexia nervosa, I was impressed by the definiteness with which mere assumptions were presented as scientific fact, in endocrinological as well as psychoanalytic writing. I looked for but did not find in my patient the postulated sexual fantasies. I explained this failure to myself as a sign of my inexperience, but I did not doubt that the complexes existed somewhere.

It was not until the 1950s that I began to see anorexic patients with any degree of regularity. They were referred to me on the basis of my psychotherapeutic work with fat adolescents, whose psychodynamic development suggested a relationship to schizophrenia. By the late 1950s, when Will's paper appeared, I had become aware of certain preschizophrenic features in some anorexics but had hesitated to express this view. Will's paper encouraged me to pursue the question of the diagnostic classification of anorexia nervosa. Clarification of the contradictory opinions became possible with increasing experience due to the more frequent occurrence of the condition.

A first step was the recognition that what clinically was called anorexia nervosa did not represent a uniform condition. I quote here from a paper I presented in 1965:

> "What is in a name?" might well be the leit-motif for my presentation. . . . The condition of self-inflicted starvation . . . is usually diagnosed as Anorexia Nervosa [in English-speaking countries]; in the German literature it is also called Pubertaets-magersucht [addiction to thinness]. These two names, focusing on the most dramatic aspects of the disorder, actually describe two essentially different problems. On the surface it may appear not to matter whether one emphasizes the refusal to eat or the resulting emaciation, or Magersucht. The aim of my presentation will be to demonstrate that it is of decisive significance whether a patient is preoccupied with his body size, with a relentless pursuit of being thin and a phobic avoidance of being fat, or whether he is preoccupied with the eating function itself and its distorted symbolic meaning, with thinness only an accidental by-product. Somewhat paradoxically, "Magersucht" is the key issue in the classical Anorexia Nervosa syndrome, which justifies to separate it from other psychiatric conditions associated with se-vere, even dramatic loss of weight, in whom the eating function is disturbed incidentally to a variety of underlying problems, often together with other physiologic and psychologic disturbances. [Bruch, 1965, pp. 70–71]

A specific syndrome, primary anorexia nervosa, could be differ-entiated from atypical forms of undernutrition that were secondary to some other psychiatric illness such as hysteria, schizophrenia, or depression (Bruch, 1973). Many of the cases reported in the older literature belong to the atypical group; they still do occur, but not more frequently than in the past. It is the primary form that is on the increase, and my discussion will be based on it. It affects mainly adolescent girls and young women from educated and prosperous homes; it occurs only rarely in males, usually in prepuberty. It looks now as if with increasing frequency and popularization the picture is undergoing some changes.

Primary Anorexia Nervosa

An important new observation was the finding that patients with primary anorexia nervosa do not suffer from loss of appetite, as the name would seem to imply. Rather, like other starving people, they are frantically preoccupied with food and eating. Relentless pursuit of thinness seems to be the outstanding motive, and to accomplish this they overexercise and deliberately, seemingly willfully, restrict their food intake. They are panicky with fear that they might lose control over their eating. When they "give in" and eat, they will devour large amounts of food, which they then vomit. However, the basic illness is not a disturbance of the eating function, though the physical and psychological consequences of the severe malnutrition dominate the picture. The deeper psychological disorder is related to disturbances in the personality, with deficits in the sense of self, identity, and autonomy.

Characteristically, anorexics are inaccurate in judging their size and appearance, indicating disturbances in the body image. They are uncertain in identifying hunger and other bodily sensations, and use the eating function for the pseudosolution of other problems of living. They also suffer from a pervasive sense of ineffectiveness. There are numerous disturbances in their gender identity and psychosexual maturation; this is part of a general maldevelopment.

By reconstructing the antecedents of the anorexic illness, as is done during psychotherapy, new concepts emerged about the nature of the underlying developmental disturbances. One puzzling aspect of this serious illness is that it occurs in individuals who, according to family and school reports, had been unusually good, successful, and gratifying as children, and who had been well cared for in stable, privileged homes. The onset of the anorexia nervosa is accompanied, or often preceded, by marked changes in behavior, as previously compliant girls become negativistic, angry, and distrustful. They stubbornly reject help and care, insisting on their right to be as thin as they want to be. They take pride in their skeletonlike appearance and vigorously defend it. They experience their body as separate from their psychological self, as something extraneous, not their own, or as being the possession of their parents. Underneath their self-assertive façade they experience themselves as acting only in response to demands coming from others, and not as doing anything expressive of their own needs and decisions.

This split between body and psychological self is a basic issue in anorexia nervosa. The illness usually becomes manifest when those at risk are faced with new experiences and thus with the need to make decisions, something for which they feel unprepared. They suffer from a deep fear of being incompetent, a "nothing," of not getting or even deserving respect. Actually they are deficient in the sense of autonomy, in the awareness of their self and core identity. Deep down, every anorexic is convinced she is inadequate, low, mediocre, inferior, and despised by others.

These developmental deficits and expressions of confusion suggest that the condition is more akin to borderline states, narcissism, or schizophrenia than to neurosis. Anorexia nervosa represents an illness in its own right in which psychological and somatic factors are closely intertwined. It represents a desperate effort to ward off panic about being completely powerless, an attempt at self-cure, to develop through discipline over the body a sense of selfhood and interpersonal effectiveness. Anorexics transform their anxiety and psychological problems through manipulation of food intake and size. The experience of underlying psychological factors is thus reduced to a narrower range than in purely psychological illness.

In spite of what looks like good intelligence they continue to function with the morality and style of thinking of early childhood, which Piaget (1954) has called the period of egocentricity, or preconceptual and concrete operations. The next step in conceptual development, which is characteristic of adolescence, that of formal operations with the ability to perform abstract thinking and evaluation, is deficient or absent in them.

Psychotherapeutic observations and direct study of the families helped to shed light on the puzzle why seemingly well-functioning, stable homes raise children who mistrust their own abilities to face the future, and who shy away from adult living. On one level child care appears to be excellent; everything is provided for, materially, psychologically, and culturally, but things are superimposed according to the parents' decisions and convictions, with little attention to a child's own expression of needs, wants, and feelings. This manifests itself in many different ways, but characteristic is the absence or paucity of confirming, validating, and encouraging responses to child-initiated cues. In modern thinking about early development the emphasis is increasingly on the infant's own contributions, on his giving the cues and signals to his unfulfilled needs. How they are responded to, gratified, or disregarded appears crucial for his becoming discriminately aware of his needs, or his failing to achieve this. Behavior needs to be differentiated, from birth on, into behavior *initiated* in the infant and behavior *in response* to stimuli. The mother's behavior is either *responsive* or *stimulating*, and the interaction can be rated as *appropriate* or *inappropriate*, depending on whether it fulfills the expressed needs or disregards or distorts them (Bruch, 1969b). Absence of regular and consistently appropriate responses to his needs deprives the developing child of the essential groundwork for his "body identity," the perceptual and conceptual awareness of his own functions.

The anorexic's defect in control and awareness of hunger is the result of inappropriate responses by the caregiving person to expressions of the child's needs. They are responded to not according to their cues but to the caregiver's decisions. Expression of feelings is also not encouraged or confirmed, and many anorexics are restricted to a narrow range in identifying emotional reactions.

In this model the development of personality and the sense of self is conceived of as the outcome of a continuous stream of circular and reciprocal interaction between parent and child. This concept fits well with other reconstructions of early development and with direct observations from recent infant studies.

Theoretical formulations that are the outcome of extensive clinical inquiries are helpful, in turn, for the dynamic understanding of the condition and serve as a guide through the maze of seemingly contradictory psychological responses. If one wishes to express an anorexic's behavior in one formula, one might view it as a desperate effort to be recognized and admired as special, unique, outstanding, extraordinary, etc. Being mediocre, average, normal, ''like everybody else,'' is something to be avoided at all costs.

As long as anorexia nervosa was rare, in a way an elite illness, the goal of being unique may have appeared attainable. But this search for uniqueness is not compatible with the greater frequency of anorexia nervosa today. Though no reliable figures are available, there is no doubt as to the increasing prevalence and greater frequency of its occurrence. One common argument points to the increasing cultural emphasis on slenderness as a determining factor. Though this may play a role, in my opinion it does not do justice to the psychological complexity of the condition, which expresses a much more severe disturbance than simple dieting that has gotten out of hand. Ordinary weight control, even if it goes too far, is distinctly different from the anorexic's frantic preoccupation with excessive slenderness.

It appears that the dilemma from which the anorexic attempts to escape is confronted nowadays by many more young women. It is my impression that changing status and expectations as regards women play a role. Girls whose early upbringing had prepared them to become accommodating wives are suddenly, at adolescence, expected to prove themselves as women of achievement (Bruch, 1978). This activates basic uncertainties and doubts about their ability to fulfill these expectations. Formerly this was faced only by the daughters of exceptionally successful homes. In their submissive way they ''choose'' the fashionable dictum to be slim as a way of proving themselves ''special,'' as deserving of respect.

The first anorexics I met during the 1950s and 1960s, and some even later, had in common that each was an original inventor of this effort at self-assertion. They had never heard about such a condition, nor had their parents or even their physicians. Yet the manifest clinical picture and the psychological reactions showed amazing similarities, in the way they described body sensations, hunger experience, and hyperactivity, as if they had been part of a secret network of communication. They all expressed the conviction that they were not sick; on the contrary, they were doing something positive about their life and resented parental and professional interference with something they considered a positive achievement.

This originality gave to the behavior of each individual patient an aura of special power and superhuman discipline. With increasing prevalence some changes seem to occur. Those who developed the illness during the 1970s or later often had "known" about it, from magazine articles or television shows. Some had observed the illness in someone they knew, a friend or a cousin. Though I am not able yet to define what it is, there is no doubt in my mind that this "me-too" picture is associated with changes; it is as if something like "passion" has gone out of the picture. Instead of the fierce search for independence, these new "me-too" anorexics compete with or cling to each other (Bruch, 1982).

A similar discrepancy can be observed in anorexic twins. Usually it is the follower twin, the weaker one, who develops anorexia nervosa, when the leader twin moves away from the twinship into independence (Bruch, 1969a). However, there are situations where the leader twin reacts with a certain envy—"She is getting away with something"—and imitates her weaker sister by beginning a starvation regime, but without genuine goals. The desire to be special, unique, extraordinary, is expressed with less vigor and urgency.

Changes are apparent in the socioeconomic features of the families, though anorexics from economically deprived backgrounds continue to be very rare. In the early descriptions family tension and discord were hidden under a facade of "happiness." In recent cases marital tension appears to be more in the open, with competition for the anorexic child's loyalty, and more frequent divorce. Not only has the socioeconomic spectrum broadened but also the age range at which the illness occurs. Anorexia is now observed in women approaching forty years or even older, and there are also more married women. It looks as if they were undergoing a midlife crisis; the absence of what they consider achievements of their own suddenly becomes a challenge.

Rivalry with siblings, schoolmates, and other anorexics is much more pronounced. The old-time anorexic would pay little attention to other anorexics; since the condition was so rare, the likelihood of in fact meeting another was quite small. The modern anorexic who knows about the condition before she becomes sick expresses enormous competitiveness and continually measures herself in terms of other anorexics. This may be a sign of the illness being less severe; anorexics who develop social relationships or friendships have a better prognosis than those who stay strictly isolated. It looks as if instead of the fierce search for independence these new anorexics compete with or cling to one another.

It is my feeling that the condition will gradually lose its specific psychodynamic meaning, namely that of representing a station in their search for uniqueness, one that ordinary people cannot share. With increasing prevalence the picture will become blurred and gradually disappear. It may not be accidental that shortly before the increase began Bliss and Branch (1960) published a book on anorexia nervosa with descriptions so bland and unspecific that it sounded as if they wanted to abolish the concept. It is quite possible that as the illness begins to dissolve, unspecific pictures will outnumber the specific primary form, until sociopsychological conditions are right again for the true anorexia nervosa to return. Recently Crisp (1981–1982) described an abnormal normal weight control syndrome and calls it ''anorexia nervosa at normal body weight.'' The picture he describes seems to resemble what I have called ''thin fat people'' (Bruch, 1973, pp. 194–208), who, though they resemble anorexics, are different from them by the fact that their weight stays within normal range and that they are less socially withdrawn.

It may well be that the sudden, nearly explosive preoccupation with bulimia is a sign of a beginning dissolution. Not all anorexics are able to maintain rigid control over their eating. When they give in to their desire for food they gorge themselves and then vomit and/or use laxatives to maintain the low weight. About 25 percent of the group on which I reported in *Eating Disorders* in 1973 showed this behavior. The anorexics who would binge did not look very different from the abstainers, though they appeared to be less rigid, emotionally somewhat more responsive, but also more disturbed. Binge eating occurs now much more often, in more than 50 percent of the cases who were seen during the last five years. There is agreement that bingeing represents a dangerous complication and makes treatment more difficult.

During the past few years a condition called bulimia has made its appearance as the great new eating disorder; it is widely discussed in the electronic media and popular press. It is presented as closely related to anorexia nervosa, and someone has coined a semantic atrocity, ''bulimarexia,'' as if to indicate that the two conditions are nearly identical, which they are not. Compulsive overeating may occur in different conditions and with different severity. I seriously doubt that bulimia is a clinical entity.

The patients with bulimia whom I have studied bear little resemblance to those with genuine anorexia nervosa, though they too are inaccurate in hunger awareness and show poor control over food intake. Display of uncontrol and lack of discipline are prominent, in contrast to the adherence to discipline of the true anorexics, even those who indulge themselves in eating binges. Modern bulimics are impressive by what looks like a deficient sense of responsibility, in contrast to the overharsh conscience with which the anorexic functions. They blame their symptoms on others, namely the person from whom they ''learned'' to binge, and particularly the one who introduced them to vomiting. Often there is only a single episode of the shared experience, but they act from then on as if they are completely helpless victims. To consider them part of the anorexia nervosa picture confuses the issues instead of clarifying them.

Application to Treatment

The distinction between different forms of eating disorder is not only of theoretical interest but also of practical importance as a dynamic guide to treatment. Anorexia nervosa has the reputation of offering unusually difficult treatment problems. On principle, these patients resist treatment: they feel that in their extreme thinness they have found the perfect solution to their deep-seated unhappiness, that it makes them feel better. They do not complain about their skeletonlike appearance—on the contrary, they glory in it and actively maintain it. In addition, they find it painful to face the underlying issues.

For effective treatment, changes and corrections must be accomplished in several areas. Refeeding must be integrated with various other factors: a certain nutritional restitution is a prerequisite for psychotherapy to be effective. But weight gain alone is not a cure, though not correcting a dangerously low weight may lead to disaster. It is unrealistic to hope that nutrition would improve by itself once the underlying problems have been identified and solved. Eventually some metabolic or pharmacological substances will be discovered that interrupt the self-perpetuating cycle of changes caused by the starvation. Thus far no such medication has been found, though there are promising leads.

Nutritional improvement and resolution of psychological problems occur in close interaction; lasting recovery requires changes in the patient's inner image of herself. As a patient becomes involved in treatment she permits herself to relax her overrigid discipline and to gain weight on her own. The stagnating patterns of family interaction need to be clarified and unlocked. But family therapy alone is not enough. Regardless of a family's contribution in the past, the patient has integrated these abnormal concepts about herself and others into her own personality. Direct work with the family and individual psychotherapy complement each other. It is necessary to clarify and correct the underlying faulty assumptions and the self-deceptive pseudosolution that anorexia nervosa represents.

The psychotherapeutic approach is derived from psychoanalysis, but its application to the needs of individuals with primary anorexia nervosa demand marked modification of the classical model. It has been recognized for some time that classical analysis was associated with unfavorable results. To these patients ''receiving interpretations'' in the traditional setting represents in a painful way a reexperience of being told what to feel and think, confirming their sense of inadequacy and thus interfering with the development of a true self-awareness and trust in their own psychological abilities. The anorexic needs to be encouraged in her search for autonomy and self-directed identity. The setting for this is the new intimate relationship with the therapist. One important factor is that what she has to say is listened to and made the object of exploration.

It is useful to give at the beginning of treatment a simple explanation of the dynamic meaning of the illness, that the preoccupation with eating and weight is a cover-up for underlying personality problems, namely doubt regarding her own self-worth. She needs to be told that at this stage the severe starvation interferes with her psychological functioning, and that the goal of treatment is to discover her positive qualities and assets. It is important to clarify from the outset that therapy is an effort to accomplish something positive for the patient's benefit, not to appease the parents. An anorexic needs to become an active participant in the treatment process, so that she can reach the point of differentiating herself from others, of discriminating bodily sensations and emotional states, and of growing beyond helpless passivity, hateful submissiveness, and indiscriminate negativism. Patients need to experience that close and alert attention is paid to what they have to say and contribute. This is essential if the individuation process, which miscarried earlier in their lives, is to take place. The therapist's task is to help a patient face the realities of her life in the past and present, instead of focusing on the symbolic significance of symptoms and behavior.

It is important to reconstruct the patient's emotional interactions and involvements in the period before her illness. If this is made the focus of inquiry, she will gradually recognize the extent to which she always did what she thought she was supposed to, thereby neglecting her own developmental needs. The excessively good behavior that is encouraged and rewarded is an early manifestation of severe maldevelopment. Faked and make-believe expressions and reactions are praised as if genuine, with the result that the ability to differentiate between genuine and pretended feelings remains unclear and confused. Deficits in encouragement and validation of expression of needs interferes with the development of a sense of self and competence. The task of therapy is to help patients discover their genuine self, and what is valid about themselves. They need to face the problems of living in the present and also reconstruct what went on in the period before their illness.

In a way each anorexic patient has to build up a new personality after all the years of fake existence. They are eternally preoccupied with the image they create in the eyes of others, always questioning whether they are worthy of respect. An attitude of basic mistrust permeates their self-concept and all relationships. Every anorexic dreads that basically she is inadequate, low, mediocre, inferior and despised by others. The efforts to be outstanding or perfect express the need to hide the fatal flaw of their inadequacies. This mistrust is usually hidden from the therapist under a façade of ingratiating cooperation.

They are convinced that people look down on them with scorn and criticism, and they feel they have to protect themselves against this.

Therapy represents an attempt to acknowledge the conceptual defects and distortions and to create a climate in which these developmental delays can be identified, a necessary first step toward their correction. An important part of this process is the reevaluation of interactional experiences within the family so that the forces that had interfered with normal development can be recognized and the overclose ties to the parents loosened. This anorexics are reluctant to do. They deny not only their own illness and the need for treatment, they deny also that there was anything troublesome in their relationship with their parents. Everything was perfect, their parents were superior and provided privileges and opportunities, and they consider efforts to look at what really happened and how they experienced it as being forced to "blame" their parents. They will, however, complain about the parents' interference with eating behavior, and also about their having made arrangements for treatment. Others are tireless in expressing blind and indiscriminate hostility toward one or the other parent.

By paying minute attention to the way a patient talks about her experiences, one may find an entry into the rigid denial. A severely anorexic eighteen-year-old had accepted treatment only because she "detested" arguing with her mother. She felt happy about her low weight and considered it a sign of superiority. She had grown up abroad and been raised by governesses who changed every two years. When I inquired about the emotional hardship of having to adjust to so many different people, she said reassuringly, "I knew they all loved me. I made sure they would." She became upset when her "making sure" of their love was discussed as implying doubt about being loved if she just behaved naturally. This led to her talking, at first tentatively and with much resistance, about her great efforts to be always beyond blame and criticism, and deserving of admiration. She would drive herself to exhaustion with her numerous activities and explained, "Only then [when exhausted] can you be at peace that you have done enough. If you have not given the last drop of strength, you do not deserve to sleep or eat." As treatment progressed and she became more relaxed about her obligations, she reviewed with much emotion the hardship of being the youngest child in a successful, wealthy home where everybody else was "brilliant," how she had felt that nothing she ever did was good enough, that she could never live up to what she felt "they" expected of her.

Reexamination of patients' erroneous assumptions about life and relationships helps them recognize that there were factual situations which interfered with their developing a sense of inner rightness, that from the beginning the scales were weighted against their becoming distinct, self-reliant individuals. They also need to learn that children will interpret such experiences as proving that they themselves are in some way undeserving, not good enough, or even defective.

Therapy involves a relatedness different from the one experienced during the years of growing up and developing a negative self-concept, and it will permit the reexamination of the unrealistic aspects of their convictions. One of them is that "Mother always knew what I felt," though the opposite is true, that their mother often disregarded their feelings. It is the task of therapy to help them discover their own needs and values. By being empathically tuned in to distortions in the patient's sense of reality, the therapist can instigate necessary reevaluations without appearing judgmental. Anorexics who have lived so long with a self-belittling assumptive reality may have become convinced they cannot change, in particular when they have been exposed to ineffective or mechanical treatment efforts in the past. They may politely agree with what has been clarified but at the same time maintain the secret conviction, "I know better—I know for me things are different."

They compensate for the self-belittling attitude with grandiose aspirations, and it requires a real sacrifice of pride to reduce their ambitious dreams of glory to human proportions. The need to be unique and super-special is so compelling that any conclusion that seems based on common human experience, or on observations of other anorexic patients, is rejected as inapplicable to them. They want to be human in a way that is different from the rest of mankind, to the point of their feeling inhuman in their demands.

This fact-finding approach, which I have called "the constructive use of ignorance," implies reconstruction of what really happened during the patient's early development (Bruch, 1963). The therapist does not know and can find out only with the patient's active participation in the inquiry. With increasing experience it will become apparent that the active involvement serves as a stimulus for the development of something that was deficient in the early interactional patterns, namely reliance on one's own thinking.

Deficits in self-concept and hunger awareness were recognized as related to certain factors in the patient's development, namely the paucity or absence of appropriate responses to child-initiated cues. This generalized formulation served as a guide for the inquiry into family interactions and attitudes, with focus on initiative and autonomy.

These formulations and their application to therapy were independently arrived at during the last twenty years. They do not stand in isolation but show many parallels with other reevaluations of psychoanalytic therapy, particularly in its application to narcissism, borderline states, and schizophrenia. Will's paper on relatedness (1959) represents an important reevaluation. Traditional psychoanalysis, too, has undergone many changes and modifications.

The considerations I have presented here bear fairly close resemblance to those expressed by Kohut (1977) in his psychology of the self. He considers favorable interaction with the environment as necessary for the healthy development of the self, and calls the positive responses to a child's expressions of his needs, "mirroring."

These modern developments have broadened the range of conditions that can be favorably influenced by psychotherapy. This is of particular importance in the treatment of anorexia nervosa and other eating disorders, where the clinical picture is complicated by the distorting influence of the abnormal nutrition on psychological processes. A clear theoretical formulation represents an indispensable guide through the maze of seemingly contradictory psychological responses.

References

Bliss, E. L., & Branch, C. H. H. (1960), *Anorexia Nervosa: Its History, Psychology, and Biology*. New York: Hoeber.

Bruch, H. (1963), Effectiveness in psychotherapy or the constructive use of ignorance. *Psychiatric Quart.*, 37:332–339.

——— (1965), The psychiatric differential diagnosis of anorexia nervosa. In: *Anorexia*

Nervosa, ed. J.E. Meyer & H. Heldmann. Stuttgart: Georg Thieme Verlag, pp. 70–87. Also published as: Anorexia nervosa and its differential diagnosis. *J. Nerv. & Ment. Dis.*, 141:555–566.

—————— (1969a), The insignificant difference: Discordant incidence of anorexia nervosa in monozygotic twins. *Am. J. Psychiat.*, 126:123–128.

—————— (1969b), Hunger and instinct. *J. Nerv. & Ment. Dis.*, 149:91–114.

—————— (1973), *Eating Disorders: Obesity, Anorexia Nervosa, and the Person Within.* New York: Basic Books.

—————— (1978), *The Golden Cage: The Enigma of Anorexia Nervosa.* Cambridge, MA: Harvard University Press.

—————— (1982), Four decades of eating disorders. Second Annual Daniel Prager Lecture, George Washington University, Washington, DC, April 16.

Crisp, A.H. (1981–1982), Anorexia nervosa at normal body weight!—The abnormal normal weight control syndrome. *Internat. J. Psychiat. in Med.*, 11:203–233.

Deutsch, H. (1981), Anorexia nervosa (with introduction by P. Roazen). *Bull. Menn. Clin.*, 45:499–511.

Eissler, K. R. (1943), Some psychiatric aspects of anorexia nervosa, demonstrated by a case report. *Psychoanal. Rev.*, 30:121–145.

Gull, W.W. (1874), Anorexia nervosa. *Trans. Clin. Soc.* (London), 7:22–28.

Kohut, H. (1977), *The Restoration of the Self.* New York: International Universities Press.

Meyer, B. C., & Weinroth, L. A. (1957), Observations on psychological aspects of anorexia nervosa. *Psychosom. Med.*, 19:389–398.

Piaget, J. (1954), *The Construction of Reality in the Child.* New York: Basic Books.

Simmonds, M. (1914), Ueber embolische Prozesse in der Hypophysis. *Arch. Path. Anat.*, 217:226.

Story, R. I. (1982), Anorexia nervosa and the psychotherapeutic hospital. *Internat. J. Psychoanal. Psychother.*, 9:267–302.

Waller, J. V., Kaufman, R. M., & Deutsch, F. (1940), Anorexia nervosa: A psychosomatic entity. *Psychosom. Med.*, 2:3–16.

Will, O. A. (1959), Human relatedness and the schizophrenic reaction. *Psychiat.*, 22:205–223.

12

The Struggle Toward Ambivalence

Clarence G. Schulz, M.D.

My patient angrily flounced into the office and after seating herself said, "I just want to go home, that's all!" Upon seeing me jot this down on a piece of paper, she, half smiling with mock suspicion, asked what I had written. She knew that I did not make notes during our sessions. I read back to her, "I just want to go home, that's all!" I did not add that I was looking for a good example to illustrate an all-or-none attitude for a paper I was writing. The subsequent exchange led us to look at the many intermediate steps she had to take before she could return to her home across the continent: being able to get up on time, to catch the bus, and to improve her appearance so she could consider applying for a job.

Freud (1912) commented on the favorable potential with the manifestation of ambivalence.

In the curable forms of psychoneurosis it [the negative transference] is found side by side with the affectionate transference, often directed simultaneously towards the same person. Bleuler has coined the excellent term 'ambivalence' to describe this phenomenon. Up to a point, ambivalence of feeling of this sort seems

[1]Contributions of clinical findings were provided by Dr. Charles Peters and Dr. Miles Quaytman of The Sheppard and Enoch Pratt Hospital staff.

223

to be normal; but a high degree of it is certainly a special pecu-
liarity of neurotic people. In obsessional neurotics an early separation of the 'pairs of opposites' seems to be characteristic of
their instinctual life and to be one of their constitutional precon-
ditions. Ambivalence in the emotional trends of neurotics is the
best explanation of their ability to enlist their transferences in the
service of resistance. Where the capacity for transference has
become essentially limited to a negative one, as is the case with
paranoics, there ceases to be any possibility of influence or cure.
[pp. 106–107]

How does treatment accomplish the task of integrating opposite
tendencies to achieve ambivalence? To what extent can we conceptualize a treatment approach that is narrowly directed toward a particular defense or symptom? Psychiatry of today has developed programs
to treat alcoholism and phobias. There are even shyness clinics and
anxiety clinics. At times we treat symptoms apart from the person. It
is my impression that attacking splitting in isolation from the total
mental structure will not be effective. One can, however, usefully
develop methods to bring about the progression toward ambivalence
if these are used in the context of treatment more broadly conceived.

The effort to devise objective criteria for DSM-III diagnostic
categories fosters the emphasis on behavior. Table 1 shows diagnostic
criteria for Borderline Personality Disorder taken from DSM-III.

The Joint Commission requires that we develop treatment plans
with specific measurable objectives and ultimate goals. On the other
hand, psychoanalytic writers approaching the problem from a developmental standpoint conceptualize specific defense mechanisms, levels
of ego organization, and object relations. I shall attempt to schematize
these concepts using the work of Otto Kernberg (1975), the acknowledged authority in this field (see Table 2).

Here one can select a particular symptom, for example depression
or narcissism, and view the diagnostic category as at the neurotic,
borderline, or psychotic level. Each level has its characteristic defense
mechanisms, level of ego organization, and object relationships. It is
characteristic of borderline patients to have several symptoms in addition to one or two primary ones. For present purposes I wish to

TABLE 1

1. Impulsivity or unpredictability in at least two areas that are potentially self-damaging, e.g., spending, sex, gambling, substance abuse, shoplifting, overeating, physically self-damaging acts.

2. A pattern of unstable and intense interpersonal relationships, e.g., marked shifts of attitude, idealization, devaluation, and manipulation (consistently using others for one's own ends).

3. Inappropriate intense anger or lack of control, e.g., frequent displays of temper, constant anger.

4. Identity disturbance manifested by uncertainty about several issues relating to identity, such as self-image, gender identity, long-term goals or career choice, friendship patterns, values, and loyalties, e.g., "Who am I," "I feel like I am my sister when I am good."

5. Affective instability: marked shifts from normal mood to depression, irritability, or anxiety, usually lasting a few hours and only rarely more than a few days, with a return to normal mood.

6. Intolerance of being alone, e.g., frantic efforts to avoid being alone, depressed when alone.

7. Physically self-damaging acts, e.g., suicidal gestures, self-mutilation, recurrent accidents, or physical fights.

emphasize that interventions altering the level of ego organization (for example, the imposition of an external structure in a hospital setting) can alter the entire symptom picture, including uncontrolled anger, impulsiveness, and self-damage.

Elsewhere (Schulz, 1980) I have suggested that the concept of splitting into "good" and "bad" self- and object representations be broadened to include a whole range of all-or-none phenomena. I presented examples of contrasting polarized positions and their corresponding more mature, integrated attitudes (see Table 3). In discussing borderline patients, I pointed out their tendency to be overwhelmed by mammoth problems and the need for the therapist to help break these down into manageable intermediate tasks. This tendency is seen in my patient, cited earlier, who wanted to leap over all the intermediate steps and enact the instantaneous end point of "going home."

	NEUROTIC (Repression, reaction formation, obsessive and compulsive defenses)	BORDERLINE (Splitting, projection, denial, idealization, primitive aggression, rage)	PSYCHOTIC (Borderline phenomena *plus* impaired reality testing, thoughtdisorder, self-representation/object-representation fusion issues, loss of boundaries, etc.)
NARCISSISTIC			
OBSESSIVE-COMPULSIVE			
SCHIZOID			
HYSTERICAL			
CYCLOTHYMIC			
DEPRESSION			

TABLE 2

TABLE 3
Two Contrasting Patient Approaches[a]

All or none	Integrated
Splitting into either "good" or "bad"	Ambivalence
Rigid overcontrol vs. loss of control	Modulated expression of affects
Attack entire problem vs. avoidance of problem	Approach by breaking down into manageable parts
Now or never	Ability to tolerate delay
Murderous rage or total denial of anger	Partial expression of anger
Infatuation (crush) or denial of dependency	Mature object dependency
	Shared responsibility, cooperation
Either my way or your way	Able to consider variety of options
Either this way or not at all	Tolerate illness or defect
Perfect health vs. death	Realistic appraisal of limitations
Complete optimism vs. hopelessness	Appropriate decision making
Impulsivity vs. failure to act	Stable interpersonal relationships
Extreme attachment vs. rejection of object	Fairly consistent moral regulations
Harsh disapproval, self-injury vs. absent moral constraint	Reasonably stable goals
Narcissistic ideal expectations vs. despair of accomplishing anything	Moderation in caloric intake
Overeating vs. starvation	Self-control in drinking
Severe alcohol intoxication vs. abstinence	Improvement by small increments, working through
Instant recovery vs. no progress	One individual among many
Special patient or feels overlooked	

[a]From Schulz (1980), p. 184.

Kernberg (1975) notes the importance of pointing out the patient's active participation in the splitting of the transference: "With these patients, it is not a matter of searching for unconscious, repressed material, but bridging and integrating what appears on the surface to be two or more emotionally independent, but alternately active ego states" (p. 96).

More specific steps in carrying out this integration are suggested in his later book (Kernberg, 1976). To summarize, the therapist must first sort out from the confusing report from the patient the predominant transference affect. Second, he must classify the various interactions of self and object in the transference. Third, part-object relations must be integrated with opposite, dissociated part-object relations leading to an integration and consolidation of the real self (pp. 164–165).

From Blanck and Blanck (1974) I have selected a few treatment tools from the long list they propose. These include ego support, improvement of the defensive function of the ego, verbalization as ego building, and confrontation "to help the observing part of the ego 'look at' the experiencing part and confront itself intrasystemically" (p. 353). Their emphasis is on the building of internal structure.

I shall be referring to Winnicott's "holding environment." Modell (1976) states, "The holding environment suggests not only protection from the dangers from without, but also protection from the dangers from within. For the holding environment implies a restraint, a capacity to hold the child having a temper tantrum so that his aggressive impulses do not prove destructive to either himself or the caretaker" (p. 290). Applying this to the analytic situation, he adds:

> there are actual elements in the analyst's technique that are reminiscent of an idealized maternal holding environment, and these can be enumerated: the analyst is constant and reliable; he responds to the patient's affects; he accepts the patient, and his judgment is less critical and more benign; he is there primarily for the patient's needs and not for his own; he does not retaliate; and he does at times have a better grasp of the patient's inner psychic reality than does the patient himself and therefore may clarify what is bewildering and confusing. [p. 291]

Adler (1977) utilizes the hospital as a holding environment but also comments that separate clinical administrator and therapist roles tend to support splitting by the patient. He concludes that sometimes, after a careful review, it is necessary to help therapist and patient end their work when it is decided that the limitations of the therapist's personality have led to an irresolvable impasse. This question came up for consideration in the following case.

Change from the Viewpoint of Individual Therapy

A young woman patient with anorexia and borderline personality organization developed an intense negative transference toward her therapist, with concurrent marked splitting of the treatment team. The therapist was all bad; other members of the treatment team were seen as all good. In the midst of the resultant turmoil, I was called to decide whether or not a new therapist should be assigned, a move supported by the patient, the nursing staff, the dance therapist, and the patient's mother. Looking into the matter, I detected in the patient covert positive feelings for the therapist, feelings she considered absurd at the time. Having recognized this, I felt that some degree of integration of feelings, positive and negative, could be hoped for were treatment continued. I recommended continuation with the same therapist.

The ensuing shift from marked splitting to a more integrated stance seems to have taken place in a series of stages, beginning with an affectless denial of anything but the most negative of feelings toward the therapist. Upon the therapist's returning from vacation, the patient stated in a matter-of-fact way, "While you were gone, I didn't miss you at all. I did better in fact. I cannot work with someone as cold as you are."

In later forays with her therapist, what might be considered a second step toward integration began to appear. Now, instead of stating her polarized position with little afterthought, she demonstrated a beginning identification with the therapist's appreciation for her all-or-none position. "I can talk to Joan [the dance therapist]. She always understands what I'm saying. You never seem to. I just can't say a thing when I'm up here in therapy. Just can't talk to you at all. Oh, I know, you're going to say I'm looking at things in my usual all-or-none way."

With the beginning emergence of integration and a state of ambivalence, the patient experienced marked anxiety and evidenced a last-ditch attempt to retain the splitting defense. "You know even though I'm coming to therapy, I still hate it most of the time. Still feel sort of panicky just before I get here, want to leave the hospital all together. I don't do it but I'm not sure why."

As the hostility abated and anxiety over the emergence of ambivalence lessened, we saw the beginning of a state of remorse at having missed something as a result of her previous all-or-none view of the world. Speaking of a new male acquaintance, someone the patient viewed in much the same negative light as the therapist, she commented, "I still get anxious when I am with him alone. I don't want to leave. He is nice, but being with him I am very afraid. I think sometimes that I have been missing something with the way I've looked at things; I've never allowed myself to go through the steps of growing up."

This progression is consistent with Melanie Klein's shift from splitting to the ambivalent depressive position. The therapist's interventions after the initial inquiry regarding an instance of all-or-none thinking helped the patient see how pervasive this attitude was. Later the therapist would begin to question whether it had to be that way, facilitating identification with his position and modification of the patient's defensive operation.

We see then a progression through a series of stages taking the patient to a point of greater integration of positive and negative object representations. Although this process takes place in a much broader way, permeating all areas of the patient's life, I have described here its manifestation in the patient-therapist relationship. It would seem that an initial affectless splitting is followed by a gradual recognition of, and identification with, the therapist's observation of the splitting process. The patient then begins to experience the emergence of considerable anxiety as her own splitting defenses attenuate. Last-ditch efforts to salvage the defensive operation yield bursts of hostility and oscillation between a splitting position and a more integrated one. As therapy progresses, one gradually sees the evolution of a state of remorse as the patient recognizes what experiences have been lost as a result of rigid enforcement of the splitting defense.

I would note that as the consultant I provided the necessary "holding" environment in this therapeutic relationship. Someone must do this. Ordinarily, the therapist provides it unless the situation becomes too tense, in which case a somewhat removed consultant may serve the same purpose. An important facilitation of integration occurred in this case when the dance therapist and the psychotherapist met together with the patient for four or five sessions. Here the patient was able to view external to herself the integrated and cooperative relationship between these two parties and gradually identify with that alliance in allowing her own polarized object representations to become more integrated.

In an episode later on in her treatment, the patient's mother visited her in her apartment. The patient found herself more able to become annoyed with her mother, although she also found it somewhat distressing. There were disagreements over such issues, as the temperature of the apartment and her mother's assumption that her daughter shared her taste, as reflected in an article of clothing she had purchased for the patient. "She said she wouldn't buy me another one, because she realized I didn't like it. She has said that before but goes ahead and does it anyway." The patient then explained to her that she was taking chances buying her clothes: "My taste is different from yours." But her mother responded, "We have always had similar tastes." When the patient noticed that she was being sharp and oppositional toward her mother, she became curious about this and viewed the disagreements as attempts to separate from one another.

Change from the Viewpoint of Hospital Environment

In the initial Stage, after an immediate period of calm, there is usually an acting-out phase in which the patient repeats in the hospital the same difficulties experienced prior to admission. For example, a patient's mother put her in the closet when she became upset. In the hospital she did things that would lead to her placement in seclusion.

In the second stage, divisions occur within the staff. Intense feelings develop around these issues, and there is polarization over whether or not to seclude a patient. One patient wrote a note to her husband saying her children would be better off without her. The question then came up as to whether we should let her children visit. Debates occurred over the interpretation of the hospital policy manual regarding such visits. When it was decided not to allow them to visit, the patient refused all visitors. (Incidentally, this turning to the manual is a seeking of external structure to allay staff anxiety and is quite akin to the patient's use of structure.) It is important to maintain communication across these inevitable staff splits. During this stage the hospital constitutes a "holding" environment in quite concrete ways, such as going after the patient who runs away or using the sedative cold wet sheet pack when patients try to burn themselves. The hospital with its secure holding environment becomes a transitional object toward which the patient both forms an intense attachment and directs hateful feelings. This often happens on a nonverbal level, as in dance therapy. The psychotherapist tries to observe what is happening as a repetition and to convey this to the patient. It takes many examples before the patient begins to see the pattern.

Finally, there is a beginning internalization with concomitant intensification of affect. A patient might first be able to see splitting as exemplified in her artwork. These initial fleeting moments of mixed feelings toward the nurse or therapist can occur only when the patient feels safe enough to tolerate the anxiety. Symptoms may exacerbate at this point, and staff feel they are back at the beginning with the patient.

The patient's barrage of criticism toward the therapist may defend against grief. The therapist recognizes the emptiness in the patient's life, and a different view of the patient's history emerges. Some of the self-destructive behavior reappears, and later on the patient improves. Integration is not achieved at once or with finality. Splitting and the all-or-none attitude alternates with that of increasing ambivalence.

McGlashan and Miller (1982) in a comprehensive article on the goals of psychoanalysis and psychoanalytic psychotherapy had the following to say:

> Tolerance of Ambivalence—This goal refers to the capacity to acknowledge, freely experience, and accept the full range of ''good'' and ''bad'' feelings within and about one's self and one's objects. It relies especially on relinquishing the mechanism of splitting whereby idealization oscillates with devaluation or glorification alternates with contempt. The result is decreased thinking and feeling characterized as polarized, either/or, all or nothing, and black or white.
>
> These split-off qualities of good and bad derive from early experiences of pleasure and unpleasure that accrue positive and negative ''valences'' or values over time. With maturation and/or treatment, one comes to a recognition of their common derivation. Related attributes are a tolerance for mixed feelings, opportunities, incongruity, gray areas, uncertainty, ambiguity, and doubt.
>
> Obviously, the goal of integrated ambivalence relates inti-

mately to many of the other clusters already outlined. For example, it reflects successful negotiation of trust and separation /individuation and is a crucial part of object constancy. Since "good" and "bad" representations and/or introjects can form aspects of ego, superego, and ego ideal, integrated ambivalence relates to conscience, self-sense, self-esteem, and parental relationships. Since a tolerance for ambivalence implies attenuated splitting and projective identification, it also involves defensive structure and functioning. Because of this "broad base of operation," successful integration of ambivalence should include all of the aforementioned dimensions. In practice, greater synthesis of "good" and "bad" valences generally does occur in several areas simultaneously—hence the rationale for differentiating it into a cluster of its own. [p. 384]

I would concur in the belief that a treatment approach should include "all dimensions." Even though we may have some specific techniques to deal with all-or-none or splitting, most of our interventions will affect almost all symptoms simultaneously. I will conclude by summarizing a conceptual scheme of hospital treatment objectives and goals that cut across a variety of symptoms of the borderline patient.

First of all, the hospital, the patient, family, staff—including the psychotherapist—must be viewed as a system. For purposes of conceptualization, the patient in this system can be seen as involved with an "external" structure and a developing "internal" structure. The borderline and psychotic patient should have an overall goal of building an internal structure to take the place of the externally provided one.

The external aspect of the system should provide the potentiality to form relationships and set limits, a program with a schedule, the ability to observe and confront (especially transferential phenomena), the opportunity for discussion, the ability to use data to predict responses, and effective communication to coordinate the efforts of a comprehensive program. I have recently utilized team supervision with regular weekly meetings of the psychotherapist, nurse, activities person, and social worker in place of individual psychotherapy supervision.

The internal structure should encourage thinking, observing, identification, understanding/integrating data, verbalization, use of defense, and sublimation.

There are some specific technical aspects connected with both "external" and "internal" aspects of the system. We of course must keep in mind that such terms as external and internal are simply for our convenience in categorizing events, when in actuality they are quite interrelated and necessarily overlapping. What follows are some details on how to achieve and maintain a holding environment even in the face of staff splitting and resulting polarization.

The staff provides an auxiliary ego function through their observing capacities as they note and try to call the patient's attention to various events that seem to recur in a pattern. Of course patients are themselves making observations about each other, in group therapy and formal meetings involving the entire community, as well as informally in the daily life of the hospital. The staff also set limits, especially to destructive acting out, whether self-inflicted injury or violence toward others. This in itself tends to promote a delay in action and to foster discussion and thought about anger and other affects that might otherwise lead directly to action. Identity issues are important with these patients. With psychotic patients and often with borderline disorders, we encounter symptoms resulting from a tendency toward fusion and confusion of self-representations with object representations, as well as defenses against such fusion. Boundary issues are sometimes quite prominent, so that the staff must keep a respectful distance from these patients and yet remain involved with them.

A milieu addressed to respond to the individual needs of patients will foster identity stabilization as well as recognition of the patient's own needs. Staff will often guard against treating some patients in a "special" manner. As a result, the patient's inability to shift from all-or-none toward a more negotiating posture is compounded by a staff arbitrarily committed to fairness for all. It is important that the staff support and reinforce patients' preliminary attempts at changing their usual patterns and not simply regard this as "going through the motions." Sometimes staff will think of this as a superficial accommodation on the patient's part and a manifestation of "denial of illness." The staff also functions to facilitate the clear definition of problems on which the patient is working in the hospital environment. We have additional external features, including an organized program which itself provides a structure in that there are certain benchmarks of expectation and accomplishment. A good activities program should provide opportunities for real accomplishments on the part of the patient. This is especially important for the vulnerable and fragile self-esteem of patients who respond with extreme all-or-none attitudes. Behavior modification can be a useful organizer, and I think that it has as much effect on the staff as on the patient. When staff tend to react in conflicted and antagonistic ways to patients' behavior, a behavior modification program dealing with such responses provides a structure that allows a comforting amount of consistency among the staff. There is, however, a certain disadvantage sometimes when staff find themselves prevented from using certain appropriate responses which happen not to be included in the behavior modification outline.

The concept of multiple function is an important one for the staff to grasp. Their realization that any bit of behavior on the part of the patient can serve multiple purposes simultaneously will prevent a great many arguments and disagreements among them, as it allows the possibility that they may all be correct in their various understandings of why a patient is behaving in a particular way. As attachments may develop in long-term treatment programs, the staff must be alert to anxieties around separation and loss in relation to the staff and other patients. Patients with all-or-none proclivities tend to feel that any loss or separation will be the end of the world, and it is only through repeated experience of the contrary that they are eventually able to come to terms with this feeling.

Negativism is an important characteristic of many borderline and psychotic patients. Rather than try to eliminate or avoid negativistic attitudes, it is important that these be allowed to develop and be understood and worked through in the treatment process. Often patients are extruded from their environment when this negativism is viewed as something manipulatory or malicious on their part. Staff must become the recipients of anger, projective mechanisms, and transference. It is here that the concept of the holding environment becomes especially crucial. The feelings become extremely intense, and even experienced staff may be caught up in counterreactions.

The resolution of splitting is important for a staff that must deal with splitting phenomena; they must continue to communicate with one another in order to facilitate integration of the patient's various split-off aspects. In extreme situations the staff will sometimes become paralyzed by their assumption of absolute responsibility for the patient's self-destructive acting out. Patients who cut themselves or set fires or swallow objects will find willing adversaries in staff who go to extreme lengths to prevent these occurrences. Often someone outside the treatment team—a consultant or a supervisory nurse—can step into such a situation and lead the group to see the impossibility of assuming total responsibility. They may make provisions for a meeting of the patient, responsible relatives, and staff to work out their shared responsibility and an acknowledgment that it is impossible to prevent such self-destruction or suicide in any absolute way.

Finally, medications are at times a useful aspect with these patients. The so-called antipsychotic medications can be helpful in diminishing extreme peaks of anxiety, and antidepressant medications can be helpful as well.

As regards internal changes, we include the process of educating the patient to various concepts, including the difference between thinking something and doing it. One must also point out to the patient, in a gradual way, his particular manifestations of anxiety and his responses to it. I have found it quite useful to alert patients to noticing the sudden shifts in their thinking or speech that might indicate the presence of anxiety. One must actually foster the patient's postponement of action and his use of thought in the period of delayed action. One example of a patient who accomplished this was a woman who for a long time had been so disturbed that she was unable to come out of the seclusion room except when the other patients were off the unit. Eventually she was reintegrated into the community and was able even to go to the dining room. The assistant director of nursing was pleased to see her and indicated that she would stop by and visit with her on the hall at some unspecified future time. A couple of weeks passed with no visit, and the patient found herself at a tea, sponsored by an adjacent hall, at which staff from various parts of the hospital were in attendance. Upon seeing the assistant director, the patient immediately reacted with her usual anger and had a series of feelings culminating in the fantasy "I will show her. I'll make her pay attention to me. I'll smash the windows, and then she'll notice me." Upon observing this in herself, however, the patient paused, thought a moment, and then said to herself, "Oh, hell, why don't I just go over and say hi." When she approached the nurse, the latter expressed her pleasure at seeing her and said she had been up to visit her on two occasions but the patient had not been available; one time she was in her therapy session, and the other time she was sleeping. This was a very impressive sequence for the patient, who could begin to see how important it is not to jump to conclusions.

We also educate the patient to approach "insurmountable" problems by trying to break them down into manageable parts and attacking each part separately. This becomes a very useful skill once achieved and can do a lot toward improving the patient's sense of self-esteem.

Other internal features I would emphasize include patients' efforts toward integrating unconnected aspects of their behavior by patterning themselves after similar efforts by the psychotherapist and other staff. In fact, identification with therapist, staff, and other patients is probably the principal internal structure-building mechanism. Encouraging the patient to use previously successful coping patterns makes it easier for him to identify with his own healthy functioning.

Finally, the establishment of a sense of self-identity through a whole variety of experiences and interventions are very important in the diminution of symptoms and the achievement of goals in treatment.

My conclusion is that the treatment approach must be global and structural rather than symptom-oriented. However, one can best monitor change occurring during treatment by observing changes in symptoms. The sequence of shifts from splitting or all-or-none attitudes toward an integration reflecting ambivalence follows an oscillating pattern. At first there is a gradual intellectual recognition of the polarities. This recognition is at the same time disowned with some such phrase as "You would say . . ." etc. When the idea begins to penetrate, there is increased anxiety and marked affect. As the integration becomes established, there is a sense of sadness and remorse at having missed something in the past. Concomitant with changes toward integration is a recognition of separateness and growing independence. There is a sense of estrangement, the patient's perception of the therapist having changed, and a diminution of affective transference intensity.

References

Adler, G. (1977), Hospital management of borderline patients and its relation to psychotherapy. In: *Borderline Personality Disorders*, ed. P. Hartocollis. New York: International Universities Press, 1979.

Blanck, G., & Blanck, R. (1974), *Ego Psychology: Theory and Practice*. New York: Columbia University Press, pp. 345–357.

Freud, S. (1912), The dynamics of transference. *Standard Edition*, 12:97–108. London: Hogarth Press, 1958.

Kernberg, O. (1975), *Borderline Conditions and Pathological Narcissism*. New York: Aronson.

———— (1976), *Object Relations Theory and Clinical Psychoanalysis*. New York: Aronson.

McGlashan, T., & Miller, G. (1982), The goals of psychoanalysis and psychoanalytic psychotherapy. *Arch. Gen. Psychiat.*, 39(4):384.

Modell, A. (1976), "The holding environment" and the therapeutic action of psychoanalysis. *J. Amer. Psychoanal. Assn.*, 24:285–308.

Schulz, C. (1980), All-or-none phenomena in the psychotherapy of severe disorders. In: *The Psychotherapy of Schizophrenia*, ed. J. Strauss, M. Bowers, T. Downey, S. Fleck, S. Jackson, & I. Levine. New York: Plenum Press, pp. 181–189.

Part IV

Otto Allen Will, Jr., M.D.

13

Illuminations of the Human Condition

Otto Allen Will, Jr., M.D.

During my years in psychiatry my major interest has been—and is—in psychotherapy. Its theories and techniques, multiple and changing, are only a part of my continuing concern with this enterprise. In a limited and fairly safe way, I am enabled in my work to witness various psychiatric disorders revealed as representations and caricatures of human living with which each of us is more or less intimately acquainted. I am being shown something about the interrelatedness of my patients' hurts with the matrix of life—physical, biological, social, and cultural. So it is that although I focus my attention in therapeutic sessions in a person's particular troubles, there are no aspects of knowledge that seem entirely foreign to my professional activities. This is a broad expanse from a narrow window. The accuracy of the view is always to be questioned and each of us has a private vision. It is essential, however, that the common qualities of these disparate views be recognized and organized into communicable sense that can be used in the general governance of human behavior. In any case, to cease looking and seeking to comprehend whatever we are permitted to see to the extent of our abilities is perilous.

People are many things—and they are also interesting. Psychotherapy is a form of involvement with them.

The following remarks by the anthropologist Loren Eiseley (1957) are relevant to the work of the psychotherapist. ''It finally comes to me," he writes, "that this is the most enormous extension of vision of which life is capable: the projection of itself into other lives. This is the lonely, magnificent power of humanity. It is, far more than any spatial adventure, the supreme epitome of the reaching out" (p. 46).

My remarks today are marked by a personal quality. There are several reasons for my speaking in this fashion:

(1) I am not a scientific investigator or theoretician and thus cannot report on research studies or refinements of theoretical issues.

(2) In my work as a therapist I have usually been very personally involved, finding it difficult to stand apart as an observer of the action. At times, greater distance on my part would have been beneficial for all concerned.

(3) I have commonly felt myself to be something of a stranger—on the periphery of events. So the personal emphasis is a kind of introduction, even to myself.

(4) I no longer experience psychotherapy as a discipline of treatment that can be practiced without constant reference to the world in which it takes place. To some extent, in my actions I live a quiet and protected life; in my feelings I do not.

(5) Finally, being at this Center is never an impersonal experience for me. I came here fifteen years ago not because of the beauty of the country, or the peacefulness of the surroundings, or even because of the first-rate professional people who had been, were then, and are now here. I came because the work that I care about was done—and would be done—here. I wanted the opportunity to learn from prolonged and serious association with people—patients and members of the staff—who had in their own ways interests similar to mine.

Of The Past

I shall attend today to certain concepts that are particularly important to me in my professional activities. As the private and the public aspects of my living are clearly related to each other, I shall continue to speak personally.

I wanted to be a physician because I saw much illness in my own family, and the doctor who gave care appeared as both powerful and good. At university I majored in the social sciences, learned at least that I was ignorant, and then wanted to learn something that was tangible, concrete, and useable in ways demonstrably practical. Despite this wish, in medical school I felt drawn to psychiatry, probably because of what I had seen—in myself and others—of anxiety, depression, anger, failed hopes, and the great variances between the overt and covert aspects of the self. There was, then, a lack of harmony between my interests. For me, philosophy and the social sciences were intriguing, but I felt inferior to my friends in engineering who were learning, for example, how to build a bridge. Psychiatry was inviting, but I was troubled by it because I wanted to be a "real doctor." Although I have, for the most part, been accepted by the groups with which I have been associated, I have usually felt peripheral to them, never quite an integral part. I am describing a quality of oscillation in my personality and we could, as is our tendency, ascribe it to early experience with the contrasting personalities of my parents. Perhaps that is the case, but that can be of no real concern to us. Of greater interest is that such swings from one attitude to another are present in our society and in such manifestations of it as our profession.

In medical school my interest in psychiatry declined. Where I studied, this "specialty" was not highly esteemed. The psychotic people were frequently dreaded, disdained, or dismissed, and the many treatments offered them—removal of faci of infection, intravenous gold salts, thyroidectomies, fever induced by various methods, prolonged sleep, metrazol, insulin, electroshock, lobotomies, and so on—did not appeal to me. Psychoanalytic teaching was discouraged and what I heard of its theories I could not apply easily to what I saw in the clinic—a reflection, of course, of my continuing hesitancy to take a closer look at human behavior. In the latter part of the Second World War I worked with psychotic military patients in an institution with a population of eight thousand. I felt overwhelmed by the mass of seemingly purposeless disorder, and I planned to return as soon as possible to the comparative security of internal medicine.

Certain events, however, brought a change in my perspective. I heard Frieda Fromm-Reichmann talk about her version of the "mentally ill" and I began to see individual persons in the masses that were crowding the facilities of the Federal hospital. Masserman, David Rioch, and Liddel showed more clearly how some aspects of human behavior resembled that of other animals. Sullivan described his views of schizophrenia and I was encouraged by what he said to take a further—and fresh—look at the events of which in many ways I had been a blind and prejudiced onlooker. I experienced something of what Helen Perry (Sullivan, 1974) was later to describe: "Sullivan became, first, the Recording Angel for the schizophrenic process in the mental hospital; and having realized some measure of hope in that chaotic world set out in later studies to find some path for order in the vastly troubled ways of the larger world" (p. xxxi).

Psychiatry, because of my particular experience and personal bias, had become for me an activity dominated by diagnosis, disposition, speculation, rationalization, organic treatments, and theories more obscuring than revealing of the hurt person. When I had been more directly concerned with anthropology, biology, comparative anatomy, and sociology, I read that the anthropologist Kroeber had described his interests as the "study of man." This idea had been to me overwhelming, but interesting nonetheless. Some later remarks by Sullivan (1953) encouraged my interest:

> the field of psychiatry is neither the mentally sick individual, nor the successful and unsuccessful processes that may be observed in groups and that can be studied in detached objectivity. Psychiatry, instead, is the study of processes that involve or go on between people. The field of psychiatry is the field of interpersonal relations under any and all circumstances in which these relations exist. It was seen that *a personality* can never be isolated from the complex of interpersonal relations in which the person lives and has his being. [p. 10]

I then felt that the undeveloped, still obscure, and seemingly conflicting interests of earlier years might be brought into greater harmony in ways that made sense. The oscillations—the swings between "hard" and "soft" ideas—were being lessened.

While still in service after the war's end, I found the opportunity to be the therapist of a young military officer who had been treated with insulin, electroshock, and barbiturate-induced prolonged sleep, with no apparent benefit. Because of his assaultiveness, self-mutilation, and refusal to eat, he spent most of his days in a pack alone in a locked room. Not knowing anything to do or say that might be useful to this man, I soon spoke less and observed more of what might be going on in the extended silences of our growing relationship. No miracles occurred, but we came to know more of each other, and his mutism and gross disturbance disappeared. This experience was professionally encouraging, but in some ways discomforting. The schizophrenic patient, in becoming in my eyes a person, had led me to hear hints of aspects of myself that could not be denied or put aside. To use a somewhat imprecise phrase, the oscillations existed within myself as well as without. I was a part of both my experience and my expectations. Past, present, and future could be seen as one and whole, rather than simply linear. The increasingly evident connections between persons labeled sick or called patients, those diagnosed healthy, the society, and their cultural-biological heritage brought with them flickering suggestions of hope for patients and all of us. It was apparent, however, that if mankind was to be more than victim this hope would have to be increased or realized, and hard decisions would be required—always on the basis of data that could be challenged as somehow less than adequate.

At first I felt supported by Sullivan's statement (1953) that ''in most general terms, we are all much more simply human than otherwise, be we happy and successful, contented and detached, miserable and mentally disordered, or whatever'' (pp. 15–16).

It seemed to me then that this remark was kindly, tolerant, pleasant, and vaguely reassuring. Perhaps, but I have come to find it insightful, provocative, and disturbing. To me, it means that there is no way out—no escape from the state of being human. Whatever what we call our faults or virtues may be, we cannot be more, less, or otherwise than human. This, for life as I witness it. As to elsewheres of speculation I know nothing. If, without exit, we are so confined, limited responsibility for existence lies with us. The enemy, as well as benefactor, being, for the moment, largely ''us,'' we must for our own preservation learn all that we can about him. Thus it is that I consider the investigation of human behaviors to be the most pressing and vital concern of research.

My own activities in the field have been clinical, not research.

With doubt and trepidation I became, as the phrase goes, a psychotherapist. I continue with uncertainty, but without regret. This enterprise has been, for me, both beneficial and costly.

Developments in Psychiatry during, Roughly, the Past Forty Years

During the past forty years there have been many developments
in the field that I have been able to witness. I shall review these briefly,
knowing that in doing so I may slight or overlook some matters of
importance.

1. The recognition of the hospital, and other organizations, as active
   social systems.
2. The study of the family as a social system vital as a fundamental
   humanizing agency.
3. The extension of field theory into general systems theory.
4. The elaboration of concepts of group processes into planned techniques of therapy.
5. Attempts at interdisciplinary collaboration—discovered to be as
   difficult as important (that is, very).
6. The application of psychoanalytic theories to a wider range of
   human problems.
7. The direct observation of the human being at different stages of
   his life cycle.
8. Further understanding of language and symbolism as communication and defense.
9. The growing science of ethology.
10. Behaviorism reawakened and emerging as behavior therapy.
11. Social studies of genetics.
12. Theories reflecting observations of the effects of attachment, sep-
    aration, and loss.
13. New approaches to the study of dreaming.
14. A proliferation of psychosocial therapeutic procedures—community
    psychiatry, halfway houses, and the approximately 250 more-or-
    less accepted brands of psychotherapy.
15. Further refinements and reevaluations of psychoanalytic person-
    ality theory, including attempts to define existentialism.

16. Recent studies in "infant psychiatry."

These developments may be looked upon as belonging in the general field of social (or socio-) psychiatry, what we call the intrapsychic being an expression of, a contribution to, and an integral, operational part of what is perceived as external. Whatever the actual or seeming differences may be, emphasis in all of these is placed on the study of man through the observation of his behavior in various social situations, and on making what is learned available for possible therapeutic application.

During these years there were other developments that influenced the theories and practices of psychiatry, although that field was not their primary focus. Among these developments were (1) increasingly sophisticated methods of investigation in biochemistry and neurophysiology; (2) genetics; and (3) pharmacology. From these studies of the physical workings of the body came, among other results, the creation of a new specialist—the psychopharmacologist.

There were changes in society that affected psychiatry somewhat indirectly, but very importantly. These included:

1. The economic depression of the 1930s with the accompanying decline of confidence in the ability of the country to control the business enterprise.
2. The Second World War and the numerous wars that followed.
3. Increases in methods of communication, making the world more rapidly visible to at least many of its inhabitants.
4. The growth of population.
5. Growing recognition of the limitations of natural resources.
6. Competing needs for attention and the provision of care and help—the young, the old, the infirm, the destitute, the criminal, the mentally retarded, the mentally ill, the poorly educated, the unemployed, the unemployable, and so on—plus the differing opinions regarding the definition of each of these groups.
7. The great increases in scientific and technical knowledge not accompanied by significant alterations in what has been called "man's nature."
8. Nuclear power and the human power and necessity to decide upon its use.

These are some of the developments that influence our profession, the ways we live, our views of the universe and ourselves, our expectations, and our hopes and despairs.

Frequently it is necessary that someone else speak for me. In this instance, Loren Eiseley (1970):

> The long slow turn of world time as the geologist has known it, and the invisibly moving hour hand of evolution perceived only yesterday by the biologist, have given way in the human realm to a fantastically accelerated evolution induced by industrial technology. So fast does this change progress that a growing child strives to master the institutional customs of a society which, compared with the pace of past history, compresses centuries of change into his lifetime. I, myself, like others in my generation, was born in an age which has already perished. At my death I will look my last upon a nation which, save for some linguistic continuity, will seem increasingly alien and remote. It will be as though I peered upon my youth through misty centuries. I will not be merely old; I will be a genuine fossil embedded in onrushing man-made time before my actual death. [p. 22]

So what of the psychotherapist who has spent so much time with so few deeply troubled people—and continues on that course? Recently I was asked to speak to a medical staff in an effort "to keep alive and well long-term inpatient psychoanalytic treatment . . . [which] due to various pressures of the times is threatened with becoming an endangered species." A few days ago I was invited to "grand rounds" at a university medical school because some of the residents wanted to hear about psychotherapy as applied to psychotic conditions. Several years ago Elvin Semrad responded as follows to my receiving such an invitation: "They want to hear you because you are a walking anachronism." So it goes.

Current Questioning of "Psychological" Treatment

Hope is a sentiment that has commonly been associated with this land, although there have always been, as there are now, many who do not share the luxury and the necessity of this notion. The idea of being bound by fate, inheritance, circumstance, or nature is not popular. We want to know, to govern, and to be in control. We feel that we should be able to do something about almost everything, sometimes not taking note of the costs of our actions.

There has been—and is—hope in American psychiatry. For example, commenting on dementia praecox (schizophrenia), Adolf Meyer (1938) wrote, "where there is life there is hope, i.e., there is something to be done. In this we do not want to fool ourselves. We want the facts. We are willing to recognize defects so as to be sure wherein we shall also find victories" (pp. 4–5).

Hope was strengthened by discovering that some of the most regressed and psychotic people could be helped to move out of the depths of disorder to more effective and satisfying living through serious attempts to discover what the troubles were about—what they meant. We found that we could assist in bringing about useful changes if we had time, knowledge, patience, belief leavened by governing doubt, at least some public support, and the help of other people concerned more directly—professional colleagues and the members of a patient's family. There were failures, but we were encouraged not to give up in our efforts to learn and to help the patient. We knew also that we must hold in check our ambitions and enthusiasms lest an overwhelming need to cure produce harm rather than benefit. We had confidence in the human relationship as a major factor in the forming of personality, and in the influencing of change in the direction of either health or sickness.

Attendant upon hope is disappointment; to dare one is to risk the other. In some quarters the idea of the human being as rational and able to care for itself and its relevant universe is declining. There is some questioning of the idea that the human being is a salvageable organism. There are many pressures—social, economic, moral—to do something in a hurry about the many needs in the society. Psychotherapy has never been a get-rich-quick method of treatment or research. As a formalized procedure, it is not available to many people, and we feel guilty because of the numbers who do not receive whatever benefits can be derived from it. We recognize that the costs of treatment lead to a form of triage reflecting, to a large extent, economic conditions.

The humanistic, interpersonal, social, environmentalist approach has not produced miracles of change, and the resulting disappointment leads to searches for more promising sources of hope. The trend today is toward a form of biologism, a search in the machinery of the body for further information about the structural and functional bases of behavior. The hope is that the knowledge gained can be put to use in treatment. In the face of this shift to biologism, writes Walter Reich (1982),

> the rest of the profession is standing aside, partly in wonder, partly in hope, and partly in fear.
>
> But those psychiatrists who are fearful probably should not be. And those who are haughty in their biological knowledge probably should not be. . . . During the now-ending reign of environmentalism, something was learned, despite its overextension. Something was learned, after all, about people—about their needs and ways of being, both in health and illness. . . . Psychiatrists learned—or stumbled upon—verbal methods for dealing with disturbances of behavior and thinking, of mood and perspective that can be effective even if the source of the effect is not, or may not be, in the words themselves, or in the special nature of the technique, but in the nonspecific elements of attentiveness and caring. . . .
>
> And, too, the biological psychiatrists and their followers have other lessons to learn from environmentalism's fall. They have to learn humility. They have to recognize that no psychiatric ideology has a claim on the whole truth at every level. If it did it would be a divine ideology, a true religion. And that, in turn, would imply the existence of some scientific god, one that has not been discovered, even in psychiatry. [pp. 195–196]

Having looked about for an illusive certainty, and finding little evidence of its existence in much of what I do, I must agree with the following comment by Lewis Thomas (1981):

> The greatest of all the accomplishments of twentieth century science has been the discovery of human ignorance. We live, as

never before, in puzzlement about nature, the universe and ourselves most of all. . . . Now, for the first time in human history, we are catching glimpses of our incomprehension. . . . It is the admission of ignorance that leads to progress, not so much because of the solving of a particular puzzle leads directly to a new piece of understanding but because the puzzle—if it interests enough scientists—leads to work! [pp. 49–52]

Reports of research in psychotherapy may be sobering, as presented in these remarks from a member of the Senate Finance Committee (quoted in Parloff, 1980): ''Based on evaluation of the literature and testimony . . . it appears clear to us that there are virtually no controlled clinical studies, conducted and evaluated in accordance with generally accepted scientific principles, which confirm the efficacy, safety, and appropriateness of psychotherapy as conducted today'' (p. 289). A recent review of outcome research by Smith, Glass, and Miller (1980) is more encouraging: ''Psychotherapy is beneficial, consistently so and in many ways. Its benefits are on a par with other expensive and ambitious interventions, such as schooling and medicine. The benefits of psychotherapy are not permanent, but then little is. . . . Psychotherapy enjoys near parity with drug therapy in treating even the very serious psychological disorders'' (pp. 183–189).

The point of all this talk, however, is that there is no true safety to be found in the extremes, or even in a middle course. I have myself come to make a belated peace with a governing principle of uncertainty.

Concepts of Particular Concern to a Therapist

Although I may properly have doubts, I must also have certain convictions—forms of belief—that govern my actions. These convictions should be subject to review and modification, but to change or abandon any of them will not be easy. As a therapist, I am guided in my professional work by certain concepts of human behavior to be discussed below. They also, of course, influence my more personal living, although it is often difficult to apply them to myself. Such ideas should be explicit, and I shall refer briefly to some of them here. Although I am not an expert in any of the subjects to be mentioned,

I hold opinions about them. What I do as a psychotherapist will reflect to a large extent my view of human beings, an idea expressed by Leon Eisenberg (1972) as follows:

> What we believe of man affects the behavior of men, for it determines what each expects of the other. Theories of education, of political science, of economics, and the very policies of governments are based on implicit concepts of the nature of man. Is he educable? Is he actuated only by self-interest? Is he a creature of such dark lusts that only submission to sovereign authority can save him from himself?
>
> What we choose to believe about the nature of man has social consequences. . . . men and women must believe that mankind can become fully human in order for our species to attain its humanity. [pp. 125–128]

The Human Being

Man is a biological organism with roots in a distant past in which he did not exist. He is the current expression of the incomprehensible phenomena that we call creation and the still unending changes known as development. Related as he is to other animals and forms of life, he is not "just a beast." Although we learn much about the workings of the body, man is not "simply a machine." To a considerable extent a personality is formed through experience, but the human is not "merely" some kind of material molded by external events. Man is not free to escape his biological heritage, but he is not entirely its victim; he can make choices and assert his will, whatever that may be. Man is a creature not only of the past and the present, but of the future. He lives in many worlds. He—and she—are puzzles, and those who try to solve this conundrum are handicapped by being part of it.

Instinct

The human being is not bound by "instincts," however defined, as are other organisms known to us. In the loss of relatively invariant instinctual responses man has gained the freedom to be creative. There has been lost also the safety of certain built-in behavioral controls or guides. The lack of such governing mechanisms requires that a person become responsible and make choices based on selections from available data. The ability to exercise such responsibility has anxiety as a partner. To avoid the experience of that unpleasantness, various systems of beliefs may serve as pseudoinstincts that can direct behavior without the painful necessity of resorting to rational thought. When beliefs become "natural" they are not questioned, for they seem to be simple statements of "the way things are." Therein lies a danger for the survival of the human being and the species.

Referring to the Renaissance mystic, Pico della Mirandola, von Bertalanffy (1967) writes:

> When creating man, Pico tells, God had pre-empted all treasures, archetypes and niches in the world, having given them, with a rigidly determined nature, to plants, animals, and angels. But man was created with the highest of gifts, as a being neither earthly nor heavenly, mortal nor immortal, but endowed with free decision. So he may become a vegetating plant, a rapacious animal, or an angel and son of God. [p. 48]

Aggression

Despite the welter of destruction which is reported to us daily, I do not think of man as an animal driven by aggressive instincts. An outstanding aspect of human behavior is the need for relationship and cooperative enterprise. For better or worse, no enterprises are devised or carried out by one person without the at least indirect participation of others. There are many views on this subject. The following is that of the biologist Dobzhansky (1956): "the view of nature, red in tooth and claw, in which every living being has only the alternative of 'eat or be eaten' is just as unfounded as the sentimentalist view that all is sweetness and light in unspoiled nature. . . . It has been said that 'Man was formed for society' . . . [and] in fact, interpersonal relations constitute the most important aspect of human environment" (pp. 69, 124). A similar statement is made by Rene Dubos (1973): "Man's propensity for violence is not a racial or a species attribute woven in his genetic fabric. It is culturally conditioned by history and the ways of life'' (p. 91).

There are, of course, other opinions, but I choose the one presented here.

Symbolism

The human being is a symbolizing animal. He has the ability to create symbols of his experiences, and to remember, dissociate, suppress, deny, disbelieve, believe, cherish, reject, live, and die in their service. On this subject I again quote von Bertalanffy (1959); man, he writes, ''lives in a universe not of things but of symbols of things . . . it is symbolic activity which distinguishes human and subhuman behavior. . . . psychopathology means disturbances not only at the biological and physiological but above all at the symbolic level'' (pp. 41–51).

Over thirty years before this last statement, Sullivan (1926) wrote:

The extinction of the mind-body problem and the affiliation of psychology, not only with biology, but with all the sciences depends upon the conception of the symbol. . . . we must elucidate our notion of the symbol if psychological consideration is to displace the sterile traditional psychology and the verbal theories. . . . Psychiatry thus rests upon the study of the origin, growth, and manifestations of symbols. [pp. 81–93]

If the ability to create and live by symbols is mankind's greatest strength it could be also its fatal weakness.

Culture

Man, the maker of cultures, has both a biological and a cultural heritage. He creates ideas and builds them into systems of thought that have an enduring quality more real than the tangible things he builds. He can learn anything, often without recognition of the antibiological nature of some of the concepts to which he becomes devoted. On this subject I quote Eiseley (1957):

We are now in a position to see the wonder and terror of the human predicament: man is totally dependent on society. Creature of dream, he has created an invisible world of ideas, beliefs, habits, and customs which buttress him about and replace for him the precise instincts of the lower creatures. In this invisible universe he takes refuge, but just as instinct may fail an animal under some shift of environmental conditions, so man's cultural beliefs may prove inadequate to meet a new situation. [p. 92]

Attachment

Many years ago, when I first left my boyhood home for an extended period, I experienced a state of extreme discomfort. I was depressed, restless, dissatisfied, preoccupied, and unable to take any pleasure in my surroundings, which were both comfortable and interesting. I was homesick. In retrospect these phenomena seemed strange in view of the fact that I had wanted to go away and had experienced living at home as very unpleasant. In brief, I found myself tied painfully to a situation that I wanted to leave. I felt bound by invisible and inexplicable bonds. In my later professional work I became impressed by the intensity and strength of the attachments that many of my patients had to family situations that were obviously unpleasant and laden with anxiety. The emotions associated with attachment, separation, and loss continue to be primary forces in my experience of living.

The investigations of John Bowlby and John Paul Scott have been of great value to me professionally, and a help and comfort to me personally. What is now called attachment theory is a vital part of my own work as a therapist. The essence of my interest is represented in the following quotations:

an individual at the proper period in life will become attached to anything in the surrounding environment, both living and nonliving. . . . an intense emotional experience, whether rewarding or punishing, will increase the speed of forming the primary attachment. . . . it is likely that the capacity to form these attachments is never actually lost in adult life but simply takes place more slowly, usually because of various interfering patterns of behavior. [Scott, 1963, pp. 37–38]

attachment theory is a way of conceptualizing the propensity of human beings to make strong affectional bonds to particular others and of explaining the many forms of emotional distress and personality disturbance, including anxiety, anger, depression, and emotional detachment, to which unwilling separation and loss give rise. [Bowlby, 1979, p. 127]

The Social Field

There is nothing static about the human being; he is in constant involvement with the environment. It is this field of transactions that is available for observation. In the words of Gardner Murphy (1947), "a personality is a structured organism-environment field, each aspect of which stands in dynamic relation to each other aspect. There is organization within the organism and organization within the environment, but it is the cross organization of the two that is investigated in personality research" (p. 8).

In psychotherapy both patient and therapist are variously participants and observers in these fields. Their behaviors and their observations are governed largely by their personal organization of past experience, by current necessities, and by estimates of future events. That is, all human relationships are experienced through a lens formed of a multitude of other experiences, remembered or not. We live in a world of transferences. In therapy we attempt to gain some understanding of the way in which the participants view themselves, each other, and what goes on between them. The therapist knows something about the story of his own life; he helps the patient devise his own story, one that makes sense in terms of available data, and that is usable for further living.

Relationship

The difficulties with which I attempt to deal as a therapist arise from the need for—and the fear of—human relationships. The actuality, or the dread, of loneliness is present or at the edge of awareness. There is no escape from a person's involvement with people, hate, love, and seeming indifference being but aspects of the entanglement. In the words of James Lynch (1977), ''Human relationships *do* matter. They are desperately important to both our mental and our physical well-being. . . . Quite literally we must learn to live together or face the possibility of prematurely dying alone. . . . Nature uses many weapons to shorten the lives of lonely people'' (pp. 3–4).

The items briefly outlined in my previous remarks are relevant to the psychotherapeutic process. Patient and therapist meet with the understanding that whatever the difficulties may be, they are acceptably human. While the partly historical, partly narrative story of a life is told, bonds of attachment form. Attempts are made to understand how and why each participant experiences what is happening between them. The self is revealed—to some extent—and the question ''Who are you?'' begins to be answered. Then comes separation.

In Conclusion

My life as a psychotherapist has been spent working with a few patients in and out of hospitals. In many ways this has been an isolated and protected existence, representations of outside storms being viewed through an individual. But those oscillations between the real and the imaginary, the concrete and the abstract, once so troublesome, become less so. The differences between these extremes are no longer of great moment, as the resemblances of one to the other become more apparent.

The work in the consulting room must be seen as having relevance beyond the ''ivory tower.'' Whatever knowledge we gain in this work should be formulated in clear and simple language, and made available to the public. Our primary concern professionally is for the welfare of our patients, but their welfare, and ours, requires a broader view.

As we learn more about human relationships, we find them threatened with extinction. Perhaps more of us are beginning to comprehend what a few have known for a long time—namely, that there is no guarantee that the species will continue to exist.

There is fear in the air. Fear of destruction of self, family, special group, or even a society is not new, but now we cannot with any confidence identify the survivors. The responsibility, if not the ability and power, to preserve life lies in ourselves. The tools that will save or kill are largely symbolic. The real question has to do with a concept of humanity. Are all human beings to be accepted as human, or are some groups to be labeled less human than others? And, in any case, do we care about other human beings, or do we, more or less covertly, despise both them and ourselves?

Many people have commented on such questions, and I will let them speak for themselves:

> The fateful question for the human species seems to me to be whether and to what extent their cultural development will succeed in mastering the disturbance of their communal life by . . . aggression and self-destruction. . . . Men have gained control over the forces of nature to such an extent that with their help they would have no difficulty in exterminating one another to the last man. They know this, and hence comes a large part of their current unrest, their unhappiness and their mood of anxiety. [Freud, 1930, p. 145]

> ours is a dangerous age in which the race between creative knowledge and destruction is closer than ever before. Destruction has not yet arrived, and knowledge still has a chance. Those of us who have scientific training and ability should do everything in our power to speed up creation and slow down destruction. [Scott, 1958, p. 134]

> We have to make sense; we, every one of us. We have to make sense not about everything, but about principles that are important in promoting harmonious human relations. . . . [p. 273] Do we want nearly everyone to die in order that the human race may begin all over? Is it seemly that we, momentarily honorable among the builders of the future, shall further by irresponsibility a schizophrenic dream of death and rebirth? [Sullivan, 1947, pp. 277–278]

> It is difficult for my generation to know how seriously you [the

younger generation] take the danger of mankind destroying his own species. But those who share the apprehension of my generation might perhaps, with us, derive strength from keeping alive the thought that has helped so many of us in the past when faced with the possibility of imminent death. Scientific research is one of the finest occupations of our mind. It is, with art and religion, one of the uniquely human ways of meeting nature, in fact, the most active way. If we are to succumb, and even if this were to be ultimately due to our own stupidity, we could still, so to speak, redeem our species. We could at least go down with some dignity, by using our brain for one of its supreme tasks, by exploring to the end. [Tinbergen, 1968]

If then, by the question "Is there hope for man?" we ask whether it is possible to meet the challenges of the future without the payment of a fearful price, the answer must be: No, there is no such hope. [p. 136]
 . . . the dangers we have discussed do not descend, as it were, from the heavens, menacing humanity with the implacable fate that would be the consequence of the sudden arrival of a new Ice Age or the announcement of the impending extinction of the sun. . . . On the contrary, as we have repeatedly sought to emphasize, all the dangers we have examined—population growth, war, environmental damage, scientific technology—are *social* problems, originating in human behavior and capable of amelioration by the alteration of that behavior. . . . [p. 61]
 Within [man's] impatient spirit lurks one final danger for the years during which we must watch the approach of an unwanted future. This is the danger that can be glimpsed in our deep consciousness when we take stock of things the way they are now: the wish that the drama ran its full tragic course, bringing man, like a Greek hero, to the end that he has, however unwittingly, arranged for himself. For it is not only with dismay that Promethean man regards the future. It is also with a kind of anger. If after so much effort, so little has been accomplished; if after such vast challenges, so little is apt to be done—then let the drama proceed to its finale, let mankind suffer the end it deserves. . . .

> [p. 142] I do not intend to condone . . . an attitude of passive resignation, or a relegation of the human prospect to the realm of things we choose not to think about. . . . the fact that the collective destiny of men pretends unavoidable travail is no reason, and cannot be tolerated as an excuse for doing nothing. [Heilbroner, 1974, p. 137]

Again, it is evident that psychotherapy with its theories and practices cannot be separated from the human vicissitudes of living in groups, however constituted. As for the ideas presented by the authors just quoted, I concur that it is imperative that we continue in our attempt to comprehend our behaviors. In this small center in Stockbridge the opportunity exists for continuing to take a close look at some aspects of troubled human living over months and years of time. That is a great opportunity and it needs to be preserved. From such observations we can learn more about what happens to children in their growing up that they become enmeshed in strange and hurtful webs of words. We should not castigate ourselves if we know that our ideas are small and our understanding deficient. Instead, I think that we should each of us observe as best he or she can, and state clearly what we see. Optimism and pessimism and cynicism we must forgo; modest hope coupled with work is for us.

References

Bertalanffy, L. von (1959), Some biological considerations of the problems of mental illness. *Bull. Menn. Clin.*, 23:41–51.
——— (1967), *Robots, Men, and Minds*. New York: George Braziller.
Bowlby, J. (1979), *The Making and Breaking of Affectional Bonds*. London: Tavistock.
Dobzhansky, T. (1956), *The Biological Basis of Human Freedom*. New York: Columbia University Press.
Dubos, R. (1973), Man's nature and social institution. In: *Man and Aggression*, ed. A. Montagu. New York: Oxford University Press, pp. 84–91.
Eiseley, L. (1957), *The Immense Journey*. New York: Vintage Books.
——— (1970), *The Invisible Pyramid*. New York: Scribner.
Eisenberg, L. (1972), The human nature of human nature. *Science*, 176:125–128.
Freud, S. (1930), Civilization and its discontents. *Standard Edition*, 21:64–145. London: Hogarth Press, 1961.
Heilbroner, R. L. (1974), *An Inquiry into the Human Condition*. New York: Norton.
Lynch, J. J. (1977), *The Broken Heart*. New York: Basic Books.

Meyer, A. (1938), Introduction to: *Analysis of Parergasia*, by G. C. Terry & T. A. Rennie, Nervous and Mental Disease Monograph 64, New York.

Murphy, G. (1947), *Personality: A Biosocial Approach to Origins and Structures*. New York: Harper.

Parloff, M. B. (1980), Psychotherapy and research: An anaclitic depression. *Psychiat.*, 43:279–293.

Reich, W. (1982), Psychiatry's second coming. *Psychiat.*, 45(3):189–196.

Scott, J. P. (1958), *Aggression*. Chicago: The University of Chicago Press.

——— (1963), *The Process of Primary Socialization in Canine and Human Infants*, Monographs of the Society for Research in Child Development, No. 85, Vol. 28, No. 1. Lafayette, IN: Child Development Publications of the Society for Research in Child Development.

Smith, M. L., Glass, G. V., & Miller, T.V. (1980), *The Benefits of Psychotherapy*. Baltimore: Johns Hopkins Press.

Sullivan, H. S. (1926), The importance of a study of symbols in psychiatry. *Psyche*, 8:81–93.

——— (1947), Remobilization for enduring peace and social progress. *Psychiat.*, 10:239–252.

——— (1953), *Conceptions of Modern Psychiatry*. New York: Norton.

——— (1974), *Schizophrenia as a Human Process*. Introduction: H. S. Perry, p. xxxi. New York: Norton.

Thomas, L. (1981), Debating the unknowable. *Atlantic Monthly*, July, pp. 49–52.

Tinbergen, N. (1968), On war and peace in animals and men. *Science*, 160:1411–1418.

14

Human Relatedness and the Schizophrenic Reaction

Otto Allen Will, Jr., M.D.

Some time past I was called upon to serve as physician to a young woman who had passed many years as a patient in a series of psychiatric hospitals. She spent the greater portion of her time in a closed room barren of furniture and decoration; she tore to pieces clothing and other objects, barricaded her door against visitors, and ran from them when she could. For many years she had not eaten freely, saying that her food was poisoned, and struggling against the efforts made to feed her. She was known by various names descriptive of fragments of her behavior, and the person which she had been was concealed behind a façade of stereotypes. Referred to as ''assaultive,'' ''negativistic,'' ''hostile,'' a ''feeding difficulty,'' as ''the one who runs away,'' and so on, she was seen more as a problem than a person.

The information about Catherine, as I shall call her, was slight, recent accounts adding little to those of earlier periods. She was said to have been an amiable, good, and intelligent child who had displayed no gross difficulties in her course of development, having been more than adequate as athlete, student, and participant in social affairs. It was evident, however, that some matters troublesome to her had not been communicated clearly to her associates; in her late teens she became markedly preoccupied, showed a distaste for the company of

263

others, and attempted to kill herself, revealing to no one her thoughts about her indisposition. Her apparent depression was then obscured by symptoms suggestive of a physical disorder; she suffered from constipation, loss of appetite, and a persistent decline in weight.

The diagnosis of a pituitary disease was made, but medications effected no cure, and she was finally hospitalized as a "mental" patient—emaciated, increasingly withdrawn, and hostile. She was moved from one institution to another, received the currently popular treatments with insulin and electricity without noticeable benefit, worsened, and was thought by some to show evidence of a "deterioration" of the brain.

Catherine cried out that she hated all things medical, and made every effort to run away from the hospital. She had little to do with her ward associates, rarely called anyone by name, and revealed nothing of her past life to others, acting as if she guarded a terrible secret. She denied that she had difficulties other than those associated with being incarcerated against her will, and resisted all approaches made to her. At times she experienced panic, acting as if she had been caught up in a horrible nightmare, assaulting those near her, and attempting to hurt or destroy herself.

Here were displayed anxiety, fear, loneliness, and the corroding effects of social isolation. But anyone who sought to help her was, without exception, driven away by her contempt or anger, or by their fear of her aloneness, seeking to account for this retreat and despair by saying that Catherine was afflicted with a strange "organic" illness, was "hopeless," "unable to love," or lacking in certain "essential human qualities." Thought of as less than human, she was referred to as "empty" and "hollow," as if she were a nonliving object.

Catherine showed no enthusiasm concerning my visits. Although I came regularly, she did not acknowledge my name or our appointments, denied that I was a physician, and turned her back on me. As I persisted she grew more tense, ran from me or attacked me, screamed that I was injuring her by my presence, was mute for long periods, and noticeably grew worse. I continued my visits, but my enthusiasm as a therapist declined on occasion. My varied approaches were seemingly ineffective, my theories were often without apparent relevance to the patient's behavior, and I frequently felt angry, discouraged, humiliated, and inept.

During the long silences—extending over many of our meetings—I would at first think of Catherine's difficulties and possible explanations for them; then I would consider our reactions together, puzzling about the reasons for our behavior; but shortly my thoughts would turn more to myself, to my own hopes and apprehensions; and in time I seemed to be abandoning all but a few repetitive and unprofitable ideas, which evidenced no clear connection to a past or future, and had their existence in an unchanging and seemingly unalterable present. Catherine was then not clear in my thinking, and I was engrossed with such generalizations as the "meaninglessness" of the situation to me and my "inadequacies" as a therapist, with anger at the institution and feelings of "despair."

What was at that time obscure later became more evident. Although I was in the room with Catherine, I was drawing back from her, it having soon become laborious for me to think of her for any length of time. Thoughts of her were replaced by abstractions, which in turn gave way to recurrent banalities and vaguely directed emotions. That which I called despair reflected difficulties in the organization and use of previous and current experience in the exercise of foresight; that is, 'hope'—which includes expectation—does not flourish when anxiety so disturbs comprehension of past and present that the concept of an evolving 'future' cannot be grasped.

Although I came to see Catherine with the purpose of helping improve her living, her responses often led me to feel ineffective and brutal. As I entered her room one day, she turned on me, saying: "I don't want to see you. You are cruel and punishing. You hurt people. You come here so you can laugh at me; you never listen to me. You are bitter and see only the dark side of things. You are unkind and you ought to be killed." I felt attacked unjustly, but as I listened I understood a little better how isolated, embittered, and pessimistic this woman was.

In this situation of anxiety and guarding, Catherine and I often held stereotyped and rigid views of each other. To me she was becoming just a patient with a diagnosis, and to her I was as follows: "You are a nothing," she said. "You are pompous, and cruel, and think you know it all, and you just want to tell people how to live as you think they ought to live. All doctors look, and act, and think alike; they aren't persons—they're just robots."

During one of the periods of silence Catherine and I, each unknown to the other, wrote about our views of what was taking place. On one occasion she wrote as follows:

> They just want to hurt you in this place and I am going mad. . . . You, doctor, are a piece of stone. . . . Your heart is ice. I shall die. . . . I shall sit and weave my fantasies into the wall. I shall never get well. . . . I feel crushed so that nothing is left. . . . I want to grow younger and younger until I don't exist any more. . . . Leave me alone; you are only a machine with all the feelings left out.

At approximately the same time I wrote:

> This woman seems brittle, cold, and hollow. With her I usually feel ignored and frozen out; I feel crushed, discouraged, and useless. I think that my personality has defects which disqualify me for this work.

Despite our silences and our withdrawals it was apparent that to some extent Catherine's experiences were being made clearer to me. It was not easy to put these matters into words, and in some instances I was reluctant to hear what she had to say, finding the message disturbing to me, and attempting to ''explain'' my discomfort by saying that my personality was unsuited to the task.

There was a period during which I felt unusually alone, isolated from my colleagues, and unable to tell them much of my work with Catherine. To one of them I said: ''I might as well not be here. It's like being in a cemetery; there isn't any life.'' Here is an excerpt from Catherine's writing at that time, read by me some months later:

> People are too terrible to live with. They have killed and the unremovable blood lies on their conscience. . . . Sorrow comes by day, and at night comes the evil. . . . I think that I am mad, because no living human being understands what I say. I feel in pieces and confused. At times I fall into the dark, going down with nothing to stop me—and then there are the voices, and I feel

that I go away for a long time. I don't know who I am. I think I have been dead for many years, but didn't know it. Maybe that's why you say I can't go home; because I am dead. Death is lonely, and I am a stranger to all of you and to me. I can't make a move; someone else will have to take the first step.

But my first steps often seemed to be misdirected or ill-timed. One day as I sat in silence Catherine suddenly turned and struck me. I held her arms and she wept, saying: "I haven't been able to hear you. You've been staying behind that wall of glass. It had to get broken somehow."

Thereafter Catherine and I spoke more freely with each other, and our isolation tentatively receded. During the several years of our meeting together she had said that she did not dream. Now she told me of a dream: "It was all very clear. I was almost afraid to look. I was afraid that it might go away, or that something would happen to it. But it was all right. It was just a picture. There was an ocean, and a white sand beach; and at the edge of the sand were some trees." I asked if there were any people in the dream. "Oh, no. Not even I. There was no one. Nothing moved—no wind—the sea was quiet; but the sun was shining. . . . But I wasn't afraid. It all seemed natural enough."

Of a later dream Catherine said: "It was like the first dream. There was the water, the beach, and the trees. But there was some surf, and I felt good. . . . And there was something else—a bird flew across the sky."

Catherine's behavior was called schizophrenic, and the events described above are not uncommon in the experience of such patients. There are certain aspects of the account which I wish to emphasize:

The patient's isolation. She was isolated, and had become involved in a situation promoting the development and maintenance of stereotyped thinking and behavior. She had great needs, but seemed to be unaware of them or denied their existence, and those who attempted to help often misinterpreted her requirements, or did not respond in ways acceptable to her. She often spoke of being free and independent, and of being separate from all people, as if her memories of relatedness were intolerable, and any hopes of comfortable closeness with another had been abandoned.

Her difficulty in communicating in words.   Catherine's difficulties in adolescence had been obscured by her social success; at that time no one thought of her as ill. She made a suicide attempt, became depressed, developed signs of an "organic" illness, and was finally called "mentally" disordered. It was as if her case could not be stated in words, her entire organism being involved in a responsiveness that included communicative as well as defensive and survival values. Thus the nonverbal aspects of our association were of great significance.

My reflections of my patient's feelings.   There were times when my own[1] sentiments—anxiety, loneliness, depression, anger, uncertainty about myself and my function—were reflections of my patient's feelings, and these shared experiences were the rudimentary beginnings of our using a more highly symbolic form of communication.

Our growing mutuality.   Our contacts were marked by recurrent approaches and retreats, without, however, a complete abandonment of a growing mutuality. Despite mutual rebuff and withdrawal I felt increasingly bound to Catherine, and she said: "You are a fool for getting caught up in this—this nothingness, this evil." Evil or otherwise, there were ties which were strengthened.

The concept of relatedness.   My earlier thoughts were concerned with such concepts as "her" ability to relate to me, or mine to her. As we went on, I thought of *our* relatedness, the mutuality of the therapeutic field becoming more apparent to me.

As Catherine and I continued our meetings, her anxiety subsided somewhat and her behavior became less disturbed. At this point some of her family members wished to terminate her treatment, saying that not enough was being accomplished; this was at the very time when there first appeared some evidence of useful change in the patient. There was no openly expressed serious complaint about the therapy, and the relatives had always spoken of their grave concern with the young woman's betterment, although they had often remarked that she was probably something to which they referred as "beyond recovery." I talked with the parents, finding them to be evasive, uneasy, and seemingly under some unclear but powerful pressure to "change things."

---

[1]"My own" is an inappropriate locution, as it seems to imply the operation of ideas apart from the interpersonal field.

I reminded Catherine's mother of her frequently expressed wish that her daughter get "well," and again asked what that term meant to her. The reply was: "I want it to be like it used to be when we all seemed all right together. She's getting different now—she doesn't seem to be a part of us any more."

I had witnessed such events before. Why should those who wished for the betterment of the patient frequently appear uncertain, anxious, and unsympathetic at the very point of his improvement and growing independence?

In thinking about this question I recalled John, a young man who improved from a schizophrenic reaction during the course of therapy with me. There was a point at which he became fearful and hesitant and wished to terminate our meetings, finally saying that he might kill me. I eventually learned from him that as our association developed he was at times afraid that I could not tolerate either his closeness to me or his independence. He stated matters this way:

I felt that there was a destructiveness in me that would involve you and kill you. I tried to tell you, but you didn't seem to hear. I'd get to feeling all right, but then we'd seem to be getting tied together so that neither one of us could be separate—or free—something like that. It was like we'd be lost, or eaten up, if we got close. So I wanted you to go away. If you stayed on and were destroyed, I'd lose you. But if you went away—I'd have you in my memory. . . . Then I got to feeling that something would happen to you if I went out on my own. It's crazy—but it's like you couldn't stand to let me get well—or go away.

In discussing John's experience, we discovered that his feelings about me resembled those he held for his mother. She had often spoken with enthusiasm about her pleasure in thinking of him as becoming more independent, but she also suggested that she could not live adequately without him, and that she might die or succumb to depression should he leave her. So it was that John grew anxious in his work with me. He needed me, but he expected that I, for my own necessities, would attempt to control him and resist his achievement of maturity and separation. We talked about all of this, and kept on with the work.

John's mother seemingly accepted the changes in her son, but thereafter grew more aloof and developed a malignancy of which she died. Referring to this, John said: "When you spoke of my getting well I felt as if you were telling me to be a murderer—that somehow you, or me, or someone—like my mother—was going to get killed. That sounds crazy, but I felt that way."

This may indeed sound crazy. I am not talking about simple cause and effect, and I do not know why John's mother sickened as she did. I do suggest that the family is a social field in which the patient plays an important functional role, subtle accommodations being made by other members to the development of his disordered ways of living, and a definite importance being attached to their perpetuation.[2] The patient, including what one may think of as his "sickness," is not only an expression of the family culture, but also an integral factor in the maintenance of its uncertain equilibrium. Changes in the patient, for example, threaten that stability, and necessitate reciprocal adjustments on the part of others, who are required to alter their behavior in some way, becoming more expressive, more participant, or more withdrawn. If the more independent, self-sufficient actions of the patient cannot be met by similar action on the part of others, those others may respond with the display of what are called "emotional" and "physical" disorders. To avoid such alterations, often felt to be disruptive and threatening, attempts may be made to reinclude the patient unchanged in the family field, the move being rationalized in terms of his being "hopeless" or requiring some other form of treatment.

In brief, the schizophrenic reaction reflects the family social sys-

---

[2]See, for example, the following incomplete list of articles concerned with family relationships. Studies of the patient's family increasingly emphasize the function of that organization as a social unit, the structure of which is mirrored in (and requires) the behavior of the patient, and reflects the larger culture of which it is a part (Caudill). The problem is considered in various ways, as follows: (1) the teaching to the children of distorted and personal family concepts of the culture (Lidz and others); (2) the involvement of various members in the anxiety of any one member (Limentani); (3) disturbances in communication systems within the family (Bateson and others); (4) the family system as a trap from which the patient cannot extricate himself without significant alteration in the system (Wynne and others). See Ackerman (1958), Bateson, Jackson, Haley, and Weakland (1956), Caudill (1958), Gerard and Siegel (1950), Kohn and Clausen (1956), Lidz (1958), Lidz, Cornelison, Terry, and Fleck (1958), Limentani (1956), Wolman (1957), and Wynne, Ryckoff, Day, and Hirsch (1958).

tem, and changes in the one require accompanying changes in the other. In such systems growth, which involves greater self-identification and accommodation to new experience, may be looked upon as productive of destruction and loss, and may lead to powerful—and seemingly hostile or meaningless—efforts to retain the status quo. One may look upon such phenomena as evidence of interrelatedness of the participants in a social field in which the pattern or mode of interaction must be comprehended in order to clarify the transactions involving any two members.[3] The parent who responds anxiously to his child's growth is not necessarily resisting change for evil motives; he may not recognize the need for alteration in himself, or he may think of himself as incapable of such development. In this last instance his child's increasing separateness may be experienced as a threat—of loss of the child, or as destruction of the parent who continues to need the child to maintain his own sense of integrity. As the interrelatedness of behavior is recognized, provision may be made for the mutuality of change, and growth will be equated with life rather than with death.

I have reported that Catherine was thought to have a pituitary disorder—sometimes called Simmond's Cachexia[4]—prior to the onset of that behavior described as schizophrenic. In the course of treatment there came to be no further evidence of such a state, and she was eventually no longer looked upon as "physically" or "mentally" ill.

I thought of other patients who had shown marked disturbances of organ systems prior to the establishing of the diagnosis of schizophrenia. Charles was eighteen years old when he developed a colitis; a year later he was obviously schizophrenic, but the colitis persisted during the first three years of psychotherapy, and then disappeared. James was thought to be suffering from multiple sclerosis before the appearance of schizophrenic behavior, and neurological signs were evident at times during the earlier period of his psychotherapy, although the original diagnosis was not confirmed.

---

[3]In this sense the schizophrenic reaction is not considered to be a reflection of an earlier (or persistent) interaction between "schizophrenogenic" mother and child, or "inadequate" father and child. The object of study becomes the character of the social field, reflecting the participation of significant members in it.

[4]Simmond's disease: Cachexia hypophysea (pituitary cachexia).

I then thought of Steven, a college student who consulted me many years ago with a complaint of pain in the groin, and the fear that he might have a rupture. I examined him, assured him that there was no evidence of hernia, and was surprised to find that he was not relieved at this intelligence. We talked further and I discovered that he had engaged recently in a sexual venture. He feared that he might have contracted a venereal infection, and hoped that in the course of my examination for hernia I might comment on the absence—hopefully not the presence—of such a disease. When I did not mention his genitals he was troubled, but was at first unable to question me because of being ashamed. But this was not all; he was concerned with the feeling that he had committed the unpardonable sin in having a sexual affair, and he was hesitant to speak of this, not wishing to appear insane. I asked him what he meant by the sin, and he said: "I felt as if I had done something very terrible, and that I'd be punished. That's crazy—but I felt as if I would lose my mind. How could I talk of that?"

"What do you mean by '*that*'?" I asked.

He gave me a plain answer: "I just wouldn't *be* any more. There would be no one."

Steven was describing his experience of severe anxiety, but he was also telling of his great difficulty in relating to another human. The physical symptom, pain in the groin, enabled him to see a physician, and because I had time and was somehow not too harsh with him, he learned more of himself, speaking finally not so much of sexual matters, but of his great need for and fear of any relationship, and his shame at being so alone.

Each of my patients displayed behavior which at times involved various organ systems and frequently required the expert consultation of the internist and other specialists. Often these physical symptoms were more pronounced when verbal communication was failing and social withdrawal increasing—as in the earlier stages of onset, prior to the appearance of clearly evident psychosis, and at intervals during the course of psychotherapy. In this sense the bodily disturbances had a quality of communication. They could not be translated directly into speech (so far as I am concerned), but they were suggestive of the patient's struggle with his need to express himself without terrible risk to his self-esteem; his contacts with others were fragile and failing, his words were not adequate for the maintenance of both security and communication, and his entire organism responded strongly to the threat of an increasing unrelatedness.

There have been instances in which the death of a schizophrenic patient has been very puzzling to me. Consider briefly a man of twenty-five whom I knew some years ago when he was a patient in a large psychiatric hospital. He was for many days in what was known as a state of "excitement," being restless, assaultive, wild, and generally incomprehensible in his speech. His behavior led him to be isolated, he had to be fed, since he did not eat, and despite our efforts to cope with his withdrawal he died. The findings at autopsy did not disclose the cause of death, and we spoke of his having succumbed to exhaustion, although he was muscular and well nourished throughout his illness (see Adland, 1947).

I think of Thomas who became depressed at the age of nineteen and suddenly assaulted a stranger, crying out that he must kill or be killed. He told me later something of how he had felt at that time: "I could see people, but they didn't seem to hear me or see me. They just looked through me. I felt like there was something bad in me and I had to kill it, or get someone else to kill it. Then I'd be free—and I'd make sense with someone. I didn't want to just kill myself—I needed things to change. After killing maybe I'd live in another way."

Thomas was in psychotherapy for about two years and seemed to improve, although his therapist once said to me: "Tom and I are still strangers. We talk, but you're never sure that the words get across."

This physician moved to another locality, terminating his work with Thomas, who showed no great distress at this, saying only, "So what?" Not long after the separation the young man quarreled with his girl friend, had little to do with other people, and gave up his work in an office. His parents wanted him to live with them, but he refused, saying: "I'd like to go with them in a way, but if I do I'll never be free. They love you, but they sort of crush you."

I then saw Thomas a number of times in consultation. One evening he said: "You'd better give up on me. I feel alone. I don't know how it's happened, but the doctor left, and the girl—and those others; and now I can't seem to reach anybody. I just don't feel connected. It's sort of like I was cursed. I'm contaminated—I'm untouchable.''

I did not see Thomas again. He died in his apartment a few days later, no cause for his death being found.

It is evident that I do not know why these two men died. It is of interest to me, however, that each of them was remarkably unrelated to his fellows. I did not learn much in words from the first man (or those like him) because we could not talk together. From Thomas, I heard that he felt as if his contacts with others were irretrievably lost, and it was my impression that he believed himself to be utterly alone. Although we spoke with each other I doubt that he felt heard by me, and I do know that he felt that I turned from him when, in my role as consultant, I referred him to another physician.

Thomas, as well as all of the people whom I have mentioned, experienced in varying degrees feelings of isolation. They feared the isolation, but they also feared human relationship. Efforts of the afflicted person to deal with such apprehension often led to the display of very odd behavior. The implication of my remarks is that humans must develop ties with their fellows in order to become human, but in doing so frequently learn to fear their attachments, recognizing in them the possibilities of hurt and loss as well as support.

William James spoke of this in saying:

A man's social me is the recognition which he gets from his mates. We are not only gregarious animals, liking to be in sight of our fellows, but we have an innate propensity to get ourselves noticed, and noticed favorably, by our kind. No more fiendish punishment could be devised, were such a thing physically possible, than that one should be turned loose in society and remain absolutely unnoticed by all the members thereof. [quoted in Cannon, 1942, p. 185]

Walter Cannon's remarks (1942) about ''voodoo'' death are relevant here. Such deaths, recurrently reported, occur after a man has been cursed, is convinced that he will die as a result, and feels abandoned by his fellows, who share his belief. Said Cannon:

all people who stand in relation with him [the cursed man] withdraw their sustaining support. . . . The organization of his social life has collapsed and, no longer member of a group, he is alone and isolated. The doomed man is in a situation from which the only escape is by death. . . . the victim . . . cooperates in the withdrawal from [the group]. He becomes what the attitude of his fellow tribesmen wills him to be. Thus he assists in committing a kind of suicide. . . . The question which now arises is whether an ominous and persistent state of fear can end the life of a man. [pp. 185–186][5]

People who are isolated from their kind, as in shipwreck, or to whom the input of such stimuli as light, sound, and touch is experimentally reduced, may experience distortions of perception, feelings of frustration, self-disorganization, and hallucinations, and may exhibit behavior suggestive of severe mental disorder. For example, such phenomena are commonly observed in patients hospitalized for eye surgery, the combination of fear, the strange environment, and the obscuring of vision creating a great sense of aloneness. Two investigators in this general field say quite simply: "Total isolation is death" (Azima and Cramer, 1956, p. 121).[6]

In a variety of studies there has been expressed an interest in the possible relationship between the integrity of the cellular structure of the human organism—in terms of bacterial invasion, membrane permeability, and cell growth—and a particular personality and emotional state. For example, in 1870 James Paget wrote:

The cases are so frequent in which deep anxiety, deferred hope and disappointment are quickly followed by the growth and increase of cancer, that we can hardly doubt that mental depression is a weighty addition to the other influences favoring the devel-

[5]Also of interest is work by Richter (1957), who reports studies of rats who die when placed in a position in which they may, from the experimenter's point of view, feel hopeless and out of touch with a known environment.

[6]For other articles concerned with problems of isolation, see: Editorial (1958), Lilly (1956), Weisman and Hackett (1958), and Solomon, Leiderman, Mendelson, and Wexler (1957).

opment of a cancerous constitution. [quoted in Leshan and Worthington, 1956, p. 50]

In 1958 Arthur Schmale wrote the following on the relationship of separation and depression to disease: "one could envision disease and depression as distinct and separate consequences or attempts at adaptation to feelings of helplessness and hopelessness" (p. 271).

I am *not* speaking of "causes" of mental disorder, of physical illness, of malignancy, and so on. I *am* saying that the development of the potential and the maintenance of the integrity of the human organism are, to an extent perhaps not yet clearly grasped, a function of the involvement of man with his fellows and his culture. What people speak of as the emotional and the physical are inseparably interwoven. The nature of man's relatedness to others is a significant factor in the etiology and form of mental disorder; it will be of interest to continue studies of the role of this factor in the inception and development of more material ailments. (See also Selwyn Brody, 1956; Fisher and Cleveland, 1956; Greene, Young, and Swisher, 1956; Hinkle, Christenson, Kane, Ostfeld, Thetford, and Wolff, 1958; Kaplan and Gottschalk, 1958.)

To return for a moment to the people I have discussed so far, they present certain qualities in common. First, although each had great needs, he was not clearly aware of their nature, could not formulate and express them adequately to others, and often was unable to accept or make use of the help offered to him. Second, his needs were expressed not only in speech—the communicative value of which may be diminished as its defensive function is intensified—but in other behavior, which might involve organ systems in what is called physical illness, and possibly death.

Third, each seemed to have great need of human contact, but behaved in such a fashion that others withdrew from him, seeming to validate his fear that his requirements could not be met. Fourth, each felt alone, but was in an obscure "involvement" with others in which his social requirements and his quest for freedom appeared to be irreconcilable. Fifth, he had his being in a social field which to some extent created and was created by him, and which was related to other social fields of past and present which often were poorly comprehended or even unrecognized by him. And last, each was at some time in his life called ''schizophrenic.''

I shall now quote briefly from a book of which I am very fond—*The Little Prince*, by Antoine de Saint Exupéry (1943). The story is relevant to the topics of loneliness, relatedness, and the fear on the part of some that closeness to another implies anxiety, separation, and death.

In this story the little prince comes to earth from a distant planet where he has lived alone, tending a beautiful flower which he loved. Other than plants he has known no living thing, being related only to a flower and the volcanic terrain of his planet; but on earth he meets a fox who rouses his interest and with whom he wants to play.

> ''I cannot play with you,'' the fox said. ''I am not tamed.'' . . . [Said the prince:] ''I am looking for friends. What does that mean—'tame'?''
>
> ''It is an act too often neglected,'' said the fox. ''It means to establish ties. . . . if you tame me, then we shall need each other. To me, you will be unique in all the world. To you, I shall be unique in all the world. . . . My life is very monotonous. . . . But if you tame me, it will be as if the sun came to shine on my life. . . . Please—tame me!'' he said.
>
> ''I want to, very much,'' the little prince replied, ''But I have not much time. I have friends to discover, and a great many things to understand.''
>
> ''One only understands the things that one tames,'' said the fox. ''Men have no more time to understand anything. They buy things all ready made at the shops. But there is no shop anywhere where one can buy friendship, and so men have no friends any more. If you want a friend, tame me. . . .''
>
> ''What must I do, to tame you?'' asked the little prince.
>
> ''You must be very patient,'' replied the fox. ''First you will sit down at a little distance from me—like that—in the grass. I shall look at you out of the corner of my eye, and you will say nothing. Words are the source of misunderstandings. But you will sit a little closer to me, every day. . . .''

And so the fox was tamed, and came the time of their parting. The fox wept, to the distress of the prince, who said:

> "Then it has done you no good at all!"
> "It has done me good," said the fox. . . . "Goodbye. . . . And now here is my secret, a very simple secret: It is only with the heart that one can see rightly; what is essential is invisible to the eye. . . . Men have forgotten this truth. . . . You become responsible, forever, for what you have tamed. . . ." [pp. 65–72]

The prince, having found friendship with a flower and a fox, then dares to risk relatedness with a man (who tells the story). But from the man who loves him he finally withdraws, returning to his lovely planet, as if to become involved with humans was wonderful and necessary—yet, for him, fatal.

I have, thus far, used the term *relatedness* a number of times, but I have not explained precisely what I mean by it. By relatedness I refer to the interaction of humans in social fields (past, present, and extended into the future; operative in awareness or otherwise) and to those ties between all humans which cannot be disregarded—their biological alikeness and their sharing of an obscure but common destiny.

Man has become a success on this planet in the sense that he has survived, has increased his numbers, and has dealt with other organisms so effectively that he now faces himself as his own major competitor, most needed friend, and most fearsome enemy. He has developed the ability to conceptualize, being able to formulate varied aspects of experience, remember the past, evaluate the present, structure a view of the future, and conceive of himself in relation to his world. Having an awareness of himself, and recognizing something of his powers and limitations, he is in a position to consider the possibilities of more actively directing the course of his own future development; he is no longer bound rigidly and helplessly to the movement of biological evolution.

Man has the unique ability to use symbols—to form an abstraction of his experience, giving meaning and value to events in accord with his personal necessities and cultural bias. Through language man transmits his ideas to others, creating symbols which may become more real and influential in his living than the events which they signify, and may serve to perpetuate not only the valid but the dangerously nonsensical. The manipulation of symbols and the accompanying distortion of perception in the service of preserving human relationships and a tolerable degree of self-esteem lead to the formation of a quality of words whereby they seem to have a life of their own; that is, man describes his living with words, but his perception of his own existence is to a considerable extent governed by the words which he has learned to use. In a sense man's behavior is largely symbolic (von Bertalanffy, 1956).

People sometimes speak of the mind as an entity localized in space, and as a something which a psychiatrist, for example, might be called upon to treat. This is a concept which requires the making of a complicated distinction between the mind, the "rest of" the person, and other persons. The mind may be thought of as evidence of the interaction of the organism with its environment, reflective, in the human, of participation in earlier interpersonal fields and, to an extent, influenced by the foresight of future participation.[7] From this point of view 'mental disorders' may be viewed as expressions of human experience—the formation of complex, inefficient forms of behavior whereby some semblance of human relatedness is maintained at the cost of interferences with learning, restrictions on growth, and distortions of perception.

Man's art, beliefs, customs, science, and so on are the expression of his organization and evaluation of experience transmitted from one generation to the next. This "culture," created by man, also molds its creators, extending beyond the lives of any of them, and giving to each a world view which is his more by accident of birth than by any calculation. Thus the personality reflects the interaction of the biologically given with the forces of a multitude of interpersonal fields, the characteristics of each of which are largely culturally determined.

Man is subject to both a biological and a cultural heritage, the extent to which the potential of the one is realized being greatly de-

---

[7]A useful definition of *mind* is as follows: "The sum total of those activities of an organism by means of which it responds as an integrated dynamic system to external forces" (Warren, 1934, p. 167).

pendent upon the influences of the other. Through his culture man learns to be human, and within it he finds grave and self-created limitations to the extent of his humanity. Intermingled in the culture are the wisdom and the folly of the past, often valued alike without clear recognition of their possible suitability to changing human needs. It may be that man's fatal weakness lies in his too tender regard for that which he has created, and that his clinging to the spurious comforts found in the maintenance of a familiar and relatively unchanging culture may interfere with his making the appropriate and timely response to the challenge of his existence. The delusions of the culture are costly—and may be fatal—for man in general, and for psychiatric patients in particular.

Despite what looks like much evidence to the contrary, I do not think that man is born to be aggressive, hostile, destructive, or "evil." The genes—so I am told—do not determine characters and traits, but influence rather the responses of the organism to stimuli, so that one's constitution is a reflection of biological and environmental influences. Human nature is to a considerable extent the nature of culture, and is malleable throughout life, being responsive to appropriate learning at all ages. Man is not born to destroy, nor does the survival of the fittest refer to the perpetuation of those organisms most effective in the elimination of their kind. Survival will very likely go to those forms of life which are able to engage in cooperative enterprises. On this subject W. C. Allee (1943) wrote as follows: "human altruistic drives are as firmly based on an animal ancestry as is man himself. Our tendencies toward goodness are as innate as our tendencies toward intelligence. . . ." (p. 521; see also Allee, 1951; von Bertalanffy, 1958; Dai, 1952; Dobzhansky, 1956; LaBarre, 1954; A. Montagu, 1950, 1955, 1958; White, 1949).

In brief, man is born with the potential of becoming effectively cooperative with his fellows, but because of anxiety, fear, ignorance, and cultural distortion, has often failed to appreciate this ability as a major requirement for his survival. The present extraordinary increase in the world's population stresses the fact that problems of improving local and international cooperation are of urgent, practical importance, directly related to man's suitability to exist in the world.[8]

The following quotation from Charles Cooley (1956) is relevant here:

> the individual is not separable from the human whole, but a living member of it, deriving his life from the whole through social and hereditary transmission as truly as if men were literally one body . . . on the other hand, the social whole is in some degree dependent upon each individual, because each contributes something to the common life that no one else can contribute. . . . A separate individual is an abstraction unknown to experience, and so likewise is society when regarded as something apart from individuals. [pp. 35–36]

Relatedness is a condition described in many ways. You may think of it as a thermal state (hot or cold), as a medical condition (healthy or otherwise), as a function of time (enduring, transient), as a system of moral values (good, bad), as associated with emotions (friendly, hostile), as reflecting economics (profitable or not), and so on. I think that relatedness is described in so many ways because it is an ingredient of all human experience, and thus does not lend itself to any but a very particular or a very general description. Whatever man does involves his relationship with others; whether he be content, unhappy, angry, fearful, lonely, or what not, he exists as he does with some reference to his fellows. Death itself is a human experience of relatedness, its interpersonal quality often being distorted as greatly by the withdrawal of the living as of the dying. In brief, relatedness is a requirement of human life, the potential for its full development being a part of the biological equipment of man. One does not so much seek for relatedness or somehow develop it in others; it is there already. Relatedness is of man; without some semblance of it he will not survive.

---

[8]The present human population of approximately 2.5 billion, reached over hundreds of thousands of years, may reach 6 to 7 billion in the next forty years. This is an ''explosion'' of population, accompanied by a decline in natural resources and a lag in social techniques. (Figures from United Nations Bureau of Social Affairs, quoted in an editorial of the *Washington Star*, July 6, 1958; p. A-22.

It is our concern as humans seeking our own welfare to comprehend those factors leading to the concealment, distortion, denial, and fear of the fact of our responsibility for—that is, our responses to—one another.

The psychotherapist is not required to create that which exists, but to understand more fully the nature of the relationship in which he joins with his patient. As the distortions and deficiencies of experience are revealed, there will be made possible the natural growth of the relationship toward a more effective and satisfying development. When the relationship functions well, it will go unnoticed, which is to say that relatedness is not the preoccupation of the related, any more than love is the major concern of those who love.

I shall now say something of the course of human development, as a preliminary to discussing how the schizophrenic way of life has its beginning. The human animal moves from one developmental era to another in gaining the experiences through which he can become more fully human. In each era readied behavioral potential must be met by the social situation appropriate to its expression in order for proper growth to occur. Defects in development resulting from inadequate meeting of ability and opportunity in one era may not be fully corrected in later periods, the resulting deficiencies in learning, dissociation of aspects of experience, and deformities of behavior being, in some instances, so prominent and troublesome that the personalities concerned are referred to as examples of mental illness.

The human infant—if he is fortunate—has much bodily contact with a mother who is happy in her love for him and somewhat pleased with herself as a person. In such an accepting situation he begins to differentiate himself from others without undue anxiety, and accepts with increasing pleasure and responsiveness the tenderness available to him. The child, increasing his linguistic skill, learns more of his particular cultural prescriptions, advances in his ability to distinguish between those matters labeled by his group as ''reality'' or ''fantasy,'' and discovers others outside his home. The juvenile improves his social skills, learns something of group activities involving competition and cooperation, hopefully corrects certain gross distortions learned in the home, discovers the often destructive shortcuts available through the use of stereotypes, and makes increasing use of foresight. The pre-adolescent refines his abilities for group participation and discovers the wonder of love and communication as he finds a friend. There follows the patterning of sexual behavior and the achieving of a greater coincidence of lustful and loving interests.

In all of these steps the human has become more involved with his fellows. So that he may feel secure—tolerably free of anxiety—he requires the approval of his kind. His need for tenderness has developed into a need for intimacy, for collaboration with others, for the giving, as well as the receiving, of affection. He has gained what he has of his humanity from others, and his fate is inextricably and finally bound to theirs. Being attached to others, he will know loss and loneliness, but these he can endure if he does not deny his relatedness.

The schizophrenic reaction may be looked upon as the expression of complicated patterns of behavior adopted by the organism in an effort to deal with a gross inadequacy in relating to other humans, the appearance of the clinical syndrome being a late expression of the accumulating disasters of many years. The behavior exhibited is a reflection of response to stress; is evidence of a disorder of personality structure—that is, the organization of the interrelatedness of person and environment; has a communicative aspect; and enables the person to preserve some sense of security and comfort.

It is my impression that the schizophrenic way of life has its beginnings in infancy, that period during which the young human is remarkably dependent upon those who care for him, is vulnerable to their anxiety, and is subject to their teaching. It is then that the fundamental pattern of relationship is formed. That pattern may be marked by anxiety, fear, and insecurity, with accompanying attempts at correction—refinements of human behavior which are referred to as sublimation, repression, substitution, obsessionalism, projection, and so on—or by relative comfort and acceptance of human associations.

By *stress* I refer to the following elements which, if uncorrected by later experience, may contribute to the deviation of personality which may eventuate in a schizophrenic response:

First, severe and recurrent anxiety in the mothering person, complicating the infant's attainment of a clear concept of himself or others (see Sylvia Brody, 1956; Goldfarb, 1955; Lowrey, 1935; Mahler, 1952; M. F. A. Montagu, 1950; Ribble, 1941; Sontag, 1944; Spitz, 1950).

Second, a multiplicity of conflicting, incomplete, and obscure messages from those who care for the infant, before he has attained much skill in the use of language. The discrepancies between action and speech lead to uncertainty about his position in relation to others and to persisting unclarity as to the significance of what is said and done.

Third, repeated threats to the continuance of the relationship of the infant with those who care for him. The result may be the dissociation of aspects of behavior which seem to jeopardize the relationship essential for survival; and the keeping of such matters out of awareness will interfere with further learning and contribute to later perceptual distortions.

Fourth, a warped and peculiarly personal view of the culture, taught to the child by members of his family through the necessities of their own anxieties.

Fifth, the development of a fear of people, interfering with learning, the verification of ideas with others, and the correction of early misapprehensions of the culture.

The human has certain *goals* toward which he tends, among which are:

First, the continuance of his growth toward a greater realization of potential.

Second, the attainment of learning which will increase the comprehension of experience and the capacity to cope with it.

Third, the maintenance of the relatedness required for survival.

Fourth, the preservation of some feeling of security and freedom from anxiety.

Fifth, the awareness of some dependable concept of himself in relation to his family, his culture, and his universe; that is, the establishing of some sense of permanency and predictability regarding the social field in which he exists.

In order to attain anything resembling such goals, the person who has experienced the stress suggested above must keep dissociated important aspects of interpersonal experience, which requires that he move with great caution among people who may threaten to increase his anxiety and disturb his precarious security, and that he distort his perception of events in the service of his prestige needs. With increasing involvement in the complexities of living and a greater need for self-identification, the defensive operations may no longer suffice to maintain anxiety at a tolerable level, and behavior characteristic of the onset of schizophrenia may appear.

There comes a time—usually in adolescence in this culture—at which one must declare himself; he must identify himself as a person apart from his family, establish intimacy with a friend or face loneliness, pattern his sexual behavior, and consider such matters as further formal education, marriage, work, and life in a community. All of these activities require increased self-identification, the ability to relate, and the revelation of self to others. The move toward intimacy involves increasing anxiety; the failure to make the move brings loneliness and the threat of unrelatedness. The extreme of either course is panic and the feeling of impending, if not actual, dissolution and death. Many of the phenomena observable during the development of disorder reflect efforts to escape the intolerables of anxiety[9] and aloneness.

[9]By the word *anxiety* I refer to an interpersonal phenomenon in which one is related to another in such fashion that his feeling of security and personal worth seems subject to that one's approval. This anxiety is man-made, having its origin and continuance in the relationships between humans. Although this unpleasant sentiment, which is so destructive to human intimacy, reflects the anticipation (and experience) of disapproval, it is, I think, more basically associated with the apprehension that separation and unrelatedness will follow upon rejection. By anxiety I do not refer to any more basic discomfort supposedly associated with growth, new experience, or death. I think that anxiety is man-made, and that processes of growth, including death, are not "naturally" accompanied by any anxiety other than that reflecting human experience.

I make these rather limited remarks in order to emphasize my concern with what I think of as the necessity for man to direct his attention to the part which he plays in the reduction and destruction of himself. Should man "explain" or seek to "justify" his destructiveness as being evidence of his "fate," or his "nature," or the unfathomable "wisdom" of unidentified forces, he might overlook his proper responsibilities and seal his own fate; that is, he might begin to accept the symbolic structure of his culture as somehow an unmodifiable reality, and die a victim of the symbolization of his personal inadequacy. The therapist, without abandoning wonderment for his universe and recognition of his own limitations, and without espousing a biological reductionism, is well advised to seek for anxiety in the interpersonal field, avoiding any tendency to ascribe interhuman discomfort to the extrahuman (see Benoit, 1959, chap. 5).

From the point of view presented here, schizophrenia is not looked upon as a disease, but as a reaction to, and an expression of, the social scenes in which an organism with certain biological endowments—usually adequate, so far as I know, to the task of becoming fully human—has its being.[10]

The schizophrenic person has become involved in a relatedness which has been complicated by his fear that he cannot measure up to expectations of him, by the anxiety associated with people, by deficiencies of learning, and by the warped views held by those who participate with him in the disorder. Such a person is not unrelated; he values relatedness and is so fearful of losing what he has that he may fail to improve his state, the anxiety of human contact being equated with the loss of all contact.

The human who develops his ability to experience some degree of intimacy with another is subject to loneliness, a tension so strong that on occasion one may endure anxiety to escape it. Loneliness, which is a refinement of intimacy in human relationship, is marked by a quality of hopefulness, in that there is the possibility of its relief through action. Unrelatedness does not have this quality, but implies the loss of human contacts without discernible ways for regaining them. The failure to develop the needed relatedness in infancy leads to the marasmic death. The loss of relatedness later in life leads to panic, to a sense of the loss of self, and, in some instances, to death.

At this point I wish to consider some aspects of treatment. Fundamental to all psychotherapy is the development of a relationship which makes possible a further evaluation of the past and an increased participation in new experience. Therapy takes place in the action of an interpersonal field marked by the increasing mutuality of evaluation, confidence, growth, and communication; it is a dialogue of variable freedom influenced by the intrusion from the past of never clearly identified shadows which distort the view of present and future.

It would be reckless, and inaccurate, to speak of relatedness as if it were some universal good, which, having been discovered and

---

[10]I do not speak of "disease of the ego," not being content with a dividing of the personality into parts, and being impressed by the totality of the organism's response to situations of stress.

embraced, would somehow lead to the resolution of man's troubles—or all of the disorders of the psychiatrist's patients. A careless seeking for something called relatedness will not lead to it, any more than happiness or contentment are discovered through their direct pursuit. Emphasis on relatedness as such in the therapeutic situation may, at times, be more in the service of the therapist than the patient, concealing anxiety and obscuring defects in treatment. On occasion the therapist may "explain" prolonged impasses by saying that he is "waiting for a relationship to develop," an outcome which may not be reached when other difficulties are masked by the anxious preoccupation with relatedness.

Humans may, on occasion, be drawn to one another by some recognition of the fact of their common humanity, their lives being illuminated by such glimpses of a simple, yet extraordinarily impressive verity. More commonly, I think, relatedness develops on the basis of interpersonal exchanges through which certain needs of the participants are met in part, and neither one suffers grave hurt from the other. The technique[11] of psychotherapy is concerned with the identification and facilitation of movements toward relatedness; with interferences to these, such as increases of anxiety; with the cultural equipment available to the participants; with learning defects; and with associated difficulties in communication.

The psychotherapist's stated technique represents the formalization of the known ways in which he deals with others in the therapeutic situation, and is but a small portion of the activity in which he factually does engage. The technique, the people concerned, and the existing relatedness are all expressions of culturally modified organisms operative in a social field, and cannot be dealt with as separate entities. This is to say that the process of interaction is the primary subject for study, the characteristics of any partner to the action not existing, in a realistic sense, outside of the field.

If the psychotherapist were to deal with a technique as an entity in its own right, distortions would occur in the therapeutic field. Any enduring preoccupation with some facet of field phenomena may be

---

[11]The relevant definition of technique is, "the formal elements, collectively, of an art," according to *Webster's New Collegiate Dictionary*, Springfield, MA: Merriam, 1949.

in the service of anxiety and favor the overlooking of more promising data.

Technique, the formulation of experience that "works," should be clearly available to the therapist's awareness; otherwise it will guide his behavior without being readily subject to correction. At best a useful and somewhat malleable tool, technique should not become an inflexible instrument encumbered by reverence and the weight of tradition.

My point is simply this: Relatedness does not just appear, but is responsive to the demonstration of skills in interpersonal affairs, such skills being spoken of by the therapist as his "technique."

Therapy is concerned with a formulation of the past, with integration of it knowingly into the present, and with its profitable use for predictions of the future. The patient dreads the integration of past and present, anticipating as its outcome only his old prediction of future calamity, marked by anxiety, loneliness, and decreasing relatedness. As the therapeutic relationship develops, past, present, and future are drawn together and self-awareness increases, which is to say that the self is always engaged in a process of becoming, of self-differentiation as a function of social participation. The patient fears nonbeing, and in the course of useful therapy forms a sense of self which can remain intact under the threats of nonrelatedness, panic, and death. The development of relatedness and of the concept of self, and the reduction of anxiety, go together. The tendency of the human is to grow toward more effective cooperation with his kind; his envy, fear, greed, hatred, and jealousy, reflections of interpersonal experience complicated in some instances by unmet physical wants, interfere with such growth. But the course of growth is toward relatedness and self-realization—not destruction and death. Man's great sense of guilt is to some extent related to his denial of this development in himself or others. His fulfillment of himself as a human is dependent upon his ability to join freely in nonfearful communication with his fellows, and no success in other fields can do away with the need for this realization of the self.

In this regard Martin Buber said:

The basis of man's life with man is two-fold, and it is one—the wish of every man to be confirmed as what he is, even as what he can become, by men; and the innate capacity in man to confirm his fellow men in this way. That this capacity lies so immeasurably fallow constitutes the real weakness and questionableness of the human race: actual humanity exists only where this capacity unfolds. [quoted in Friedman, 1955, p. 81]

In speaking of relatedness, I do not refer to a type of cooperative living in which one person is bound to another in such a fashion that the sense of individuality—of being—is lost. The cases which I have cited were of people feeling distant, estranged, lonely, and threatened by unrelatedness, yet bound to others by obscure ties that permitted little aloneness, freedom, growth, or sense of self. In these people there is such a need for relatedness, so great a fear of it and preoccupation with it, that the rest of living is seriously deranged. Only as man can accept himself and his relatedness to others can he stand apart and tolerate aloneness; learning that he can be both related and lonely, he may at times embrace his loneliness, knowing that it is not cause for shame, but reflects certain personal—and perhaps situational—limitations restricting his participation, and in itself may have value and offer great comfort.

Although I shall not discuss details of treatment, I shall outline, as follows, certain phenomena which have characterized my therapeutic relationships with schizophrenic patients:

1. The patient displays a great need for and fear of the relationship. In our approaches to each other, his anxiety may so increase that perception is disturbed, and I am required, as best I may, to make clear to him my identity, and to improve his orientation to his surroundings. At the times of his withdrawal, although I do not abandon him, I shall respect his need for aloneness and independence.

2. The relationship is marked by a drawing together in which mutual identification will occur, and by a moving apart so that the concept of self may grow through separation. A factor in what is called negativism is the need to say no and to assert oneself when one feels threatened by involvement with another. In brief, relatedness and self-identity develop together through a process of advance and retreat.

3. The patient is to learn that the therapeutic field, unlike that

of the family, is tolerant of change and growth in each of the participants. At some point in the work the patient will fear that the relationship will be destructive to him or his therapist, and that the outcome will be death or unrelatedness. If matters go well, both therapist and patient will discover that, although each can need and enjoy the other, each can exist apart.

4. The patient, fearing nonbeing, may involve his physician in this fear, and may engage in various kinds of behavior, such as assault, to obtain a response and confirm his existence. When such a fear is present, the physician must also be present, with verbal, vocal, and, at times, physical contact, opposing his patient's alienation from the nonhuman world, from his fellows, and from himself.

5. The patient anticipates dealing with a confusing multiplicity of unclear and often conflicting messages, and he responds in kind. His fear of closeness to another is in part a fear of becoming involved in such disorder, and therapy is directed toward the resolution of needless ambiguity.

6. Although the view of the present will be influenced by reflections from the past, the reality of the present will be emphasized at the same time that the truth of the past is accepted.

7. The behavior of the patient may be looked upon as an effort to communicate a need and preserve some semblance of security. The therapeutic task involves the following: (a) identifying the need; (b) providing a prompt and adequate response, with the goal of helping the patient recognize his own need and extending his foresight; (c) encouraging him to express his need clearly so that a useful response is obtained from others; (d) enabling him to accept the suitable response from others without an unrealistic fear that in doing so he will be controlled or injured; and (e) helping him mold the expression and satisfaction of his needs to the requirements of the culture without becoming subservient thereto.

8. The therapeutic process is concerned with the development of the relatedness of patient and therapist and a study of the antecedents, the course, and the vicissitudes of that development. It will be noted that therapy involves growth; as previous experience is recalled and evaluated, deficiencies in learning revealed, distortions of the culture corrected, anxiety lessened, and dissociated symbols of significant

interpersonal events brought into awareness, growth will occur, assuming that opportunities are provided for the exercise of available potential. Growth takes time, and cannot, as far as I know, be accelerated without end. The decrease in anxiety enables the patient's understanding to increase, and his knowledge is consolidated and expanded as he tries himself in action. Relatedness, insight, and action increase together. Therapy is a process of growth marked by mutuality, in which one participant cannot alter without change in the other. The therapist learns from his patient, and grows with him; it could not be otherwise. Having said that psychiatric illness requires in its origin and continuation the participation of others, so is the healing process one of participation. Again I refer to Martin Buber (1951): "A soul is never sick alone, but always through a betweenness, a situation between it and another existing being" (quoted in Friedman, 1955, p. 191).

9. The therapist does not attempt to define the exact nature or form of relatedness, but can only attempt to open ways for its development; how it grows will vary with each situation. Relatedness, in this sense, is not a proper subject for control or precise definition.

Should the treatment become unduly mechanistic and deterministic the therapist might deal with his patient as an object to be manipulated and subjected to his power. In such case therapy would simply reflect the highly technical culture, carrying with it elements of fragmentation and impersonalization whereby "doing what is good for" the patient becomes control, freedom becomes slavery, and depersonalization is called love. When the therapist speaks of the "mature" patient, or of a "completed" analysis, he must be warned that his goal is not the creation of a robot to fit a culture or to satisfy the therapist's own needs for the fragile security of perfectionism. The goal of therapy is *not* the attainment of a particular requirement set by the culture, or the advancement of the therapist's prestige, or the achievement of the community "good" apart from the patient's own self-realization.

I do not expect to comprehend myself or others in any deep sense, and by that idea I am not dismayed. Sometimes when I make a "wrong" interpretation, or a patient eludes my "plans" for him, I feel a sense of triumph at his refusal to be bound by me even as he seeks freedom from the restrictions of his anxiety. I *do* look for a greater understanding of man in his biological and cultural heritage, and I do expect to apply that knowledge usefully in therapy. But I do not expect to find in such the essence of man—his strength that will resist subjugation. Even as I emphasize relatedness I remember the words of Job (13:15): "Though he slay me, yet I will trust in him; but I will maintain mine own ways before him."

I am opposed to the disordered way of schizophrenic living, to the painful experiences leading to it, and to the expense in human potential it entails. But the alternative is not conformity to some well-structured world in which are found, as Arthur Schlesinger (1957) once said, "the bland leading the bland" (p. 37). Relatedness leads to freedom—even to the freedom to be alone and to be "different." A pseudorelatedness leads to the loss of a sense of self, to control, and to a frightened and desperate attempt to merge one's identity with that of the group.

I feel somewhat presumptuous in talking about man's ways of living and in considering the possibilities of modifications in what I think of as a useful direction. I am ignorant of much of my culture, to say nothing of others, and I am uncertain of the future. Listen to what Robert Oppenheimer says of our times: "One thing that is new is the prevalence of newness, the changing scale and scope of change itself, so that the world alters as we walk in it, so that the years of a man's life measure not some small growth or development or rearrangement or modification of what he learned in childhood, but a great upheaval" (Brown, 1957, p. 8).

In the face of uncertainty the therapist may seek for the assurance of precision and predictability—in a fixed concept of himself, in a theory of personality, in the performance of his patient. His ambition may be to establish order, resist change, make "rational sense," induce conformity, and consolidate the conventional as a "new freedom." He may seek a "togetherness" which may be no more than alikeness. In this way "results" may be "produced" in therapy that are far more hopeless than the disorder treated, in that despair may be encouraged to mask as health.

The schizophrenic reaction is characterized by an anxious struggle in which is sought an adjustment of the need for relatedness to the fear of control and depersonalization. This struggle is of interest, not only as a disorder of the person, but as a reflection of the stress within the culture. The therapeutic problem (of the patient) is concerned with the harmonization of three concepts: (1) freedom from enslavement to anxiety, without (2) subjugation to a crippling and deadly conformity, and with the (3) attainment of the ability to grow, to be with others, and to differ and stand apart from them.

One need not, out of concern with problems of anxiety and loneliness, become unduly fearful of being anxious and alone. As each person stands alone, he may evaluate his living, find rest, and in separation confirm his being. Should he fear aloneness, being afraid to listen to the voices of the world as heard through himself, he might huddle together with others, fearful of looking to the stars, dreading growth and a sense of his own existence. Although communication requires others for its completeness, only as he becomes so related that he dares to be alone can he speak meaningfully to others.

The therapist should not seek to enshrine a concept of relatedness—an honorific term applied only to the elect and subject to use in the service of envy, leading one to derogate another by the implication that "I am more related than you." Relatedness is a function of interpersonal communicative and need-fulfilling activities, and is not in itself an exclusive goal that one should seek in an effort to solve economic, social, and psychiatric problems. We psychiatrists will concern ourselves with such matters as the meeting of our patients' basic needs—sometimes (in hospitals) with the provision of their food, clothing, and shelter—with the understanding of interferences to adequate communication and of hindrances to effective action, and with the identification of expensive, if not dangerous, cultural delusions—all with the idea that relatedness, being consistent with the biological nature of man, and in keeping with his proper functioning, will develop as opportunity is provided. By this I do not imply the assumption of a passive, vaguely optimistic attitude that all is for the best, and that man's development will inevitably lead him toward increased cooperation with, and love for, his fellows. I am very much of the opinion that man may take an active part in determining his own future, and that he may turn toward life or death, having in his hands the power for his own destruction or salvation. I do not think that psychotherapy will progress for the benefit of anyone through a placid "belief" in an assumed relationship that is supposedly attendant upon two people doing little more than meeting together at intervals throughout time. Relatedness is inevitable for man, but it can be marked by anxiety, cruelty, destruction, hatred, horror, and a control in which man becomes at the most a creature of his culture, bound to the proposition that the goal of living is the perpetuation of his particular cultural mythology. This is to say that one cannot avoid a valuation of relatedness as good or evil; therein man faces his greatest responsibilities, and is required to take not only thought but action, accepting the prospect of defeat if he does not dare to envision a life consistent with the actualization of his potential.

In the disorder of "mental" patients can be seen caricatured the disorder of the world. Even though it were somehow possible to do away with "mental illness," problems of cultural variation, change, and derangement would still have to be dealt with. The individual responds with his attitudes and his behavior to the nature of his society, and should schizophrenia be eliminated, other distortions of human living under other designations would have to be devised to cope with turmoil in the family and the state. A danger in the seeking of "cures" for psychiatric and social disturbances lies in discovering techniques which would produce a seeming quietude at the cost of reducing man's capacity for growth and individual self-realization.

Psychiatry is itself an expression of the culture in which it exists; it is man looking at himself, in his biased fashion, in an attempt to comprehend, and perhaps alter, his rather narrow and odd view of things. The psychiatrist works for the development of man's expressiveness in a social field in which the growth of one can be enabling to the growth of others. Psychiatry is concerned with medicine, with the social sciences, and with the humanities. It is also concerned with the wayward spirit of man. Although the psychotherapist respects and must wisely develop formulae, basic rules, and theory, he may take not only interest, but some delight, in those aspects of man which are unique and unpredictable, and which elude conformity and rule.

Should it be that much of man's anxiety originates in his fear of loss and separation, this sentiment may indicate the human's requirement for relationship with his kind, and symbolically with the universe unknown to him. Anxiety heralds the threat of unrelatedness, and a death which is more than simply biological, being born of the culture and the symbol. Guilt, so commonly an accompaniment of man's living, has, I think, its roots in man's denial of relatedness, and thus of his fellows, and of himself. Anxiety, relatedness, and guilt are of man—not afflictions from on high, as I see it, but indications of his knowledge and his fear that in his "commonness" lies his greatness; which is to say that the inhibition and destruction of the essential relatedness is man's curse upon himself and his gods.

Loneliness is part of the life of man, as are change, uncertainty, and anxiety. But unrelatedness is destruction. As men dare to consider the possibility that to be unrelated is to die, the responsibilities of their living may be seen more clearly, and the chances for their survival improved.

References

Ackerman, N.W. (1958), Toward an integrative therapy of the family. *Amer. J. Psychiat.*, 114:727–733.

Adland, M.L. (1947), Review, case studies, therapy, and interpretation of the acute exhaustive psychoses. *Psychiatric Quart.*, 21:38–69.

Allee, W.C. (1943), Where angels fear to tread: A contribution from general sociology to human ethics. *Science*, 97:521.

———— (1951), *Cooperation among Animals, with Human Implications*. New York: Schuman.

Azima, H., & Cramer, F.C. (1956), Effects of partial perceptual isolation in mentally disturbed individuals. *Dis. Nerv. Syst.*, 17:117–122.

Bateson, G., Jackson, D., Haley, J., & Weakland, J. (1956), Towards a theory of schizophrenia. *Behav. Sci.*, 1:251–264.

Benoit, H. (1959), *The Supreme Doctrine: Psychological Studies in Zen Thought*. New York: Viking.

Bertalanffy, L. von (1956), A biologist looks at human nature. *Scientific Monthly*, 82:33–41.

———— (1958), Comments on aggression. *Bull. Menn. Clin.*, 22:50–57.

Brody, Selwyn (1956), Psychological factors associated with disseminated lupus erythematosus and effects of cortisone and ACTH. *Psychiatric Quart.*, 30:44–60.

Brody, Sylvia (1956), *Patterns of Mothering: Maternal Influence During Infancy*. New York: International Universities Press.

Brown, J.M. (1957), The writers of 1984. *Saturday Review*, June 1.

Buber, M. (1951), Heilung aus der Begegnung. *Neue Schweizer Rundschau*, 19:382–386.

Cannon, W. B. (1942), "Voodoo" death. *Amer. Anthropologist*, 44:169–181. Reprinted in *Psychosom. Med.*, 19 (1957):182–190.

Caudill, W. A. (1958), *Effects of Social and Cultural Systems in Reaction to Stress.* New York: Social Science Research Council (Pamphlet 14).

Cooley, C. H. (1956), Human nature and the social order. In: *The Two Major Works of Charles H. Cooley: Social Organization; Human Nature and the Social Order.* Glencoe, IL: Free Press.

Dai, B. (1952), A socio-psychiatric approach to personality organization. *Amer. Sociolog. Rev.*, 17:44–49.

Dobzhansky, T. (1956), *The Biological Basis of Human Freedom.* New York: Columbia University Press.

Editorial (1958), Sensory deprivation. *N. Engl. J. Med.*, 258:1314–1315.

Fisher, S., & Cleveland, S. E. (1956), Relationship of body image to site of cancer. *Psychosom. Med.*, 18:304–309.

Friedman, M. S. (1955), *Martin Buber: The Life of Dialogue.* Chicago: University of Chicago Press.

Gerard, D. L., & Siegel, J. (1950), The family background of schizophrenia. *Psychiatric Quart.*, 24:47–73.

Goldfarb, W. (1955), Emotional and intellectual consequences of psychologic deprivation in infancy: A revaluation. In: *Psychopathology of Childhood*, ed. P. H. Hoch & J. Zubin. New York: Grune & Stratton, pp. 105–119.

Greene, W. A., Young, L. E., & Swisher, S. N. (1956), Psychological factors and reticuloendothelial disease: II. Observations on a group of women with lymphomas and leukemias. *Psychosom. Med.*, 18:284–303.

Hinkle, L. E., Christenson, W. N., Kane, F. D., Ostfeld, A., Thetford, W. N., & Wolff, H. G. (1958), An investigation into the relation between life experience, personality characteristics, and general susceptibility to illness. *Psychosom. Med.*, 20:278–295.

Kaplan, S. M., & Gottschalk, L. A. (1958), Modifications of the oropharyngeal bacteria with changes in the psychodynamic state: II. A validation study. *Psychosom. Med.*, 20:314–320.

Kohn, M. L., & Clausen, J. A. (1956), Parental authority behavior and schizophrenia. *Amer. J. Orthopsychiat.*, 26:297–313.

LaBarre, W. (1954), *The Human Animal.* Chicago: University of Chicago Press.

Leshan, L. L., & Worthington, R. E. (1956), Personality as a factor in the pathogenesis of cancer: A review of the literature. *Brit. J. Med. Psychol.*, 29:49–55.

Lidz, T. (1958), Schizophrenia and the family. *Psychiatry*, 21:21–27.

——— Cornelison, A., Terry, D., & Fleck, S. (1958), Intrafamilial environment of the schizophrenic patient: IV. The transmission of irrationality. *Amer. Med. Assn. Arch. Neurol. & Psychiat.*, 79:305–316.

Lilly, J. C. (1956), Mental effects of reduction of ordinary levels of physical stimuli on intact, healthy persons. *Psychiatric Research Reports*, 5:1–9. American Psychiatric Association.

Limentani, D. (1956), Symbiotic identification in schizophrenia. *Psychiatry*, 19:231–236.

Lowrey, L. G. (1935), Personality distortion and early institutional care. *Amer. J. Orthopsychiat.*, 10:576–585.

Mahler, M. S. (1952), On child psychosis and schizophrenia: Autistic and symbiotic infantile psychoses. *The Psychoanalytic Study of the Child*, 7:286–305. New York: International Universities Press.

Montagu, A. (1950), *On Being Human*. New York: Schuman.
———— (1955), *The Direction of Human Development*. New York: Harper.
———— (1958), *Education and Human Relations*. New York: Grove Press.
Montagu, M. F. A. (1950), Constitutional and prenatal factors in infant and child health. In: *The Healthy Personality*, ed. M. J. E. Senn. New York: Josiah Macy Jr. Foundation.
Ribble, M. A. (1941), Disorganizing factors of infant personality. *Amer. J. Psychiat.*, 88:459–463.
Richter, C. P. (1957), On the phenomenon of sudden death in animals and man. *Psychosom. Med.*, 19:191–198.
Saint Exupéry, A. de (1943), *The Little Prince*. New York: Reynal & Hitchcock.
Schlesinger, A. M. (1957), Liberalism. *Saturday Review*, June 8, pp. 11–12, 37.
Schmale, A. H. (1958), Relationship of separation and depression to disease: I. A report on a hospitalized medical population. *Psychosom. Med.*, 20:259–277.
Solomon, P., Leiderman, P. H., Mendelson, J., & Wexler, D. (1957), Sensory deprivation: A review. *Amer. J. Psychiat.*, 114:357–363.
Sontag, L. W. (1944), Differences in modifiability of fetal behavior and physiology. *Psychosom. Med.*, 6:151–154.
Spitz, R. A. (1950), Anxiety in infancy: A study of its manifestations in the first year of life. *Internat. J. Psycho-Anal.*, 31:138–143.
Warren, H. C., ed. (1934), *Dictionary of Psychology*. Boston: Houghton Mifflin.
Weisman, A. D., & Hackett, T. P. (1958), Psychosis after eye surgery: Establishment of a specific doctor-patient relationship in the prevention and treatment of "black-patch delirium." *N. Engl. J. Med.*, 258:1284–1289.
White, L. A. (1949), *The Science of Culture*. New York: Farrar, Straus.
Wolman, B. B. (1957), Explorations in latent schizophrenia. *Amer. J. Psychother.*, 11:560–588.
Wynne, L., Ryckoff, I. M., Day, J., & Hirsch, S. I. (1958), Psudo-mutuality in the family relations of schizophrenics. *Psychiat.*, 21:205–220.

15

The Reluctant Patient, the Unwanted Psychotherapist—and Coercion

Otto Allen Will, Jr., M.D.

In a review of my experience as a psychotherapist, I find that it has been marked, in many instances, by a peculiar—and intriguing—quality. I refer to the absence of enthusiasm—or to the presence of ill-concealed or openly displayed antagonism—characteristic of diverse people who are led (for one reason or another) to have something to do with me professionally. Although colleagues, friends, and others may (within limitations) speak well of me and, on occasion, urge someone to see me in consultation, a number of those who are (or eventually become) my patients would shun me if they could. Often I meet with someone who is (at best) reluctant to become a patient, in which case I find myself to be the unwanted therapist, now confronted by problems of influence, persuasion, and coercion.

In the more conventional tradition of medical practice (or the healing arts), I should not expect to have to deal with matters involving force, but rather with events customarily occurring in the following sequence:

1. Someone notices that his effectiveness in living is decreased, or altered in ways that are painful or troublesome and often not clearly understood by him. Should he himself overlook such changes, they

may be observed and brought to his notice by those who are in some way affected by them.

2. He may then speak to others about his observations (except in situations in which concealment might seem to be required by custom and prejudice) and in ensuing discussions decide that "something is wrong"; that is, he may be confirmed as one having an "ailment."

3. Being thus defined or identified as possibly being sick, he becomes a candidate for the services of an expert who can hopefully determine what ails him and, in so doing, extend somewhat the definition of himself as a person.

4. The expert generally has some publicly recognized and accepted status; that is, it is all right to consult him and to let selected others know something about the visit to him and its results. If the consultation is held, various "tests" are made and a conclusion is reached, including a definition of the problem (diagnosis), a prediction of its course and outcome (prognosis), possibly a statement as to what brought it about (etiology), and a recommendation for action (treatment).

5. In these operations the person seeking help is himself subject to a modification of his concept of who he is. Thus, he may find that he has become aware of phenomena that are not rightly labeled symptoms but are common to "anyone" and for some unclear reason have now become apparent to him, or that reflect some transient disturbance readily dealt with and necessitating little change in self-concept—such as the effects of fatigue. Should the conclusion be that "nothing is the matter," he may feel reassured and yet be concerned by the implication that he is overly sensitive, "weak," or "neurotic" in some way not clearly evident to him. Should he be found to be "sick"—"really sick," as we sometimes say—a redefinition of himself may be required as at least vulnerable to ills (if he has not accepted that fact already) and perhaps as diabetic, tubercular, or whatever, requiring a change in the way he has looked upon himself.

6. In this last eventuality, treatment is recommended, and the person now accepts (however reluctantly) the role of patient, implying his cooperation in a program designed to prolong his life, or ease it, or restore him to a state recognized by him and others as good health or "normalcy." The roles of physician and patient are established by

custom and law; within limits each accepts his own role and that of the other, and knows something of what he can expect as the result of behaving "properly" in the professional interaction.

However, even in the conventional practice of medicine, such clarity of role recognition is not always present. In such a case, the person may not seek help, failing to recognize or acknowledge the presence of a condition requiring it, may resist efforts to give him care, and may challenge the "right" of anyone to interfere with his living. I recall seeing many years ago a child with extensive pulmonary tuberculosis whose parents, because of religious convictions, refused medical treatment for him. Despite their heartfelt objections the child was hospitalized, the reasons for so doing including the following:

1. Symptoms, signs, and laboratory studies confirmed the existence of a disease, medically and (to a considerable extent) publicly recognized, with known course and prognosis, and with an accepted form of treatment.

2. The welfare of the patient (and that of others in a public health sense) were at stake, a factor taking precedence over certain desires, personal beliefs, and moral values, and leading to the enforcement of a program.

3. Costs associated with such coercion—distrust, fear, resentment—went unrecognized, or were not considered as important as those anticipated as arising from a lack of any treatment. The physician who takes part in this procedure may feel professionally correct (which he is) and any sadistic or power-seeking motives that may exist are carefully concealed, "justified," or repressed.

Although I have participated in events such as the above, I have never felt entirely at ease in so doing, and my discontent is more marked in dealing with psychiatric disorders to which the medical model is not so clearly applicable. Recently I served as consultant in circumstances that brought more clearly to my awareness some of the concerns that cannot well be avoided when there is a seeming incompatibility between a person's desires and beliefs and what appears to be therapeutic desirability, if not necessity.

There follow brief descriptions of individuals who strongly disagreed with me about their need for psychiatric help. There is nothing novel in these presentations. However, the very fact that they are commonplace may serve to provide a useful basis for later discussion.

Three Persons Reluctant to Become Patients

Mr. A.

When I first met Mr. A., he was forty-five years of age, married, and had young children. Several years prior to our meeting, he had undergone a marked, radical change in his behavior, becoming depressed, suspicious, withdrawn, and finally "delusional," hallucinated, and assaultive. He was hospitalized, treated with insulin coma and electroshock, and within a few months discharged as improved. After a year his disturbed behavior reappeared and the treatment was applied as before. Again he improved, only to worsen despite the addition of ataractic drugs. He was then remanded to a large state institution, where he became "regressed," mutilative, suicidal, violent, and so on, many terms being used to describe his despairing and wild way of living. Friends, dismayed at his condition, determined that he should "have" psychotherapy and brought him, against his will, to the institution in which I worked. On our first meeting he spoke to me, in part, as follows:

> I'm not talking with you and I'm not staying here. I don't want any part of you. You're not a doctor and, besides, I don't need one anyhow. I'm not a patient. I don't require treatment—and if I did, I wouldn't take yours. I didn't ask for you. I had nothing to do with coming here. Get out of my life.

In this case there was little open staff disagreement about what should be done, although some thought that no procedures could be of real value. Mr. A. had long been labeled as sick, his behavior being grossly deviant from that regarded as socially acceptable and in keeping with what is commonly recognized as "crazy." Most of those who saw him agreed that he was ill and needed hospital care, meaning that he should be locked up until he would cooperate with those who lived more conventionally than he did, changed his mad behavior, developed insight, and accepted his status as a patient. Before we met, he had been hospitalized nine years without fulfilling these requirements. Frequently he was accessible and charming and often spoke with fellow scientists so clearly about professional interests that one wondered why, on other occasions, he had to appear so disordered. However, his behavior was generally such that the role of patient seemed to be appropriate, and it was agreed by staff members and others that he was a chronic paranoid schizophrenic (as well as being Mr. A.), that he could not properly care for himself, that he was potentially a public nuisance, and that if he were not in one hospital he'd soon be in another. With none of these ideas did Mr. A. agree, and his refusal to be a patient was held to be further evidence of his actually being one.

Miss B.

Miss B. was twenty-two years old when she was brought to my office. Although a good student, a leader, and popular in high school, she grew increasingly antagonistic toward her parents, rebellious, and sexually promiscuous as an expression of her intense anxiety. In college she was depressed and withdrawn; she dropped out after making several suicide attempts. She failed in her efforts to hold jobs or friends. Diagnosed as schizophrenic, she was in treatment briefly with a series of psychotherapists, each of whom was unsatisfactory from her point of view, and was finally hospitalized as assaultive, hallucinated, and in panic after another attempt at suicide. Ataractic drugs and insulin coma brought no appreciable relief, and I met her after she had been in and out of a number of hospitals and had no enthusiasm for anything psychiatric.

At first Miss B. was pleasant with me, but she shortly reminded me that she had been forced to come to my office, that she was not ill, that she did not wish to see me, and that she would unrelentingly resist coercion. She said:

I'm not sick as you call it. Psychiatrists have tried to force their ideas on me—and in the long run they make you sick. There's nothing wrong that I can't handle. I never sought you out and I don't like your kind. Let me go. You aren't seeing me to help me; you're just doing it for yourself—for money, or to get some kind of perverse sexual kick out of me. I think you're crazy yourself, but you can't admit it, can't face up to it. I'll get out of here, or I'll kill you. Leave me alone, or I swear I'll destroy you.

Much of the time in the hospital, Miss B. showed no evidence of psychosis; she did well in studies and art and, except for a certain arrogance and haughtiness, appeared to be a charming young lady. Staff members and others did not as readily agree on her identity as they had on that of Mr. A. She was referred to as neurotic, psychopathic, schizophrenic, a spoiled child, a malingerer (a term she herself favored), and possibly a sufferer from temporal lobe dysfunction. With the uncertainty about "what was the matter" went indecision about "what to do" and, the prognosis being unclear, some thought that she should have no formal treatment. For Miss B. the role of patient was not always clearly suitable, and could even appear to be inappropriate.

Miss C.

Miss C. was a twenty-year-old woman to whom I served as consultant. She was a good student in high school, but left college to wander about the country with friends, hiding her whereabouts, and tantalizing and worrying her parents through occasional fragmentary, cryptic, and troubled notes. None of her friendships was durable; she lost interest in studies and work, used marijuana and LSD freely, joined a hippie colony, concerned herself with astrology and Hindu mysticism, and finally suffered an acute hallucinatory episode in which she was confused, assaultive, and in a state of panic. Hospitalized, she quickly "recovered" with the use of Thorazine and insisted on her release.

I was called by her relatives to serve as consultant about the course that she should follow. Miss C. herself had no wish to see me, but agreed to do so with the hope that I would be "on her side."

During the course of several meetings she reviewed her "history," finding it (she said) little different from that of many others of her age who were not hospitalized or labeled sick. She did not feel able to live in her home, which was marked by anxiety and depression, and she did not wish to conform to her parents' ideas of the good life—finish college, have a career, marry, adopt middle class virtues, and be an acknowledged "success." She opposed the mechanization and depersonalization of the culture, the destructiveness and hatreds of international and racial war, and sought a simpler life with people who shared her beliefs. Her goal in living was to be happy, and the drugs gave her a sense of freedom and power otherwise not experienced by her. She was determined not to commit herself to any person or cause (save that of "freedom")—not to parents, elders, society, lover, husband, or career; to do so, she felt, would be to accept coercion, to replace her values with those of others, and to lose her sense of being a person.

She had had "a bad trip" with LSD, but insisted that she was not ill, and that she had been told lies and tricked into entering a hospital. She passionately said that she was "fed up" with being labeled as bad, irresponsible, rebellious, or sick, never being seen as a person beyond the stereotypes applied to her. She saw me as her parents' agent (which was true), and said that I would never have met her had she come from a less well-to-do and psychiatrically sophisticated family. Gently enough, she told me that I was blind, bound by tradition, and sick of mind and soul, imperfectly concealing my disorder with a facade of professionalism. She spoke as follows:

> Please don't try to force yourself on me. You may mean well, but you can do terrible harm just by being ignorant—and so damn "self-righteous." If I'm forced to be in a hospital, I'll die—or kill myself—or I'll cooperate until you have to let me go, and then I'll hide myself forever from all of you. I won't be pulled back into your life anymore, because I know too much about it and it's intolerable to me.

I did not find my task with Miss C. to be simple. She had been diagnosed as schizophrenic through observation of the behavior that led to her hospitalization and through psychological testing. However, that behavior was complicated by the effects of marijuana, LSD, amphetamines, barbiturates, a bout of influenza, her parents' pursuit of her for several months, fatigue, and other factors associated with her search for an acceptable and durable concept of herself. After a brief course of Thorazine, she did not appear obviously ill; although some of her speech sounded ''sick,'' it was also hippie and acceptable to those with whom she had been living in a community of disaffiliated youth. Her condition, unlike Mr. B.'s, was not (so far) episodic, there being only the original period of disturbance.

Staff members (and relatives) were willing to accept her as sick because the doctor said that she was, but others did not see her as such and she did not accept a patient role. There had been no serious threat to others in her behavior, and when I met her she denied any threat to herself; thus, there was no clear ''social'' need to keep her hospitalized. The prognosis was not clear-cut; we could only say that her chances for greater ''self-realization'' would be better with psychotherapy, and that a possibly more grave psychotic development could thereby be prevented. The issue of coercion and deprivation of freedom was now inescapable, it being evident that we could not be certain that one course of action was demonstrably preferable to another.

Elements Common to These ''Cases''

Each of the persons to whom I have referred above has engaged in behavior that led him into ''trouble''; each has broken certain rules of the community within which he lives. These rules are related to a multiplicity of behaviors so built into the culture that they are usually accepted without question as being normal, ''the way to do things'' and, seemingly, God-given or innate. Violations of these prescriptions for living, common though they may be, are generally looked upon as being almost beyond the pale of human understanding, and thus may be called (depending upon the historical age of their appearance) evidences of possession by spirits, innate evil, witchcraft, mental illness, or disease. (What they may be named in years to come—providing that civilization survives—is not now clear, but the concept of disease in the traditional sense may not endure.)

In the ''trouble'' just mentioned, the individual's sense of identity seems threatened. He attempts to hold on to his ''old,'' established role (perhaps not well formed and not clearly a "part" of himself), to deal with new problems (such as growing up in a world of turmoil), to maintain required social relationships, to keep anxiety at a tolerable level, to avoid obviously disturbed action, and to function and even learn in the midst of uncertainty and what is experienced as a threat to personal security and self-esteem. Should these efforts fail, there may for a time be a loss of role structure—of self-concept—which may be resolved in a variety of ways: a regaining of the old role (recovery); a construction of a new and potentially more promising role (growth); a fantastic and discouragingly unalterable role (as in the paranoid resolution); or the acceptance of the role of patient which may, or may not, be modifiable in an acceptably "healthy" direction.

I, too, have a role—as psychoanalyst, psychiatrist, therapist, consultant, and concerned human being. The professional roles have to do with caring for the "sick." Thus, he who consults me is pushed in the direction of assuming a role complementary to mine—that of patient. At this juncture a struggle may occur, as if the therapist felt required to force the other into a patient role in order to confirm himself in his own role. If the idea of being a patient is equated with hopelessness or disgrace, it will not be an acceptable substitute for what is (until hope itself fades away). There will thus develop resistance against the threat of both the role and the coercion associated with it.

The Consultant's Experience With Coercion (Operational Account)

A person who permits himself to question what he does—and what many others say it is all right for him to do—will discover that it is his lot to attempt to act with assurance in dealing with uncertainties. Should he ignore the fact of uncertainty, he will come to rely on stereotypes and platitudes, detaching himself from the realities of his existence. Should he fall victim to uncertainty by becoming uncertain himself, he will renounce action and thereby assign it to others. Neither course is satisfactory—and, in a sense, none is. Perhaps it will be of some slight use to say something of my experience as a consultant (as with Miss C., for example) without attempting to explain or justify all that I recall of it.

As in that case, someone turns to me for help—not the troubled person, but a parent. My task (in conventional terms) is to observe, define a state of affairs, estimate possible outcomes, and prescribe a course of action. The trouble I have to deal with is described to me by a variety of interested parties—the potential patient, concerned relatives, involved friends, complaining public, and so on—and their accounts are colored by obscure motivations, by bias, by anxiety and fear, by the need to be "rational and make sense," by the desire to conceal, or whatever. There is, almost invariably, an effort to fit the behavior into a socially defined and seemingly meaningful compartment; "it" has to be "something," such as naughty, perverse, normal, sick, crazy, and the like. The assumption of a pseudocertainty thus surmounts the lack of definition.

The person who is brought for help often feels that he faces judgment; others will determine that he is normal, or that he is neurotic or psychotic and insane, a decision that will seriously influence his future. But it is not only his role that is at stake; those closely associated with him will also find their identities challenged. Family members are scrutinized and may emerge as being excessively anxious, overly solicitous, schizophrenogenic, destructively permissive or restrictive, sick, normal, or what not. The consultant may feel that *he* too is somehow on trial, discovering that he is viewed as professionally competent or otherwise, as one seduced by the patient or "bought" by the relatives, as a conservative or a liberal, as a Freudian or Sullivanian (for example), as a "nut," as one out of touch with the times if he is not a behaviorist or a group expert, and so on.

These multiple, often shifting identities reflect the complexities of behaviors in a social field and emphasize the idea that psychiatric disorder, whatever its "causes," can be studied as an interpersonal, social involvement. The struggle for clarity as to "who I am—you are—we are" is particularly noticeable in working with someone who, like Miss C., does not fit readily and consistently into an established category around which other behaviors can be conveniently organized.

The consultant, once engaged, cannot readily remove himself from the entanglement. He must express an opinion, knowing that whatever he does will influence the lives of others. At times he may be reluctant to do this, feel ashamed and apologetic for being coercive or simply uncertain, and want to be "neutral," or to wash his hands of the affair. Nonetheless he must act, realizing that whatever he does will have consequences for better or worse, and that for the most part he must operate with uncertainty as to both the meaning and the outcome of events.

During the time of my visits with Miss C., I experienced a variety of emotions and had time to consider these as well as the nature of my task. As she talked of freedom and "rights," I knew how strongly I resented any infringement of my own freedom; I also thought of how little leeway I had in the complex professional and personal world which had grown up around me. I resented being an enforcer and I was angry (irrationally, if you will) at Miss C., her parents, the psychiatric "system," and myself. Perhaps I was annoyed at her wish to escape from a system which so many of us accepted and usually managed not to look at too critically. I didn't like to have my attention called to it.

As we talked I grew more aware of the multitude of factors involved in this situation. Miss C. was not a medical case in the usual sense of "having a disease," and I was thus required to be more than an "objective" physician; I was confronted with moral values and problems of ethics that could not be comprehended in terms of my simply treating someone with a disorder.

The young woman's behavior seemed to be influenced by a number of factors. From one point of view, she was involved in a crisis of adolescence, not yet having established herself in terms of separation from her family, choice of career, dependable patterning of sexual activity, and interpersonal intimacy. She lived in a "mechanized" society in which there is much talk of loss of identity, at a time when a revolt of youth against the standards of their elders is prominent. Her rebellion was also against her family, being unable to accept dependency, give it up, or work out some viable compromise. To her I was a "square," a member of the establishment, a "shrink" so bound by training and ideology that anyone not sharing my values was sick and likely to be locked up until he saw things in the "right" way. The problem was further complicated by Miss C.'s recent use of marijuana and LSD, and by psychological studies (as well as clinical observation) that diagnosed her behavior as evidence of an acute schizophrenic reaction.

As our interviews went on, I was sympathetic with Miss C.'s wish to be free of what she experienced as crippling and restrictive forces in her life. At times I found myself struggling against being cast in the coercive role—a threat to my own sense of identity as a psychoanalyst and a freedom-loving man. I felt out of step with the young and realized that, in part, my sympathy arose from wanting to be accepted and thus to fancifully regain an aspect of my earlier years. Attempting to avoid the unfortunate influence of sympathy on the exercise of good judgment, I could seek to be more objective and removed, only to be looked upon by the patient as withdrawing from her. Through these movements Miss C.'s alienation was recognized more clearly; as I identified with her, I felt a threat of alienation from my "group," and as I attempted to "correct" myself, I felt alienated from her and the spirit of youth that she seemed to represent.

I could say that I was simply indicating a problem of countertransference in need of resolution, and that the moral issues were not my concern, being left for decision by the patient once the psychiatric difficulty had been settled. I thought, however, that a consideration of such issues was necessary as a part of that settlement, and that my own responses were not simply evidence of neurosis but an indication (however vague) of the presence of an existential dilemma.

As Miss C. spoke of her feelings of isolation, of the horror aroused in her by war, and of her attempts to escape from the impersonality of the culture, my own sense of aloneness and my half-hidden apprehensions about aging and death came to the fore. I then knew that, were I not cautious, I might subtly encourage this woman to act out for me an escape from events that I could not effect for myself. Once again I was reminded that more than professional goals and values are influential in reaching what may seem to be a rational decision about the life of another person; there are personal motives that cannot be denied and which, when clearly in awareness, may enrich the quality of the decision to be reached. Thus I spoke to Miss C. of my responses to what she described, placing both my wisdom and my ignorance at her service. What was "good" for her we could never truly know; any action had its risk and cost and there was to be no surety in what we did.

Of course, a consultant can lessen what doubts he has and seemingly reinforce himself in several ways. He can remind himself of his professional identity, gaining relief from tradition, the approval of some colleagues, and the sense of being "right." He can refuse to look or act beyond the stereotyped concepts of doctor, patient, sickness, and "safe" treatment, unwilling to accept uncertainty as a factor in reaching a decision. He can assign the task to someone else, or he can become lost in a variant of obsessional doubting, hiding behind a spurious concept of wisdom in which all can be stripped of meaning and reduced to nothing. It is well for a man to hesitate when he finds himself doing the "right thing"; it may be that his accompanying sense of comfort comes from following the acceptable and established course, and not from having acted in the better interests of his patient. Many a person has become the victim of "right" decisions made out of ignorance, prejudice, or self-interest.

The consultant (and others in this work) must at times assume a responsibility that seems to be beyond his professional competence but cannot be put aside. He need not unnecessarily decorate his patient with his doubts, but on occasion it may be useful to share with his patient the limitations of his knowledge, the possibilities that he envisages, and the hope that enlightens the task to be done.

A relevant comment, attributed to Robert Frost, was evoked on an occasion when the poet was asked to give a definition of wisdom. His final version, he said, was a paraphrase of a comment of many others throughout the ages, that true wisdom was the ability to act, when it was necessary, on the basis of incomplete information (Levine, 1960, p. 245).

Traditionalism and Reasons for Coercion

If I am to be coercive, I expect to explain why I am. From the traditional point of view, I can simply say that I am an expert in psychiatric matters and that I am required to act for the patient's good. I have no doubts about what to do if a person attempts to kill himself; I do what I can to prevent the act without reference to my right to violate his right to do so.[1]

---

[1]Does this mean that I would interfere with the seeking of death by a patient dying in great pain of a malignancy? For me, that is another question.

But in the case of Miss C., for example, my problem is not so simple. There is always a danger that words will suffer from a spread of meaning. Thus, being "expert" in dealing with anxiety in a psychiatric situation does not necessarily mean that I am an expert on how to live, on how to be happy, on what values should be adopted, and so on. And "good" can be a dangerous word; when I say that something is "good for you," I may actually mean that I will feel better if you follow the course I recommend, in which case the result may be good for me but not necessarily good for you. To be specific, it may be good for Miss C. to remain in a hospital, but a factor in this decision is that I would feel more at ease if I knew that she was under cover and not wandering about the streets.[2]

A reason commonly given for being coercive is that one acts for the public good, in which case the public is protected from possible depredations by the patient—and he is protected from the public which wants to get rid of him. As Erving Goffman (1961) states,

> Mental hospitals are not found in our society because supervisors, psychiatrists, and attendants want jobs; mental hospitals are found because there is a market for them. If all the mental hospitals in a given region were emptied and closed down today, tomorrow relatives, police, and judges would raise a clamor for new ones, and these true clients of the mental hospital would demand an institution to satisfy their needs. [p. 384]

Sometimes hospital care is offered—or enforced—as a means of providing shelter for someone who cannot "make it elsewhere." Then the hospital is a haven; it provides a home when none exists elsewhere, although one may be required to be crazy to gain admission—an interesting commentary on any society.

Coercion may be the force that brings together the agents of treatment and the person in need of them. The justification for the use of force arises from the idea that there is a disease that is harmful to the person and that there is a treatment available that may produce

---

[2]I do not mean to imply that the needs and comfort of a therapist (or parent) are to be ignored in caring for a patient (or a child). In all such situations, a mutuality of needs must be recognized and met for a useful relationship to develop.

results more desirable both for the patient and the public than is the untreated disorder. The patient's wishes may be overruled because his welfare is of concern to society; that is, the welfare of society (in the sense of preferring a healthy citizen to a sick one) takes precedence. This has been a useful concept, despite its abuses; like much that is useful, however, it may suffer from becoming enshrined as an absolute rule that is not to be investigated or departed from.

Research interests may lead to people being housed in particular institutions, as in the transfer of a depressed patient from a state hospital to a center in which depressive states are under study. Occasionally such interests may properly cause the hospitalization of someone previously cared for in his home, but such a person may be held overlong as a patient out of unconscious or rationalized motives to "study" him further. If the research motives leading to coercion are openly investigated, it may be discovered that they sometimes mask something else, such as a voyeuristic interest.

Goffman (1961) has suggested that psychiatrists are trained to provide service and that people must be available to receive it:

> I am suggesting that the nature of the patient's nature is redefined so that, in effect if not by intention, the patient becomes the kind of object upon which a psychiatric service can be performed. To be made a patient is to be made into a serviceable object, the irony being that so little service is available once this is done. [p. 379]

The burden of these remarks is that it may become too easy for the psychiatrist to see the patient in the person rather than the reverse; to make note of what is wrong with too little attention paid to what works well. The consultant must be wary here; he can almost assume that the fact that he has been called is indication that disorder is present. It is not common for him to find *no* disorder.

Relevant to this topic is the following observation by Thomas Scheff (1966):

> Members of professions such as law and medicine frequently are confronted with uncertainty in the course of their routine duties.

In these circumstances, informal norms have developed for handling uncertainty so that paralyzing hesitation is avoided. These norms are based upon assumptions that some types of errors are more to be avoided than others—assumptions so basic that they are usually taken for granted, are seldom discussed, and are therefore slow to change. [p. 105]

In brief, in some instances I may feel safer if I judge someone to be sick rather than well, the mistake being considered greater if I mistake sickness for health than health for sickness. Such a view is understandable when disease is thought of as an entity within a person, that unattended it may progress, that the outcome may be hurtful, and that further study (and even treatment) will produce no lasting ill effects. The tendency to declare that a person is ill may be reinforced by a number of factors that, despite their seeming triviality, irrelevance, and unsuitability, can influence the consultant's task. I shall outline these factors briefly in terms of my own experience, which is probably not unique.

1. It was necessary for me to travel a long distance to consult with Miss C., requiring an expenditure of effort, time, and money, as well as postponement of other activities. The fact that so much had to be arranged added an air of "importance" to the job (and to me). Anxious people looked to me to "do something," as it had already been determined that "something was wrong." In such a climate there seemed little room for there being "nothing wrong"—or in finding that trouble lay not in the putative patient but in others. Miss C. was well on the way to being a patient long before I saw her, and to alter this newly acquired identity would be troublesome to a number of people, if not to herself.

2. I am, in a sense, one of the world of disease, being better acquainted with the paraphernalia of sickness than of health. Most of the people I see (at least professionally) are "sick" (or troubled—not uncommon in times of stress and self-scrutiny); some get better, others are said to be "too sick" to change, but few are thought to require no help. Somewhat sadly I find that I am a better diagnostician of sickness than of health, and that I tend to do what I can do best. This being so, it is well to keep in mind such comments as Goffman's:

"I think that most of the information gathered in case records is quite true, although it might seem also to be true that almost everyone's life course could yield up enough denigrating facts to provide grounds for the record's justification of commitment" (1961, p. 159).

3. As I am in a hurry, other interests than those with the patient competing for my attention, I push for a "solution."

4. My own anxiety and uncertainty decline if I define a situation, diagnose disorder, hospitalize someone as a patient, and finally turn him over to the care of professional persons recognized as competent. In doing so, I am confirmed in my own role as an effective psychiatrist. For me to say that Miss C. is not sick is to question the judgment of others, and it may be easier to agree than to face their opposition—simpler to add a brick of confirmation than a gust of dissent. Decision is also influenced by belief in the "scientific" and technical, and by pride in the power of medical knowledge as superior in some ways to friendship and love. (Miss C. insisted that the latter could be more helpful in her case than the formalized techniques of psychotherapy.)

5. Convenience is another factor. The patient is now in a hospital, where her activities are centralized and she is, in a conventional sense, "safe." There she can be controlled, observed, and treated; it may be easier—and seemingly less risky—to continue this program than to make a change.

6. Miss C., like many others, is in a sense "suitable" for psychotherapy; she is intelligent, well educated, sensitive, in turmoil, at a critical period in her life, and without close attachment to anyone. Once her opposition is reduced, she should make good use of treatment. By and large, I won't be seriously criticized for recommending therapy, whereas if I did *not* recommend it and matters went badly for her I might be vulnerable to criticism. If she did poorly in treatment, the "explanation" might be that she was too resistant, that her ego was weak, that there was a fault in the way the procedure was conducted, and so on; but we could say that we had done our best and, without becoming preoccupied with self-criticism, would try to improve our methods for use in other cases. We should also consider the possible good as well as bad that might have ensued had Miss C.'s suggestions been followed—namely, that she run her own life as best she could.

7. The pleasure in doing the work of a consultant—the gratifi-

cation derived from accomplishing a well-defined professional task—also enters into decision-making. Satisfaction may come from pulling together a complexity of events into a neatly defined statement leading to a solution, making "sense" out of nonsense, and pushing aside (for the time being, at least) uncertainty. Sometimes there may be poorly recognized personal needs to capture and hold on to a person, as if keeping him (or her) in a "safe place" reassured one. This might be something like attempting to capture a quality (a bit of youthfulness, perhaps) and holding it, like a gem in a box, to look at occasionally. This motive may operate more often than one cares to acknowledge.

8. I suppose that the role of money and prestige must be mentioned, unpleasant though the thought may be. At least the patient will voice it, so it cannot be pure invention. Said Miss B.:

> How can you really be for me? A hospital pays you, not I. My parents bought your opinions, and your psychiatric organization made them for you long ago. You're not your own man at all; you only pretend that you're free.

There is some truth in what she says; I must face up to it and deal with it as best I can. Scheff (1966) makes a comment that seems appropriate: "The process of psychiatric screening would appear to be more sensitive to economic, political and social-psychological pressures on the screening agents than to most aspects of the patient's behavior" (p. 176).

Control: Concepts and Methods

The psychotherapist often feels uncomfortable at the thought that he is an agent of control; he prefers (usually) to think of himself as a source of freedom or that the control he does exert and the "self-control" he may advocate lead to freedom. He feels more at ease with such matters as education, the investigation of moral values, the modification of behavior through experience and insight, and so on. For the moment, however, let us consider control and its more unpleasant associate, coercion.

Control has been defined as the exercise of directing, guiding, or restraining power. Coerce means to restrain by force (especially by law or authority), to compel, curb, enforce, and repress. Among other words associated with coerce are intimidate, bulldoze, bully, browbeat, con, threaten, menace, drive, and restrain. These words have a "bad" connotation and are frightening: nonetheless, they are descriptive of actions more common than otherwise, and they have all been applied to me by patients. True, I am often the object of transference responses, but transference does not exist without some reality in the present as well as the past.

In psychotherapeutic work in particular, and in psychiatry in general, considerable emphasis is placed on the need for controlled behavior. The psychoanalytic patient must subscribe to various rules of control so that he can be less controlled in his thinking (at least in his sessions); the hospitalized patient must subscribe (or submit) to varieties of controlling forces until he demonstrates enough control to live in a controlled society "outside." Brief mention of some of the forms of control (coercion) that exist in the field of psychiatry will serve as a reminder of the powers that we psychiatrists hold over others and the danger of taking them too lightly, and coming to accept them as "natural" to us or God-given.

1. We expect a person to "control himself"—that is, to act generally in ways that are, within certain limits, predictable and in accordance with the rules and customs of the group in which he lives. Certain forms of "losing control" are tolerated if their duration, destructiveness, or annoyance potential is limited. Thus, one can "act crazy" in certain situations for a brief span of time (illustrated by the legal concepts of "temporary insanity" and "irresistible impulse") and "get away with it." But if the behavior persists beyond certain prescribed social limits, the person involved is redefined (as patient, for example) and placed in a special location designed (supposedly) to modify the behavior in a favorable direction or at least to contain it (the hospital).[3]

2. Closely related to the concept of self-control is that of cultural and social controls through customs that are so accepted by a group as to seem "natural" and therefore hardly require formalization,

---

[3]How such "self-controls" originate is a matter of psychiatric-sociological interest, but need not be discussed here.

through publicly acknowledged rules for "right" living, and through more formal laws. Violation of the mores—implicit or explicit—is responded to in a multitude of ways, from nonverbal indicators that push the offender back into the proper path, through such means as ostracism, a complexity of rewards and punishments, to the formal agencies of coercion, segregation, and limitation (such as the hospital, prison, and the like). The controlling agencies include family, school, peer groups, the local community, and the larger society.

In order to respond adequately to such pressures, an individual must value himself as having some worth, be able to foresee a future that could be for him either better or worse, and be able to entertain hope as well as anxiety and fear in relation to his behavior. Otherwise, the threat to self-esteem, personal reputation, future advancement, and so on will have little significance for him.

Whatever may be the causes of his difficulties, the psychiatric patient is a social deviant in that he has not acted in accord with group customs and rules that are not clearly categorized and, moreover, include covert as well as overt behavior. The violation of certain clear-cut rules leads one to be labeled a criminal or an alcoholic, for example, but the progress toward becoming a psychiatric patient entails the breaking of subtle regulations in such a way that the person may at first be called odd, then impulsive or withdrawn, then crazy (when some action is so out of place that its modification or regulation is required), and finally declared insane—through a panoply of legal-medical procedures (Erikson, 1966).

3. There is today a resurgence of interest in control through social reinforcement, personality being viewed as "primarily a function of the outside environmental stimuli, social interactions and social roles" (Krasner, 1963, p. 25). Referring to research in this field, Krasner (1962) states: "The essential element of behavior control studies is the influence, persuasion, and manipulation of human behavior" (p. 57). Under the term "social reinforcement" are included psychotherapy, hypnosis, operant conditioning, attitude influence, placebos, and brain-washing. Variants of this approach have operated in and out of institutions under other names and often without open recognition or acknowledgment. Recently there has been a more precise formulation of theory and technique, with patients being systematically exposed

to these methods of control, applied both overtly and covertly. In view of the rapidly expanding field of literature on the topic, it is unnecessary to elaborate it further here.

4. Influence and control may also be exerted through the use of physical devices such as direct stimulation of the brain. Although such studies are experimental, human subjects are used and there is no doubt that control is exerted over the patient without his being able to do much about it. In some instances, as in the work described by Robert Heath (Heath and Mickle, 1960), the patient may even operate the machinery that modifies his own behavior.

5. Control is exerted through hospital programs in which some degree of conformity is sought through a variety of methods, including physical restriction, punishment and reward, group pressure, treatment with drugs and other agents, isolation, and so on. Despite the established purpose of such institutions to treat and cure, they employ practices that tend to perpetuate the disorders of patients rather than to alleviate them.

Although there are ''open'' and ''closed'' hospitals, the degree of conformity enforced in the former may be greater in some instances than in the latter. A hospital may be kept ''open''—that is, the patients ''voluntarily'' live in accord with its rules despite the absence of locked doors—through the forces of community pressure, convulsive therapy, drugs, and so on. Of importance in the present context is simply the recognition of the coercive nature of aspects of hospital care.

6. The use of drugs to control behavior both in and out of institutions is a practice of long standing. It is interesting that we currently are much concerned about curtailing the use of certain of the drugs that modify behavior, such as alcohol, marijuana, and LSD, while advocating the use of others, ataractics, barbiturates, and so on. As the variety and usage of drugs increase, we must deal with some fine distinctions between addiction, ''proper'' usage, the nature of the behavior we choose to mold, and the direction in which it should be molded.

7. Other ways to modify the action of the central nervous system include electroconvulsive treatment, insulin coma, and lobotomy. The history of psychiatry offers many examples of procedures of more or less transient popularity that are designed to modify behavior in a

controlled direction. The mutilative character of some procedures (such as surgical interventions for the elimination of alleged foci of infection) emphasizes how closely the therapeutic may be aligned with the sadistic forces of life. In all of these instances, the coercive element cannot be disregarded, particularly when many of them may be applied without the consent or knowledge of the patient.

Embarking on a Coercive Course: Attendant Considerations

Despite many objections, doubts, and hesitations, one may decide upon the coercive course. I became the therapist of Mr. A. and Miss B. despite their objections, and I recommended that Miss C. begin psychotherapy in a hospital. Having reached such a conclusion, we must note that certain hazards must be faced.

In the first place the patient will resent—and usually resist—coercion. It is true that some people seem to invite being forced, that others will (despite expressed objections) welcome care and refuge, and that some don't seem to attend to what happens. Nonetheless, I have not known anyone who did not in some way resent the imposition of authority that drove him to psychiatric treatment, and I have not been content with the idea that such resentment can be explained purely in terms of unresolved oedipal conflicts. This resentment, with its ''realistic'' and ''neurotic'' components, must be openly included in any psychotherapy other (possibly) than the behavioral ''shaping'' of action.

As already noted, the therapist who assumes the coercive position does so with particular goals and values in mind. He is not neutral and cannot assume an attitude of impartiality. Bergin (1963) writes:

We never have and, I believe, never will strictly agree upon the goals or outcomes to be strived for, but to me it is folly to suppose that the research enterprise in psychotherapy will become optimally fruitful until it includes an enlarged devotion toward valued ends. . . . There are no such phenomena as culture-free or value-free people; consequently it seems inevitable that specific attention and action are required on the part of both practitioner and researchers with regard to these facts. This involves becoming explicit about the values to which we are committed, doing all we can to specify their meaning in precise psychological terms and finally devoting ourselves to developing ways of achieving those ends. [p. 164]

This lack of neutrality, this open declaration of values accompanying the coercive posture, must also be integral facets of the ensuing psychotherapy; they cannot be denied or explained away.

Having coerced someone into a course of action, we could assume it is generally accepted as offering reasonable promise of achieving desirable ends. If I "coerce" a person into the role of patient in psychotherapy, I do so with the expectation that the outcome will probably (or at least possibly,) be worth the cost. Such expectations, hopefully, will be reinforced by knowledgeable colleagues and some public approval. However, despite such support, there are contrasting views of the procedure that cannot be ignored; these salt the undertaking with a sharp doubt which may be useful if it leads to critical observation and questioning.

There is no need for us to review here the many criticisms of the psychotherapeutic approach—often justified, at times heated and bellicose, and not always easy to answer. To cite just two brief examples: Dr. D. N. Malan of the Tavistock Clinic states: "There is not the slightest indication from the published figures that psychotherapy has any value at all." H. J. Eysenck (1964) comments: "All these studies reinforce my conclusion that there is no difference in outcome between treated and non-treated groups." We could attempt to deal with such criticisms by declaring them completely invalid, by ignoring them, or by derogating the critics as simply being unable to see the truth. The fact is that if we are to do psychotherapy we must go ahead and do it, not with blind belief, but with confidence in the potential usefulness of a human relationship, being unafraid to doubt as well as believe. My point is simply that one can't be a psychotherapist torn by doubts or caught up in an all-inclusive eclecticism, but belief should be placed in the essence of the matter rather than in technical variables that may well be modifiable.

The psychotherapist cannot rely on technique alone. The results of his efforts cannot be correlated clearly with how he does what, and seem to have something to do with the kind of a person he is. In other words, the effective agent in the psychotherapeutic transaction is not clearly identifiable. Therefore, in our coercion, we do not engage a person to be treated by clearly defined and demonstrably effective techniques; rather, we attempt to involve him in a relationship that will differ to some extent with each therapist and has the potential of being destructive as well as beneficial. The task of consultant in referring a patient for treatment is, from this point of view, a notoriously complicated one.

It has been pointed out that therapeutic establishments may injure as well as help, and that hospitalization is no guarantee that good will outweigh the damage done. The consultant is therefore well advised to know intimately the place (the hospital) as well as the therapist when he assigns a patient for treatment. As Goffman (1961) cautions,

> current official psychiatric treatment for functional disorders does not, in itself, provide a probability of success great enough easily to justify the practice of institutional psychiatry as an expert service occupation, as here defined, especially since the probability that hospitalization will damage the life chances of the individual is, as already suggested, positive and high. [p. 362]

To repeat: when I coerce a person into becoming a psychiatric patient, I know that he will resent my action, that he will be exposed to my concept of values, that many colleagues and others will not approve of the treatment prescribed, that there is a chance of harming as well as helping, and that the personality of therapist, as well as patient, will be factors in the outcome. Nevertheless, I can't pass the buck to someone else or to ''circumstances.'' It is required that I take a stand, asserting myself with the belief that affection and confidence develop in a human relationship along with anxiety and doubt, and that much that is known as psychiatric disorder has been learned and can be modified by learning.

The Coerced Patient

Coercion is directed not only toward restraint but involves the acquisition of a new role—in this instance that of patient. Psychiatric disorder is derived, as I now view the problem, to a great extent from past experience in living, and is perpetuated through remembrances of what has been, through present circumstances that seem to confirm the past and require its continuance, and through anticipation of a future not strikingly better than the present. The patient role often carries with it the curse of past, present, and future. It is a socially derogated and poorly defined role (awkwardly bearing with it elements of the medical model that may be outmoded, remnants of belief in devil-possession, the mark of wickedness, the continuing struggle between free will and determinism, nature and nurture, sociological concepts of role-playing and game theory, and so on), and it is tinged with a quality of hopelessness and despair. Many persons feel that to assume the patient role is to be marked for life, to become further a victim of social prejudice, and to be disadvantaged in all future social relationships. In a sense, this view is correct. Why then, assume such risks when, to some, the promise of help may seem so slight?

The patient's view of the therapist's role is usually not one that is marked by an anticipation of much help, and matters are worsened by coercion. This view reflects the general social attitude toward the psychiatrist (the "shrink"), which is for the most part uncomplimentary. It reflects too distrustful and resentful attitudes toward authority, parents, and anyone who has the power to control and enforce. If there has been previous experience with psychiatrists, it has often not been useful; otherwise, the patient would not be in this present position. To the transference aspects of the psychiatrist's role is added the reality of the coercive act.

Many of the people who consult me speak of being caught up in an impersonal, machinelike society that they cannot comprehend or control, and within which they feel impotent. Such a person may try to "fit in" by attempting to be like the machine he fears and distrusts; that is, he tries to be efficient, detached, objective, unemotional, goal-directed, and productive in a conventionally accepted sense. In the process, he may further lose his sense of self and, being more machinelike, become a caricature of a human being. As the sense of helplessness increases, so do anxiety, anger, despair, and alienation. Escape may be sought by withdrawal into deviant subgroups, by isolation, by the use of drugs, by psychosis, by suicide, and so on. The intrusion of the psychiatrist, the threat of treatment and hospital, can be fitted easily into one's fear of the machine.

Miss C. felt that she would be captured rather than helped—captured by an impersonal, uncomprehending group of ''experts'' who would apply predetermined techniques in an effort to force her into conformity with a system which, she believed, had already come near to destroying her. Even if she ''got well,'' this might only mean (from her point of view) that she had really ''sold out'' to the establishment, and that she would thereafter live in a ''healthy'' way that would be a travesty of her concept of herself as an honest and worthy person. In that case, the therapist is at a disadvantage; his professional role is not accepted, and he is suspected and mistrusted as a person.

Nevertheless, the patient may at times continue usefully in the disliked treatment. Why? To begin with, he has no choice. He is locked up and, despite his objections, the therapist does visit with him.

As such meetings continue, a number of developments may take place that make satisfactory therapy possible. The personality of the therapist may be experienced as attractive, and no longer seen in a stereotyped fashion as only coercive. Some interest in the therapeutic process may develop, most likely following actual changes in behavior that are demonstrable improvements in living (such as recurrent, and eventually persistent, reductions in anxiety). In the prolonged encounter of patient and therapist, relational bonds are formed and some of the values of each are taken in by the other, leading in some instances to improved understanding and the basis for a cooperative, and eventually collaborative, enterprise. The likelihood that the relationship will prosper is increased if its goals are formulated as it develops, thus avoiding the application of preconceived goals to a conventional concept of what a patient is and ought to become. In other words, goals are identified as they are derived from experience in the therapeutic relationship and are found to be suitable for that particular person.[4]

It is well to note that therapeutic results are to some extent related

---

[4]In some instances, however, the patient's behavior seems to be designed to provoke a coercive response, as if one were desired. Such a person may have become so accustomed to a coercive atmosphere, as in his home, that he feels ''comfortable'' only with what has seemed ''natural.'' He may therefore act in such a way as to re-create, in the hospital or in the relationship with the therapist, a replica of the past.

to a patient's expectations. The patient who expects to find no help
is usually able to document his views through his observations of the
treatment procedure. Similarly, the therapist and others can seemingly
find support for their anticipations of patient betterment or failure. In
the coercive situation, enough resentment may be stirred up to reveal
the previously hidden motives of both parties; it is better that their
expectations be out in the open than concealed.

Much of what has been said can be summed up in terms of
motivation. Motive implies goal and direction. The unmotivated patient
may be so anxious that he can't contemplate anything as complicated
as a goal, or so despairing that a future goal can be seen only as a
continuation of the miserable present. In such a case, one doesn't talk
about goals for the moment, but gets busy with developing the rudi-
ments of a relationship so that anxiety and despair can be reduced.
Then, with some dawning of hope, goals and motives can be considered. The therapist works in such a fashion that his patient can envisage
change, and then move in a certain direction, being encouraged to do
so by exposure to the therapist's goals, by recognition and reevaluation
of his own, and by the impetus derived from observation of profitable
improvement in his own performance.

The Coercive Therapist

When a therapist is confronted with the need to assume a coercive
position he may do so, or abandon the case, or seek some different
way of dealing with it; whatever he does, he may find it necessary to
take a long look at the concept of his personal and professional self.
Should he himself set forceful limits, he can no longer claim to be
neutral; he becomes (at least at the beginning) an enforcer rather than
a helper, usually being met with the distrust and hostility of the patient.
Then the therapist's stance, despite its public acceptance, is not a
popular one, as he seems to move toward the position of prison-keeper
rather than healer.

In assuming the responsibility of controlling another person—of
imposing one's ideas on him—the therapist declares his interest in the
patient's life in a powerful and often dramatic fashion. His coercive
posture proclaims that for the moment his own opinions are to be

valued above those of the patient, that he will override all objections to do what he thinks is for the patient's good, and that he will insist on establishing the roles of doctor and patient somewhat (despite variations) in a medical tradition that is obviously not well suited to all aspects of the problems to be dealt with. It is difficult to act thus without feelings of doubt and guilt; the therapist arrogates to himself powers that cannot be assumed with comfort. By such actions, the therapist intensifies the relationship with his patient; there is a confrontation between the two which can be useful or otherwise but which cannot be neutral, mild—or denied. More than in his usual work, in these instances the therapist becomes for the patient an ideal, model, and teacher to be accepted, used, or resisted as a representation of all that is evil.

The coercive consultant or therapist must ask himself how he managed to get into this position and why he is willing to accept it. After he says that he has made a diagnosis of psychiatric disorder requiring help and that he (or someone) must provide that help, he can look for other motives. He might become aware of some of the following:

1. Perhaps the therapist has himself had long experience in controlling and being himself controlled, with the result that the process seems natural and almost beyond question. In hospital work we run the risk of losing our perspective about freedom; it becomes too easy to lock people up, and in doing this to become locked in ourselves. In a sense the psychiatrist can be no more free than his patients.

2. In some instances one is coercive to others out of revenge for having oneself been coerced.

3. Others of us may doubt their ability to gain or hold a relation with another person and thus seek to capture him by force, fearing that otherwise he will abandon us.

4. The need for a variant of a sadistic-masochistic relationship may figure in the use of coercion, an unhappy satisfaction being derived from the patient's protests and the therapist's experience of power.

5. An interesting attachment can arise between a patient who is kept on a hospital ward and the therapist who comes to the patient's room to see him in privacy. A feeling of possessiveness is often increased, and the intrusion of others resented, until the patient may feel

(and be looked upon) almost as belonging to the therapist. The development of this form of relationship may be subtle and to some people very attractive. A therapist who finds it so should consider the possibility that he has an undue need to be "bound in" to another person in this manner.

6. There are therapists who require "action" and thus find the assertive, coercive role to their liking. Wanting to "do something," they may be attracted to the idea of going forth and capturing someone to be a patient, then struggling to "tame" that person, and finally with some reluctance settling into the more passive role of observer and interpreter. In these circumstances, the desire to rescue someone in distress may operate, fed by the fantasy of taking him against his wishes away from an unsympathetic and uncomprehending world and then revealing a better one in which the therapist plays a dominant part.

7. Therapists, like others, enjoy praise for attempting the difficult. It may therefore seem heroic (on a modest scale) to oppose someone, to enforce a point of view, and to attempt treatment against strong opposition. Therapy complicated by coercion is not an easy task, but the seeking of praise is not a very useful motive for assuming the coercive role.

8. A therapist's need to display himself, to reveal his anxiety, anger, fear, and so on may lead him to enter into a coercive situation to attract attention.

9. There are some who find satisfaction in establishing dominion over others. Out of a need to be dominant, they are driven to seek power, usually convinced that they act for the "good" of the subject person. It is difficult for such a therapist to accept the patient's contrasting point of view, for to do so would be to lose the powerful position.

This list could be expanded; indeed, the reader may be able to add to it from his own experience. The motives listed are not necessarily "bad" in themselves. In varying degrees most of us, I suspect, have needs to control, to seek revenge, to rescue, to display ourselves, to engage in action, to win praise for attempting the difficult, to possess another person, to convince others of our virtues, and so on. There must be a motive for what we do, and usually it is not so simple as a pure drive to serve as an understanding and helpful therapist. Hopefully, the motivations noted above have been discussed in the therapist's personal treatment; at least they should be in his awareness so that he does not deny them while responding to them. Of course, should these motivations be persistently dominant and powerful, some field other than psychotherapy might prove to be more suitable for one who finds himself strongly drawn to the coercive mode.

The psychiatrist will usually resist being associated with such concepts as coercion, control, and conformity. He would probably agree with John Whitehorn (1959): ''The ideal human condition toward which Freud's therapy aimed appears to me to have been a state of freedom in which a person could, through understanding, hold himself inwardly free from the coercive prohibitions of society and free also from the coerciveness of blind biological impulses.'' Perhaps the therapist, after his long years of training, has more personal knowledge of subtle coercion and the pull toward conformity than he can comfortably accept, and thus must champion a freedom no longer his. In doing so, he could perhaps go too far. Again Whitehorn provides a useful comment:

> In admitting to some feeling that there is something shameful in conformity, I think that we manifest our unwise submission to one of the prejudices of our time and of our culture. I misdoubt the presumed ignobility of conformity. . . . the suckling infant conforms to mother, and mother to infant, with an eagerness which gives one warrant to think that conforming behavior may be confused with an inner glow of enthusiasm quite as genuine and noble as is the aspiration for freedom. So, too, in the infinitude of human interactions, domestic and social, many transactions and relationships of sustenance and sharing may come to partake also of this inner eagerness for conforming. [pp. 5–6]

The ''coercive therapist'' needs not only to be aware of what he does and have some degree of insight into why he does it; he must also beware of being intimidated by his coercive position or his patient's claim to a nobler view of the universe. For example, Miss C. spoke eloquently and movingly of freedom and grieved for me as a stodgy, conforming, tradition-bound sellout to the establishment. She seeks happiness, a feeling of security, and predictability, finding an apparent expression of the self, increased awareness, and comfort through association with a group who agree with her, and through the use of drugs. The therapist has, in a sense, so little to offer, and he knows this. He can provide no certainty, no knowledge or wisdom beyond the limitations of his own experience and narrow view, and no hope except that derived from acceptance of his own being and a determination to do what he can without requiring his patient's gratitude as a reward. The patient will come to face (not alone, but with the therapist) a feeling of void and the concept of nothingness. At the confrontation of the fear of nothingness he will, if all goes well, assert himself to be at least something—achieve a definition of self more permissive of growth and satisfaction than the neurotic or psychotic resolutions.

To quote Rollo May (1967):

As he [the patient] becomes more conscious of the infinite deterministic forces in his life, he becomes more free. . . . *Freedom* is thus not the opposite to determinism. Freedom is the individual's capacity *to know that he is the determined one*, to pause between stimulus and response and thus to throw his weight, however slight it may be, on the side of one particular response among several possible ones. . . . Freedom is thus also not anarchy. . . . Freedom can never be separated from responsibility. [p. 175]

The therapist need not feel guilt, except perhaps at refusing the attempt to engage his patient in a human relationship in which the chances for greater freedom do lie. He cannot provide certainty, but he can help to do away with the fear of living with uncertainty.

Psychotherapy

The problems of psychotherapeutic intervention with the patient who feels, or has been, coerced require more adequate consideration than I can give them here. Nonetheless, a few brief remarks should be made for the record. Let us recall the three persons I mentioned earlier. What happened to them?

For several years Mr. A. remained in a hospital—recalcitrant, hostile, obdurate, persistently critical of me, and never accepting the role of patient. Somehow, however, he was able to go back to his work. He wrote me years later that life was good for him. Before leaving the hospital, he said to me, ''We are students and teachers—the two of us—each to the other.''

Miss B. battled with me and often found no good in me. Many a time she discharged me, but I did not accept dismissal. On leaving me after a few years to return to school, she said: ''Perhaps you did more harm than good. But you gave me hope and you kept me alive.''

Miss C. did not go into treatment. She went on her way with her hippie friends. We keep in distant contact. I don't know what will occur.

When I become the therapist of a coerced person, I don't pass the buck to anyone; I say that I accept my position willingly and I share, more or less directly, the responsibility for setting limits to behavior. If I knew something better to do, I'd do it. Perhaps I represent to the patient an impoverishment of ideas, or a painfully narrow view of life, but for the moment I can do no better than curtail his freedom, being aware of some of the costs and risks in so doing. I agree that I am coercive, and that, oddly enough, I so act in the pursuit of freedom. There is not much to say about all of this; words will not allay a distrust and fear of the enforcer.

I do not deny that I am a prison-keeper, but I do suggest that the patient is also one. He lives within a prison of the self—keeping himself in and others out. I often have some reluctance to become involved with this imprisoned person, as I know that he will for a time imprison me in his own fears and hates, and that he will beat on me as a substitute for all of those people and ideas that have led to his incarceration. But I gladly seek his true freedom because only through it can I find my own.

Despite objections and protests about the uselessness of it all, I persist in meeting with my patient, knowing that as time goes on bonds of relationship will develop, and that these can be used as a bridge toward improved living—that is, an increased ability to learn and a loosening of fixed and stereotyped concepts of other people. I do not insist on an acceptance of the roles of patient and therapist, but I do not deny the existence of these roles or that, in my opinion, they are in some ways suitable to the therapeutic enterprise. The role per se need not determine what one is, unless one feels too small and weak to exist apart from a publicly declared role or name. One can be sick, a patient, a human being, and also free—what one cannot be is anything other than a transient, alone in a universe that is largely unknown.

Thus, in the spending of time together, in the increased exchange of our views, and in our observations of what goes on between us, there may come escape for both from the prison in which the patient has lived and into which the therapist has found his way.

References

Bergin, A. E. (1963), The effects of psychotherapy: Negative results revisited. In: *The Investigation of Psychotherapy: Commentaries and Readings*, ed. A. P. Goldstein & S. G. Dean. New York: Wiley, 1966.

Erikson, K. (1966), *Wayward Puritans: A Study in the Sociology of Deviances.* New York: Wiley.

Eysenck, H. J. (1964), The outcome problem in psychotherapy: A reply. *Psychotherapy*, 1:97–100.

Goffman, E. (1961), *Asylums: Essays on the Social Situation of Mental Patients and Other Inmates.* Garden City, NY: Doubleday.

Heath, R. G. & Mickle, W. A. (1960), Evaluation of seven years experience with depth electrode studies in human patients. In: *Electrical Studies in the Unanesthesized Brain*, ed. E. R. Ramey & D. S. O'Doherty. New York: Hoeber.

Krasner, L. (1962), Behavior control and social responsibility. *Amer. Psychol.*, 17:199–204.

———— (1963), Reinforcement, verbal behavior and psychotherapy. *Amer. J. Orthopsychiat.*, 33:601–613.

Levine, M. (1960), Oedipus, Cain and Abel, and the geographic full-time system. *J. Med. Ed.*, 35 (March):245.

May, R. (1967), *Psychology and the Human Dilemma.* Princeton, NJ: Van Nostrand.

Scheff, T. J. (1966), *Being Mentally Ill: A Sociological Theory.* Chicago: Aldine.

Whitehorn, J. C. (1959), Goals of Psychotherapy. In: *Research in Psychotherapy*, ed. E. A. Rubinstein & M. B. Parloff. Washington, DC: American Psychological Association.

16

The Schizophrenic Patient, the Psychotherapist, and the Consultant

Otto Allen Will, Jr., M.D.

Few psychiatrists develop or maintain an interest in the intensive psychotherapy of psychotic people. This work may not seem personally rewarding to a therapist, and he may resent the fact that such individualized efforts—often prolonged and tedious—are not available to the populations of our crowded mental hospitals, and even if they were, in many instances would not be demonstrably helpful. Nonetheless, such therapy need not be looked upon as impractical and unjustified. It is enough that some seriously disturbed persons can be benefited significantly by interested and capable physicians; the alleviation of human misery, even for the few, does not require justification, and it is useful that there be repeated demonstrations that psychosis need not be equated with a "living death." Furthermore, the therapy of psychoses is also the study of psychoses, the information derived therefrom being relevant to the understanding of human behavior in general and to the care and prevention of mental disorder in particular. Experience gained in the psychotherapy of psychoses will further the physician's knowledge of psychopathology and improve upon the effective use of technical skills.

In this presentation I shall discuss matters that are of special significance to me both as therapist and as consultant to others who

333

work with psychotic patients; that is, the subject has relevance to both education and psychotherapy. My own experience as a consultant has been with the colleague, psychiatric resident, candidate in psychoanalytic institute, hospital staff member, or private practitioner—who is somewhat sophisticated as a clinician, is acquainted with theories of personality development, psychopathological formations, and therapeutic techniques, and to a considerable extent already earns his living through the practice of psychotherapy. Although such therapists usually work with a variety of patients, I shall comment on the treatment of psychotic patients in a hospital setting, with particular emphasis on those labeled schizophrenic. I think that much of what I have to say is applicable to the practice and teaching of psychotherapy in general and the themes will be presented with these two considerations, education and practice, in mind.

Variations on the Medical Theme

In considering the problems dealt with by the psychotic patient and his therapist, it is useful to remind ourselves of certain contrasts between the psychiatric therapeutic situation and the classical medical model. In traditional medical circumstances the patient, suffering from something referred to as a disease, seeks help from a qualified expert, the physician, who uses his skills in an attempt to remove (as we put it) the sickness from the patient, restoring him (if all goes well) to a state of health, agreed upon by those concerned as recognizable and desirable. The patient voluntarily seeks treatment, cooperates in its application, and is able to evaluate it in terms of publicly recognized standards. Therapy is carried on in a locale designed for the care of the patient and protected from the intrusion of destructive external influences. The therapeutic program is a benign constellation of events unmarked by coercion and social stigma. The disorder itself (with notable exceptions) is not a source of the patient's feeling shame, humiliation, or fear of social disapproval. It is expected that upon his improvement he can return to his previous—or some other—mode of living without being ostracized or socially estranged by virtue of his disablement.

In a number of ways the above description does not apply to the psychiatric patient in general, and to the psychotic patient in particular. For example, the signs and symptoms of schizophrenia are multiple and variable; there is no consistently verifiable underlying disorder of structure, and there is still some question about the existence of such an entity in accord with the classical concept of disease. The therapist is of necessity unclear as to the nature of the ailment, is often uncertain as to the needs of the patient, discovers that therapeutic techniques are not always well-defined or readily taught, and must accept the fact that the outcome of treatment is not clearly predictable (Goffman, 1961).[1] There may be disagreement among patient, therapist, and others concerned as to the significance of the disorder, the proper treatment to be used, and the definitions of states of health and sickness, such that what is held desirable by some is opposed by others as threatening or even wicked. Often the psychiatric hospital has not been designed with an understanding of patient needs, is not easily modifiable, and may be intruded on by external destructive forces. Treatment is frequently coercive and influenced by prejudicial moral traditions; the disorder generally is looked upon as shameful and evidence of inferiority, and the patient's future life may be handicapped by his reputation of having been "crazy." The therapist may receive little appreciation from his patients and their relatives, and often meager support from colleagues and others who may consider him deficient in choosing this work, just as the patient is thought of as being deficient for "having" the disorder.

Characteristics of the Therapist

I do not know what would be the "best" training for those who would work with the gravely disordered. I favor a background of medical education, as in that training one participates as observer and helper in the major events of human living—birth, growth, injury and sickness, separation and loss, behavioral accompaniments of love and hate, aging, and death; one develops the ability to take some personal

---

[1]Consider the following remarks by Goffman: "current official psychiatric treatment for functional disorders does not, in itself, provide a probability of success great enough easily to justify the practice of institutional psychiatry as an expert service occupation, as here defined, especially since the probability that hospitalization will damage the life chances of the individual is, as already suggested, positive and high" (p. 362).

responsibility in the life of another, acquires a sustaining sense of professional identity, and comes to recognize that in some situations he is unable to help, save by being present. Should the physician become rigidly bound in a professional role marked by impersonal distance and a devotion to a pseudoobjectivity whereby interpersonal events are of less moment than physical and laboratory phenomena, his education may appear at times to be more handicap than advantage, and to work effectively as a psychotherapist, unlearning as well as learning may be required. In brief, medical training does not in itself necessarily lead to the development of an accomplished psychotherapist.

Thus I know of no formal training that regularly produces a therapist demonstrably competent in the treatment of psychotic people. I think that the good physician brings with him a combination of factors—experience in living, education, and certain value systems and moral attitudes that will stand him in good stead in this work. I doubt, as we know matters now, that we can ''train'' a person for this, but perhaps we can help those who, through experience and inclination, wish to engage in it to improve their efforts to the benefit of their patients.

It is difficult to determine who is best suited to be the therapist of psychotic patients, and the scope of this paper does not allow for a detailed discussion of this subject. The studies of Whitehorn and Betz (1954) regarding the helpful characteristics of the therapist of the schizophrenic patient are illuminating, as indicated by the following quotation:

> in the psychotherapy of schizophrenic patients success is to a large extent determined by the differences found among physicians in the extent to which they are able to approach their patients' problems in a personal way, gain a trusted, confidential relationship and participate in an active personal way in the patient's reorientation to personal relationships. Techniques of passive permissiveness, or efforts to develop insight by interpretation, appear to have much less therapeutic value.

Those who speak to me of an interest in the psychotherapy of schizophrenic patients have usually completed part or all of their formal psychiatric training. They are not bound to an unyielding regard for the conventional, and are not astonished that life in this world is often troubled, uncertain, and not devised for the accommodation of man. They eschew despair as well as bland optimism. Although they welcome learning, they are not likely to extend reverence to the teacher, having no expectation that he will present them with the final word in therapeutic theory or technique. Such a person has had enough experience with personal anxiety that he wants to learn more about "it," and is not excessively disturbed by observing its varied manifestations in himself as well as in others. Being able to consider his own motives as often obscure but nonetheless influential in the behavior of other people—such as his patients—he will engage in a directed scrutiny of his own character and intentions through personal analysis, knowing that the results may be as discomforting as enlightening. He is compassionate and attempts to be of help to the ailing, but is not driven to convert them to his views; he does not identify with his patients to the extent that he completely accepts their despair, their estimation of their own destructiveness, or their fear of the world and its inhabitants; recognizing psychotic experience as no more or less than human, he does not look upon it as necessarily evidence of special gifts and powers; he has no conviction—or need to prove—that his patients will somehow be cured by exposure to his love; he does not seek the companionship of mental hospital inhabitants as a solace for his own loneliness; and he is not driven to exert power or establish dominion over assorted victims locked in an institution. Having spent several years on a hospital staff and perhaps having completed psychoanalytic training, this physician will probably depart into a more conventional practice, likely being less troubled by, and more skilled in, dealing with the so-called "borderline" patients than would have been the case had his earlier professional experience been otherwise.

The following comments by Gabriel Marcel (1963) are relevant to our concern with the characteristics of a psychotherapist:

> It is an undeniable fact, though it is hard to describe in intelligible terms, that there are some people who reveal themselves as "present"—that is to say, at our disposal—when we

are in pain or in need to confide in someone, while there are other people who do not give us this feeling, however great is their goodwill . . . the distinction between presence and absence is not at all the same as that between attention and distraction. The most attentive and the most conscientious listener may give me the impression of not being present; he gives me nothing, he cannot make room for me in himself. . . . The truth is that there is a way of listening which is a way of giving, and another way of listening which is a way of refusing, of refusing *oneself.* . . . Presence involves a reciprocity which is excluded from any relation of subject to object. . . . The moment I think: After all, this is only a case . . . it is no good, I can feel nothing.

But the characteristic of the soul which is present and at the disposal of others is that it cannot think in terms of *cases*; in its eyes there are *no cases at all.* [pp. 39–40]

On the Teaching Encounter

Learning is a process extending throughout the life of a person, beginning in rudimentary form before birth and continuing until death. Education, in the more formal sense, involves student, teacher, and subject matter, is dependent upon man's unique ability to create, elaborate, and transmit symbolic representations of experience, and is directed toward ends more or less explicitly stated and understood. A commonly accepted goal of education is the learning by the student of what are considered to be the essentials of a subject. A second goal—often not clearly defined—is the development "in" the student of ideals, standards of conduct, and value systems acceptable to himself, his teacher, and the culture of which both are a part. Associated with any scheme of education are these two general concepts: (1) the acquiring of information and skills by the student, and (2) the molding of his personality in ways held to be somehow best suited to the possession and exercise of these achievements.

The following comment by Bertrand Russell (1926) is relevant to the above:

Before considering how to educate, it is well to be clear as to the sort of result which we wish to achieve. . . . We must have some conception of the kind of person we wish to produce, before we can have any definite opinion as to the education which we consider best.

One of my aims in the teaching of psychotherapy is that the student become informed—that is, knowledgeable—in regard to theory and techniques relevant to the comprehension and performance of his professional tasks. Our work together should lead to an increase in his therapeutic effectiveness, and enable him to make observations that can be conceptualized, formulated, and transmitted to others. Another aim—an accompaniment of the first—is concerned with the student becoming, or continuing to be, one who seeks and values wisdom—that judicious expression of experience, learning, and understanding in practical affairs and philosophical speculation which includes, and is beyond, knowledge. While appreciating the accomplishments of the past and their expression in the present, the wise man can accept the alteration and expansion of what he has learned and looks for change; disquieting as this attitude may be, in this sense he is something of a revolutionary and, at the least, a discontented evolutionist.

Although the psychotherapist may seek greater certainty and precision in his work, he must be able to live with the imprecise and the unpredictable, taking care that he does not devalue human behavior which, in its complexity and subjectivity, may appear unworthy of the scientist. Despite his speculations and his theories, he will often be ignorant of the origins, causes, and outcomes of the phenomena with which he must deal. Being human, he can observe only with human equipment, recognizing that, as Bridgman (1959) says, "The brain that tries to understand is itself a part of the world that it is trying to understand" (p. 7). At times, in attempting to make sense of the complex circumstances of his professional living, he may wish to say, along with Dixon (1958): "What bubbles we blow and call it thought! Human thinking, high and low, is worm-eaten with prejudices and fallacies" (p. 55). If he is to be worth his salt, however, he cannot seek refuge in self-indulgent despair, excessive optimism, or rigid adherence to overly simple reductionistic formulae; he must labor with determination in a universe marked by the indeterminate. His must be, in the words of Whitehorn (1961), an "education for uncertainty."

The teacher, having but passing contact with his student, attempts to lead him to observe and comprehend what currently can be apparent to both, and to lift his vision to horizons perhaps never to be known to the teacher. In this regard Eiseley (1962) says:

> the teacher is fighting for an oncoming future, for something that has not emerged, which may, in fact, never emerge. His lot is worse than that of the sculptors in snow. . . . Rather, the teacher is a sculptor of the intangible future. There is no more dangerous occupation on the planet, for what we conceive as our masterpiece may appear out of time to mock us—a horrible caricature of ourselves.
>
> The teacher must ever walk warily between the necessity of inducing those conformities which in every generation reaffirm our rebellious humanity, yet he must at the same time allow for the free play of the creative spirit. It is not only for the sake of the future that the true educator fights, it is for the justification of himself, his profession, and the state of his own soul. . . . He is giving shapes to time, and the shapes themselves, driven by their own inner violence, wrench free of his control—must, if they are truly sculptured, surge like released genii from the classroom or, tragically, shrink to something less than bottle size. [pp. 24–25]

In this presentation I am not directly concerned with the teaching of techniques—those expert methods useful in the execution of the details involved in accomplishing a given task. Such a concern would be with the *how* and the *when*—and less certainly, the *why*—of the therapist's behavior in anticipation of—or in response to—certain actions of his patient. Recommendations regarding technique, usually referent to experience that is common, observable, and subject to formulation, can be stated in simple language. Thus we may make suggestions—or teach "principles"—relevant to the "setting of limits," the avoidance of argumentation in response to denial and delusion, the maintenance of "distance" in dealing with the paranoid person, and so on. Although the methods of such teaching may be diverse, the teacher should know what he wants to teach, why he wants to teach it, and the results to be anticipated. The student, on the other hand, can be expected to know what he wants to gain from the experience and should be able to comprehend the reasonableness of the teaching process. The degree of personal involvement in the extreme of the situation just described may be minimal, and the participants need not know much of each other. Such a transaction may be marked by little anxiety, its success depending largely upon at least one of the participants having a clear idea of the significances of major movements in the social field with which both are concerned, and his being able to make a succinct formulation for the other. Even in these seemingly clear-cut states we do well to remind ourselves, recurrently, that formulations labeled as the truth may turn out to be otherwise.

In general terms, the consultant is interested in data related to the following areas: (1) "what goes on" in the therapeutic sessions; (2) the ways in which the colleague views the treatment field—his conceptualization of the patient's difficulties, his notions about the patient, and his awareness of his own attitudes and emotions; (3) the consultant's own reactions to the account presented; (4) the divergencies and similarities of theory, technique, and value systems that characterize colleague and consultant; and (5) the ways in which the data can be used by the therapist in conformity with the structure of his own personality and his current needs.

My first interest as a consultant in psychotherapy is to discover what works well in the treatment situation in addition to what goes "wrong." Rather than emphasizing the "right" and "wrong," I look for what "is." I am not as intent upon teaching precise techniques as I am in furthering comprehension, by all concerned, of what goes on in the patient's life largely as reflected in his dealings with the therapist.

In order to discover anything very useful about this complex process of someone else's therapeutic intervention, I try to promote an atmosphere in which there will develop an increasing freedom of observation and reporting. Such a situation is one of mutual respect in which the attitudes and views of both participants can be revealed without serious threat to the self-esteem of either. This concern of mine will be more comprehensible if we remind ourselves of the following characteristics of the therapeutic field: (1) the verbal expressions of a psychotic person may be unclear at times and not readily translatable into conventional modes of speech; (2) much of the therapeutic transaction may be nonverbal and may escape observation and reporting; (3) occasionally the therapist will experience emotions so startling in terms of their intensity and seeming inappropriateness that their recounting will be difficult and embarrassing; (4) in some instances the therapist may think it useful to engage in activities that are not in keeping with conventional therapeutic procedures, and later hesitate to reveal what may appear to be extravagant and possibly ill-advised behavior; (5) the patient's observed activities may prove difficult to formulate and may not fit easily into the usual theoretical frames of reference; and (6) the consultant will himself often be uncertain as to the significance of material and unclear as to the action most suitable to the events described. In the setting marked by the characteristics just outlined, both therapist and consultant, recurrently feeling frustrated and ineffective, may impair the work by withdrawing from the field in protest against their supposed helplessness, or by taking action on the basis of hypotheses developed more in response to their own anxieties than to data reflecting observations of a patient's needs.

As a consultant I hope to discover something of the therapist's way of living—of looking at things—and thereby learn something about his patient's lifestyle. I refer here to an attitude—a concept of himself and others, of his world and his philosophy; these are matters so much a part of him as to exist outside his awareness, or when he is reminded of them, seem so ''natural'' that their formulation, communication, and questioning appear to be unnecessary, if not irrational. Such attitudes and philosophies are influential in determining the behavior of a therapist, and it is part of the teaching encounter to bring them into his awareness. As psychiatrists we deal with symbolic representations of experience, the referents of which may be distant, obscure, unknown, and often beyond precise identification. We attempt to clarify the meaning and further the formulation of certain symbols—those of immediate and major significance to the effectiveness of communication and relationship. Thus I am interested in a therapist's fundamental assumptions regarding himself, other human beings, ethnic groups, and so on, as these are symbolic reflections of the basic structure of his personality—who he is—through which will be exerted much of his influence on his patient. So it is that in consultation with a colleague I ask not only ''What do you do?'' and ''Who is your patient?'' but also ''Who are you?'' The being and the doing are woven one into the other. In raising such questions, however, I have no intention of intruding myself into the role of the colleague's analyst; as consultant I am not therapist.

Elements of the Therapeutic Predicament

In working with the hospitalized psychotic patient, the therapist must attend to, and often becomes involved with, elements of the therapeutic field with which he has little direct contact in his office practice of psychiatry. His attitudes toward these, as well as his ways of dealing with them, will influence the course of treatment, and thus are of interest to the consultant. Among such elements are: (1) the concept of schizophrenia, (2) the patient himself, (3) his family, (4) the hospital, (5) the extrahospital culture, and (6) the coordination of these in the patient's transactional field. Each is worthy of greater consideration than the brief mention to be given here.

The Concept of Schizophrenia

As used here the term *schizophrenia* does not refer to a specific disease entity residing within a person, but to a complex process of operations manifested in social fields, and reflecting, no matter what ''basic'' and as yet undetermined biological defects may exist, deficits and distortions in learning, acculturation, and the use of interpersonal skills. The person with whom we are concerned has managed to reach the era of chronological adolescence without having revealed gross evidence of grave psychiatric disorder. Failing in the adequate organization and execution of the required tasks of adolescence—such as the gaining of a satisfying and durable sense of identity and the patterning of sexual activities consistent with needs for intimacy—he develops a form of social estrangement, characterized by a decrease in the integration of behavior (Shakow, 1963) defects in the ability to communicate, the persistence of autistic ideation, the revealing of dissociated symbolic systems essential to the establishment and continuance of human intimacy by obscure representations (as in dream and hallucination), by restitutional movements as reflected in delusion and denial, by deficiencies in learning, and by recurrent failures of dissociation. The schizophrenic disaster is, at best, a form of personal bankruptcy in which there is little security and ample reason for the growth of despair. Fundamental to the therapeutic problem is the introduction of hope.

The Patient

Many of the patients of whom I speak were grossly disturbed for months or years before entering into psychotherapy. Usually they were hospitalized and exposed to currently popular forms of treatment which had resulted in varying transient responses, none of which, however, had had any lasting benefit. The previous treatment not having been notably helpful, such a patient will not expect good to come from further association with a hospital, psychiatrist, or other attending personnel. If hospitalization has been prolonged, the original disorder is complicated by chronicity, despair, and low morale. In such cases, the therapist finds himself dealing with a schizophrenic patient whose illness is compounded by complications attendant upon therapeutic failure and prolonged social estrangement.

The patient's sense of his own identity is usually unclear, shifting, or pathologically fixed, with associated difficulties in role-taking. In time, his personality becomes lost in a stereotype, and as his own sense of self is threatened, others become for him caricatures of human beings. This person has a low opinion of himself and grave doubts as to the possibility of finding any security or satisfaction in contacts with others. It is with such a one that the therapist seeks to establish a communicative, growth-promoting relationship.

The Hospital

The hospital may not have been designed for the needs of psychiatric patients, and may resemble a prison or a repository for the hopelessly misfit and recalcitrant, rather than a therapeutic institution. Despite talk of sickness, treatment, improvement, cure, and hope, there is usually an undercurrent of doubt, discouragement, and resentment. The patient, often angry and ashamed at what he has become, is confronted by the anger and shame of staff members who are caught up with him in the sense of futility and puzzlement characteristic of the institutional morass into which, with time, one tends to sink. In the hospital a large part of significant communication is covert; behind a front of assumed knowledge and proclaimed hopefulness all too often exist envy, jealousy, competitiveness, self-doubt, conflict between private and public modes of intercourse, and feelings of personal and professional ineffectiveness. Here, then, is a human situation which, in effect, simulates many aspects of home, prison, and refuge—on the one hand, it is marked by anxiety and strife, on the other, by efforts to make of it a demonstrably therapeutic structure. In such a social organization, the state of being of patients—as well as of those who care for them—may be bettered, although improvement cannot be guaranteed.

The Patient's Family

The patient is an integral part of the social field of his family, his "sick" behavior frequently being a caricature of interrelationships in the home. The patient's behavior, attitudes, value systems, and general view of life, learned in large part within the family, are functional components of that social system. If we consider the patient's disorder to be a function of his cultural-social-interpersonal environment, we expect that alterations in his behavior will require concomitant adjustments by others associated with him. Thus his getting "better"—becoming more assertive and independent, for example—may be experienced as destructive by other family members whose own sense of self-integrity apparently requires the continuance of the patient's dependency. The withdrawn patient may be more tolerable than the one who "acts out," blatantly expressing distaste for the world and those who reared him, as he unsteadily seeks a semblance of self-identity and independence. Thus his improvement may be more disturbing to the equilibrium of a social field than his continued hospitalization in his withdrawn state.

The social fields of family and hospital organization may be remarkably alike in adjusting to, and perpetuating, the patient's disorder, covertly and "automatically" operating to maintain the status quo while publicly seeming to promote useful change. Thus psychotherapy of the hospitalized psychotic patient is intimately involved with the lives of members of the patient's family, and less obviously with the lives of those who care for him on the ward.

The Extrahospital Culture

The hospitalized psychotic patient has been removed from "normal" society; against his will he has been coerced into "accepting" care. Despite his often proclaimed contempt for society, his contempt and blame for himself are greater; he looks upon himself as a failure, doubts that he can conform to the customs and demands that seem to be a necessary part of the "freedom" of the "world outside," and wonders if he will ever be accepted by the "sane," who now know, or later will discover, that he has been "crazy" and "put away." Having been judged incompetent to care for himself, he has given up many "rights," and will be required to "confess" his inadequacies and "demonstrate" to those who care for him that he will not be a social danger or a community charge. There is no doubt that he will be disadvantaged in the public domain by having been a mental patient. Despite much verbiage to the contrary, his "illness" will not be looked upon as "any other sickness," and he will frequently feel that he is the victim of a social leprosy or carries within himself representations of evil and the devil.

In general terms, these are the elements of the therapeutic situation with which the therapist must deal. He is required to possess conceptual and functional clarity about the concept of disorder and the roles played by the patient, the family, the hospital structure, and the greater society in the overall therapeutic field. Whereas he may at one time have thought of himself as a unique individual, a physician, attending to another individual, a patient, in efforts to modify or remove a state of disease, the therapist may now come to appreciate more fully the complexity of interlocking social fields within which he plays a role, somewhat inconstant, often obscure. He will not be content with the idea that he always "conducts" psychotherapy; sometimes "it" will conduct him, when forces outside of the therapeutic sessions take over as more or less transient determinants of the patient's living. The social field will be seen as a transactional system, rather than one of action, reaction, or interaction. Of this, Lawrence Frank (1958) says:

> In *transactions* we are concerned with the activity of an organism which evokes messages from the environment, including persons, and responds to those messages in terms of their meaning for him, with patterned activities that are not naïve reactions, but are the products of past experience under adult guidance. Thus the transactional process involves reciprocal, circular relations, like a feedback, with the participating persons tuned or prepared for such circular, reciprocal communications. The messages are governed as much by the intent of receiver as by the intent of the sender, and each message evokes a response from the other, as contrasted with a linear reaction or interaction.

Coordination within the Patient's Transactional Field

My first experience as the psychotherapist of a schizophrenic patient was in a large psychiatric hospital where such attention to a single patient was, of necessity, a rarity. In that situation I supervised all of the arrangements for the patient's living, talking with members of his family, meeting daily with nursing staff, and being directly responsible for all administrative-medical decisions. Through frequent discussions of our varied observations of the patient, an effort was made to coordinate the work of all who cared for him.

Later I worked in a situation in which an attempt was made to divide the therapeutic functions, one physician serving as therapist and another as ward administrator. The administrator was in charge of the patient's daily living and worked with nursing staff and family members in conjunction with a social worker. More recently, administrator, nurse, social worker, patients, and others are concerned with developing a milieu, the structure of which can be formulated and directed as a therapeutic instrument in itself. In the extreme of this plan, the therapist deals with his patient in the form of the more traditional psychoanalytic model; he is there to listen, to interpret, and to further the patient's understanding of behavior. Limit-setting, processes of education, concern with patient's relatives, and so on, are left to others, the therapist attempting to keep himself in a somewhat neutral role.

It has been my observation that often such neutrality cannot be maintained. At some point in the treatment program the therapist is drawn into at least a consultative role with others who work with the patient. For example, the patient "acts out" violently, or is unable to come to the therapist's office, or there is disagreement about ward care, or relatives decide to discontinue support. In such instances, the therapist's refusal or inability to take action is sometimes followed by the removal of the patient and the termination of therapy.

In working with regressed, disturbed psychotic patients, I favor a simplified social milieu in which the functions and authority of those who care for the patient are clear and explicit. I do not isolate myself from the general therapeutic activities, but am in close association with those who exercise power over the patient, participate in decisions concerning him, and discuss treatment plans and goals with his relatives. In the early part of the work I am active in setting limits, make clear wherein my authority lies, have an interest in the learning aspects of therapy, and recognize that I shall be something of a model for the patient. In later stages I fill a more conventional and less participant role.

It is well to remember that a hospital milieu is not constant. In prolonged therapeutic ventures extending over several years, the patient may be exposed to shifting administrative policies, and will be cared for by many people—nurses, aides, administrators, and others—who come and go without direct relevance to his needs. In such circumstances, the therapist provides a necessary thread of continuity, as does a parent in the growth of a child. At times the therapist—like a parent—must assert himself and be strong in his determination if the life of therapy is to continue.

In the hospital the therapist will be the constant, but not the single, therapeutic agent, and must be able to coordinate his activities with those of others who share in the care of the patient; he cannot remain aloof from the hospital-family-community field. This working with others is not easy or consistently pleasant. Competitiveness with attendant envy and jealousy, struggles for personal and group power, and open or covert efforts to diminish or destroy rivals, are commonplace in the hospital, often being strikingly reminiscent of aspects of the patient's home and the community at large.

As consultant, I attempt to bring matters such as these to my colleague's awareness, helping him to observe and report them accurately. I expect that he will have difficulty in being a careful observer and a compassionate but somewhat uninvolved therapist. He, too, may experience the distress of untoward ambition, envy, and competitiveness, and may be tempted by the seeming certainty and spurious comfort of partisanship. Such phenomena can be dealt with only when they are in the open; they are common—if not inevitable—constituents of the hospital scene.

Modes of Communication

In the treatment of the hospitalized psychotic patient, it is useful for the therapist to become aware of the various modes of communication available to him and his patient. Often, the modalities of communication characteristic of conventional circumstances are disordered—some others becoming prominent in the behavioral repertoire. If the therapist focuses on one mode such as the verbal-vocal to the exclusion of others, he may overlook available opportunities for communication, the neglect of which may lead to the patient's further discouragement and withdrawal. If the patient is unable to use the style of approach employed by the therapist, the latter must be able to adjust himself to the current capacities and needs of the former. Conflicts in messages transmitted by different modes must be recognized and reconciled; for example, what is said in words may be destructively denied by space, time, sound, and so on. Frequently a therapist discovers that he is uncomfortable with certain forms of communication, which, for the time being, are characteristic of the patient, and that he tends to avoid these and show distaste for them; the patient may then feel disparaged by the therapist's attitude. It is useful to remember that much of what we come to accept as natural in our living is denied the hospitalized patient, or has become distorted for him by his disorder or the circumstances of his existence. Very briefly, consider again the modes of communication as observed in therapy with the psychotic person.

Space

The patient in a hospital is confined—to a room, a living unit, the institution grounds; he may be isolated, but he cannot attain privacy. He has little or no choice of the form or size of space; he cannot choose his companions, he cannot adjust spatial arrangements as his needs may require, and his perception of space may be recurrently distorted. In that there is never enough of it, space is regarded as an important factor, although therapeutic significance has been neglected.

In the past few years much has been done in the investigation of the territorial requirements of human and other animals. It is becoming apparent that the human being has spatial needs that are fundamental to him as a biological organism (although in this regard, as in others, he may have more flexibility in adaptation than do other forms of life), that are molded by custom within a culture, and that vary with the individual's personal state—degree of anxiety, current needs, and the constancy of his perceptual ability. Edward T. Hall (1963), the anthropologist, has this to say:

> Man has many needs, drives, or tropisms. Of these, food, sex, and affirmation are perhaps those most commonly considered. The need to lay claim to and organize territory, as well as to maintain a pattern of discrete distances from our fellows may be just as basic. [p. 422]

In working with the disturbed patient the therapist must attend to his patient's spatial needs and be able to adjust to a variety of situations; he may meet with his patient in the office, in a ward room, hallway, or porch, or in the open, depending in part on what spatial size and configuration is required and can be tolerated. Although spatial arrangements on a hospital ward are often treated as if they were not influential in the careers of patients—or staff members—the messages conveyed by the form, size, and furnishings of a room, a ward, or a building may so contrast with the words spoken therein that the sense and significance of the latter are intensified, reduced, or vitiated.

Time

Time has biological, cultural, family, social, and personal significances. Although time is said to pass slowly or rapidly (as we think of it on a linear scale) we usually expect it to have a certain constancy; while we may speak of timelessness in the unconscious, we know that we can return to our time-bound state on demand.

The psychotic person's perception of time may vary with his state of anxiety, his despair, and the degree to which he has become immersed in the chronicity of hospital life, detached from the events that we routinely use as septations of time. The experience of time is influenced by the anxiety of the perceiver, his social role, and the situation in which he exists. Thus, time for the doctor, the nurse, the patient, and the expectant relative is not a unity. Although a therapist, for example, may oppose chronicity, he may, without being aware, become adjusted to timelessness, be disturbed by its alteration, and resist any changes in the "time set." He may himself become lost in time, be threatened by change, and wish to cling to the peculiar timeless intimacy that can be found in long immersion in a hospital room with a disordered person. Perhaps there is reawakened the wish to return to privacy with an object—a mothering one—who was available, at times incomprehensible, familiar, often vocal rather than verbal—and "mine."

Touch

Touch is the earliest communicative mode of the human being, conveying affection, intimacy, distance, anger, hostility, fear, disgust, contempt, and the like. There is a reciprocal quality to skin touching, as he who touches is touched, reflecting the reciprocal aspect of all human relationship. There are various types of touching, contact being made through the skin, sound, smell, eyes, and intermediate objects that form a bridge between people.

Although we begin life with touching, we are soon exposed to a variety of prohibitions regarding this mode of contact, and one learns not to touch—as well as not to hear, or see, or smell, or taste—many important aspects of one's living. The touching prohibition is continued by the therapist in keeping with the customs of his culture and profession. There is an accepted physical distance between the participants, the patient being asked to speak, to listen, and to feel (in the emotional sense) but otherwise not to touch.

In the hospital one is often impressed by the patient's physical as well as social isolation, by his need for bodily contact, and by his resistance to it and fear of it. Some assaults and states of regression seem to provide an outlet for the need to touch, as do the traditional sheet packs, sedative tubs, and massage (Frank, 1958).

Smell, Sound, and Taste

Odor as communication may not play a prominent part—at least in awareness—in the conventional psychotherapeutic encounter, but frequently is unavoidably apparent in the treatment of the psychotic patient. The odors of the ward, of the incontinent or unwashed patient—intensified by the bodily contact often required in such work—cannot be ignored, but must be dealt with as part of the communicative process (Kalogerakis, 1963).

It is evident that *sound* on a ward is not controlled as it usually is in the consulting room. The sounds of the hospital, part of the patient's life, intrude themselves into the therapeutic situation, and there may be a recurrent shattering of conventional niceties. Taste also becomes more of a reality, as the patient presents eating problems, and at times may share food with the therapist.

Each of the above briefly mentioned modes of communication has been of importance in our growing up, but may have become so modified through acculturation as to go relatively unnoticed, and, in some instances, marked by disapproval as socially unacceptable. Sometimes, as I sit in my usually quiet office, I am struck by the degree of organization and control that exists there. Sounds are muted, speech is somewhat comprehensible, odors are faint, touch is limited mostly to the feel of furnishings, vision is gratified by objects selected for pleasure as well as utility, and taste is probably that of tobacco. Then I am reminded of my past in caring for sick infants and children, with whom close personal contact was commonplace, and of experiences in war when sound, smell, touch, and taste burst into the open as convention was abandoned in our efforts to care for the severely injured. I think also of the development of my own children, recalling something of both the sweet and the troubled contacts of youth, long unused and faded in my memory. In the care of the psychotic patient the old ways of relating—perhaps previously denied or ignored—come again to the forefront to be used as circumstances and personalities require.

As consultant I wish to observe with my colleague his awareness of, and ways of dealing with, these modalities. I am interested in evidences of attraction or avoidance, fascination or revulsion, knowing that such tendencies may indicate the existence of dissociated systems relevant to the therapeutic task.

Difficulties with Identity and Role in the Hospital Milieu

In this brief report I make no attempt to deal with the more common transactions of consultant and colleague—the study of symbolic significances, perturbations in the therapeutic field labeled transference or parataxic distortion, problems of interpretation, evidences of anxiety such as assaultiveness and mutism, complications of ''acting out,'' and so on. My intent is to outline selected broad areas of experience commonly observed to be troublesome in the therapy of hospitalized psychotic patients, suggesting that these phenomena characterize the involvement of the psychotic person in a social system, and that a study of both person and system may be enlightening. Disturbances in the concept of self—in terms of identity and role—constitute one of these areas of interest.

In the conventional medical model the professional identities and roles of the various participants are clearly defined and usually supported by tradition; ''personal'' attributes and needs of those concerned may be recognized as important and influential but are clearly secondary to professional requirements. The physician conducts the overall program, prescribing and more or less directly administering the definitive treatment; the nurse and others are in ancillary positions, and there is little difficulty in determining who anyone is and what he is expected to do.

The situation in a psychiatric hospital frequently differs from the classical model. Formal roles are less clearly defined, as it is difficult to distinguish precisely the therapeutic activity of one person from another. If it is felt that strong role identification interferes with the development of useful relationships between staff and patients, efforts are made to reduce the attachment to a role. Thus a nurse who is bound to a traditional and rigid concept of nursing duties may have difficulty in adapting her attitudes to the often unpredictable and unconventional behavior of the psychotic patient, who in turn may be handicapped by his own prejudiced and stereotyped view of nurses. In an effort to modify rigid role hierarchies in staff and to deal with the unyielding roles adopted by some patients, nurses and aides may dress in clothes other than uniforms, and in ward and other hospital groups there is encouraged an easy exchange of ideas without reference to seniority or position as staff member or patient. The patient is "pushed" to take an active, assertive part in the hospital community; he is not expected to be a passive recipient of treatment.[2]

For many people adjustment to this social structure is difficult; they may feel lost in it and, in attempting to retain a more traditional role, become further estranged from the group, even to the point of abandoning it. A question commonly raised in this situation by both staff members and patients is simply, "Who am I?" and there may be much talk about identity "diffusion," identity "crisis," the "establishing" of identity, its loss, and so on. The patient is often uncertain as to his own identity; the roles of his past life have not been well developed or consistently satisfying and may be lost in the disorganization of personality; the role of patient itself seems to offer little hope and fails to bolster self-esteem; roles assigned to the future when he is "better" or "well" are unfamiliar and unreal; in a sense he is looking for himself, but from his anxiety and experience tends to reject roles presented to him. Staff members, often finding that their traditional roles are not fully adequate to the task at hand, and unsure in their new, less well-defined roles, may express their anxiety in such comments as, "I don't know what I'm doing here. You can't distinguish patients from staff." Patients tend to cling to their old familiar roles, unhappy though these may be, and personnel defend their positions, unproductive though they often are. Each group—nurses, phy-

---

[2]This model is derived from practices at Chestnut Lodge and a few other places.

sicians, patients—while covertly envious of other groups, will seek to retain its own attributes, resisting change, however therapeutically promising it may be said to be.

Recurrent shifts in institutional administrative policy at times seem to reflect problems of identity. For example, there may be a period in which patients and staff operate with considerable freedom and little regard for role adherence. All seems to go well until, at some juncture, patients engage in behavior disturbing to the hospital equilibrium, and there then arises an outcry to the effect that no one knows his place, and that authority is no longer recognized or even identifiable. There usually follows a period of "pulling things together," with demands for nurses to wear uniforms, patients to conform to a recognizable patient role, administrators to clearly specify and enforce policy, and therapists to stick rigidly to their function of sitting down, listening, and interpreting. A semblance of order is thus attained and tension subsides. After a time, the hospital atmosphere is felt by some to be stifling, and the complaint is heard that improvement cannot occur in this "controlled" environment. There then follows, accompanied by struggle, some relaxing of restraints justified by explanations that have the ring of rationalization. The recurrent pattern of such changes may go unnoted, with the result that each shift is felt to be a "crisis" involving grave moral issues. Unfortunately, such blind shifts in policy may be destructive to morale in an institution, and indicate a lack of awareness of social structure and needs.

The therapist may have other difficulties in finding an enduring and satisfying role for himself. If he is young he is not far beyond his basic medical training, and the role of physician may never have become entirely his. As an intern he was emerging awkwardly from his position as student, accustoming himself to being a doctor. As a resident, a combination of student and practitioner, he was on the way to acquiring the role of psychiatrist before he felt assured as a physician. If he is in psychoanalytic training he is in the process of assuming a new professional identity which will not be fully his for several years. Patients will ask if he is "really" a doctor, or a psychiatrist, or a psychoanalyst; some colleagues may suggest that being a psychiatrist is a far cry from being a physician, others, that being an analyst is a form of escaping the grim realities of psychiatry through retreat to an "ivory tower," and still others, that his particular brand of psychoanalytic experience may not be as significant or profound as some other.

The activities of the psychotherapist in a hospital are not consistently and conventionally medical, psychiatric, or psychoanalytic, although elements of each discipline may be identified therein. If he does not use somatic therapies and is not an administrator, the psychotherapist may sense a weakening of his psychiatric role. His role as analyst will be challenged by patients unable to conform to conventional psychoanalytic requirements; such a patient won't come to the office, doesn't lie on a couch, grows anxious at discussions of past, present, and future, evidences more transference distortion than can be dealt with, and shows little ability to develop the relationship fundamental to treatment. Therapeutic techniques are often ineffective, leading the therapist to feel that he is not clearly physician, psychiatrist, or analyst; he may then hope that his goodness of heart and ability to exhibit love will favorably influence the patient. However, there may be little evidence that the patient finds worth in the physician as a human being. At this point the therapist may feel stripped of much of what he has come to depend upon as himself, being denied in his professional roles as well as his more private identity. A therapist may then abandon the work, saying, for example, that the patient is hopeless. Again, he may seek greater definition for himself by taking action, by asserting himself, and by attempting to force another—such as the patient—into a role that will help to define his own. Such assertive movements, arising from anxiety, can be disadvantageous to treatment in that they may be experienced by the patient as further evidence of his supposed unsuitability for human relationship.

Of interest to the concept of identity is the covert shifting of the therapist's role in response to his own anxiety during a session with a patient. Such movements are not readily observed, often seem to be of no moment if successful in allaying anxiety, and are likely to escape reporting. For example, during a portion of an interview in which the patient is speaking freely, the physician may picture himself as an analyst—which he, in fact, is. Later, in response to the patient's behavior, he may take action (as in the setting of limits), either observing that a parameter has been created, or abandoning the analytic role for that of the psychiatrist. Should he feel persistently discouraged by his therapeutic efforts, he may conveniently picture himself as a scientist—a research observer rather than a healer—thus avoiding the anxiety associated with maintenance of the former role. Such shifts, often not observed by the therapist, are not openly announced to the patient, but may be manifested in behavior noticeable to the patient, who is unaware of its motivations and origins. As neither participant is clearly aware of what is going on, the complexity of the interview is likely to be increased, which fact, if noted, may be "explained" by irrelevancies.

The consultant can be of use to his colleague in clarifying these problems of identity and role. Often the therapist experiences such matters as evidence of his unsuitability for the work, or the work's unsuitability for anyone. He may have little awareness of what has been discussed, and experience only anger, anxiety, or despair. The consultant need not teach his colleague what to "do," but must lead him to discover the characteristics of the situation in which he is involved. The answer to these problems is not to be found in a rigid adherence to professional roles which may be used by all concerned to maintain destructive interpersonal distance. Nor is it useful to abandon all roles with the pretense that there are no differences between people and that roles are meaningless. There will need to be a restructuring of roles which can be identified and formulated, can undergo change as required, and which favor communication. Thus the therapist may discover that he is indeed a physician, a psychiatrist, a psychoanalyst, and (if he is to succeed) a trustworthy and kindly human being; he can make good use of the skills of all these designations. He will also find that he must come to peace with uncertainty and change; his theory, his technique, his role, and his concept of self will be repeatedly challenged and often found wanting; if he does not deny this challenge, or retreat before it, he will experience continued growth in the mutuality of the therapeutic experience.

Distance and Feedback

Another area of interest in the psychotherapy of the psychotic patient is indicated by such words as *distance* and *lack of feedback*. A frequent complaint by the therapist is the following: "I've been working with X for a long time, but there's no evidence that we're getting anywhere, or that I mean anything to him. I'm not sure what his behavior means, and I can't tell if what I do makes any impression on him.'' The patient, who is thus unresponsive and withdrawn, may be referred to as aloof, distant, cold, narcissistic, and rejecting, and the therapist, failing to communicate meaningfully with the patient, may come to feel that he is himself distant and somehow lacking in human warmth.

The word *distance* may refer to physical space between objects, or to remoteness on any scale—such as that of human interest. The words *distant* and *remote*, indicating that an object is alien, aloof, foreign, separate, or inaccessible, may be applied to a person or a situation. Although distance may be desirable in some circumstances, its prolonged continuance in any marked degree in psychotherapy is often experienced by one or both of the participants as frustrating, painful, and eventually intolerable. Ultimately, it may become equated with ''coldness'' and ''hardness'' in contrast to a more desirable state of ''warmth'' and ''softness.'' This tendency to describe features of human relationship in terms of linear measurements, thermal variations, and states of density suggest the inadequacy of observation, description, and formulation of such relationships as field phenomena.

In response to distance and obscurity, or lack of feedback, the therapist may become so active that he soon deluges the patient with interpretations, suggestions, theories of pathology and plans for living, which are often more puzzling than illuminating to the patient, and frequently go unattended. In his impatience to cross this *distance*, or break down the *barrier*, the therapist may in effect attack the patient (''anything to make an impression on him''), or he may withdraw, feeling that he is faced by a void in which he will become lost if he does not take flight.

Although we often speak of distance as a quality existing *in* a person, it may be thought of as a term describing movement in a social field, in which the interpersonal integration is marked by anxiety, distrust, uncertainty, and a persistent doubt that human relationships can be other than destructive. In the developing therapeutic encounter there is a degree of identifiable reciprocity, of confirmation of each by the other, of the exchange of tenderness as well as other sentiments—that is, a recognition of and response to the needs of self and other. The expression, recognition, and meeting of reciprocal needs in psychotherapy reflects the earliest interpersonal experience of the human being—the infant-mother relationship—which early in life is structured as a fundamental need for mutuality in relatedness. For long periods in the work with some patients, the therapist's need in this regard is not met—he does not receive adequate confirmatory feedback. The continued frustration (and sometimes denial) of the need may provoke the therapist to withdraw or engage in other behavior disadvantageous to the therapeutic operation.

The consultant can help his colleague recognize the fundamental importance of the need for confirmation, the patient's anxiety as its expression, and the inadvisability of trying to force him prematurely to meet needs of the therapist. The therapist will learn to wait, to observe the recurrent small but significant evidences of the patient's responsiveness, and to have confidence that relationships do exist and grow, however slight and obscure their early manifestations may be. All of these may be carried out more effectively as the therapist accepts and respects his own needs for feedback, discovering in his own feelings of frustration and despair something of his patient's condition.

Conclusion

In these remarks I have outlined a few areas of interest to the therapist and consultant engaged in the psychotherapy of hospitalized schizophrenic patients whose enthusiasm for such intervention in their lives is minimal. This is a sampling; there is more to the story than has been told here—and without doubt, a good deal of which I know little or nothing. I do not expect that we shall, in this work, cure large numbers of the sick; they have come by their illness through long, tedious, and painful experience, and there is much that must be unlearned, learned, and understood before they can once again capture the freedom to grow. In our efforts, however, we have the opportunity to observe, and often to usefully modify, the complex and subtle intermingling of the biological-cultural-social influences that produce the human being—the animal who must learn to live—disastrously or otherwise—in his self-created universe of symbols.

References

Bridgman, P. W. (1959), *The Way Things Are*. Cambridge, MA: Harvard University Press.

Dixon, W. M. (1958), *The Human Situation*. New York: Oxford University Press.

Eiseley, L. (1962), *Mind as Nature: The Fifth John Dewey Society Lectureship*. New York: Harper & Row.

Frank, L. K. (1958), Tactile Communication, etc. *Rev. Gen. Semant.*, 16:31–79.

Goffman, E. (1961), The medical model and mental hospitalization: Some notes on the vicissitudes of the tinkering trades. In: *Asylums*. Garden City, NY: Doubleday, pp. 323–386.

Hall, E. T. (1963), Proxemics: The study of man's spatial relations. In: *Man's Image in Medicine and Anthropology*. New York Academy.

Kalogerakis, M. G. (1963), The role of olfaction in sexual development. *Psychosom. Med.*, 25:420–432.

Marcel, G. (1963), On the ontological mystery. In: *The Philosophy of Existentialism*. New York: Citadel, pp. 39–40.

Russell, B. (1926), The aims of educating. In: *Education and the Good Life*. New York: Avon, pp. 31–51.

Shakow, D. (1963), Psychological deficit in schizophrenia. *Behav. Sci.*, 8:275–305.

Whitehorn, J. C. (1961), Education for uncertainty. Paper presented at the Celebration of the 150th Anniversary of Massachusetts General Hospital, February.

———— Betz, J. (1954), A study of psychotherapeutic relationships between physician and schizophrenic patients. *Amer. J. Psychiat.*, 111:321–351.

Chronological Bibliography
of
Otto Allen Will, Jr., M.D.

Psychoses in naval inductees with less than fifteen days' active duty. *U.S. Navy Med. Bull.*, 43:909–21, November 1944.

Electroencephalography in the study of chronic behavior problems. *U.S. Navy Med. Bull.*, 44:341–352, February 1945.

Certain psychiatric reactions in operators of antisubmarine sound gear. *U.S. Navy Med. Bull.*, 44:746–748, April 1945.

The psychotic naval prisoner. *U.S. Navy Med. Bull.*, 46:680–689, May 1946.

The value of the social service history in the detection of those psychiatrically unsuited for military service. *U.S. Navy Med. Bull.*, 46:1403–1407, September 1946.

Remarks on current problems of psychiatric therapy. *Quart. Rev. Psychiat. Neurol.*, 1:438–449, October 1946.

The use of electro-shock therapy in psychiatric illness complicated by pulmonary tuberculosis (with Addison M. Duval, M.D.). *J. Nerv. Ment. Dis.*, 105:637–646, June 1947.

A consideration of the significance of hallucinations. *U.S. Navy Med. Bull.*, 47:622–633, July-August 1947.

Psychotherapy with a schizophrenic patient: Summary of a case in progress. *Quart. Rev. Psychiat. Neurol.*, 2:122–128, October 1947.

A fatality in electro-shock therapy: Report of a case and review of certain previously described cases (with Frederick Cooper Rehfeldt. & Meta A. Neumann). *J. Nerv. Ment. Dis.*, 107:105–126, February 1948.

"Data" and the psychiatric patient. *J. Clin. Pastoral Work*, 2:91–107, Summer 1949.

A report of a recorded interview in the course of psychotherapy (with Robert A. Cohen). *Psychiat.*, 16:263–282, August 1953.

Introduction to *The Psychiatric Interview* by Harry Stack Sullivan. New York: Norton, 1954, pp. ix–xxiii.

Psychotherapeutics and the schizophrenic reaction. *J. Nerv. Ment. Dis.*, 126:109–140, 1958.

Book review: *Schizophrenia*, by Manfred A. Sakel. In: *J. Nerv. Ment. Dis.*, 128:473–478, April 1959.

Human relatedness and the schizophrenic reaction. *Psychiat.*, 22:205–223, August 1959.

Processes in psychoanalytic education. In: *Science and Psychoanalysis*, Vol. 5, ed. Jules Masserman, New York: Grune & Stratton, 1960, pp. 84–102.

The schizophrenic reaction and the interpersonal field. In: *Chronic Schizophrenia*, ed. Lawrence Appleby, Jordan M. Scher, and John Cumming. Glencoe, IL: Free Press, 1960, pp. 194–224.

Process, psychotherapy, and schizophrenia. In: *Psychotherapy of the Psychoses*, ed. Arthur Burton. New York: Basic Books, 1961, pp. 10–42.

Paranoid development and the concept of self: Psychotherapeutic intervention. *Psychiat.*, 24:74–86, 1961, Supplement to No. 2.

Psychotherapy in reference to the schizophrenic reaction. In: *Contemporary Psychotherapies*, ed. Morris I. Stein. Glencoe, IL: The Free Press, 1961, pp. 128–156.

Comments on the psychotherapeutic intervention. In: *Contemporary Psychotherapies*, ed. Morris I. Stein. Glencoe, IL: The Free Press, 1961, pp. 157–189.

Hallucinations: Comments reflecting clinical observations of the schizophrenic reaction. In: *Hallucinations*, ed. L. J. West. New York: Grune & Stratton, 1962, pp. 174–182.

Problems in the psychoanalytic treatment of depressions. Panel Discussion: Paul Hoch; George Gero; Sandor Rado; & Otto Allen Will, Jr. *Bulletin: The Association for Psychoanalytic Medicine*, Vol. 2, No. 3, February 1963, pp. 35–40.

Schizophrenia and the psychotherapeutic field. *Contemp. Psychoanal.*, 1:1–29, Fall 1964.

The beginning of psychotherapeutic experience. In: *Modern Psychotherapeutic Practice*, ed. Arthur Burton. Palo Alto, CA: Science and Behavior Books, 1965, pp. 3–35.

The schizophrenic patient, the psychotherapist, and the consultant. *Contemp. Psychoanal.*, 1:110–135, Spring 1965.

Discussion of "A case of depression in a homosexual young man," by Walter Bonime, M.D. In: *Contemp. Psychoanal.*, 3:14–20, Fall 1966.

Psychotherapy and schizophrenia. In: *Comprehensive Textbook of Psychiatry*, 1st ed., ed. Alfred M. Freedman & Harold I. Kaplan. Baltimore: Williams & Wilkins, 1967, pp. 649–661.

Schizophrenia: The problem of origins. In: *International Conference on Schizophrenia*, ed. John Romano. New York: Excerpta Medica, 1967, pp. 214–227.

The milieu in the psychiatric hospital—therapeutic and otherwise: Comments on "Ego psychology and the milieu at the mental hospital," by Lewis L. Robbins. In: *Psychotherapy in the Designed Therapeutic Milieu*, ed. Stanley H. Eldred & Maurice Vanderpol. International Psychiatry Clinics, Vol. 5, No. 1. Boston: Little, Brown, 1968, pp. 88–94.

The beginning of a psychotherapy (and discussions). Report of Eleventh Annual Seminar at Dikemark Hospital, Solberg, Norway. In: *Kontrollsvikt og grensesetting ved psykoterapi av hospitaliserte pasienter*, Referat fra Dikemark-seminaret 7–8, mai, 1968.

Schizophrenia and psychotherapy. In: *Modern Psychoanalysis: New Directions and Perspectives*, ed. Judd Marmor. New York: Basic Books, 1968, pp. 551–573.

The reluctant patient, the unwanted psychotherapist—and coercion. *Contemp. Psychoanal.*, 5:1–31, Fall 1968.

Proposal for a psychotherapeutic center: Comments on "the future of the private psychiatric hospital," by Lawrence S. Kubie. In: *Internat. J. Psychiat.*, 6:442–448, December 1968.

Book Review: *Sickness and Society*, by Raymond S. Duff & August B. Hollingshead, 1968. For Behavioral Science Book Service.

Book review: *Violent Men*, by Hans Toch, and *Human Aggression*, by Anthony Storr, 1969. For Behavioral Science Book Service.

The therapeutic use of the self. *Medical Arts and Sciences* (journal of Loma Linda University School of Medicine), 24(1,2):3–14, 1970.

Excerpts from papers by Dr. Will. In: *Psychoanalysis and Interpersonal Psychiatry: The Contributions of Harry Stack Sullivan*, ed. Patrick Mullahy. New York: Science House, 1970, pp. 621–630.

The psychotherapeutic center and schizophrenia. In: *The Schizophrenic Reactions: A Critique of the Concept, Hospital Treatment, and Current Research*, ed. Robert Cancro. New York: Brunner/Mazel, 1970, pp. 153–167.

The relationship of schizophrenia to psychotherapy. *J. of the National Association of Private Psychiatric Hospitals*, 2(3):18–24, Fall 1970.

Psychotherapy, schizophrenia, and the identity of the therapist: Transactions of the Topeka Psychoanalytic Society. *Bull. Menn. Clin.*, 34(5):387–389, 1970.

The patient and the psychotherapist: Comments on the "uniqueness" of their relationship. In: *In the Name of Life*, ed. Bernard Landis & Edward S. Tauber. New York: Holt, Rinehart & Winston, 1971.

Psychotherapy and schizophrenia: Implications for human living. In: *Psychotherapy of Schizophrenia: Proceedings of the Fourth International Symposium on Psychotherapy of Schizophrenia, Turku, Finland, 1971*, ed. David Rubinstein & Yrjo O. Alanen. Amsterdam: Excerpta Medica, 1972, pp. 25–37.

Comments on "Schizophrenia disorders: The influence of conceptualization on therapy," by Theodore Lidz. In: *Psychotherapy of Schizophrenia: Proceedings of the Fourth International Symposium on Psychotherapy of Schizophrenia, Turku, Finland, 1971*, ed. David Rubinstein & Yrjo O. Alanen. Amsterdam: Excerpta Medica, 1972, pp. 22–24.

Discussion of "Paranoia or persecution: The case of Schreber," by Morton Schatzman. In: *Family Process*, 10(2):207–210, June 1971.

Discussion of "Schizophrenia as a defense against conflict: Implications for research and therapy," by Jack L. Rubins. In: *Science and Psychoanalysis*, Vol. 21, ed. Jules H. Masserman. New York: Grune & Stratton, 1972. (Also in: *Internat. J. Psychiat.*, 10(3):85–88, 1972.)

Catatonic behavior in schizophrenia. *Contemp. Psychoanal.*, 9(1):29–58, November 1972.

Changing styles in the treatment of schizophrenia. In: *Amer. J. Psychiat.*, 130(2):152–155, February 1973.

Foreword to *Schizophrenia as a Life Style*, by Arthur Burton, Juan J. Lopez-Ibor, & Werner M. Mendel. New York: Springer, 1974, pp. vii–xi.

Individual psychotherapy of schizophrenia. In: *Strategic Intervention in Schizophrenia*, ed. Robert Cancro, Normal Fox, & Lester E. Shapiro. New York: Behavioral Publications, 1974, pp. 17–33.

Schizophrenia: Psychological treatment. In: *Comprehensive Textbook of Psychiatry*, 2nd ed., ed. Alfred M. Freedman, Harold I. Kaplan, & Benjamin J. Sadock. Baltimore: Williams and Wilkins, 1975, pp. 939–955.

The conditions of being therapeutic. In: *Psychotherapy of Schizophrenia*, ed. John G. Gunderson & Loren R. Mosher. New York: Aronson, 1975, pp. 53–66.

Panel discussion: In: *Schizophrenia 75—Psychotherapy, Family Studies, Research: Proceedings of the Fifth International Symposium on the Psychotherapy of Schizophrenia, Oslo, Norway, August 13–17, 1975*, ed. Jarl Jorstad & Endre Ugelstad. Oslo, Norway: Universitetsforlaget, 1976.

Psychiatry at the Austen Riggs Center. In: *Long-Term Treatments of Psychotic States*, ed. Colette Chiland. New York: Human Sciences Press, 1977, pp. 361–374.

The future of the therapeutic relationship as an agent of change. In: *Psychotherapy and Behavior Change: Trends, Innovations and Future Direction*, ed. O. Lee McCabe. New York: Grune & Stratton, 1977, pp. 5–19.

Clinical considerations in the treatment of adolescent psychosis. In: *Annual Review of the Schizophrenic Syndrome*, Vol. 5, ed. Robert Cancro. New York: Brunner/Mazel, 1978, pp. 581–599.

Responsiveness of the schizophrenic to the planned use of the human relationship. In: *Controversy in Psychiatry*, ed. John Paul Brady & H. Keith Brodie. Philadelphia: Saunders, 1978, pp. 621–659.

Comments on the professional life of the psychotherapist. *Contemp. Psychoanal.*, 15:560–576, 1979.

Schizophrenia: Psychological treatment. In: *Comprehensive Textbook of Psychiatry*, 3rd ed., ed. Alfred M. Freedman, Harold I. Kaplan, & Benjamin J. Sadock. Baltimore: Williams & Wilkins, 1980, pp. 1217–1240.

Comments on the ''elements'' of schizophrenia, psychotherapy, and the schizophrenic person. In: *The Psychotherapy of Schizophrenia*, ed. John S. Strauss, Malcolm Bowers, T. Wayne Downey, Stephen Fleck, Stanley Jackson, & Ira Levine. New York & London: Plenum Med. Book Co., 1980, pp. 157–166.

Values and the psychotherapist. *Amer. J. Psychoanal.*, 41:203–212, 1981.

Foreword to *Principles and Practice of Milieu Therapy*, ed. John G. Gunderson, Otto Will, & Loren R. Mosher. New York: Aronson, 1983, pp. vii–x.

Ackerman, N. W., 270*n*
Adler, G., 228
Alanen, Y. O., 141
Allee, W. C., 280
Anna O., 170
Antonio, 163
Arnold, F., 144
Astaire, F., 101

Balint, M., 83
Bally, G., 6
Bateson, G., 270*n*
Beck, J. D., 144
Benedetti, G., 6, 7, 185-196
Beres, D., 155
Bergin, A. E., 320-321
Betz, J., 336
Bird, B., 170, 171
Blanck, G., 227-228
Blanck, R., 227-228
Bleuler, M., 6
Bliss, E. L., 215
Boss, M., 6
Bowen, M., 83
Bowlby, J., 3-4, 19, 23, 50, 51, 54 55-56,
    63-79, 87, 255-256
Branch, C. H. H., 215
Bridgman, P. W., 339
Bruche, H., 7, 205-222
Bruner, J., 113
Buber, M., 83*n*, 88-91, 288-289 291

Cain, A. C., 75
Cairns, R. B., 44
Camus, A., 204
Cannon, W., 274-275
Carroll, L., 81
Casteneda, C., 114
Caudill, W. A., 270*n*
Clausen, J. A., 270*n*

Cooley, C., 281
Crisp, A. H., 215

Davoine, F., 108, 110-111
de Chateau, P., 44
Delbruck, B., 158
Deutsch, H., 208
Dixon, N. F., 69
Dixon, W. M., 339
Dobzhansky, T., 253
Don Juan, 114
Dubos, R., 253-254

Eagle Elk, J., 111-112, 115
Einstein, A., 157
Eiseley, L., 241-242, 248, 254-255 340
Eisenberg, L., 252
Elliot, O., 48
Engel, G. L., 82, 123
Erdelyi, M. H., 69
Erikson, E., 4, 83, 86, 88-89, 129
Eysenck, H. J., 321

Fairbairn, W. R. D., 29, 30, 83, 94
Fast, I.75
Fisher, A. E., 46
Fleener, D. E., 44
Fleming, Sir A., 168-169
Foster, B., 6-7, 197-204
Frank, L., 347
Freud, S., 1, 17-18, 21-25, 26, 29 31, 64-
    65, 71, 73-74, 125, 130 158-160, 163,
    165, 170-171, 193 223-224, 258, 328
Fromm-Reichman, F., 9, 243
Frost, R., 311
Fuller, J. L., 55

Gaudilliere, J.-M., 108
Gedo, J. E., 30, 78
Gerard, D. L., 270*n*

Gill, M. M., 2-4, 17-41, 82, 94
Goffman, E., 312, 313, 314-315, 322 335*n*
Goldberger, L., 27
Golden, S., 144
Gunderson, J. G., 5, 139-153

Hackett, T. P., 275*n*
Hall, E. T., 350
Harlow, H. F., 19, 46
Harlow, M. K., 19, 46
Heath, R., 319
Hegel, G. W. F., 109
Heibroner, R. L., 260
Heidegger, M., 115
Herman, B. H., 53
Hermann, I., 19
Hersey, J., 164-166
Hickey, 166-168
Hoffer, W., 171
Hoffman, I., 33-35
Holtzman, P., 27
Honnegger, A., 168

Jacobson, E., 29
James, W., 274
Jespersen, O., 158
Job, 292

Kant, I., 195
Kennell, J. H., 44
Kernberg, O., 29, 224, 225-227
King, J. A., 48
Kingston, M. H., 100-107, 109, 115
Klaus, M. H., 44
Klein, G., 27, 32
Klein, M., 28, 30, 192, 230
Knapp, P., 140
Koch, E., 78
Kohn, M. L., 270*n*
Kohut, H., 17, 30, 32-33, 129, 221
Krasner, L., 318
Kris, E., 27
Kuhn, T., 18

Lacan, J., 4, 17, 99-101, 109-110 113
Lasch, C., 82
Leonard, J., 100
Lewis, C. S., 204
Lidz, T., 270*n*
Lilly, J. C., 275*n*
Limentani, D., 270*n*
Lipton, R., 129

Loewald, H. W., 29, 171, 172-173
Lynch, J., 257ˌ

Mahler, M., 29
Malan, D. N., 321
Malipiero, G. F., 168
Marcel, G., 337-338
Matisse, H., 161-162
May, P. R. A., 148
May, R., 329
McGlashan, T., 232-233
Meringer, R., 158
Meyer, A., 249
Miller, A., 76
Miller, Arthur, 163-164
Miller, G., 232-233
Mintz, T., 66
Mirandola, Pico della, 253
Mohatt, G., 114-115
Mujeeb-ur-Rahman, M., 17
Muller, J. P., 4, 99-116
Murphy, G., 256

Norman, D. A., 69

O'Brien, C. P., 141
O'Neill, E., 166-168
Olson, D., 83
Oppenheimer, R., 292
Orff, C., 168

Paget, J., 275-276
Pankesepp, J., 52, 53
Pasteur, L., 168-169
Paul, H., 158
Paz, O., 115
Perls, F., 82
Perry, H., 244
Peterfreund, E., 17, 78
Piaget, J., 211
Picasso, P., 161-162
Pollack, J., 162
Portia, 163
Provence, S., 123, 129

Rees, K., 78
Reich, W., 250
Reitman, W. R., 168
Richter, C. P., 275*n*
Ricoeur, P., 17
Rioch, D., 243
Robertson, J., 63
Roentgen, W. C., 168

Rogers, C., 141
Rosenblatt, A., 17
Rosoff, A., 142-144
Rothenberg, A., 5-6, 155-181
Russell, C., 83
Russell, B., 338-339

Saint Exupery, A. de, 277-278
Schafer, R., 17, 32
Scheff, T., 313-314, 316
Schlesinger, A., 292
Schmale, A., 276
Schönberg, A., 168
Schulz, C. G., 8, 223-238
Schwartz, D. P., 5, 117-136
Scott, J. P., 3-4, 43-62, 87 255-256, 258
Searles, H. F., 130
Semrad, E., 139, 248
Shakespeare, W., 126, 163
Siegel, J., 270n
Singer, M., 84-85
Smith, M. L., 251
Sokolowski, R., 109-110, 113
Solomon, P., 275n

Spitz, R., 129
Sprinkle, D., 83
Stanton, A., 140
Strauss, R., 168
Sullivan, H. S., 9, 20, 30-32, 33 244-245,
    254, 258
Sutherland, J., 17

Thomas, L., 250-251
Tinbergen, N., 258-259

Virgil, 159
von Bertalanffy, L., 253, 254, 279
von der Gabelentz, G., 158

Weigert, E., 155
Weisman, A. D., 275n
Whitehorn, J., 328, 336, 339
Will, O. A., Jr., 8-14, 31, 38, 59 73, 86,
    107, 139, 185, 197, 205 206-207,
    209, 221, 241-360
Winnicott, D. W., 29, 30, 228
Wolman, B. B., 270n
Wynne, L. C., 4, 81-97, 270n

Subject Index

Abandonment, threat of, 77-78
Abnormal normal weight control syndrome
    215
Acting out, 132
    patient's responsibility for, 235-236
Action
    psychoanalytical concept of, 5
    language, 17, 19, 32
Active play, 55
Adapatability, 90
Adopted babies study, 123
Aggression, 129-130, 253-254
    of psychotic patient, 193-195, 196
    sexual, 23
    therapeutic, 193-195
Agoraphobia, 72
Alice in Wonderland, 81, 95
All-or-none patient approach, 227, 230 233,
    235, 237
Amae, 82
Ambivalence
    acquisition of, 8
    definition of, 223-224
    Freud on, 223-224
    struggle toward, 223-237
    tolerance of, 232-233
American Psychoanalytic Association
    symposium, 66
Amphetamine sulfate, 52
Anger and separation distress, 54, 67-68
Anorexia nervosa
    changing picture of, 205-221
    dissolution of, 215
    history of, 207-210
    increasing incidence of, 213
    misdiagnosis of, 207
    primary, 210-216
    psychoanalytic treatment of, 7-8
    schizophrenic features of, 209
    as search for uniqueness, 213-214, 215

    symptoms of, 205-207
    treatment of, 216-221
    in twins, 214
Anorexic personality, 210-213
Antidepressant drugs, 51-52, 236
Antipsychotic medications, 236
Anxiety
    definition of, 285*n*
    origin of, 294-295
    in schizophrenic patient, 272
    separation, 51
Appersonation, 188, 192
    unconscious, 194
Art, errors in, 161-162, 163
Articulation, definition of, 157
Assertiveness, 92
Asymmetries, 127-128
Attachment
    avoidance of new, 56-57
    beyond critical period, 44, 45
    biologically based beginnings of, 3
    from close contact, 46-47
    critical period for, 44-45
    disturbance of, 91-95
    emotional basis of, 45-48
    emotions associated with, 255
    evolution of, 43
    fear of, 72-73, 274-275
    forces leading to, 3
    interpersonal, 19 *see also* Person
    paradigm
    late in life, 48
    in marriage, 48
    mating behavior and, 45
    need for, 255-256
    pathological, 48
    physiological basis of, 45-48
    in psychotherapy, 6-7, 59-61
    site, 3, 43
    social, 3, 23, 43, 44-45, 47-48

survival and, 48-49
in voluntary associations, 47
in working situations, 47
see also Emotional bonding;
Relatedness; Relationships
Attachment behavior, 65-66
Attachment theory, defensive processes
in, 63-78
Audio-recording therapy sessions, 31, 38
Austen Riggs Center, 10
environment of, 59
symposium on human condition, 8
Autism, 61
Autistic death, symbol of, 187

"Bather, The," 161
Behavior
bodily, 28
controls of, 253
limits on, 130-132
maladaptive, 11-12, 56-59
range of permissible in child, 129-130
Biologism, 250
Biopsychosocial model, 82
Birth
attachment immediately after, 44
emotional excitment during, 45
Blank screen model, 33-35
Bodily behavior, 28
Bodily drive, 32 (*see also* Drives)
Bodily interaction, 32-33
Body
Freud on role of, 31-32
in human development, 21
importance of in psychoanalysis, 23
Body image, disturbances in, 210
Body paradigm (*see* Body schema)
Body schema, 2, 82
Bohr's principle of complementarity, 157
Borderline Personality Disorder
criteria, 224, !225!
Brain opioids, 52-53
Bulimarexia, 216
Bulimia, 215-216

Caregiving, 87-88
Chance and creativity, 169
Change
from hospital environment viewpoint 231-237
from individual therapy viewpoint 228-231
Chestnut Lodge, 10

Child, effects of separation and loss
on, 3
Child-mother relationship, 65, 66
origin and evolution of, 3
see also Infant-mother attachment
Child-parent relationship
inversion of, 77
China Men, 100-106
Chlorpromazine, 51
Coercion
considerations in, 320-322
consultant's experience with, 307-311
patient and, 322-325
reasons for, 311-316
resistance to, 320
therapist and, 325-329
in therapy, 299-331
traditionalism and, 311-316
Cognition, understanding of, 27
Cognitive functions in creative process 5-6
Cognitive psychologists, 69
Cognitive system, 71
Communication
in creative process and psychotherapy
155
definition of, 85
deviances in, 85-86
difficulty of in schizophrenics, 268
disturbances of, 91, 111
with hospitalized psychotic patient 349-353
and human fulfillment, 288-289
modes of, 349-353
physical, 351-352
reciprocal, 347
relatedness as function of, 88, 293
sensual, 352-353
subliminal, 199-200
see also Language; Relatedness
Conflict and psychoanalysis, 27
Conformity, 292
Consultant, role of, 341-343, 357
Contentiousness, 92
Control
cultural and social, 317-318
definition of, 316-317
methods of, 316-320
physical, 319
of self, 317
techniques of, 318-320
by therapist, 325-326
through drugs, 319
see also Coercion

Control system, 64, 65
    deactivation of, 69
Conversion hysteria and anorexia
    nervosa, 207
Coping responses, 50
Corrective emotional experience, 29-30
Countercathexis, 64
Counteridentification, 190
Countertransference, 33, 118
    articulation of error of, 174-175
    as distortion of reality, 35
    in neurotics, 190
    schizophrenics and, 179
Countertransferential aggression 193-195
Creativity
    cognitive functions in, 5-6
    and error, 155-169
    freedom for, 252
Critical period, 3, 44-45
Crying, suppression of, 76
Culture, 254-255
    as controler, 317-318
    creation of, 279-280
    psychiatry as expression of, 294

Death
    as abandonment, 78
    as experience of relatedness, 281
    of parent, 75-76
    relationship with naming, 109-111
    and unrelatedness, 273-274, 275-276
    "voodoo," 274-275
Defensive processes, 63-78
    Freud on, 64
    therapeutic changes in, 72-73
Delusion, 192
Depression, 51, 58, 72
    and disease, 276
Desensitization techniques, 57
Destructiveness, 195-196
Detachment, 63-64, 66, 71
    case history of, 67-69
Developmental deficits in anorexics 210-211
Distance in psychotherapy, 357-359
Distress vocalization, 49
Distrust, 76
Divergence, 89-90
Dreams, 159
Drives
    ambiguity of, 28
    definition of, 19, 29
    discharge, 3
    in normal development, 32

versus person paradigm, 19
Drug abuse, 304-306
Drugs, use of to control, 319
Dynamic unconscious, 25n, 71

Eating Disorders, 215
Ego
    need for recognition of, 100-101
    relations of with objects, 19
    organization and interventions, 225
Emotional bonding, 87-88
Emotional detachment (see Detachment)
Emotional isolation, 73
Emotions
    as basis of attachment, 45-48
    exclusion of from consciousness, 76-78
    expression of by anorexics, 212
    intense, 48
    separation distress and, 50-55
    sexual, 48
Endopsychic perception, 125
Energy
    repressed, 64
    discharge, 17-38
    definition of, 20-21
    Freud on, 23
    object relations and, 29
    see also Drives
Energy metapsychology, 17
Error
    articulation of, 5-6, 157-158
    as artist's signature, 156-157
    in creative process, 160-169
    Freud on, 158-160
    meaning of, 158-160
    in psychotherapy, 169-180
    purpose of, 160
External object relations, 28, 30, 31
Extratransference, 18

Failure-to-thrive syndrome, 129
Family
    of anorexics, 206, 213, 217
    conflict with therapist, 149
    disturbed communication in, 111
    dysfunctional, 84-85
    normal and pathological functioning, 4
    pseudorelationships in, 92-95
    rigid structuring of roles in, 84
    of schizophrenics, 270-271, 345-346
    schizophrenogenic, 271n
    subculture, 92-93
    support of patient's therapy, 149, 152

of troubled person, 308
Family therapy
    development of, 81
    early formulations of, 83-86
Fear
    of loss and separation, 54, 294-295
    of relationships, 284, 288-289
Feedback
    need for, 359
    in psychotherapy, 357-359
Flexibility, 90
Food in relief of separation distress 53-54,
    55
Forgetting, 74-76
    as defense against psychosis, 110-111
Freedom, definition of, 329
Freudian clinical theory, 29
Freudian paradigm, revision of, 32
Fusion of individuals, 128-129

Genetic fallacy, 23
"Gestalt Prayer," 82
"Group Psychology and the Analysis of
the Ego," 22
Guilt, 295

Hallucination, 192
Hallucinatory episodes, 304
Healing ceremonies, native American, 4
Hermeneutics, 24-30
    definition of, 25-26
Heterosexual gratification, 31
Holding environment, 228, 230, 231-237
Hospital
    as agent of control, 319
    difficulty with identity, 353-357
    effects of setting, 148
    as holding environment, 231-237
    as jail, 203
    milieu of, 348
    role in treatment of psychotic
    patients, 344-345
    roles in, 353-357
    social structure in, 353-357
    staff function, 234-235
Hospitalization, involuntary, 301, 303, *see
    also* Patient, reluctant
Human being, concept of, 252
Human condition, illumination of, 185-
    196, 241-260
Human contact, 55, *see also*
    Relationships

Human development, 4, 21, 127-132 282-
    283
    body in, 21
    conditions of, 127-132
Human goals, 284-285
Human nature, 280
Human reality, registers of, 4
"Human Relatedness and the Schizophrenic
Reaction," 205
Hunger
    in anorexics, 212, 221
    and separation distress, 53-54, 69

Iceman Cometh, The, 166-168
Identification process, 189-190
Ignorance
    constructive use of, 220-221
    discovery of, 250-251
I-it relationships, 88-89, 90
    and I-thou relationships, 90-91
"Illumination of the Human Condition"
symposium, 8
Imaginary, the, 4, 100
Imipramine, 51
Inadequacy, fear of, 211, 218-219, 220
Individuality in therapeutic process, 31
Infant-mother attachment, 44-45
    interaction, 31
    physiological and emotional basis of 45-
    46
    see also Child-mother relationship
Information, exclusion of from
consciousness, 74-78
Information theory metapsychology, 17
Insight-oriented therapy (EIO), 140 146,
    147, 151
Instinct, 19, 252-253
Integrated patient approach, 227
Integration
    change toward, 228-237
    emergence of, 229
Intention, 25
internal object relations, 28
Internal structure-building mechanisms 236-
237
Interpersonal interaction
    and bodily interaction, 32-33
    in psychoanalytic process, 33-35
    see also Interpersonal
    relationships; Relationships;
    Relatedness
Interpersonalism, 30-32
Interpersonal relationships, 19-20

bodily behavior in, 28
  see also Person paradigm;
    Relationships
Intimacy, 89, 90
  illusion of, 91-92
  loneliness and, 286
  move toward, 285
  and therapy, 95
Intrapsychic structure, 117
  in anorexic patient, 7-8
  changes in, 5
  conditions of development of, 120
  imposed organization of, 118
  imposition of in therapy, 121-133
  integration of, 133
  need to exercise, 118-120
Isolation
  emotional, 73
  of schizophrenic patient, 264-267
  see also Unrelatedness
I-thou relationships, 89
  and I-it relationships, 90-91

Kleinian theory, 28

Language
  and death, 109-111
  as defense against psychosis, 105, 115
  from intrapsychic structure, 133
  as mediator of relationship, 101
  as mediator of the Real, 106-107
  in psychoanalysis, 4
  and psychosis, 99-115
  shaping of reality with, 113
  transmission of ideas through, 278-279
  see also Communication; Symbolic
      order
Libido, 29
Life of dialogue, 89, 90
Limits, 130-132
Literature, error in, 163-168
Little Prince, The, 277-278
Loneliness, 295
  and intimacy, 286
Loss, 3 (*see also* Separation)
Love
  childhood deprivation of, 77
  falling in, 46
  Freud on, 22
  sexuality as, 31
  supplying to patients, 29
  therapeutic, 193
Love-hate relationships, 61

Lust dynamism, 31

Macbeth, fixity in, 126
Maladaptive behaviors, 11-12
  and separation distress, 56-59
Marriage, 48
  intrapsychic structure in, 124
Mating behavior and attachment, 45
Matrix, 18
Meaning, Freud on, 24-25
  see also Hermeneutics
Medical model versus psychiatric model 334-
  335
Medicine man, practice of, 111-115
Memory
  hallcinatory, 192
  paradox of, 111
Mental hospitals, need for, 312
  see also Hospitals
Mentally ill, individuality of, 243-244
Mental processes, psychical context of 25
Meprobamate, 51
Merchant of Venice, The, 163
Metapsychology, 17
  abandonment of, 19
  definition of, 26
  in explaining psychology, 28
  see also Natural science
Milieu
  effects of on success of therapy, 149 152
  fostering of identity stabilization
  by, 234
  see also Hospital, milieu
Mind
  definition of, 279*n*
  relation of to person, 279
Mirroring, 221
Morphine, 52
Mother-child relationship, 65-66
  origin and evolution of, 3
  schizophrenogenic, 271*n*
  see also Parent-child relationship
Mother-infant attachment, 31, 44-45
  physiological and emotional basis of 45-
  46
Music, error in, 168
Mutuality, 4, 81-95
  as component in relatedness, 90-91
  definition of, 84
  Erikson on, 129
  need for, 359
  prerequisites of, 86, !87!
  with schizophrenic patient, 268, 286-

287, 289
and therapy, 95
tolerance in, 90
Mystical experience, *see* Medicine man practice of; Spiritual experience and psychosis

Naloxone, 52
Naming things, 109-111
Narcissism, culture of, 82
Natural science, 24-30 (*see also* Metapsychology)
Negativism, 235
Neurotic symptoms, fixed organization of, 126
Niobrara Institute meeting, 107
Nonmutuality, 84

Object loss, effects of, 66-69
Object relationship, 20
definition of, 28
as supraordinate to energy discharge 29
theory, 19
theories, 17, 30
Odd Couple, The, 124
Odor as communication, 352
Oedipus complex
definition of, 130
Kohut on, 32
Omnipotence, 194
Opioids, 52-53
"Oral impregnation" fantasies, 207-208
Organismic aims, 30
"Outline of Psycho-analysis, An," 23
Overdependence, 61

Pain of separation, 52-53, 54
Paranoid behavior, 57
Parapraxes, 159
Parental loss, 75-76
Parental separation, 76
Parent-child relationship
inversion of, 77
range of permissible action in 129-130
see also Mother-child relationship; Mother-infant attachment
Past, formulation of, 288
Patient
confrontation of with image of self 186-188
expectations of, 323, 325
identification of with therapist 189-190
new self-image of, 188-189

reluctant, 299-331
resistance of, 118
role of, 322-325
steps of in seeking help, 299-301
suicide of, 197-204
unmotivated, 325
Patient-therapist relationship, 33-35 118
attachment in, 60-61
creative collaboration of, 169-180
interpretation of, 36-37
pseudomutual, 93
separation distress in, 59-61
see also Countertransference; Transference
Penicillin, discovery of, 168-169
Perception, understanding of, 27
Person, defined, 19-20
Personality
creative integration of, 170, 174
defined in terms of ongoing social relationships, 31
Person paradigm, 2-3, 4, 17-38, 82
definition of, 21
difficulty in accepting, 24
Freud on, 22-23
see also Interpersonal relationships
Physiology of attachment, 45-46
Physiology of separation distress, 50-55
Positivisation, 189
Presence and Absence, 109
Presentational truth, 170
Primary object love, 30
Progressive psychopathology, 191-192
Pseudohostility, 93-94
Pseudoinstincts, 253
Pseudomutuality, 81-85
characteristics of, 91-92
definition of, 84
"Pseudo-Mutuality in the Family Relations of Schizophrenics," 83
Psyche, 21
Psychiatric disorders, nature of, 11
Psychiatry
developments in, 246-248
disappointment in, 249-251
hope in, 249
influences on, 247
nature of, 244
social, 247
Psychic energy, 3, 64, 73-74,
see also Energy
Psychoanalysis
in America, 82-83

criticism of revisionist schools of 32
dealing with meaning, 24
definitions of, 27
goals of, 232-233
hermeneutics of, 24-30
language of, 4
as natural science, 26-28
point of view and, 17-34, 35-37
without psychodynamics, 32
schools of, 28-32
social nature of, 34
see also Countertransference;
      Patient-therapist relations;
      Therapist; Transference
Psychoanalytic research, 37-38
Psychoanalytic theory
   clinical investigations and, 1-2
   clinical issues in, 6-8
   different schools of, 2
   history of, 1
   need for modification of, 2-5
   research in, 5-6, 37-38
Psychology, psychoanalysis as, 27
Psychopathology
   as disturbance at sumbolic level, 254
   nature of, 11-14
   progressive, 191-192
   roots of, 11-12
   treatment of, 7-8
Psychosexuality, 22
Psychosexual maturation disturbances 210
Psychosis
   and catastrophe in social disorder 106-109
   and illumination of human condition 185-196
   and language, 99-115
   nature of, 108
   positive phenomena of, 190-191
   as word slippage, 105
   see also Schizophrenia
Psychosynthesis process, 194
Psychotherapeutic process, 13
Psychotherapy
   articulation of error in, 169-180
   attachment and separation in, 59-61
   coercive, 329-331
   creativity in, 169-180
   criticism of, 248-251, 321
   damage done by, 322
   development of, 81
   distance in, 357-359
   effects of on schizophrenics, 139

goals of, 14, 232-233
illumination of human condition in 241-260
importance of attachment in, 6-7
nature of, 11-14
point of view and, 35-37
process of, 13, 127
of psychotic patient, 139-152, 185-186
reciprocity in, 185-186
role of error in, 155-180
schizophrenics in, 139-152
symptom-specific, 8
"Psychotherapy and Schizophrenia:
Implications for Human Living,"
   185
Psychotherapy-milieu interaction, 149
Psychotherapy of Schizophrenia, Fourth
International Symposium on, 185
Psychotherapy Outcome Study, 139-140
Psychotic delusion, sharing, 189-190
Psychotic patients (*see* Schizophrenic
patients)
Purpose, 25

Randomness and error, 162
Real, the, 4, 99-100
   mediated by language, 106-107
   overcoming, 103
   passage of into language, 113-115
   and reality, 101-105
Reality-oriented, adaptive/upportive
therapy (RAS), 140, 146-147
Reciprocity, 185-186
Refeeding, 216
Reification, 190
Rejection, fear of, 73
Relatedness, 4
   components of, 86
   death and, 281
   definition of, 278
   epigenesis of, 86-91
   as human condition, 280-282
   in human development, 282-283
   perturbation of, 91-95
   and schizophrenic reaction, 263-295
   theory of, 84
   types of, 4
Relationships
   asymmetries in, 127-128
   biological bases of, 3, 87
   divergence in, 89-90
   fear of, 256-257
   I-it, 88-91

between I-it and I-thou, 90-91
I-thou, 89, 90-91
need for, 83, 256-257
problems with maintaining, 85
pseudohostile, 93-94
pseudomutual, 91-93
in psychotherapy, 13-14
transferences as basis of, 171
see also Interpersonal
    relationships; Relatedness
Relativity, theory of, 157
Religion and psychosis (*see* Spiritual
experience and psychosis)
Repetition, "re-creative," 172-173
Repetition compulsion, 118
Representation
    in developmental play, 132
    process of, 125-126
Repressed energy, 64
Repression, 71
    Freud on, 73-74
    interpretation of, 187
Research interests, 313
Ridigity, 126-127
Ritual, 114 (*see also* Medicine man practice
    of)
Role structure, 88-89
    loss of, 307

Schizophrenia
    anorexia nervosa and, 7
    articulation of error in treatment of 177-
        179
    characteristics of, 5
    concept of, 343-344
    creative articulation of transference
    error in, 6
    influences on psychotherapy for, 5
    lack of relatedness in, 263-267 272-273
    personality stereotypes of, 263
    as reaction, 283-295
    stress and, 283-285
    Sullivan on, 244
    treatment of, 286-292, 333-334
    uncertainty of symptoms of, 335
Schizophrenic patient
    characteristics of, 141-144, 344
    characteristics of therapist for 335-338
    communication with, 349-353
    discontinuance of therapy by, 151
    disordered life of, 292, 294
    elements of therapy of, 343-349
    engagement of in psychotherapy 139-152

families of, 84-85
perception of time of, 351
treatment of, 286-292, 333-334
undefined role of, 353-357
Scientific discovery and error, 168-169
Self
    concept of, 30
    evolution of, !87!
Self-creation, 188
Self-esteem
    low, 11
    struggle to maintain, 11-12
Self-identification, 285
    difficulty with in hospital, 353-357
    establishment of, 237
    threat to, 306-307
Self psychology, 17, 30, 32-33
Self-realization as therapeutic goal 292, 294
Sensitive period, 44
Sensory inflow, 69-71
    suppression of, 74-77
Separation
    chronic, 58, 59
    depression from, 58
    development of, 49-50
    and disease, 276
    processes, 3
    in psychotherapy, 59-61
    situations, 58
    see also Death; Divergence; Loss
Separation distress, 3, 51
    biochemical basis of, 53
    during development, 49-50
    emotional effects, 50-51
    emotional response to, 53-55, 66-69
    in infants, 49-50
    and maladaptive behavior, 56-59
    nature of, 51
    physiological and emotional bases of 50-
        55
    physiological reaction to, 50, 53
Sexual aggressiveness, 23
Sexual behavior, 129-130
Sexual bonding, 46
Sexual emotions and attachment, 48
Sexuality, 20
    Freud on, 22-23
    phenomena relating to, 32
    prepubertal, 31
    regressively avoided, 122
    rejection of primacy of, 30, 31-32
Sharing
    attention and meanings, 88

tasks, 88-89
Sick, defining patient as, 313-316
Site attachment, 3, 43
Slip of tongue, 158
Smell, 352
Social attachment, 3, 23, 43, 47-48
Social disorder and psychosis, 106-107
Social field (*see* Social interaction
as separation distress reliever;
Social relationships;
Transactional system)
Social interaction as separation
distress reliever, 55, 58-59
Social psychiatry, 247
Social reinforcement, 318-319
Social relationships, 256
    ongoing, 31
    psychiatric disorders and, 308
    schizophrenia and, 343-346
Social structure in psychiatric
hospital, 353-357
Society
    control through, 317-319
    fear of destruction of, 257-260
Soft toys in relief of separation
distress, 55
Somatic stimulus, 21
Sorrow, repression of, 76, 77
Sound, 352-353
Southern belle, 120-122
Space, 350
Speech, 4 (*see also* Communication;
Language)
Sphere of the between, 89
Spirit, the, 100
Spiritual experience and psychosis 99-115
Splitting, 191-192, 228, 232-233
    resolution of, 235-236
    shift from, 229, 230, 237
    of transference, 225-227
    see also Ambivalence
Stress and schizophrenia, 283-285
Subjective aims, 30
"Subtleties of a Faulty Action, The,"
    160
Suicide
    and anorexia nervosa, 205
    impact of on therapist, 7, 197-204
    parental, 75
Survival and attachment, 48-49
Symbolic, the, 4, 100
Symbolic order, 103-104
Symbolism, 254

Symbols, creation of, 187-188, 278-279
Symptom-specific treatment, 8
System theory, 82

Taste, 352-353
TAT
    of families, 84
    relationship of score to engagement in
    therapy, 142-144
Teaching encounter, 338-343
Technique
    definition of, 287*n*
    in therapy, 287-288
Therapeutic impasses, 118
Therapeutic symbiosis, 188
Therapist
    as agent of control, 316-320
    alliance with patient, 149, 152
    characteristics of those whose
    patients remain in therapy 144-146
    coercive, 320, 325-329
    concepts of concern to, 251-257
    conflict with patient's family, 149
    education of, 338-343
    error of, 175-177
    impact of suicide on, 7, 197-204
    interaction of with patient, 33-35
    (*see also* Countertransference;
    Transference)
    isolation of, 257
    as observer, 33 (*see also* Blank
    screen model)
    as participant-observer, 33
    patient criticism of, 232
    role of, 307, 355-357
    unwanted, 299-331
    willingness of to work with psychotic
    patients, 333-334
    working with schizophrenics, 335-338;
    355-357
Therapist-patient relationship, 118
    creative collaboration of, 169-180
    pseudomutual, 93
Therapy
    achievement of ambivalence in, 223-237
    of anorexics, 216-221
    characteristics of patients who remain
    in, 141-144
    coercion in, 299-331
    effects of social context in, 147-152
    effects of type of on patient
    continuance, 146-147
    emotional demands of on patient, 146

flexibility of patient response in 131-132
of hospitalized psychotic patients 343-
349
ineffectiveness of techniques of, 356
interactions between, 148-149
lack of coherent theory in, 81-82
limits in, 130-132
patient's intrapsychic structure in 118-
133
questioning of, 248-251
role in mutuality and intimacy, 94-95
of schizophrenics, 263-295
transference in, 171
see also Insight-oriented therapy
(EIO); Reality-oriented adaptive/upportive
therapy (RAS);
Psychoanalysis; Psychotherapy
Thinness, obsession with, *see* Anorexia
nervosa
Time, 351
Too Far to Walk, 164-166
Touch, 351-352
Traditionalism and coercion, 311-316
Tranquilizers, 51
Transactional system, 347
of schizophrenic patient, 347-349
Transference
affectionate, 223
analysis of in here-and-now, 31
articulation of error of, 172-174
balance with extratransference, 18
based on person paradigm, 20
as basis of human relationship, 171
blank screen model and, 33-35
as distortion of reality, 35
evolution of, 118
Freud's discovery of, 170-171

negative, 223, 228
patient's perspective and, 34
from person point of view, 37
of schizophrenics, 179
splitting of, 225-227
understanding of, 2, 33-35
Transference errors, 6
Transformation, symbol of, 187-188
Transitional objects, 188
Transitivism, 192
Trauma, 126
Trial-and-error thinking, 161
Truth, presentational vs. explicated 170

Unconscious
creativity and, 166
errors and, 158-160
Freud on, 111
processes, 25
Union, facilitation of, 128-129
Unrelatedness
death and, 273-276
definition of, 286
in schizophrenics, 263-295
treatment of, 286-292
see also Isolation
Uprootedness, defense against, 124-125

Vision quest, 111-112
Voluntary associations, 47-48
"Voodoo" death, 274-275

Wandering, 162-163, 171
recognition of, 172
separation and, 174
" 'Wild' Psycho-Analysis," 22-23
Wisdom, definition of, 311